# RESOURCES FOR TEACHING

# The Writer's Presence
## *A Pool of Readings*

SEVENTH EDITION

CONTRIBUTORS

**Donald McQuade**
*University of California, Berkeley*

**Robert Atwan**
*Series Editor*, The Best American Essays
*Emerson College*

Joanna Imm
*University of Arizona*

Sam Ruddick
*University of Massachusetts Lowell*

MaryJo Thomas

Bedford/St. Martin's                    Boston ♦ New York

6  5  4  3  2  1
f  e  d  c  b  a

*For information, write:* Bedford/St. Martin's, 75 Arlington Street, Boston, MA 02116
(617-399-4000)

ISBN: 978-1-4576-0063-0

# Preface

We have designed *The Writer's Presence* to be a thoroughly accessible book for both students and instructors. As a collection of highly readable essays and stories, *The Writer's Presence* invites undergraduates to engage in intellectual dialogue with many of the best minds and writers on some of the most provocative issues and subjects in contemporary life. We decided early on in developing our plans for this project to provide students with direct—and unencumbered—entry into the world of ideas contained in each essay or short story. This accounts for our organization of the selections: alphabetical by author and by four types of writing—personal, expository, and argumentative essays, as well as short fiction. This same principle guides the number and nature of the questions we pose following each selection. We're interested in providing students with a broader and richer intellectual access to what they read rather than determining beforehand specifically what they should think and write about a particular essay.

This same commitment to access and excellence informs our design of *Resources for Teaching The Writer's Presence*. We would like our work—and that of our colleagues Cassandra Cleghorn, Alfred Guy, Joanna Imm, Jon Roberts, Shelley Salamensky, Alix Schwartz, MaryJo Thomas, and Sam Ruddick—to be equally inviting to you as an instructor. In the pages that follow, we want to create a broad spectrum of promising teaching opportunities, ranging from a closely integrated, hands-on initiation to the thematic and compositional "matters" of each of the selections in *The Writer's Presence*, to a comprehensive compilation of strategic advice on how to work effectively with each selection in diverse classroom settings. If we are reasonably successful in achieving these goals, we will have encouraged you and your colleagues not only to open this companion volume to *The Writer's Presence* at moments other than when no one is watching but also to think of its strategies and recommendations as occasions for fruitful discussions with one another and with your students.

As anyone who has labored to create one of these volumes knows, an instructor's guide represents a considerable—and concerted—effort. We trust as you peruse these pages, you'll find a fresh approach to a favorite essay or perhaps develop an interest in teaching an unfamiliar one. We expect that you will not always agree with either the opinions we express or the teaching strategies we propose, but we are confident that your disagreement will stimulate new ideas and open new avenues for productive discussions with your students.

*Resources for Teaching The Writer's Presence* provides comprehensive essay-like entries on each of the selections in *The Writer's Presence*. This compilation of specific teaching strategies and writing exercises demonstrates our concerted plan to weave together classroom-tested practices and speculative — and we hope innovative — suggestions about teaching each essay.

Each entry in *Resources for Teaching The Writer's Presence* begins with "Approaching the Essay," which describes the essay (and especially its instructional potential) in detail; discusses ways to help students gain full access to the work; suggests strategies for examining its subject, structure, and style; and provides ancillary information about some aspects of the essay or its author. Following this is a section titled "Additional Activities," a discussion of the essay's connections to other selections in the book, writing assignments, and collaborative projects for classroom discussion.

The next section, "Generating Writing," offers a wide range of writing exercises from informal writing to full-length essay topics and ideas for research papers. A section called "The Reader's Presence" comes next; it addresses the questions that follow each essay in the text. The entries in this section discuss each question in detail, pointing to illuminating passages in the essay and anticipating possible student reactions to what they're reading.

We have included the essay "Writing Informally About Reading" at the end of *Resources for Teaching The Writer's Presence* to help you help students use journals and other informal writing forms to establish more practiced confidence in their reading and writing.

We hope this compendium of instructional resources for *The Writer's Presence* will facilitate an open, unencumbered, and mutually respectful dialogue between you and your students and an encouraging environment in which learning can flourish through productive conversation, reading, and writing.

Donald McQuade
Robert Atwan

# Contents

Preface   iii

## Part 1   PERSONAL WRITING: Exploring Our Own Lives   1

**Chris Abani**, *The Lottery*   1

**Sherman Alexie**, *The Joy of Reading and Writing: Superman and Me*   4

**Maya Angelou**, *"What's Your Name, Girl?"*   7

**James Baldwin**, *Notes of a Native Son*   10

**Augusten Burroughs**, *Absolutely Fabulous*   13

**Raymond Carver**, *My Father's Life*   17

**Judith Ortiz Cofer**, *Silent Dancing*   20

**Bernard Cooper**, *A Clack of Tiny Sparks: Remembrances of a Gay Boyhood*   23

**Frederick Douglass**, *Learning to Read and Write*   26

**Anne Fadiman**, *Under Water*   29

**Henry Louis Gates Jr.**, *In the Kitchen*   32

**Michihiko Hachiya**, *From* Hiroshima Diary   35

**Edward Hoagland**, *On Stuttering*   37

**Langston Hughes**, *Salvation*   39

**Ha Jin**, *Arrival*   42

**Jamaica Kincaid**, *The Estrangement*   46

**Geeta Kothari**, *If You Are What You Eat, Then What Am I?*   48

**Nancy Mairs**, *On Being a Cripple*   51

**Malcolm X**, *My First Conk*   53

**David Mamet**, *The Rake: A Few Scenes from My Childhood*   55

**Adam Mayblum**, *The Price We Pay*   58

**Dinaw Mengestu**, *Home at Last*   61

**Manuel Muñoz**, *Leave Your Name at the Border*   64

**George Orwell**, *Shooting an Elephant*   67

**Richard Rodriguez**, *Aria: A Memoir of a Bilingual Childhood*   70

**Marjane Satrapi**, *My Speech at West Point*   72

**David Sedaris**, *Me Talk Pretty One Day*   74

**Brent Staples**, *Just Walk on By: A Black Man Ponders His Power to Alter Public Space*   76

**Andrew Sullivan**, *The M-Word: Why It Matters to Me*   78

**Manil Suri**, *Keys to the Kingdom*   80

**Amy Tan**, *Mother Tongue*   84

**Robert Vivian**, *Town*   86

**Alice Walker**, *Beauty: When the Other Dancer Is the Self*   89

**Jerald Walker**, *Scattered Inconveniences*   91

**E. B. White**, *Once More to the Lake*   94

**Elie Wiesel**, *Eight Simple, Short Words*   97

**Tobias Wolff**, *Prospecting*   99

## Part 2   EXPOSITORY WRITING: Shaping Information   103

**Joan Acocella**, *A Few Too Many*   103

**Daniel Akst**, *What Meets the Eye*   106

**Akhil Reed Amar**, *Second Thoughts: What the Right to Bear Arms Really Means*   109

**Dave Barry**, *Beauty and the Beast*   112

**Michael Bérubé**, *Analyze, Don't Summarize*   115

**Charles Bowden**, *Our Wall*   118

**David Brooks**, *People Like Us*   120

**Stephen L. Carter**, *The Insufficiency of Honesty*   123

**Michael Chabon**, *Faking It*   125

**Amy Cunningham**, *Why Women Smile*   128

**Don DeLillo**, *In the Ruins of the Future: Reflections on Terror, Loss, and Time in the Shadow of September*   131

**Joan Didion**, *On Morality*   134

**Annie Dillard**, *The Death of a Moth*   137

**Brian Doyle**, *The Greatest Nature Essay* Ever   140

**Lars Eighner**, *On Dumpster Diving*   142

**Joseph Epstein**, *The Perpetual Adolescent*   146

**James Fallows**, *Throwing Like a Girl*   148

**Daniel Gilbert**, *Next to Nothing*   150

**Malcolm Gladwell**, *Small Change: Why the Revolution Will Not Be Tweeted*   153

**Cynthia Gorney**, *The Urge to Merge*   155

**Stephen Jay Gould**, *Sex, Drugs, Disasters, and the Extinction of Dinosaurs*   158

**Nathaniel Hawthorne**, *My Visit to Niagara*   161

**Siri Hustvedt**, *Eight Days in a Corset*   164

**Stephen King**, *Everything You Need to Know About Writing Successfully—in Ten Minutes*   168

**Maxine Hong Kingston**, *No Name Woman*   170

**Dan Koeppel**, *How to Fall 35,000 Feet—And Survive*   172

**Steven D. Levitt and Stephen J. Dubner**, *What Should You Worry About?*   175

**Michael Lewis**, *The Mansion: A Subprime Parable*   178

**Abraham Lincoln**, *Gettysburg Address*   181

**James McBride**, *Hip-Hop Planet*   183

**N. Scott Momaday**, *The Way to Rainy Mountain*   186

**Azar Nafisi**, *From* Reading Lolita in Tehran   189

**Danielle Ofri**, *SAT*   191

**George Orwell**, *Politics and the English Language*   193

**Walker Percy**, *The Loss of the Creature*   196

**Katha Pollitt**, *Why Boys Don't Play with Dolls*   199

**Eric Schlosser**, *Why McDonald's Fries Taste So Good*   202

**James Shreeve**, *The Greatest Journey*   205

**Charles Simic**, *The Life of Images*   207

**Calvin Trillin**, *A Traditional Family*   210

**Barbara Tuchman**, *"This Is the End of the World": The Black Death*   212

**Sherry Turkle**, *How Computers Change the Way We Think*   213

**William Speed Weed**, *106 Science Claims and a Truckful of Baloney*   216

**Tom Wolfe**, *Hooking Up*   218

**Virginia Woolf**, *The Death of the Moth*   220

## Part 3   ARGUMENTATIVE WRITING: Contending with Issues   223

**Nicholas Carr**, *Is Google Making Us Stupid?*   223

**Jared Diamond**, *The Ends of the World as We Know Them*   225

**Barbara Ehrenreich**, *Will Women Still Need Men?*   228

**Nora Ephron**, *The Boston Photographs*   231

**Jonathan Safran Foer**, *Let Them Eat Dog*   234

**John Taylor Gatto**, *Against School*   237

**Adam Gopnik**, *Shootings*   239

**Vicki Hearne**, *What's Wrong with Animal Rights*   241

**Christopher Hitchens**, *Believe Me, It's Torture*   244

**Pico Iyer**, *The Inner Climate*   247

**Thomas Jefferson**, *The Declaration of Independence*   250

**Martin Luther King Jr.**, *I Have a Dream*   252

**Martin Luther King Jr.**, *Letter from Birmingham Jail*   254

**Laura Kipnis**, *Against Love*  257

**Thomas Lynch**, *Into the Oblivion*  259

**Walter Benn Michaels**, *The Trouble with Diversity*  262

**Errol Morris**, *Liar, Liar, Pants on Fire*  264

**Martha Nussbaum**, *Veiled Threats?*  266

**Barack Obama**, *Grant Park Victory Speech*  268

**Camille Paglia**, *The Pitfalls of Plastic Surgery*  270

**Michael Pollan**, *What's Eating America*  272

**Michael J. Sandel**, *Designer Babies*  275

**Scott Russell Sanders**, *The Men We Carry in Our Minds*  278

**Barry Schwartz**, *The Tyranny of Choice*  281

**Leslie Marmon Silko**, *In the Combat Zone*  283

**Peter Singer**, *The Singer Solution to World Poverty*  285

**Lauren Slater**, *The Trouble with Self-Esteem*  288

**Jonathan Swift**, *A Modest Proposal*  290

**David Foster Wallace**, *Consider the Lobster*  294

**John Edgar Wideman**, *Street Corner Dreamers*  297

**Howard Zinn**, *Stories Hollywood Never Tells*  300

**Part 4   THE SHORT STORY: Seven Modern Classics   303**

**Sherman Alexie**, *This Is What It Means to Say Phoenix, Arizona*  303

**Raymond Carver**, *What We Talk About When We Talk About Love*  306

**Jamaica Kincaid**, *Girl*  308

**Joyce Carol Oates**, *Where Are You Going, Where Have You Been?*  312

**Tim O'Brien**, *The Things They Carried*  315

**Flannery O'Connor**, *A Good Man Is Hard to Find*  318

**John Updike**, *A & P*  320

**Writing Informally About Reading**   323

# PART 1

# PERSONAL WRITING
## Exploring Our Own Lives

## Chris Abani
### THE LOTTERY

### APPROACHING THE ESSAY

Because the central event of "The Lottery" is so ugly, it will probably provoke a visceral response in many students. But there is something philosophical about it as well, an idea that is evident in the title and articulated in the fifth paragraph. As a piece of writing, "The Lottery" is worth studying largely for the way it manages to balance its visceral and intellectual elements. Abani's timing and restraint are essential to the essay's success. He is careful to say what he has to say about mob justice in Nigeria (para. 5) before proceeding with the most horrifying part of the narrative: the capture and subsequent immolation of the accused man. By placing the background information before the immolation itself, Abani provides us with an intellectual context in which to interpret the event. But perhaps more important, he avoids interrupting his description of the event with abstraction. If, for example, he had interrupted his description of the accused man's pleas for mercy (para. 7) or his eruption into flame (para. 8) with the ironic observation that editorials about the horrors of mob justice could be of little use to a man at the center of its wrath, the film-like quality of Abani's description of the event would have been disrupted, and some of the emotional intensity might have been lost, watered down by irony. Directly related to this issue of timing is the issue of restraint. There is no shortage of opportunity for Abani to comment on the event. More plentiful, still, is the opportunity to sentimentalize it. But Abani is careful to avoid judgment. In paragraph 8, he says that he was afraid, and that he was ashamed of his fear. That aside, there is precious little to tell us how he felt about the event, or how we should feel. The event speaks for itself. The ending is particularly important because Abani does not spare himself complicity in the accused man's death, even though it is clear that (1) he is too young to do anything about it, and (2) he is obviously disturbed, and wonders, in paragraph 6, why no one (with the exception of one elder, who is ignored by both the crowd *and* the remaining elders) tries to stop the vigilante execution. The conflict we are left with, between individual opinion and the desire or need to conform to the expectations of the community, might link well with the Langston Hughes selection, "Salvation" (p. 118), which deals more explicitly with the topic, albeit in a different context.

1

Although there is no direct reference to an actual lottery in Abani's essay, the title of the essay's piece has much to say about its meaning, and, although it is not included in *The Writer's Presence*, the Shirley Jackson story of the same title, "The Lottery," also offers an entry to a thematic discussion of the text. Many of your students have probably read Jackson's story and will immediately see the connection, so it might be worthwhile (and even unavoidable) to begin your discussion with Jackson's famous tale. Ask the students whether they have read it and, if any of them have, ask for a brief summary of the plot. If you can't get a volunteer, you can summarize the plot for them, and ask them what connections they see. This might serve as a gateway into the larger conversation about how a piece of nonfiction can deal with an event such as the one Abani describes. In Jackson's short story, there is no need to provide context or make an intellectual judgment. Everything is suggested by the story. Abani's piece requires the context, as well as some measure of moral and intellectual judgment, to be *written* into the text. The question is how to do this without boring the audience with background or alienating them by preaching. Raising these two problems can lead directly into the discussion of timing and restraint.

## ADDITIONAL ACTIVITIES

1. Abani was arrested in connection with his writing three times in his native Nigeria. You might spend some time talking about writers working under repressive regimes and writing as a political act. Have the students research other writers who worked under repressive regimes. Examples include Aleksandr Solzhenitsyn, Isaac Babel, Anna Akhmatova, Ngũgĩ wa Thiong'o, José Rizal, Steve Biko, Huang Xiang, and Herta Müller. Why were these writers persecuted? Why were their writings suppressed? What does this say about the power of the written word to challenge authoritarian regimes? authority in general?

2. Have the students read Shirley Jackson's short story, "The Lottery." Ask them why Abani might have chosen to use the same title for his brief essay. In what way is the man in Abani's essay the victim of a lottery? The community seems to unite around an act of horrific violence against a single man. To what extent is the selection of the individual to be "punished" arbitrary? What needs does the community serve by punishing him?

## GENERATING WRITING

1. Have the students select an author whose writings led to problems with the authorities. The writer can be one of those mentioned in Additional Activity 1, or a writer of the student's choosing. The student should research the writer, then write an essay explaining who the writer was and what it was about his or her writing that led to the confrontation with government (or other) authorities. The paper should answer the questions posed in Additional

Activity 1: What does the writer's experience say about the power of the written word to threaten authority structures and/or repressive regimes?

2. Have the students use Abani's essay as a model to write a brief essay describing a meaningful event. Like Abani, they should limit the amount of exposition, relying principally on the description of the event itself to convey the meaning. Call their attention again to the pivotal paragraph 5, which is the only place where Abani allows himself to editorialize in general terms about the state of affairs in Nigeria. Encourage your students to similarly confine their "thematic" comments to one paragraph, letting the physical details of the event do the work instead.

## THE READER'S PRESENCE

1. Although there is no direct reference to a lottery in the text, Abani probably called this piece "The Lottery" to reflect the random nature of mob justice. It is also likely that "The Lottery" refers to Jackson's story of the same title, in which the residents of a small town hold an annual lottery to determine which member of the community will be stoned to death as a sacrifice to ensure a good harvest.

2. Paragraph 5 is central to the text. It is the moment in the narrative at which Abani pauses to contextualize the central event. He provides background information about mob justice in Nigeria, suggesting that the victims of such justice were not always guilty. Mob justice, while common in Nigeria at the time, was not justice at all. Without paragraph 5, many readers would not realize that such events were commonplace or that Abani's father had made him aware of the injustice of these on-the-spot trials. Abani might have saved the information in paragraph 5 for last to avoid interrupting the narrative, but then he would have forfeited the visceral power of the ending as is.

3. Langston Hughes ("Salvation," p. 118) and Abani both conclude their essays with disheartening episodes of "faking it" in order to conform to the expectations of the community. Both essays deal with boys on the cusp of adolescence, losing their innocence. Both boys are encouraged by matriarchal family members (specifically, their aunts) to take part in a community activity, activities that neither boy can believe in or support. Although the young Hughes apparently *wanted* to see Jesus, he did not see him, and in the end pretended that he did, only to stop the admonishing encouragement of his aunt and the members of her church. Abani, however, is horrified by the execution of the accused thief but spits on the burning corpse just the same, at his aunt's command. Both boys began the day peacefully enough and ended the day with their worldviews forever altered. Both boys wake up innocent, one of them going to bed a liar and an atheist and the other the witness of a brutal killing, a killing in which he, in some sense, participated in, or at least outwardly condoned by spitting at the murdered man's burning corpse.

# Sherman Alexie
## THE JOY OF READING AND WRITING: SUPERMAN AND ME

### APPROACHING THE ESSAY

The topic of Sherman Alexie's essay is one of the favorite topics of American writers: how one's childhood reading gives rise to the writing adult. This kind of essay has existed almost since printing itself was invented. In Montaigne's famous essay "Of Books" (c. 1570), the essayist details his literary likes and dislikes, and European writers after Montaigne cataloged their libraries and took inventory of their education. But what sets the American version of this type of essay apart is the way it links literacy with social or political freedom. American stories of education are often as much about the unlikelihood of that education as they are about the particulars of the curriculum. Thus, although Montaigne portrays himself as simply inhaling the contents of his wealthy family's lavish library, Alexie emphasizes the haphazard state of his father's collection: homemade bookshelves filled with a "random assortment" of everything from western novels to political tracts, books stacked in "crazy piles," all purchased indiscriminately, "by the pound" (para. 2). But if the selection of books was random, Alexie's use of them was not. His education was largely self-generated, it seems, and certainly deliberate. "I decided to love books," he proclaims at the end of the second paragraph.

The contradictions in this paragraph are worth exploring: Alexie determines to *love* reading, an emotion usually thought of as beyond rational control; he teaches himself to read *on his own*, but he does so in imitation of his father's passionate devotion to books. Alexie chooses to characterize his early education as an independent act. Compare his account, for example, to that of Frederick Douglass ("Learning to Read and Write," p. 86), who, for all his self-reliance, depicts his education as a result of serendipity and lots of help from those around him.

Through the rest of the essay, Alexie develops what we might call the essay's "plot," that of the unlikely young hero fighting against the odds. In this case, the hero is an Indian boy living on the Spokane Indian Reservation in eastern Washington in the 1960s and 1970s. The odds are material and ideological: poverty and the racist expectations of both American Indians and non-Indians that American Indian children are inherently stupid and doomed to failure.

Alexie elaborates the structure of this conflict through the use of the Superman motif. He begins the essay with the outrageous claim that he "learned to read with a Superman comic book," outrageous because by the time Alexie writes this essay he has established himself as an important young writer. He then underscores the primal nature of the comic strip for his developing consciousness: details of particular plots and characters fall away, memories about how he even managed to get his hands on the comic books fall away; all that matters is that by means of their vivid visual appeal Alexie made the imaginative connection between words and actions, between characters on the page and himself.

4

Alexie's move in paragraph 4 from "Superman is breaking down the door" to "I am breaking down the door" is a great example of how identification works in the reading process. (It also recalls a line from Walt Whitman's "Song of Myself" (1855), in which the poet warns the reader of his arrival: "Unscrew the locks from the doors! / Unscrew the doors themselves from their jambs!" [lines 502–503].) In moving from the third- to the first-person pronoun, the young Alexie tries on the voice of Superman and takes on some of his power. "Breaking down the door," for Alexie, is another way of saying, "learning how to read." He extends the reach of this physical metaphor in the description of his attachment to books as a child: "I read with equal parts joy and desperation. . . . I was trying to save my life" (para. 7).

Buried in the essay is a nuanced account of how a young child's preliterate mind works. Unable to read, Alexie still recognizes the peculiar arrangement of words on the page, in clusters he would later come to know as paragraphs. "I realized that a paragraph was a fence that held words" (para. 3). He goes on to apply the central logic of the paragraph to the world around him, geographically, politically, and personally.

At this point, Alexie has not yet made explicit the idea that being an American Indian was what threatened his achievement. He seems to be describing a general account of early cognition that is available to all readers, American Indian and non-Indian alike. But, finally, we cannot read any part of the essay as "neutral" on the subject of race; the notion of being fenced off from educational opportunities, of fencing oneself in, recurs throughout the essay as a function of the centuries-long history of racism in America. Alexie's repeated mentioning of the reservation serves to remind us that the establishment of American Indian reservations at the end of the nineteenth and beginning of the twentieth centuries reflected a policy of removal and containment.

The essay ends with Alexie's account of his involvement with reservation schools where he goes to teach creative writing. He is embraced by most of the children and is encouraged by how many of them think of themselves as readers and writers—a self-concept he found foreign when he was their age. Some of the children, however, resist his attempts to turn them on to books, and he sees in their determined spirit of isolation and suspicion a reflection of how he and his classmates acted in their youth. "I throw my weight against their locked doors," he writes, "The door holds. I am smart. I am arrogant. I am lucky. I am trying to save our lives" (para. 8). As the first-person pronoun shifts from the singular to the plural, Alexie leaves behind the myth of Superman to embrace a more modest, more contingent heroism. He admits to his own as yet unfinished education, and he reaffirms his connection with his readers through his writing.

## ADDITIONAL ACTIVITIES

1. Alexie is a poet and filmmaker as well as a novelist and an essayist. Have students find a poem or two of Alexie's (the author has a strong Internet presence, including his own very informative Web site: www.fallsapart.com) and watch the film *Smoke Signals*, for which he won several awards. His story, "This Is What It Means to Say Phoenix, Arizona" can be found on page 873

of *The Writer's Presence*. What continuities do students see between these different forms of expression?

2. Have students research local literacy programs in community centers, churches, and prisons. Encourage them to learn about programs such as Literacy Volunteers of America and Teach for America. Students who have already been involved in such programs—either as tutors or as students—may want to share their experiences with the others.

## GENERATING WRITING

1. Have students write a short essay about how they learned to read or to write or to do both, following Alexie's example. Encourage them to focus on a particularly vivid moment in the long process of learning to read—from their earliest memories of sounding out words to more sophisticated problems of learning how to interpret layers of meaning. Tell them to be as specific as possible: Alexie doesn't identify comic books in general; he names Superman in particular as the action figure who ushers him into the world of books. Which specific book does each student identify as the most formative of his or her reading life thus far?

2. Have students write an essay in which they compare Alexie's account of learning to read and write with that of Frederick Douglass ("Learning to Read and Write," p. 86). Have them pay particular attention to how and why these writers associate literacy with some sort of liberation. The historical distance between the two accounts is enormous; what are the commonalities between the accounts?

## THE READER'S PRESENCE

1. Alexie describes how he read before he actually knew how to read; that is, at age three he has an intense awareness of books, of people reading, and of the look of words on the page. This prereading stage is an important part of learning to read. His highly metaphorical linking of syntactical units to family members is a harbinger of the poet and writer he will become. As closely as possible, he writes himself into the essay that is his family, his reservation, his country; in this, his identity is absolutely bound up with reading and writing.

2. Alexie picks up Superman "at the same time" that he enters the most intense stage of prereading. He learns to read by means of Superman; he finds his best metaphor ("breaking down the door"; para. 4) in the hero's actions; he identifies with this figure of extraordinary strength who masquerades as a regular guy. Explore with your students how the Superman figure and his actions hold together the essay itself (as opposed to the "character" or "personality" of Alexie).

3. Alexie's model of literacy is at once easier and more embattled than Douglass's. That is, Alexie had ready access to books and instruction; his only barrier was the stereotype of the "dumb Indian." By comparison, he begins

his quest for literacy in a "freer" state than Douglass. Alexie's struggle is internal. Douglass, on the contrary, was explicitly prohibited from learning to read and write; slaves were often killed for such infractions. Once he does learn (in clandestine and ingenious ways), Douglass is still unable to make the freedom he now knows more about into a reality. Alexie is freed from a limited sense of himself when he learns to read and, especially, to write; Douglass, having been freed from ignorance, is eventually able to achieve freedom from slavery as well.

# Maya Angelou
## "WHAT'S YOUR NAME, GIRL?"

### APPROACHING THE ESSAY

It may be difficult for students to comprehend the historical significance of naming in African American culture. You might want to begin the discussion by reading or handing out the passage from *The Autobiography of Malcolm X* (1965) in which Malcolm outlines his reasons for changing his last name from *Little*—his "slave name"—to *X*. Or you might want to show the class the second episode of *Roots*, where Kunta Kinte chooses to be beaten rather than accept the slave name *Toby*. It was routine for slaveowners to change the names of enslaved persons, and the pattern continued for decades after the Emancipation Proclamation. Does this help explain why, as Margaret* says, "Every person I knew had a hellish horror of being 'called out of his name'" (para. 30)?

Another important aspect of the name problem is how closely being called the wrong name is to being called an *insulting* name. Maya Angelou goes on to say "It was a dangerous practice to call a Negro anything that could be loosely construed as insulting because of the centuries of their having been called niggers, jigs, dinges, blackbirds, crows, boots, and spooks" (para. 30). You might want to begin discussing the selection with this passage. One point to explore in class is the connection that Angelou makes here between a personal name and a racist epithet. If your class doesn't see why Margaret finds the name Mary insulting, then the point of the selection is lost.

Be sure, though, that students understand that it is nothing about the name Mary itself that stirs Margaret's anger. Some students might assume that Margaret hated the name or that she saw it as an unflattering nickname. Some discussion, then, is required about the motives for Mrs. Cullinan's calling her "out of [her] name." What level of respect does Mrs. Cullinan show to Margaret by calling her Mary? What level of respect is Margaret expected to show by calling her employer

---

*Angelou's first name is actually Marguerite.—EDS.

Mrs. Cullinan? Once Mrs. Cullinan's motives are understood, the class can consider how the episode ends. They should now be able to see that Margaret's anger is legitimate—the wrong name, Mary, is immediately followed by a racist epithet, "little black nigger" (para. 40), as though the two were indeed equated in Mrs. Cullinan's mind. In other words, to Margaret, being called Mary was always equivalent to being called "nigger." Why, then, does Mrs. Cullinan finally scream, "Her name's Margaret, goddamn it, her name's Margaret!" (para. 42)? Clearly, Margaret has won her point; but there seems to be more to this ending than just that sort of victory. Trying to interpret the episode's conclusion could lead to some interesting open-ended discussion about the extent of Mrs. Cullinan's own awareness of what her calling Margaret "Mary" actually meant. Ask the class, too, if they find it significant that the broken plate Mrs. Cullinan throws actually hits Miss Glory, rather than Margaret.

Another larger issue raised by this selection is how the self-definition of the African American women Angelou describes was shaped by the standards of the white community. The essay's first two paragraphs describe how Angelou's African American peers "were given as extensive and irrelevant preparations for adulthood as rich white girls shown in magazines" (para. 1). Draw the class to Angelou's irony at the end of the second paragraph: "During my tenth year, a white woman's kitchen became my finishing school." (You may need to explain the definition of *finishing school* to your class.) How is the world of finishing school diametrically opposed to a world where ten-year-old girls worked as paid servants?

Ask the class to look closely at the ways Angelou uses language to underscore this point. Students may not see the connection between the first two paragraphs and the naming episode. It might be a good idea to point out how out of place the word *debutante* is in the context of Margaret's childhood (para. 1). Students should begin to see how Angelou establishes a pattern of ironic metaphor to reveal Margaret's position through the language forced upon her. For example, Margaret learns the proper names for Mrs. Cullinan's fancy tableware, which, as Margaret says, "were additions to my vocabulary and in fact almost represented a new language" (para. 8).

The central issue in this selection is *control*. White society controls the aspirations of African Americans, and white employers like Mrs. Cullinan even try—often successfully—to control the names of their African American employees. Margaret's response to that control, as her brother advises, is to stage an act of terrorism against Mrs. Cullinan's prized possessions. Her act of defiance is in some sense successful, as Mrs. Cullinan angrily acknowledges her real name. You might also want to discuss with the class how the essay is itself an act of defiance against the white control of language: does Angelou, by relating the episode, have the power to define it? She gains a command over her identity that Mrs. Cullinan dreams of having over her housekeeping.

## ADDITIONAL ACTIVITIES

1. You might want to ask the class to read further in *I Know Why the Caged Bird Sings* (1971) and discuss how this episode relates to others in the book. What theme does Angelou raise here that she develops elsewhere in her work?

2. Langston Hughes's "Salvation" (p. 118) is another depiction of an African American childhood. Ask students to discuss how Hughes's world differs from Angelou's. Do the differences stem solely from the difference in gender?

## GENERATING WRITING

1. This essay might serve as a helpful springboard into personal writing about race, gender, and identity. Ask students to consider how Angelou depicts her identity as shaped by her gender, by her race, and even by her age. What assumptions does Mrs. Cullinan make about her as an African American? What assumptions does Glory make about her as a young person? How does Margaret challenge these assumptions? Once the class has discussed these questions, invite them to draft an essay about how they have responded and reacted to the preconceptions of others. What impact have these preconceptions had on their development?

2. Angelou's writing is outstanding in its use of dialogue to convey character, and this selection is no exception. Have the class analyze the different voices that appear in this essay. How does each character's speech differ? What traits does each person's speech reveal? Ask the students to characterize Angelou's own narrative voice. What similarities do they see between the character of Margaret and the character of the essay's author? How has Angelou changed?

## THE READER'S PRESENCE

1. To work in Mrs. Cullinan's kitchen, Margaret needs to learn new names for objects, as she writes in paragraph 8: names for plates and utensils were "additions to my vocabulary and in fact almost represented a new language." The necessity of cultural translation underscores the distance between white and African American experiences in Arkansas in the 1930s; it becomes more personal, and thus more emotional, when Mrs. Cullinan, in effect, refuses the reciprocal responsibility of learning Angelou's name (mistaking Marguerite, Angelou's original first name, for Margaret, and then simply resorting to Mary because the other is "too long"). "The very next day, she called me by the wrong name," Angelou writes (para. 25). She holds her personal response at bay, leaving that for the reader to intuit. Instead she writes about the African American associations with naming, that is, "being called out of [one's] name" (para. 30). Mrs. Cullinan's act joins centuries of racist insults of blacks by whites. The misnamers and the misnamed line up along racial lines. Miss Glory, too, was renamed by her mistress "and it stuck" (para. 32).

2. Margaret's deliberate smashing of the casserole and the two green glass cups (para. 37) is her direct, if not immediate, response to Mrs. Cullinan's earlier direction "to carry it carefully" (para. 29). The act of destroying the china is especially appropriate because the china is a symbol of Mrs. Cullinan's heritage. Mrs. Cullinan considers refinement and gentility her heritage; Margaret sees it as racism and oppression. The china is also associated with

the theme of names and language through its link with the ideals of gra-
cious living that Angelou discusses in the opening paragraph of the essay.
In rebelling against her employer's command, Margaret engages in her own
subversive act of renaming. Throughout most of the essay, she feels pity for
Mrs. Cullinan, who can't bear children. By the end, however, she not only
stages dramatic and symbolic reparations and escapes but also scares Mrs.
Cullinan into calling her Margaret, a nearly perfect victory.

3. Both selections establish a clear connection between power and language.
In the Angelou selection, the young Angelou believes that Mrs. Cullinan has
mispronounced her name, calling her Margaret, instead of Marguerite. What
is implied, however, is that the white woman and mistress of the house has no
real need to pronounce Angelou's name correctly. She holds the power and,
in a sense, controls the language as well. The new vocabulary that Angelou
learns in paragraph 8, for example, is in the main related to dishware. The
implication here seems to be that, prior to working in Mrs. Cullinan's house,
Angelou never had need of language to distinguish one type of spoon from
another or a regular plate from a serving platter. An expanded vocabulary is
available to, required for, and controlled by the upper (white) class. Angelou
doesn't need the vocabulary until she goes to work for privileged people.
Language becomes a defining element of both class and race.

# James Baldwin
## NOTES OF A NATIVE SON

### APPROACHING THE ESSAY

James Baldwin remains essential to American writing, despite the fact that he
spent most of his life in self-exile in France. Some have argued that it was his distance from America that gave Baldwin the opportunities to explore racial issues
in the country and the freedom to become a great writer. His was one of the most
important voices on the struggle of African Americans in the twentieth century.

Baldwin's essay deals foremost with his struggle with his father's legacy. He
opens with a striking juxtaposition of events: "On the twenty-ninth of July, in 1943,
my father died. On the same day, a few hours later, his last child was born. Over
a month before this, while all our energies were concentrated in waiting for these
events, there had been, in Detroit, one of the bloodiest race riots of the century"
(para. 1). In reflecting on his father's death, Baldwin describes his father as a stern,
bitter minister whose fear and hatred have also infected his son.

When Baldwin leaves New York for a job in New Jersey, he experiences more
pronounced racism than he had in New York, continually being refused service in
restaurants. It was here that Baldwin "contracted some dread, chronic disease," a

"rage in his blood" that he claims is inherent in every African American who experiences discrimination (para. 15). Nearly crazy with this rage, he finally lashes out at a waitress after being refused service. "I saw nothing very clearly but I did see this," he writes: "that my life, my *real* life, was in danger, and not from anything other people might do but from the hatred I carried in my own heart" (para. 22).

In the second section, Baldwin returns to New York at the height of racial tensions and describes a whole range of people on the streets of Harlem amid a heavy police presence. He also visits his father near the end of his life. In the third section, Baldwin describes his father's funeral and reflects on his father's faith, his own choice to write rather than preach, and the incident that sparked the Harlem riots. In the light of the riots and his father's legacy of bitterness, Baldwin concludes that hatred is ultimately destructive to the hater: "It was necessary to hold on to the things that mattered. The dead man mattered, the new life mattered; blackness and whiteness did not matter; to believe that they did was to acquiesce in one's own destruction" (para. 45). Baldwin in the end chooses the notions of acceptance and empowerment in order to keep his heart "free of hatred and despair" (para. 46).

Ask your students how Baldwin makes sense of his father's legacy. What connection does he make between the race-based violence on the streets of Harlem and Detroit and his father's death? between his own anger and bitterness and that of his father? between the choices his father made and the ones apparent now to Baldwin? Baldwin writes that he fears giving up his hatred of his father because he imagines "that one of the reasons people cling to their hates so stubbornly is because they sense, once hate is gone, that they will be forced to deal with pain" (para. 27). Why might Baldwin make this statement in the light of the racial tensions within the United States during this period? Does he see his familial turmoil and racism as symptoms of the same problem? How is his treatment of the two kinds of hate similar and different?

Ask your students to analyze the structure of the essay. What themes are introduced and developed in each section? How do the sections work together to form a single, cohesive essay? Why might Baldwin have chosen to structure his essay in this way? How does Baldwin characterize his father throughout the essay? How does the reader's understanding of him change throughout the essay? Ask students to list words and phrases that Baldwin uses to describe his father. Why does Baldwin choose to use the phrase *native son* in his title?

## ADDITIONAL ACTIVITIES

1. Encourage students to read other essays from Baldwin's collection *Notes of a Native Son* (1955) and his later essays in *The Price of the Ticket* (1985). How does Baldwin develop the themes first introduced in the essay "Notes of a Native Son"? How do his ideas about race in America change over the years? What effect does his exile have on his feelings about America?

2. Have students research the race riots of the 1940s that Baldwin refers to in his essay. What were the political and social factors that contributed to the violence? What were the consequences of these factors?

## GENERATING WRITING

1. Five years after the events described in "Notes of a Native Son," Baldwin left the United States for France. He remained there for ten years, until he returned to work for the civil rights movement. Have students write a short biography of James Baldwin, placing events of his life in the context of events in modern African American history.
2. The strength of Baldwin's essay comes from his conflation of personal history and national history. Have students write a personal essay about an event of national or local importance and the personal associations it holds for them. Ask them to reflect on what personal meanings the event has in the context of their lives today.

## THE READER'S PRESENCE

1. Baldwin opens his essay with an account of the events leading to his nineteenth birthday; these include the death of his father, the birth of his youngest sibling, and the Harlem race riots of 1943. These seemingly disparate occurrences are linked by the common theme of waiting. Both his father's death and his sister's birth are long overdue, and the streets of Harlem are pregnant with the anger and unrest that will lead to the destructive uprising. By the end of the essay, Baldwin is able to make a potent connection between his father's isolating bitterness and the devastating rage of his Harlem neighbors. Writes Baldwin: "Life and death so close together, and love and hatred, and right and wrong, said something to me which I did not want to hear concerning man, concerning the life of man" (para. 41). Baldwin decides on that fateful day to divest himself of the same hatred and bitterness that almost led him to an earlier act of violence in a New Jersey restaurant. He rejects complacency in the face of racism but decides to keep "[his] own heart free of hatred and despair" (para. 46).
2. Baldwin's paternal legacy is the familiar verse he remembers at his father's funeral: "But as for me and my house, we will serve the Lord" (para. 45). In the dismal aftermath of the funeral and the riots, Baldwin finally realizes that he must choose whom he will serve. He can follow his father's (and Harlem's) self-destructive path of gangrenous hatred, or he can reject it. With this insight comes the author's first acknowledgment of his grief at losing his father: "This intimation made my heart heavy and, now that my father was irrecoverable, I wished that he had been beside me so that I could have searched his face for the answers which only the future would give me now" (para. 46).
3. As an African American and a native of Harlem, Baldwin describes the buildup to the riots as an observer who can note the gatherings of people on the street without changing the behavior he observes. He recognized that the incongruous groups of people on the street are a manifestation of growing anger in his community. *Poisonous, smashing, exploding,* and *swelling*

are terms that Baldwin uses to describe Harlem in the period leading to the riots. According to Baldwin, the insurrection is the inevitable result of the powerlessness and anger that shape the ghetto experience. It is also the nature, and perhaps the purpose, of the ghetto to contain this rage within its boundaries. As Baldwin explains, the violence of the ghetto will not explode further because such hatred is ultimately "exhausting and self-destructive" (para. 44).

Baldwin shows how racism took a personal toll on him and his estranged father, leaving bitterness in its wake. In his response letter, Martin Luther King Jr. defends nonviolent actions to end desegregation, discussing the effects on those around him, and ending with a hopeful tone (Letter from Birmingham Jail, p. 716). King would probably concur with Baldwin's assessment of the riots and looting that "None of this was doing anybody any good" (para. 43). However, Baldwin is mostly referring to the wastefulness of the looting and cedes that the riots were inevitable, maybe even necessary, "for Harlem had needed something to smash" (para. 44). The rioters target white businesses in Harlem, an observation that helps Baldwin realize their anger is also economically driven. King, too, later realizes this and uses the power of boycott to persuade white businesses to capitulate to black demands for equality.

King's argument is laid out logically, addressing the points made in the letter from the Alabama clergymen. Baldwin's essay avoids chronology as it divulges personal memories and anecdotes about him and his father. Although King expresses disappointment that stems from love, Baldwin experiences bitterness and, for a long time, hatred, recognizing its self-destructiveness but also that "this does not mean . . . that love comes easily" (para. 44). He approaches King's philosophy, however, when he says: "It goes without saying that injustice is commonplace. But . . . one must never . . . accept these injustices as commonplace. . . . It now [has] been laid to my charge to keep my own heart free of hatred and despair" (para. 46).

# Augusten Burroughs
## ABSOLUTELY FABULOUS

### APPROACHING THE ESSAY

Burroughs has documented his struggle with alcoholism in his memoirs, and indeed the principle of excess, specifically as it relates to the author's alcoholic past, informs the selection here. Its brand of humor is disturbing, and some students are likely to be more disturbed than amused. Other students are likely to miss the humor altogether, and you may find yourself confronted with a classroom full of young people vehemently condemning Burroughs for his vanity. It will be important to keep this sort of moralizing to a minimum if the essay is to be fully understood, and you may have to illuminate some of the areas where Burroughs, through irony, demonstrates an awareness of the emptiness of his obsession with getting "the perfect abs." He is fairly clear about it by the final paragraphs of the essay, but through the front, depending on the relative reading comprehension skills of your students, it may not be entirely clear to all but the most astute readers that Burroughs is half-kidding. In spite of all this, it is also important to remember that Burroughs is not kidding entirely. In fact, it is precisely through humor that Burroughs is able to get the reader to take vanity (and, more important, the needs that drive it) seriously to begin with: the irony allows for a ruthless honesty, which, in turn, forces the reader to take the piece seriously. In Burroughs's self-obsession we recognize a bit of our own.

You might emphasize this irony by drawing the students' attention to paragraph 2: "Elsewhere in the world bombs explode, villages flood, mothers and children are tortured to death and their bodies abandoned to rot in the sun." Ask the students how the close juxtaposition of this image and Burroughs's image in the mirror serves the essay. It trivializes his vanity, to be sure. But doesn't it also trivialize most of the concerns of the average reader? In this sense, "Absolutely Fabulous" is an excellent example of how irony can be used to deal candidly with self-incriminating or otherwise uncomfortable subject matter.

At the end of the essay, after confronting the reader with the bald ugliness of his (and therefore, our own) self-obsession, Burroughs connects his vanity to his alcoholism, explaining that, while abstaining from drink has put an end to his addiction to alcohol, it has not put an end to the sense of need that drove it. He understands his compulsion to work for perfect abs as another manifestation of this abstract, more elusive need. Seen in this light, is his quest for the perfect abs entirely superficial? Or is it part of a larger struggle to give his life meaning? Burroughs himself recognizes that the abstract need will not be fulfilled by achieving the concrete objective: in paragraph 25, the third paragraph from the end, he says he knows how he will feel ("oh"), and here the essay is able to achieve a poignancy the reader would not have expected from a man who (in paragraphs 5 and 6) callously discussed bulimia. In extending a bit of compassion and understanding to himself, Burroughs has also forgiven the reader. In the last paragraph, he calls his pursuit of beauty "a fool's marathon." The statement resonates, in part, because—in addition to (or instead of) pursuing beauty—every reader will know what it is like to pursue something and will be able to sense, in some way, that he or she is really after something more abstract and that we all continue to chase the things we want despite the knowledge that we will never be satisfied.

This sense of unfulfilled desire is accentuated by the fact that Burroughs writes his essay immediately prior to achieving his goal. In one month, he will have the abs: he doesn't have them yet, but he can see them on the horizon. With his ideal body just out of reach, Burroughs is able to capture both the overpowering desire for perfect abs *and* his awareness of the lack of fulfillment he'll feel upon reaching his goal.

## ADDITIONAL ACTIVITIES

1.  Ask the students to think about goals they have set for themselves. How did they feel when they achieved or failed to achieve their goals? How did they expect to feel? To what extent is setting a goal an artificial way to make sure one is perpetually "going" somewhere? toward (or away from) something? In what way is the "fool's marathon" (para. 27) comparable to normal, every-day activity? It's obviously different in the details: in most cases, we don't willingly starve ourselves. But in what way is the goal itself arbitrary? Ask the students to list some of their goals and to think about why they set them. Many students will naturally say that they want to finish college. You might remind your students that although Burroughs did not finish college, he is a best-selling author: he already *has* a career. He has to set *different* goals if he wants to keep striving for something. What kinds of goals might your students set if they already had everything they wanted in the way of education and career?

2.  The obsession with body image has become a fixture of American life. The obsession with obesity has as well. Are these two facts related? You might ask students to collect advertisements for diets or exercise machines that promise a perfect body. You might discuss the trend and relate it to Burroughs's essay. Despite the irony in paragraph 2, for example, there is some truth to it: we are, as a nation, obsessed. Meanwhile, wars are raging, people are starving, and so on. Is our fixation on body image related to our desire to avoid other, more pressing subjects? Or are we really just vain? If so, why? The advertisements might be particularly useful here: we are constantly bombarded with images of "perfect" bodies. How has this affected the way we see ourselves?

## GENERATING WRITING

1.  If you feel comfortable getting to know your students personally or if you can set guidelines that will prevent terrible moments of too much informa-tion, you might have your students write a personal essay about an obses-sion. This assignment might bear interesting fruit. It can also be risky: some students will be dying to tell you things you don't want to know. Make sure you either prepare yourself for overly personal information or establish rea-sonable guidelines to avoid it. You might advise students to stay away from subjects like sex or drug use. You might also stress that they should keep the tone of their essay humorous, relying, like Burroughs, on exaggeration to make the point. Students might benefit from such an assignment without feeling it necessary to bare their souls in ways that might be inappropri-ate for the classroom. You might warn them that their peers will read their work, thereby discouraging all but the most eager students from airing dirty laundry.

2.  Have your students write a research paper on some aspect of dieting, body image in America, or both. Ask them to find statistics: How many people

**15**

are dieting at any given time? What is the percentage of Americans who feel uncomfortable with their bodies? What are the statistics for women? for men? Why are Americans so obsessed with appearance? Are they more obsessed with appearance than, say, Swedes or South Africans? What does our obsession with diets, dieting, and body image say about our culture? What message do your students draw from the rate of obesity in the United States?

3. Burroughs writes that he has asked women how to make himself vomit after meals and hinted that many of them—more than one might expect—have practical knowledge in that area. Is bulimia that common? Or is it more likely that it is common not so much in the general population but among Burroughs's acquaintances? Burroughs draws a straight line between his alcoholism and his obsession with perfect abs. Is there a connection between dieting and addiction? obesity and addiction? addiction and bulimia? Have your students write a paper exploring the relationships between the various afflictions, behaviors, or disorders.

## THE READER'S PRESENCE

1. At the end of the essay, Burroughs makes it clear that his pursuit of the perfect abs is driven by the same need that drove his alcoholism. However, that need is never clearly defined. It seems as though this lack of definition is part of the point of the essay. Burroughs *feels* a need. It is not a rational need, nor is it a need for any one specific thing. It could perhaps be said that it is a need *to need*: a compulsion to chase *something*, in what Burroughs recognizes as the futile hope that achieving the goal will somehow remedy the compulsion. Students may or may not find this explanation satisfactory. Some students may understand all too well, while others will be unable (or unwilling) to sympathize. In any case, the explanation for Burroughs's actions is not logical, nor does it attempt to be, beyond the extent to which he recognizes that it is a self-perpetuating sort of agony—"a fool's marathon" (para. 27)—which nonetheless gives him direction and focus, and in so doing imbues his life with at least some fragile sense of meaning.

2. Writing the essay prior to achieving the goal makes it possible for Burroughs to fuel the prose with a sense of urgency that might otherwise be lacking. This urgency drives the essay (and the reader) forward: the tone is as compulsive as the need, which makes the essay exciting to read. Part of the point of the essay is that the abs themselves don't matter: the need is all consuming. Once Burroughs has identified the nature of the need, relating his quest for perfect abs to his alcoholism, the essay has served its purpose. One could argue that the essay is not about abs but, rather, about addictive/compulsive behavior: the mad groping for *something* that Burroughs recognizes as futile, yet finds necessary to fill some vague space in his life. When Burroughs has resolved that question—identified the need, its purpose—he's finished thinking about the subject. Whether he eventually gets the abs is irrelevant. Readers who find Burroughs's explanations (Question 1) unsatisfactory are

likely to find his conclusions unsatisfactory, as well, but much of the internal logic (and therefore the success) of the piece rests on persuading the reader to accept that some emotional principles are both irrational *and* true.

3. In "What Meets the Eye" (p. 293), Daniel Akst explains our attraction to physical beauty in biological and evolutionary terms. In this sense, Akst's argument is not particularly helpful: although there is evidence to suggest that people are hardwired to find certain traits attractive (symmetry, for example), Burroughs discounts all that by stating, emphatically, that he is not particularly attracted to men or women with "perfect abs." However, Akst makes an important point early in his essay, when he says that the same part of the brain that is activated by gambling and other addictions has been seen to respond to images of beauty. This bit of information might be judged to shed a great deal of light on Burroughs's essay, because he specifically links his efforts to develop his abs to his history of addiction. The difference is that, in Akst's view, the desire for beauty is an instinctive, mechanical response to stimuli, while Burroughs seems to suggest that there is a less tangible principle at work: an almost spiritual yearning, not explicable in pat, biological terms.

# Raymond Carver
## MY FATHER'S LIFE

### APPROACHING THE ESSAY

One of the most important facets of personal identity is our knowledge and understanding of our parents and our relationships with them. This moving autobiographical essay by Raymond Carver should inspire students to consider the echoes of their parents' lives in their own.

You might want to get into the essay by asking the class to discuss Carver's tone. What does his relationship with his father seem to have been like? How does his language convey that relationship? Have your students look closely at Carver's descriptions of his father and make a list of the adjectives he uses. They may be quite surprised at the way Carver avoids evaluative, and especially negative, language when relating incidents that must have been shocking or upsetting to him as a child. In paragraph 11, for example, Carver describes a night when his father, drunk, forces his way into the house and is knocked out by Carver's mother. Ask the class to reread this paragraph carefully. Only two adjectives appear: *drunk* and *heavy*. Why might Carver have chosen to tell this story in such unadorned language? Do students feel that his spare style weakens or strengthens the emotional impact of the incident?

This essay also provides an excellent illustration of literary characterization. Ask students to supply their own descriptions of the people Carver portrays—his father, his mother, and himself—and list them on the board. Have them go back to the essay and point out specific passages that led them to their judgments. You might want to focus on the way Carver uses incidents to reveal character. A great deal is said about his mother, for instance, in paragraph 16, where she sticks her husband's hand in warm water so that he will talk in his sleep. Here, too, Carver avoids evaluating her behavior, even through the use of adjectives. What conclusions about Mrs. Carver does the reader draw? Why does Carver leave his readers to draw their own conclusions?

Carver finally begins to evaluate his father's behavior in paragraph 18: "My dad had grown restless. . . . Things had gotten a little too predictable for him in Yakima." Point out that the paragraph begins with Carver's statement that he was about to graduate from high school. Could this change in the essay's structure mirror Carver's own growth and his developing judgment and independence? It is difficult, after all, for children to put their parents' behavior into context because the parents are the primary context of their lives. By the time Carver was eighteen, though, he might be expected to have the ability to consider and draw conclusions about his father's life.

One of the threads that ties this essay together is the idea of names and naming. The names of towns, cars, employers, restaurants, and streets give the essay a rich foundation in experience. Ask students to consider why Carver is so careful to name and date his past and his father's. Then ask them if they notice any notable omissions of names. It may take them a few minutes to realize that Carver's mother is not named in the essay, and neither is his wife. How are these omissions significant?

It might be an interesting exercise to have the students write a short abstract of the essay, using a detached third-person point of view as though they were composing, for example, an encyclopedia entry on Raymond Carver. In what ways would that text differ from this essay, and why? How is personal history more than a recital of facts and incidents?

## ADDITIONAL ACTIVITIES

1. In this essay, as in Alice Walker's "Beauty: When the Other Dancer Is the Self" (p. 244), the author includes a poem inspired by a particular experience in the context of a discussion of that experience. How does Carver present his father in the poem? How does that presentation differ from that in the essay? How does the approach Walker takes in her poem differ from that in her essay? What qualities are similar in poem and prose? Carver also supplies his own critique of his poem. Why might he have included that?

2. You may wish to discuss with your class the nature of a personal narrative like Carver's and its relation to the author's memory. Ask your students to what extent Carver's essay is structured by the order in which he remembers the events of his and his father's lives. Are there any indications that he left certain details out of his essay? Have students try to unveil Carver's criteria for the selection and inclusion of family anecdotes in the essay. Are there

any indications that Carver changed certain details about his father's life or his own? What artistic or personal reasons might have accounted for these alterations?

## GENERATING WRITING

1. Have the students write a brief biography of one or both of their parents. It might be worthwhile devoting one class to freewriting on the topic, asking students to brainstorm a list of significant or revealing incidents in their parents' lives. Have them develop that material into a polished second draft, paying close attention to their characterization of their parents and themselves.

2. Discuss the manner in which Carver has chosen to relate the events of his childhood. Then ask students to recall interesting or formative moments from their own childhood and write an essay to organize and recount those events in a coherent fashion. They might end the essay by explaining why they structured the events in the way they did.

3. Near the end of his essay, Carver adds that there are things he did not get to say to his father before he died. Moreover, there is a very strong sense throughout the essay that Carver never got to know his father as well as he would have liked to have known him. To some degree, all fathers and mothers remain mysteries to their children. Ask students to write a short personal essay that describes a family member whom they feel they have never truly known or understood.

## THE READER'S PRESENCE

1. In the essay's opening paragraph, the author recalls how he as a boy did not want to share a name with his father. This stemmed mainly from the desire to have his own identity. In the last paragraph, however, the author reports that he is comforted at his father's funeral by having the same name. His desire for closeness with a man he never really knew is fulfilled in part by sharing a name with his father.

2. Aside from a few very brief exchanges, the only real conversation between the author and his father occurs in paragraph 26 when Carver tells his father about his intention to become a writer. Carver writes that "I might as well have told him I wanted to become a plastic surgeon." Apparently, the father did not know how to react to the son's announcement, yet he tried to be encouraging by offering advice on what to write about and by asking his son to send along some of his writing. All in all, however, the conversation's tone reveals two people who really don't know each other well enough to talk intimately.

3. Carver's poem, like his essay, is composed of plain words and unremarkable meter. He says that he wrote it as "a way of trying to connect up with [his father]" (para. 29), implying that for Carver the poem is a more intimate form than the story or the essay. (Note that Carver doesn't write the poem *for* his father—that would be another sort of connection, one that is now lost to the

writer.) From the reader's point of view, Alice Walker's poem in "Beauty: When the Other Dancer Is the Self" (p. 244) is like Carver's in that they are composed of the same stripped-down language, images, and ideas found in her prose. Both of these writers move easily between forms and genres.

# Judith Ortiz Cofer
## SILENT DANCING

### APPROACHING THE ESSAY

This complex essay depicts an essential process in the construction of identity — the reconstruction and interpretation of the past. Judith Ortiz Cofer's memoir traces her imaginative return to her childhood through the medium of a home movie. One way to start discussion of the essay might be by asking students to characterize Cofer's tone. How does she feel about her past and that of her family? Encourage the students to find specific passages in support of their opinions. Have them focus on Cofer's language; what judgments does it express?

Cofer makes her past live again through the masterful use of detail. You might ask students to single out the two or three details they found most arresting. How are these details presented? What knowledge does Cofer take for granted in her readers? A good place to start would be paragraphs 20 through 23, in her description of the night the home movie was taken. Talk about Cofer's appeals to the senses, and have the class discuss the power of her sensory images. How do the descriptions in these paragraphs differ from Cofer's description of the home movie? How do the two descriptions enhance each other?

You may also want to discuss Cofer's use of Spanish words and names. How does this help her characterization of her family? If she had translated each Spanish phrase into English, how might the essay have been different?

The selection's structure is central to its effectiveness. Make sure that students understand who the voices of paragraph 24 are. How does Cofer's dramatization of the voices of her past help reveal her own, and her family's, character? Discuss the impact this section of the essay has on the work as a whole. Do students find Cofer's choice here a daring one? How does this passage make the essay's title ironic?

Cofer's shifts in time also contribute to the complexity of her essay's structure. There are several time frames operating here; try to get students to separate and comment on them. They should notice the time of Cofer's childhood, the night the home movie was taken, the times Cofer watches the home movie with her mother, the times Cofer reflected on these events, and the time of writing. Which of these times are depicted directly, and which are alluded to indirectly? Juxtaposed against these real times are the timelessness of the home movie and the dream time of the voices of the dead. What is the impact of these unreal time frames? What balance do they offer to Cofer's personal history? Ask the class to discuss this issue in detail. Some students may be put off or offended by what they see as a fictional intrusion into an autobiography. Others may argue that personal history is much more than a summary of facts. You might want to point out that most personal stories have a strong component of mythology—Cofer makes the link explicit in paragraph 25, when she likens her encounter with the home movie to the Greek hero Odysseus's visit to Hades. Ask the class to think about the ways they mythologize their own lives.

Another point you may wish to introduce is Cofer's portrayal of the gulf between image and reality. Does her presentation of the home movie prepare us for the revelations the voices eventually make? Students may be shocked that Cofer's cousin, who appears in the home movie as "gorgeous" (para. 11), confident, and in control of her life, would die soon after from a self-induced abortion (para. 24). Why might Cofer have saved that information for the essay's end? In general, the atmosphere of family happiness and self-sufficiency we get from the home movie, as Cofer describes it, and from her own childhood memories of deliciousness and warmth, is profoundly complicated by what the voices tell. Ask the class why Cofer might have included a discussion of the families on television (para. 15) and their relation to her own. Are they, too, an example of the distance between the simplicity of appearances and reality's deep complexity?

Have the class talk in depth about the essay's conclusion. Why does Cofer present this material in the context of a dream? Does it seem as if this was an actual dream, or is the act of dreaming a symbolic one? Ask them to look closely at changes in Cofer's language and tone. Do they find the end of this selection comforting? disquieting?

## ADDITIONAL ACTIVITY

1. Some students may want to read further in the memoir from which this essay was taken, *Silent Dancing: A Partial Remembrance of a Puerto Rican Childhood* (1990). Another work students may find interesting is Oscar Hijuelos's *The Mambo Kings Play Songs of Love* (1988), a novel about a Cuban man's reconstruction of his family's past.

## GENERATING WRITING

1. Ask students to find or recall an artifact from their past. It may be a home movie or photograph; it might also be an article of clothing, a letter, or a favorite toy. Have them write a brief essay describing the object in detail, with special focus on sensory appeals. What did the object mean in the past? What does the object mean to them now? If the object could talk, what would it say?

2. Students may be interested in Cofer's description of television's role in shaping her early perceptions of her family. Ask the class to think carefully about

**21**

how the models presented by television affected their images of their own families. Were their families defined by their likeness or their opposition to the fictional norms of the small screen? Assign a short essay in which students present and analyze the impact that television families had on their ideas about families, and on their actual families.

## THE READER'S PRESENCE

1. You might want to encourage students to focus especially on paragraphs 1 through 9, 12 through 15, and 20. At the time Cofer's father arrived, he was rejected by an anti-Latino landlord; by the time Cofer was old enough to remember, however, Paterson had a self-contained Latino community. As Cofer's mother grew more firmly entrenched in the life of the barrio, Cofer's father was encouraging his children to assimilate—a risky process, as the death of Cofer's cousin shows.

2. Some advantages of the home movie as a vehicle for the essay are its depiction of people in groups, its ability to evoke specific sensory memories, and its portrayal of particular relations between people (for example, the cousin's confidence and the *novia's* shyness). Also, the color of the images helps keep Cofer's memories vivid and satisfies her "obsession for assigning symbolism to everything" (para. 10). It also presents limitations: Cofer can present only the lives of those who appear in the home movie, and the home movie can depict and replay only one moment in time. These limitations may help to explain why Cofer alternates between passages of relatively strict narration of the film and those in which she elaborates on the film's flashes of the past. At the end of the essay, Cofer describes the dreams that have occurred to her "in the form of this home movie" (para. 24). With these closing images and sounds, she breaks free from the confines of that particular film, if not from its haunting form.

3. Draw students' attention to Cofer's explicit intrusions into the past, such as her questions to her mother and her comments on the home movie. You might also want to talk about the ways in which Cofer juxtaposes the events of her early life (as they must have been related to her later) with her memories at the time.

4. Although they are from very different cultures, Cofer and Maxine Hong Kingston ("No Name Woman," p. 458) share some similar experiences. Both women learn of a relative who became illegitimately pregnant and was punished for it by her family. Both punishments involve forgetting about or not speaking of the guilty relative. It is up to the narrators to infer and glean what happened from competing and at times unreliable sources. For Cofer, the story of her cousin's pregnancy appears to her in a dream anchored in the memory of a family party she attended as a child. In her dream, there are competing viewpoints that tell the cousin's story. As the dream narrative progresses, it becomes clear the cousin's original perspective is naïve and incomplete. The older relatives tell of the true consequences of her actions.

In Kingston's story, her mother, who tells of the adulterous relative, is an unreliable source who imparts the story as a warning. However, Kingston infers the details of the story herself and questions some of her mother's facts. Infusing the story with context and depth, Kingston's narration provides a contrasting perspective from the judgmental viewpoint of her mother. Both Kingston and Cofer are immigrant writers, but Kingston focuses on recreating the experience of a Chinese relative who never left China, whereas Cofer concentrates on the trials of a Puerto Rican woman living in the United States.

# Bernard Cooper
## A CLACK OF TINY SPARKS: REMEMBRANCES OF A GAY BOYHOOD

### APPROACHING THE ESSAY

Discoveries and decisions about whom, and how, we are to love are vital steps in the construction of identity. Some students may be uncomfortable with the topics raised in this selection. Try to help them see that the essay is meant to capture Bernard Cooper's perspective on his own life. They may not share his views, but they have an obligation to respect them; after all, each of us must be allowed to speak authoritatively about our own lives.

The best place to begin discussing the essay might be its title. Ask the class what they thought it meant before they had read the essay. Did their interpretation change after they had finished? The subtitle, too, is important. Talk about what Cooper means by the phrase "a gay boyhood." Is it more likely, in students' opinions, that he means a boyhood shaped by sexual preference or a boyhood that helped him develop into the gay adult he is today? What might be the differences between the two? You may want to talk about the ways in which the phrase is threatening—our culture has assumed that childhood is a time free from sexuality, even from sexual preference. Is that stereotype accurate? How can it be hurtful? Why might Cooper have chosen to challenge it?

Have students reread the essay, paying careful attention to how it is structured. One pattern they are sure to pick up on is that Cooper reveals his personality and emotions by depicting his encounters with others, then discussing his reactions to them. What do his encounters with Theresa Sanchez reveal about him? about her? What about his encounters with his family? with Grady? with Debbie? with Gerald and Mr. Kendrick? Ask the class to talk about this approach to autobiography, outlining some of its advantages and disadvantages. Would they tell their own life stories this way?

It could be very helpful to talk about the stereotypes and preconceptions about homosexuality that Cooper evokes here. Go over his account, and ask students to tease out these preconceptions; you might guide them toward the description of Bobby Keagan (para. 8), Cooper's speculations about Gerald and Mr. Kendrick (para. 32), or Grady's folkloric characterization (para. 34). Are these stereotypes still widespread today? Ask students to think about how deeply they are ingrained in their own consciousness.

Much of the essay is devoted to depicting Cooper's quest for information about himself and others like him. Ask the class to reread paragraph 33, where Cooper looks up *homosexual* in the dictionary. How is this episode funny? ironic? sad? Invite the students to turn to the closing paragraph, where Cooper regrets not having been open with Theresa Sanchez. Point out the connection between Cooper's failed attempt to research himself in books and Theresa's superior information and sophistication. Encourage students to make the link between Theresa's well-researched dinner parties and the recipe for living that Cooper was seeking.

If the class finds it comfortable, it could be productive to discuss the ways in which Cooper depicts Grady as an object of desire. Reread the paragraphs that introduce Grady (paras. 7–9). What does Cooper find attractive about him? Is this at all surprising? What is the adult Cooper's perspective on that attraction? Many students will probably recognize some elements of their own first crushes—the desired person is popular, athletic, or graceful; has a perfect family life; and is, above all, "normal." Why is this so ironic here? You might want to juxtapose Cooper's presentation of his time alone with Grady with his depiction of the make-out party. Ask the class to characterize Cooper's tone here. How does it capture his reaction to the party? Are there conclusions to be drawn about the adult Cooper's relationship to the heterosexual world?

Ask the class to look at the essay's concluding paragraphs, and discuss the ways in which Cooper links his past and his present. What are the implications of that link? How effective do your students find the essay's conclusion?

## ADDITIONAL ACTIVITY

1. Students who want to read more gay, lesbian, and bisexual autobiographies could be encouraged to read *Growing Up Gay* (1993), an anthology of personal narratives edited by Bennett Singer. Ask them to consider what special obstacles bisexuals, lesbians, and gay men face in their personal growth and development. How does society challenge their self-image? What sources of support can they find?

## GENERATING WRITING

1. Some interesting personal writing could be produced by assigning a short essay in which students tell the story of their first crush and the feelings it evoked. How did that first attraction help set the pattern for their romantic

lives? What did they learn from the experience? What did it teach them about themselves at the time? What insights do they have on it now?

2. You might also ask students to report on the images of gay men, lesbians, and bisexuals that they encounter through the media and in their own lives. What assumptions and preconceptions do they see? What impact do these assumptions have? What issues are discussed openly, and which are left unspoken? (This could be a good assignment for in-class freewriting.)

## THE READER'S PRESENCE

1. Swimming is symbolic of sexuality to Cooper, a connection he makes explicit in paragraph 38, when he describes touching his lover as "the pleasure a diver feels the instant he enters a body of water." Swimming, with its implications of power, freedom, strength, and control, provides Cooper with an excellent range of imagery for sexuality and sexual connection.

2. Cooper attends the make-out party in the hope that he will catch on to heterosexuality. The "tiny sparks" (para. 25) are a metaphor for the sexual electricity between his straight classmates, who enjoy the world of accepted sexuality from which he is excluded in his "gay boyhood."

3. Cooper and Andrew Sullivan ("The M-Word: Why It Matters to Me," p. 223) write essays about previously unknown and feared aspects of themselves that now are essential to their very beings. Both authors have written powerfully about their homosexuality—especially about how the bigotry of one's culture can produce profound shame in the outcast. The shame they both express in their writing is of a very different sort than their earlier, perhaps more naïve self-consciousness, however. This shame comes with the "outing" of the particular people who—perhaps unknowingly, or with good intentions—delayed their full development as people and as writers. When Cooper describes the acute attention he paid to details of carriage and habit in order to make himself into a person he knew he could not be, readers may laugh at the cartoon portraits of his parents; but we also realize that these are the people who helped to keep Cooper from himself. Cooper's resorting to a dictionary to look up the word *homosexual* reminds us that not just his parents but the dominant culture of postwar America was bent on defending a narrow definition of "normal" in respect to race, class, gender, and sexuality.

   Frederick Douglass's desire to learn the meaning of *abolition* ("Learning to Read and Write," p. 86) and Cooper's self-conscious attempts to uncover the meaning of *homosexual* take similarly circuitous routes to fulfillment. For Douglass, the definition is empowering, long-hoped-for proof that others support his quest for freedom. For Cooper, however, the definition provides him with unwelcome information about how he sees himself and about how others see him.

# Frederick Douglass
## LEARNING TO READ AND WRITE

### APPROACHING THE ESSAY

This selection serves as a powerful illustration of how central reading and writing can be in creating an identity. It might be necessary for you to remind students that in many slave states it was actually a crime to teach African Americans—whether enslaved or free—to read or write. Frederick Douglass's own experience, as he relates it here, bears out the fears that inspired those restrictive laws. Reading gave him his first hope of liberty (paras. 5 and 6), and, as he predicts in paragraph 7, he eventually wrote his own pass to freedom.

One of the larger questions you might introduce with this selection is the role of autobiography in the creation of identity. Ask your students how they think these are related. Doesn't a large part of who we are come from the stories we tell about ourselves? Point out that it is an act of rebellion for Douglass, a formerly enslaved person, to take the initiative to write his own story. His style and diction are those of an educated person of the nineteenth century; yet, as his testimony indicates, he acquired them entirely through his own efforts. Talk with students about how Douglass extends the American ideal of self-reliance to include himself as a representative African American. How was that a challenge to the prejudices of his day?

Douglass makes good use of irony in his account of the "stratagems" he used in learning to read and write. He shows the hypocrisy underlying the paternalistic structure of slavery; his struggle to become a "civilized," literate person is mirrored by his mistress's progressive hardening to the role of slaveowner by obeying her husband's commands to keep Douglass from the knowledge he seeks. The selection's first paragraph might be a good place to begin discussing Douglass's use of irony. You might ask the students to characterize the tone of voice they hear, for example, in the phrase "It is due, however, to my mistress to say of her . . ." (para. 1). Does his attitude toward his mistress remain consistent throughout the essay, or does it change?

Perhaps the most bitterly ironic moment in the selection is Douglass's account of his mistress's ambition. He writes that "She was not satisfied with simply doing as well as [her husband] had commanded; she seemed anxious to do better" (para. 2). Douglass's own desire for self-improvement is here most painfully subverted.

There are several other moments in this passage where Douglass develops a similarly strong ironic attitude toward his own self-education. The main fact of slavery was that it "proved as injurious to [my mistress] as it did to me" (para. 2). Some other points—particularly when Douglass talks about the disadvantages of educating himself and how he "envied [his] fellow-slaves for their stupidity" (para. 6)—might inspire further productive discussion of irony, a compositional skill with which students may have difficulty.

The Douglass selection is also an excellent help in teaching other compositional skills, including organization, sentence structure, and diction. It might be helpful to ask the class to map the overall structure of the selection. Direct students to the opening paragraph, and encourage them to notice that Douglass organizes his account of learning to read and write around this statement: "I was compelled to resort to various stratagems." Ask students to list each "stratagem," and to describe it in detail. Invite them to discuss the word *stratagem* itself. You may want to read a dictionary definition aloud. What are the implications of this word choice? What do they say about how Douglass viewed his struggle to learn to read and write? How might the essay have seemed different if Douglass had used the word *trick* here?

Discussing the organization of the Douglass selection might lead easily into consideration of his sentence structure. Have students describe how Douglass builds sentences in the opening two paragraphs. Once they can break down the construction of these sentences, they are ready to take up the larger question of the effects such structures can elicit in readers.

Douglass's use of figurative language is also worthy of notice. Ask the class to read closely the anecdote of how he "finally succeeded in learning how to write" (para. 8). When Douglass was sent on errands, he always brought a book and bread: "This bread I used to bestow upon the hungry little urchins, who, in return, would give me that more valuable bread of knowledge" (para. 4). This passage could open discussion of the advantages of drawing on figurative language—especially metaphor—to make a crucial point clear. You might ask students to find other metaphors in the selection and to identify what makes each successful.

A narrative's effectiveness depends on its use of telling details, enhanced by the writer's clear sense of direction and purpose. You might want to discuss the effects of Douglass's choice of details in the incidents he recounts. Try to get students to see the connection between the details Douglass selects and his purpose in writing the piece.

It is likely that this selection will inspire productive class discussions and writing assignments on the issues of education, enslavement, racism, and autobiography. You may encourage students to reflect on the circumstances in which they learned to read and write, and create their own accounts of how they developed these essential skills.

## ADDITIONAL ACTIVITIES

1. Several essays in this section deal with questions of African American identity. Two that might be productive to consider with Douglass's are Maya Angelou's "'What's Your Name, Girl?'" (p. 31) and Malcolm X's "My First Conk" (p. 153). How did white society's preconceptions about African Americans change between Douglass's era and the time in which Angelou and Malcolm X wrote? What prejudices remained the same? How does each essay depict language as a medium of oppression?

2. You might also want to consider Douglass's essay as a story of the struggle to self-knowledge through language. Ask students to compare Douglass's

experience with Amy Tan's, as she describes it in "Mother Tongue" (p. 232). How can gaining mastery over language be a process of self-definition? What kinds of obstacles stand in the way of that process?

## GENERATING WRITING

1. The central event of this selection is the profound change that occurs in Douglass's self-image once he discovers the enabling acts of reading and writing. You might ask your students to draft a personal essay in which they re-create their own experience of learning to read and write. Urge them to be as specific as possible about their sociocultural and political circumstances at the time. What forces encouraged them or barred their way? They will need to reflect on events in their personal lives while placing the events in a comprehensible social, cultural, and political context for their readers.

2. As the selection demonstrates, the myth of American success, and the personal ambition that recharges that myth, can often be complicated or frustrated by racial and sexual stereotypes and discrimination. Ask students to analyze how contemporary media can exclude and silence the ambitions of certain groups. Have them draw on their readings of Douglass in coming to their conclusions. They might examine a recent issue of a popular magazine and select an advertisement promoting some aspect of the American dream of success. After studying the ad, they could write an expository or argumentative essay in which they first analyze the individual success imagined in the ad and then demonstrate how that ideal trades on (or is subverted by) a racial or sexual stereotype.

## THE READER'S PRESENCE

1. Douglass seems to anticipate a sympathetic audience whose members are less than fully briefed on the conditions of slavery. (You might point out his explanation of slavery's effect on his mistress, in paragraphs 1 and 2, or his statement in paragraph 4 that "it is almost an unpardonable offense to teach slaves to read.")

2. One of the most important books for Douglass is *The Columbian Orator*; he learns from it not only the form of methodical argument but also "a powerful vindication of human rights": "The more I read, the more I was led to abhor and detest my enslavers" (para. 6). Douglass's reading of this book raises his awareness of his condition and sharpens his consciousness of its injustice. Indeed, his very thinking becomes a source of almost unbearable pain: "Freedom now appeared, to disappear no more forever. . . . It was ever present to torment me with a sense of my wretched condition" (para. 6). In paragraph 8, Douglass describes his ingenious methods of learning to write, using "board fence, brick wall, and pavement" as his copybook. In learning to imitate his master Thomas's hand, he prepares quite literally for his escape to freedom (beyond the scope of this excerpt) when he will forge his own pass to the North.

3. Although Douglass is first taught to read by his mistress, she ceases this at her husband's demand. We can deduce the master's motives from Douglass's depiction of the wife. The master likely sees his slaves as "mere chattel" (para. 2) that should not be empowered through education. Ultimately, Douglass reads Sheridan's speeches on Catholic emancipation, and it is his education that serves as the key motivation for his escape to the North. Simply learning the word *abolition* is a step toward understanding the possibility of slaves' freedom.

In the excerpt from *"Reading Lolita in Tehran"* (p. 511), Azar Nafisi's female students confront the challenges of a religious state that demands that women remain inconspicuous and segregated from men. Iranian universities, intent on limiting internal rebellion, are also forbidden to teach anything Western or potentially subversive. Like Douglass, Nafisi's students find ways to educate themselves and, in doing so, they redefine their identities in opposition to what their society expects of them.

# Anne Fadiman
## UNDER WATER

### APPROACHING THE ESSAY

"Under Water" is an excellent example of a personal essay about a significant event. It tells a clear story and meditates on what the story might mean. By carefully placing the passages of meditation, Fadiman adds resonance to the story without getting bogged down in abstractions: she is introspective, not navel-gazing. Drawing your students' attention to this tightrope act might be a helpful way to lead them away from some of the typical traps novice writers fall into when composing personal essays.

In the first paragraph, for example, Fadiman reflects briefly on her childhood but uses very little abstraction. Indeed, the paragraph is full of physical details: clogged drains, catsup bottles. The only abstract word Fadiman uses to describe herself is "impatient." A lesser writer may have been inclined to say "I couldn't stand to wait for anything," or "I was always in a hurry," but Fadiman goes directly from the abstract adjective to the myriad concrete exemplifications of it. The paragraph also resonates nicely because the image of the twig going downstream connects well with what happens later. Most of the essay is concerned with what happens: Fadiman tells the story of Gary's drowning with very little scaffolding, allowing images to conjure the feelings she's trying to re-create for the reader.

The central paragraph seems to be paragraph 7. Here Fadiman gives us a little bit of exposition, explaining how she felt and what she thought about rather than simply telling the story. It might be worthwhile to talk about why she chooses this moment in the essay to interject a little reflection, and for guidance on this you might look to the entry dealing with Abani's "The Lottery" (p. 25), but first it will be important to talk through what happens with the students. As Fadiman watches Gary drown, she is reminded of a picture she saw in a textbook. The exposition tells us that she feels as though the thought itself was dishonorable. Why? What does that mean? Reader's Presence Question 2 touches on the answer to these questions. Take time to discuss the "crime of inattention" with your students. Do they agree with Fadiman's self-evaluation? *Was* the thought dishonorable? Why or why not?

After paragraph 7, Fadiman proceeds through the end of the story and Gary's death. Why does she choose to end the essay with regret? This regret seems to be more generalized than the regret over thinking about a picture in a textbook while Gary was drowning: What does she regret? How do these regrets relate to the central event of the essay? How do they tie in to the childhood recollections with which Fadiman opens the piece? Why doesn't Fadiman explain herself in more depth? How does limiting the amount of exposition affect the essay? How would it be different if, instead of three paragraphs of exposition and ten paragraphs of story, she'd done it the other way around, telling the story in three paragraphs and making broad generalizations about life and regret for the other ten?

## ADDITIONAL ACTIVITIES

1. Depending on your comfort level, you may want to have students talk a little about their own experiences. Have they had dispassionate thoughts in crisis moments? How did those thoughts make them feel? What do they tell us about ourselves? about people in general?

2. Have the students get into groups and analyze the structure of the essay. Viewed as a machine, what does the essay *do*, paragraph by paragraph? It might be especially useful to compare it with Chris Abani's "The Lottery" (p. 25). How are the essays alike, structurally? How do the authors depend on or manipulate structure to get their ideas across effectively?

## GENERATING WRITING

1. Have your students write a personal essay about a significant event in their lives, limiting the amount of abstraction and reflection they may include. You may even go so far as to specifically forbid any more than, say, four or five abstractions. For example, Fadiman uses the adjective "impatient" to describe her childhood self. One cannot see, taste, touch, smell, or hear "impatience," but Fadiman is careful to provide several examples of what she means. You might do well to impose similar limitations and requirements on your students. Don't allow them to explain how they felt about the event until the end of the essay. Rather, insist that they simply *tell the story*. Once they've done that, it might be interesting to talk to them about whether they really need their last paragraphs. Does the point still come across without the exposition?

2. Have your students write an essay comparing "Under Water" to either Augusten Burroughs's "Absolutely Fabulous" (p. 57) or Abani's "The Lottery" (p. 25). How do the authors criticize themselves? What do they hope to communicate about life, in general, with such criticisms? In a sense, this assignment would be the opposite of the one above: in this assignment, students would be asked to draw abstractions out of specifics, comparing them in order to determine author intent; in the assignment above, students would be required to practice communicating the specific without any reliance on abstraction whatsoever.

## THE READER'S PRESENCE

1. Paragraph 1 resonates nicely with the rest of the essay for a number of reasons. The most obvious is probably that the image of the twig floating downstream, snagged on a rock, is repeated in slightly different form when Gary is snagged between two rocks. The word *obstructions* is repeated at the end of the essay (para. 13). As an adult, Fadiman says she minds them less. The idea seems to be that, as she has grown older, she has learned not to be in a rush. She has learned patience, and, if she had it to do all over again, she might have handled her life differently: she says the regrets wash over her like water, one possible implication being that, having rushed through life, she's made many mistakes, and that now she is sort of drowning in regret, the same way Gary drowned in water. Obstruction seems to be a keyword, but the key *idea* might be patience. Regret is also central; Fadiman seems to regret the way she handled the central event of the essay: whether she could have saved Gary is not the point. The point is that her *thoughts* at the time were "dishonorable" (para. 7).

2. The thoughts are dishonorable because they are aesthetic. A young man is drowning before her eyes and Fadiman is thinking about a picture she saw in a book. The "crime of inattention" is simply explained by the clause preceding the phrase: "to think about anything outside the moment"—in other words, anything other than trying to save Gary—demonstrates a detachment from what's happening and, therefore, a kind of selfishness. A lack of compassion, perhaps. Her priorities are all wrong. This sentiment is repeated in the last paragraph of the essay, when Fadiman refers to all the "harsh words, foolish decisions, and moments of inattention" she would take back if she could. It's worth entertaining the thought that most people's lives are full of such moments, and almost no one lives perpetually in the moment, regardless of what's happening in front of them. In this sense, Fadiman is perhaps a little hard on herself. By the same token, it is only the honesty of the essay, Fadiman's willingness to cop to the "crime of inattention," that causes the reader to sympathize in the first place. It's a tricky principle, and one that might take some explaining. By exposing her "crime," Fadiman makes herself vulnerable, hence we sympathize. One might look to the brutal honesty of Burroughs's "Absolutely Fabulous" (p. 57) for a parallel. Burroughs exposes his vanity so baldly that it presents as weakness, and we refrain

from passing judgment. We give him, and ourselves, a little break for our imperfections.

3. Both Fadiman's and Abani's essays steer clear of a lot of reflection and abstraction. Abani's fifth and pivotal paragraph contains the precious little exposition we have to contextualize the event and get a sense of his true feelings toward it. Similarly, Fadiman limits most of her reflection to paragraph 7, where she tells the reader that she was reminded of a painting, then explains how she feels about being "the sort of person who . . . in a crisis, thought about something from a textbook." The limits imposed on abstraction and introspection, on reflective exposition, in general, serve to heighten the emotional power of both essays. The writers rely on images to do the work, and in that way the narration is similar from one to the other. Students are likely to have varied opinions about how the authors reacted to the situations they describe, but it is safe to say that neither writer seems to feel as though he or she behaved admirably.

# Henry Louis Gates Jr.
## IN THE KITCHEN

### APPROACHING THE ESSAY

Gates's essay is remarkable for the balance it maintains. It critiques the notion of "good" hair while admiring the resourcefulness of those who sought it. It provides a historical overview while remaining sharply focused on the author's personal experiences. It celebrates black resistance to assimilation through an analysis of an activity that, to many, is archetypally assimilationist. It does all of this while blending reverence and good-natured irony.

One place to begin students' deeper inquiry into this piece is to have them trace the ways Gates uses the word *kitchen*. The primary split is between the portion of hair on a black person's neck and that place in the house where cooking is done. But the latter meaning represents both the place where blacks attempted assimilation—where Gates's mother helped folks straighten their hair, and a source of strength and identity, which are the necessary qualities for resistance. His mother's friends developed intimacy and solidarity from their time together in the kitchen; Gates clearly drew upon that intimacy for his own sense of worth and well-being. The kitchen is also the place where Gates's grandmother maintained her importance to the family, despite her advanced age and failing eyesight; strong family and community ties are an invaluable defense against how an oppressive social and political environment can encroach on individual integrity.

Students may resist such a politicized reading of life in the kitchen. Gates himself is not explicit about it, and students, regardless of their background, may identify with or dissociate themselves from such a strong sense of cultural-family identity. To help them to recognize how this subject is politicized, it may be necessary to direct the students' attention to the section of the essay where Gates discusses, rapidly, how black hairstyles changed through the 1960s and 1970s. The significance of the Afro as a political statement may be lost on them, but it is a clear indicator that no black writer of Gates's age and educational background can write about hairstyles without an awareness of deeper implications. If the hairstyle itself can be seen as a loaded topic, then life in the kitchen may also be acknowledged to have political resonance.

Gates confirms his awareness of this subject's charged nature with his reference to Malcolm X's *Autobiography*, where the author's introduction to the teachings of Elijah Muhammed begins when a prison inmate asks him about his "process." Gates's essay is striking in its acknowledgment of these political implications while maintaining respect for those who had their hair straightened. After establishing the political context of this subject, ask students to trace Gates's attitude toward the activity in his mother's kitchen, the attempts of Gates and his friends to achieve straight hair, and—especially—Nat King Cole. Although there is an ironic skepticism about the effort that went into trying, as Gates describes it, to disguise one's "African past," there also seems to be admiration for the ingenuity and pride associated with such efforts. To some degree, the criticism leveled at Michael Jackson and Sammy Davis Jr. taints the process itself and makes its adherents suspect. In this light, Gates's tears in the last scene seem ironic, intended, humorously, to make suspect his nostalgia for a questionable practice. At the same time, his admiration of Nat King Cole seems genuine. By distinguishing "straight" from "stringy" hair (with a biting rejoinder to white characterizations of the makeup of *The Mod Squad*), Gates carves out some space for "the process" to be something other than purely assimilationist; it is not as simple as wanting to look like white people, and, therefore, perhaps it is something that needs less fervent denunciations than it has sometimes attracted.

## ADDITIONAL ACTIVITIES

1. In exploring the relationship between politics and appearance in African American experience, it would be valuable to have students view some representations of African Americans on television and in film, or the appearance of popular black entertainers during different time periods. How does Nat King Cole's image compare with that of James Brown or Stevie Wonder, and what do these comparisons suggest about how each performer dealt with the issues that Gates identifies? During the 1960s and 1970s, often the only film and television roles for African Americans were in crime dramas. You might show in class a film or two of this type and ask students to examine the representations of those on either side of the law, and those of men and women. Which characters seem more likely to have "processed" African physical features and dress, and which have unprocessed ones? How do these characters compare with the representation of blacks on 1980s television programs such as *The Cosby Show*?

2. Several of Spike Lee's films, including *School Daze* (1984), address such complex racial issues as assimilation. Because Lee also directed an acclaimed version of Malcolm X's *Autobiography*, you might ask students to discuss how the treatment of assimilationist issues in one of Lee's films compares with the tone of Gates's essay.

## GENERATING WRITING

1. Ask students to write about some aspect of appearance that they learned about in their families—perhaps one related to hair or about ways of dressing. Can they detect ways in which this aspect is culturally coded? Who are their parents teaching them to look like and, by implication, be like? How have they struggled against this, and who did they find themselves imitating? What do they think these "looks" suggest about the "nature" of the person adopting them?
2. Ask students to write about a cultural icon of their own choosing and to try to understand the message of that person's appearance (Madonna and Michael Jackson are obvious examples). Who is this person imitating, and who, in turn, have they been imitated by? To what extent does this "look" aspire to the "natural"?

## THE READER'S PRESENCE

1. Having a sense that the question of "good" and "bad" hair has been a loaded subject for many years, some readers will be anticipating a discussion of its social consequences and will be reading for irony from the beginning of the essay. In this case, a description such as "as straight as God allows kink to get" in paragraph 6 may already be an indication of irony. Even without such suspicions, however, the statement in paragraph 7 that the kitchen "was one part of our African past that resisted assimilation," though somewhat lighthearted, makes the political aspect of the subject explicit. Gates seems proud of both this resistance to assimilation and the ingenuity people displayed in taming that resistance. Recognizing that his own hairstyles reflect a larger movement that has political overtones ("From Murray's to Duke to Afro-Sheen," para. 21), Gates nonetheless does not entirely condemn anyone for merely trying to get straight hair. He does criticize some performers whose hair did not look good on them; given the political overtones of the essay, this criticism does seem to extend, somehow, beyond style. But despite the ironic exaggeration of his tears in the last scene, Gates manages to maintain a genuine admiration for Nat King Cole's hair, even while calling it a "tiara" (para. 36) that demonstrates a majestic degree of assimilation.
2. Gates's tone is primarily one of gentle irony. Although the idea of "good" hair is a loaded issue, Gates gives it some space. He clearly loves and respects his mother, and he is proud of both her resistant kitchen and his own process. At the same time, the last line seems pretty ironic, with the irony directed at both Gates and Cole. By 1971, when "good" was supposed to have meant

Afros and not straightness, Gates reports still feeling some nostalgia. Even writing the essay, he remembers that nostalgia fondly. As he critiques assimilationist styles, Gates proposes the idea of "straight" as an aesthetic that is less dependent on aping "whiteness" than discussion of hair usually allows (especially when he distinguishes black "straight" from "stringy"). Identifying many such touchstones with quotation marks to show his awareness of their complex context, Gates nonetheless indulges in a "straight" appreciation for the process as well.

3. Gates's essay about his mother "doing hair" in his kitchen is mostly nostalgic. From his portrait of Mama as a hairdresser to his list of the greases he applied to his head ("Murray's was some *serious* grease," para. 21), Gates shows none of the bitterness and self-recrimination evident in Malcolm X's account of hair straightening (see "My First Conk," p. 153). Does Gates mention Malcolm X's version as a shorthand reminder of the other side of the story? In ending with an unabashedly adoring portrait of Nat King Cole (whom many African American artists viewed as selling out to his white audience), Gates puts a sentimental cap on the essay. It's interesting to consider the essay in the light of his claim that he always has "two conflicting voices within [him], one that wants to be outrageous and on the edge . . . and another that wants to be loved by the community for that outrageousness" ("The Writer at Work," para. 4). Where do students see evidence of multiple voices or of irony in "In the Kitchen"?

# Michihiko Hachiya
## *FROM* HIROSHIMA DIARY

### APPROACHING THE ESSAY

Michihiko Hachiya describes his experience just previous to and following the dropping of the atomic bomb. He was enjoying his garden when he was startled by a large flash of light. Afterward he found himself disoriented and half-naked. He collected his wife and they fled; a moment later, their house fell. He found his way to the hospital, where he sought help and then began seeing patients. The doctors carefully categorized their patients' mysterious injuries but at the time were still unsure what had befallen them.

You may wish to ask students why Hachiya might have decided to keep a diary. How does the description of the garden prefigure and symbolize the events to come? How does the reader come to share Hachiya's initially confused perspective on the bombing? Through what means is Hachiya's growing awareness made evident? How does reading about the bombing from a personal perspective, and in its immediate aftermath, affect the reader in ways in which a historical account would not? How is Hachiya's scientific turn of mind evident throughout, even in the wake of one of the world's greatest disasters? Does reading this piece affect students' perspectives on warfare or human nature in general? Why or why not?

## ADDITIONAL ACTIVITY

1. Have students view the film *The Day After* (1983; directed by Nicholas Meyer), which illustrates what it would feel like to experience a nuclear explosion. Why are Americans in general so unconcerned about nuclear weaponry?

## GENERATING WRITING

1. Have students research America's role in World War II for a two- to three-page opinion essay. Was America justified in dropping the bomb? Why or why not? Have students prepare four-minute distillations of their positions for class discussion. (If you feel Japanese or Japanese American students will be made uncomfortable by this assignment, you may wish to choose a different one.)
2. Have students investigate the problem of nuclear proliferation for a two- to three-page research paper. How likely is it that a nuclear weapon might be used? What would be the local and global effects of such an event?

## THE READER'S PRESENCE

1. Hachiya's diary, chronicling patients' complaints, may help scientists to better understand the effects of the atomic bombing and may serve as a warning for the future. A patient's diary might offer a more subjective perspective than Hachiya's, with perhaps stronger emotion.
2. The entry written on August 6 is impressionistic, subjective, and emotional in tone, although it has the control and orderliness of reflection. The slight drama given to clues to the nature of the bomb, such as the silence (para. 27), indicates that the entry may have been written later, when more was known and the fear and confusion had lessened.
3. Most students will not have learned much about America's bombing of Hiroshima; this reading may inspire considerable emotion. Do students know about the American internment of Japanese and Japanese American citizens after the bombing of Pearl Harbor? This excerpt is an occasion to discuss these events in the history of World War II. How does Hachiya's highly personal account prepare a reader for further education about the war? Hachiya's account also reminds the reader of the World Trade Center disaster of September 11, 2001. Comparing the rawness and immediacy of Hachiya's account to Don DeLillo's composite essay on the collapse of the World Trade Center towers ("In the Ruins of the Future: Reflections on Terror, Loss, and Time in the Shadow of September," p. 355) may make vivid to students how

the *framing* of a detail shapes a reader's sense of the event under description. It might be useful to focus on tone. Hachiya's matter-of-fact prose style is not the simple answer to the question, "What is Hachiya's tone?"; this is a piece of complex evidence that shows how the fractured nature of experience gets sorted out through the process of writing. If some of your students have lived through a disaster (an event whose size and duration were temporarily unknowable), have them write a description of their experience for their fellow students. If possible, have both writers and readers then discuss how writing, reading, or both may be therapeutic—reviving the event, making sense of the event, perhaps even defusing some of the overwhelming power of the event.

# Edward Hoagland
## ON STUTTERING

### APPROACHING THE ESSAY

In the course of his long career, Edward Hoagland has written fiction and non-fiction on subjects as diverse as infidelity, the natural world, life in the circus, and the cultures of the Pacific Northwest. And yet in "On Stuttering," Hoagland presents the capacity for speech as the most fundamental feature of human life. Go too long without expressing yourself, Hoagland writes, and "a core in you will hemorrhage" (para. 4); life itself "can become a matter of measuring the importance of anything you have to say" (para. 2). At times, he says, "I felt I simply had to talk or die" (para. 6).

Stuttering is a physical, not a psychological, infirmity, Hoagland insists; it doesn't correspond in any simple way to physical exhaustion, insecurity, or any other discrete cause. But it is still an unexpectedly dire handicap, one that threatens Hoagland's participation in the human community. With maturity, Hoagland tells us, he managed to live with his impediment, which over the course of time grew less severe in moments of passion or anger, during sexual arousal, and after he became a father and a successful writer.

Stuttering itself is "rather like mortality" (para. 7), one more instance of human vulnerability. Yet at the same time it is a source of Hoagland's gifts, forcing him to become a keen observer, turning him into "a kind of tuning fork, vibrating to other people's anguish or apprehensiveness" (para. 5). Hoagland is aware of the irony here: that the impediment that affects his ability to speak sharpens his eye and makes him feel the suffering of others; that the circumstances that inhibit his verbal contact with other people also foster the tools he needs to communicate with his readers.

## ADDITIONAL ACTIVITIES

1. Have students prepare a selected bibliography of Hoagland's works. Have each student read one other short work by him and come to class prepared to describe it to the class. Discuss the range of Hoagland's writing and find commonalities between this essay and the pieces the students have read.
2. Read Hoagland's piece included as "The Writer at Work" (p. 117). This essay includes, among other things, a detailed account of Hoagland's family history. Have students follow Hoagland's model and create several versions of a favorite family story.

## GENERATING WRITING

1. Hoagland's essay is an excellent example of a description of a physical infirmity or limitation. Have students write a short essay in which they describe a period or an occasion in which they experienced the limitation of their bodies. After the first draft, have them rewrite the essay, using a key metaphor (like Hoagland's football game in the mind) that both gives the essay more complexity and holds it together.
2. Assign a comparative essay in which students analyze and interpret Hoagland's piece with another piece (of their choosing) in this anthology that focuses on the body. The essays by Nancy Mairs ("On Being a Cripple," p. 142) and Alice Walker ("Beauty: When the Other Dancer Is the Self," p. 244) are good possibilities. Have students pay special attention to the tone each writer adopts when discussing his or her injury, disease, or condition.

## THE READER'S PRESENCE

1. The football-game metaphor is at first glance one of the more obvious of Hoagland's metaphors; it suits almost any form of ambivalence (within oneself) or division (between oneself and another). In the case of Hoagland's stuttering, the internal nature of this "game" is most important. Hoagland is *not* saying that his ideas are on one team and his stutter is on the other. He is saying rather that two versions of his ideas are pitted against one another: on one side are "bland words" and the vague "approximations" of his ideas; on the other side are the "exact" and "accurate" words that require a bit more time to set up their offensive strategy. "Being glib and sloppy generates less blockage," he writes (para. 4). His stutter is, perhaps, the field on which the game is being fought or the stadium in which it is played. Or perhaps it is a condition that descends on both teams—unpredictably, as he says—a condition that the "glib and sloppy" words withstand more easily than their agile but weaker opponents. In the application of the metaphor—the unpacking of it into vehicle and tenor—Hoagland turns a simple metaphor into one that retains some strangeness and interest.
2. It's difficult to find any evidence of Hoagland's condition in his writing. Indeed, Hoagland attributes much of his success in writing, and his prolific

output, to the fact that writing on the page is one thing that *doesn't* inhibit him. A representation of stuttering on the page would be only an approximation and one, moreover, that was produced by an "unstuttering" flow of ideas.

3. It's hard to judge the seriousness of David Sedaris's "speech impediment" as he presents it in "Me Talk Pretty One Day" (p. 212). His ignorance of French when he starts his first language class has a hint of reality about it, but as the essay progresses, the reader falls sway to the comedian's liberties with "the world around him" and becomes less concerned about the extent to which Sedaris is documenting an actual episode in his life. In Hoagland's essay, however, the pain of stuttering is undeniably present; that pain is what fuels Hoagland's essay. Sedaris writes elsewhere about painful experiences—in which his homosexuality is the subject of ridicule, for example—but his time in the French class is more uproarious than pitiable. Do students think Hoagland is providing his readers a chance for "schadenfreude" (para.1), a kind of thrilling pleasure that comes with learning about someone else's pain?

# Langston Hughes
## SALVATION

### APPROACHING THE ESSAY

Langston Hughes presents, in this selection, one of the most significant dramas of childhood—the struggle to resolve the conflicts that exist between self-perception and community expectations. Some students may be unfamiliar with the context of Hughes's memoir and the importance of religion to African Americans in 1915. Ask the class to discuss how acceptance by a religious community can be a powerful rite of passage. The bar mitzvah and bat mitzvah of Judaism, the confirmation ceremonies of Catholicism and Mormonism, initiation rites in many Native American societies, the ritual baptism of some Protestant denominations—all mark the transition between childhood and adulthood. Encourage students to share their own experiences. Why do so many cultures choose the years between twelve and sixteen for the coming-of-age rituals? Certainly Aunt Reed's friends and fellow worshippers seem to have thought Hughes ready to take the step of joining the church. What do your students think? Might it not be difficult for a twelve-year-old to think seriously about such issues as salvation and damnation?

Hughes is best known today for his influential poetry; ask students if they are familiar with his work. How is his prose poetic? Read the opening paragraph aloud with students, and ask them to discuss the strategies Hughes uses to capture the rhythms of speech. The paragraph includes diction that evokes the thirteen-year-old

Hughes ("going on thirteen," "my Auntie Reed's") as well as the rhetoric of the revival meeting ("very hardened sinners," "brought to Jesus"). What is the effect of this allusion to the spoken word? How does it help to characterize the author as a boy?

What do the students make of the young Hughes's conviction that he would, when he was saved, see Jesus? How do they interpret the statement "I had heard a great many old people say the same thing and it seemed to me they ought to know" (para. 2)? Is Hughes the adult writer being ironic at the expense of his younger self? What kind of comment is Hughes making about the way in which children receive religious training?

The turning point of the essay is the moment when Hughes decides that he will pretend to be saved. Why does he do this? How much influence does Westley's pretense, and the congregation's response to it, seem to have on him? How great an influence does embarrassment seem to have? Hughes rationalizes his decision, saying, "God had not struck Westley dead for taking his name in vain or for lying in the temple. So I decided that maybe to save further trouble, I'd better lie, too" (para. 11). How would the class characterize the tone of this passage? What was the attitude of the young Hughes? What is the adult Hughes's take on it? Discuss the impossible situation Hughes found himself in. What might have happened if he had waited until he saw Jesus, in some satisfactory way, before he said he was saved? How did the congregation's pressure toward piety work against the young Hughes's actual piety and belief?

How does Hughes react to the success of his deception? Talk about the effectiveness of the essay's final paragraph. Does the closing run-on sentence convey the voice of a frightened, upset twelve-year-old? How does Hughes create that voice? Invite students to analyze the essential paradox of Hughes's revelation and the irony of his "salvation." Can those nurturing institutions—a loving family and a devout and caring church—end up doing a child tremendous harm?

## ADDITIONAL ACTIVITIES

1. This essay might well be looked at in conjunction with George Orwell's "Shooting an Elephant" (p. 180). How does each writer present the tension between behaving honestly, in accord with one's feelings and beliefs, and acting as the community expects? What roles do embarrassment and humiliation play in each essay? In what ways can the differences in the writers' experiences be attributed to the difference in their ages? Ask the class to talk about the ways in which Orwell and Hughes present the distance between the present self who describes an event and the past self who experienced it. Which of the authors is more self-critical?

2. Students who were moved by this essay might be encouraged to read further in Hughes's work and report on it in class. Do the themes raised here recur throughout Hughes's writing? Someone may want to give a short presentation on how Hughes depicts the world of childhood in his poetry. Others

might want to discuss his treatment of religion or his characterization of the African American community.

3. James Baldwin's *Go Tell It on the Mountain* (1985) might be a good assignment for students interested in outside reading. The novel traces a young African American boy's coming of age and his struggles with religion, family, and community. If the film *Marjoe* (1972; directed by Howard Smith and Sarah Kernochan) is available, you may want to schedule it for class or individual viewing. (The film is distributed by RCA/Columbia Pictures Home Video.) This documentary biography of a child evangelist provides an interesting contrast to Hughes's depiction of an early religious experience.

## GENERATING WRITING

1. How would students describe the mood of this essay? Ask your students to write a brief essay analyzing how Hughes uses language to create this mood. They should pay special attention to diction; what kind of vocabulary does he use? Are Hughes's family and the congregation portrayed sympathetically? How does their portrayal help heighten the essay's sense of conflict?

2. Have students discuss an incident from their own life in which community expectations caused them to go against their own conscience. How did the experience make them feel? Did it force them to reexamine some of the community's values? How can too much goodwill produce bad results?

## THE READER'S PRESENCE

1. Most students will be struck by the simple, declarative tone of the opening two sentences. Hughes's diction thrusts us into the world of the going-on-thirteen-year-old, where the clear distinctions of childhood ("saved from sin") are starting to be questioned profoundly ("but not really"). "Not really" introduces the question of deception. The class will probably be quick to say that the congregation and Hughes's aunt are being deceived; try to get students to see how the deception extends to God (or Hughes's idea of him), the reader, and Hughes himself.

2. Hughes's account of this episode is brief, but it is full of shifts in point of view. The exclamation points in the second paragraph indicate the use of "free indirect discourse"; that is, they signal that the narrator has switched over to his aunt's voice. *She's* the one who tells him that Jesus will come into his life, but by reporting the words as if *he's* speaking them, Hughes suggests his susceptibility to her message.

3. Westley is, in a very literal way, the "devil's advocate." His commonsense approach to a problem Hughes sees as a moral dilemma contributes to Hughes's own decision to deceive. Without Westley, the issue of peer pressure would be left unresolved and Hughes's action would seem unmotivated. The character of Westley is structurally necessary to the essay. Similarly, Theresa

in Bernard Cooper's essay ("A Clack of Tiny Sparks: Remembrances of a Gay Boyhood," p. 78) and Shorty in Malcolm X's essay ("My First Conk," p. 153) are necessary to the development of the two narrators. Secondary characters often foreshadow where the narrator is heading; the friends of both Cooper and Malcolm X know important things the naïve narrators will go on to learn. Secondary characters can also represent something the narrator will rise above; thus, for Malcolm X, Shorty is eventually revealed to be self-deluding, and he represents an externalization of Malcolm's fears about himself.

# Ha Jin
## ARRIVAL

### APPROACHING THE ESSAY

Depending on the demographics of your classroom and the various levels of academic preparation with which your students are equipped, the first thing you might want to do, possibly even before you have them read "Arrival," is give a brief talk about China's Cultural Revolution and Chinese Communism. You may have some students who are familiar with the history, maybe even more familiar with it than you are. You might also have some Chinese students in your class, students who have had direct experience with the Chinese government or whose parents have told them a great deal about what China was like during the years of Ha Jin's youth and early college years. In that case, you might be able to engage the class in a fruitful discussion, which will provide a background for a later discussion of the essay. However, in many cases, you will be confronted by a classroom full of students who know very little, if anything, of China's twentieth-century history. In that situation, you will need to "give a talk" or possibly assign some sort of small research project before you proceed with the reading. It will probably be very helpful, not only to facilitate reading comprehension but to generate interest in the assignment. Ha Jin's commitment to his writing is at least partially responsible for his decision to work away from the country of his birth. In the light of his military service, his opposition to the regime he holds responsible for the massacre at Tiananmen Square may capture the imaginations of your students. "Arrival" is principally concerned with Ha Jin's struggle to adapt to life in America. The essay, as such, does not go into detail about China's history or Ha Jin's ultimate decision to remain in the United States. It doesn't touch on his conception of himself as a writer. But if those things are understood *before* the students read the essay, it might help them understand what *is* there, putting Jin's struggle to adapt in a sharper light, and, perhaps most important, helping them to see how writing can become important: how writing is a political choice or a philosophical position, an essential mode of self-expression, and a necessary part of one's identity. In other words, this essay might help you teach them, in one way or another, that writing isn't just "homework."

## ADDITIONAL ACTIVITY

1. When first faced with the prospect of coming to America, one of Ha Jin's principal concerns was that he would not be able to live a meaningful life: that he could not have, in his words, "a meaningful existence" (para. 4) in the United States. You might lead the class in a discussion of what this could mean. The fact that Ha Jin is worried about being able to have a meaningful existence outside his own country suggests that—for Jin, at least—meaning has something to do with China. Is Ha Jin invested, therefore, in his national origin? To what extent does meaning in our lives depend on our sense of identity? And to what degree does that identity depend on national origin? on being, say, Chinese? or American? or Chinese American? Or is Ha Jin's concern more properly connected not to his national origin in any patriotic or general sense but rather to the more arbitrary fact that because he is Chinese, the people who matter to him—his wife and family and friends—all happen to live in China? Does bringing his wife to America solve the problem of leading a meaningful life in the United States? Or does he begin to have a meaningful existence when he starts making friends? When he discovers that he has friends, people who are friendly enough with him to loan him money, has he found a meaningful existence? What makes existence meaningful? How does the question of "home" or "country" figure into the need to feel as though one's life has meaning? You might consider pairing "Arrival" with Dinaw Mengestu's "Home at Last" (p. 170) as a way of expanding the discussion.

## GENERATING WRITING

1. Have the students write a research paper on communism in China, with particular attention to the Cultural Revolution. What was it? What were its goals? Why did Chinese Communists want to purge society of capitalist thought? What did they hope to gain? What was gained? What was lost?

2. Have the students write a research paper on some aspect of the immigrant experience. They should limit their research to a particular ethnic group or national origin, and maybe even to a certain period of time or a specific destination within the United States. How were Irish immigrants received, for example, in the Eastern United States in the mid-nineteenth century? Why did so many Irish immigrants come to the United States during that particular time? What conditions did they generally come into? Did they gravitate toward particular industries? How were Vietnamese immigrants received in the aftermath of the Vietnam War? How were Cambodians received? You

might have students present their research to the class, and compare notes: In what ways have different ethnic groups or people of different nationalities had similar immigrant experiences throughout U.S. history? In what ways have their experiences been unique?

3. Have the students write a personal essay in which they describe a major change in their lives and how they adjusted to it. It doesn't have to be anything as dramatic as immigration, although you will probably have some students who can write productively and authoritatively about the subject, and they should certainly be given free rein to do so. Some students might simply write about leaving home to attend college. Others may write about moving to a new town or a new house or about adjusting to some change at home, like a divorce. You probably won't want to suggest anything as specific or sensitive as that, but some students might come to it naturally and, again, should be given free rein as long as you think they can have productive writing experiences focusing on issues of a personal or sensitive nature. The idea is simply to get them to tell a story about adjusting to a change. Ha Jin's essay begins with his concern that he will not be able to live a meaningful life away from his home in China. It ends with him somewhat settled in his new home, having established some meaningful relationships and taken some steps to bring his family to live with him in America. The students should be able to write a narrative that reflects a similar progression, even if it has nothing to do with immigration.

## THE READER'S PRESENCE

1. Ha Jin never actually explains what he means by "a meaningful existence" (para. 4), at least not in any concrete way. It does seem, however, that he is less concerned about the issue by the end of the selection. We must therefore infer that the problem has been solved, that he has indeed found a way to have a meaningful existence in America. If your students have trouble addressing the question, you might ask them what has changed, from the beginning of the essay to the end. It is probably important to note that Jin has made some friends, that he has people in his life whom he feels comfortable loaning to and borrowing from: What does this say about the way he defines "meaning" in his life? Does it have to do with money? You might draw your students' attention to paragraph 28, which begins "For new arrivals in America, there was always the sinister attraction of money." Jin explains that, finding themselves in the United States, with the potential to earn much more money than they could in their native countries, many immigrants lose themselves completely in various menial jobs. He calls it "the money-grubbing trap." It seems logical to infer from this statement that money is not what gives his life meaning. In fact, most of what we learn from this essay, we learn by inference. At the end of the essay, we can be reasonably assured that Jin will be able to bring his family to America. It might be obvious to students that, for Jin, bringing his family to America (and forming

friendships with other immigrants) gives his life meaning. For those to whom it is less clear, you may have to connect the dots.

2. Again, Jin is careful not to state his meaning directly: most of the meaning that he attaches to the image is suggested, rather than flatly stated, and the students' ability to answer this question will depend greatly on inference. The young woman is the wife of an official. To get out of China, Jin had to bribe the official with cigarettes. The unpleasant exchange reveals a number of unpleasant things about life in China. First, bribery is essential when it comes to getting things done. Second, luxury goods, such as foreign cigarettes, are in limited supply. Taken together, these two pieces of information paint a portrait in which poverty and corruption are essential components of life in China. Furthermore, cigarettes are, if nothing else, bad for one's health. The fact that a young woman's face is haggard suggests that she may be in poor health. The fact that her hair is bedraggled suggests that she doesn't bother to "clean up." Not only is she unhealthy, she's apathetic. The fact that she is the wife of an official tells us that, even at the higher levels, life in China is *hard*, or was, at least as Jin saw it. All of this information — poverty, corruption, ill health, apathy — is captured by a single image: the haggard young woman smoking the expensive cigarette. To some extent, the image even gives us a picture of the corrosive influence of the West and of capitalism (as emblematized by the foreign cigarettes) and the dangers of communism (the value placed on those cigarettes as a consequence of their relative unavailability). In this particular image, Jin gives us a wonderful example of descriptive writing, demonstrating its capacity to convey a lot of information in a single sentence, suggesting any number of complicated ideas, much more efficiently than a sentence of exposition could.

3. Dinaw Mengestu's experience ("Home at Last," p. 170) is substantially different from that of Jin. Jin came to America as a young man; Mengestu came as a very young boy. Nonetheless, there are some common themes. Jin forms friendships with immigrants from a variety of countries, and Mengestu moves to a neighborhood where many nationalities are represented. Both writers feel a sort of kinship with other immigrants in a general way, regardless of national origin. On the particular subject of family, several interesting parallels are apparent, even if there are no direct correlations. Mengestu's parents immigrated with the entire family, and Mengestu's father was emphatic about maintaining an Ethiopian cultural identity ("Remember," he says, "you are Ethiopian," para. 2). Having grown up in the United States, Mengestu feels uncomfortable identifying himself as Ethiopian, but it is interesting, perhaps, to note Jin's yearning for family, and the fact that he never seems to question his Chinese identity. The connections are perhaps more precisely drawn, then, between Jin and Mengestu's *parents*. Nonetheless, a discussion of the question should lead to some interesting contrasts, not all of which you will be able to anticipate.

# Jamaica Kincaid
## THE ESTRANGEMENT

### APPROACHING THE ESSAY

Because of the brevity of Kincaid's essay and the powerful emotions she expresses, students will most likely feel impacted. Because Kincaid discusses motherhood, both her own and, from her experience growing up, her mother's, students should immediately relate. The key here is to get students thinking about the complexity of Kincaid's message: it might be easy for them to say, "Well, she had a bad mother." But at certain points in the essay, Kincaid says that her mother could be tender and caring at times. For instance, in paragraph 8, Kincaid explains that her mother "quarreled with" and "disparaged" her brother. Yet, when he became seriously ill with AIDS and was dying, her mother cared for her son with "the greatest tenderness." What does this mean? How can a person be cruel at one moment, throughout most of a child's life, then turn around to be a kindhearted and gentle caretaker the next? These questions should yield complex and thoughtful answers. What does it mean to be a mother?

Direct your students to the construction of the essay. Is Kincaid putting forth an argument? What is her goal with this essay? Students should find it to be a kind of cleansing of her soul, almost a confession. She has, after all, disowned her mother, in a sense. After years of disparaging remarks, she cuts off contact with her mother: Why does she do this, you might ask. What are her motivations? One of the most effective rhetorical techniques of the essay is what is left unsaid. Kincaid never explicitly details what her mother did to her: she hints, alludes, and keeps her mother mysterious. Your students should consider the effect of leaving out such information. Does it make it more or less clear that the things Kincaid's mother did were anything but motherly? Your students should also be able to see that Kincaid's efforts to be a particular kind of mother are a direct reaction to the kind of mother she had: it should be clear that Kincaid doesn't want to be like her mother—that she makes a conscious effort to distance herself from her mother, to be different.

Near the end of the essay, Kincaid writes, "I believe every action of a certain kind that I make is completely influenced by her, completely infused with her realness, her existence in my life" (para. 12). It is here that students should begin to see Kincaid's real concern. Not only does Kincaid want to avoid ending up like her mother, she wants to make sure her children don't end up like her (Kincaid), dreading the idea of spending eternity with their mother. The frightening thing for Kincaid is *how much* of her mother is in her. How much of her mother will her children see through her? Kincaid acknowledges that she does not know. Ask your students what they think. In what ways might Kincaid's willingness to sever her connections to her mother demonstrate that, in fact, the two are very much alike?

## ADDITIONAL ACTIVITIES

1. Get your students to consider the complexities of motherhood by having them read the poem "The Mother," by Gwendolyn Brooks. Although it is not in *The Writer's Presence*, it is easy to find and could serve as a nice companion piece to Kincaid's essay: Brooks's poem deals not only with abortions but also with mothers who are both cruel and kind. In what other ways does Brooks's poem relate to Kincaid's essay? In what ways are the two works different—in scope, in voice, and in outlook?

2. Kincaid's essay is filled with different types of emotions concerning mothers and motherhood. Ask students, in a short journal entry, to define *mother*. They should not give a dictionary definition; instead, they should focus on the connotative implications of the term *mother*.

## GENERATING WRITING

1. Have students write a personal-narrative essay about either one of their parents. The goal of the essay should be linked to Kincaid's idea that "every action of a certain kind that I make is completely influenced by her [Kincaid's mother]" (para. 12). In the same vein, students should write a personal-narrative essay, a kind of confession, that traces how parts of their parents' behavior or personality is evident in them. They should explore the attributes of a parental figure that they wish to imitate in their own lives as well as attributes they want to avoid and see as flawed. By the end of the personal narrative, students should come to a larger idea both about their lives in the world and how they were and are influenced in their living by their mother or father.

2. At one point in her essay, Kincaid shares that her own children misunderstood her message to them at the beginning of one of her books. She says she wrote it with great love, but they were angered by it. Ask students to write a reflective essay in which they experienced a misunderstanding with a parental figure or another adult in a position of authority. Ask them to explain the situation, both from their own perspective and from the parent's. What was the outcome of the misunderstanding? Did they learn anything about themselves? About their parent?

## THE READER'S PRESENCE

1. Kincaid's repetition of phrases and language here highlights her complex and deeply felt emotions toward her mother. After her mother's death, she repeats, "I could not believe that such a presence could ever be stilled" (para. 2), highlighting the god-like vision she had of her mother. For Kincaid, her mother is an awe-inspiring force, one capable of great kindness and great cruelty—a force that will live on inside her. When she repeats the word *eternity* at the end of the essay, the reader should be feeling Kincaid's awful connection to her mother, one that could possibly last forever.

2. Kincaid favors nothingness to her mother's company, which is why, early in the essay, she stops talking to her mother. The remark is sort of kōan-ish, though, in that her mother is dead. So, if Kincaid were to die, how could she not "spend eternity" with her mother? Really though, the statement is that Kincaid would probably prefer the nothingness of death, or the horror of dying, to spending the rest of her days, months, and years with her mother.

3. It's not possible to say whether the story is autobiographical for certain, but a strong argument could be made for that interpretation. The story clearly tells about a girl who is controlled, dominated, and often disparaged by the person the reader must take as her mother. In this way, the short story could act as a key to the essay, opening some of the hidden nastiness that her mother inflicted on Kincaid, which Kincaid leaves out of the essay.

# Geeta Kothari
## IF YOU ARE WHAT YOU EAT, THEN WHAT AM I?

### APPROACHING THE ESSAY

Ask students to use the opening quote by Michael Ignatieff to summarize Geeta Kothari's thesis. For the American-born Kothari, the search for identity is a delicate balance between the "tacit codes" of two cultures. Her dilemma manifests itself specifically in her relationship to the two cuisines of her childhood: the intimate food customs practiced by her Indian parents and the evasive customs of her American environment.

You may want to first draw students' attention to passages that suggest Kothari's changing attitudes toward Indian and American cuisines. Have students isolate passages that demonstrate the author's tastes at a particular time and place. How do the sections deal with the changes in Kothari's or her family's relationship to food? What kinds of food is she eating in section II? In sections IV and V, we see the clearly Americanized tastes of the author's sister. How do the children's food preferences change when they visit relatives in India? Why? What does this tell us about the children's need to belong? What do they do differently in India than in America? How does the appetite of the contrary Kothari change when she goes to an English boarding school that stresses "strict rules about proper behavior" (para. 37)? Why? The nine-year-old Kothari in section I is said to have a "longing for American food" (para. 1). However, by section XVI, the adult Kothari says that "living far from the comfort of people who require no explanation for what I do and who I am, I crave the foods we [her family] have shared" (para. 54). Ask students to find passages where Kothari has to explain what she does and who she is. How does her self-image change as she grows up and moves away from her family?

Clearly, taste has something to do with belonging, with a recognition of and an identification with a particular culture.

Kothari uses humor effectively to make her point. What is funny about Kothari's relationship with her husband-to-be in section XII? Have students find at least two humorous lines in this section and explain why they are funny. In section XVI, Kothari returns to her relationship with her husband with humor. Why does she use her husband and their relationship humorously? Is she making any serious points in these two sections, or are they strictly comedic?

Point out the structure of this essay: the use of sections and the apparent lack of transitions between sections. Note, too, that the narrative is not linear. Is this style stream of consciousness? Does it evoke journal entries? Do your students find it hard to follow? How effective is the essay's structure and why does the author choose to write this way? Discuss with your class how the form of the essay informs its content and message. What is that message?

## ADDITIONAL ACTIVITIES

1. *Babette's Feast* (1987; directed by Gabriel Axel), based on a story by Isak Dinesen, is a fine example of the cultural relevance of food. Providing varying perspectives, this film works well for a class discussion. Set in nineteenth-century Jutland, this Danish film concerns the clash of two cultures: the cook's (Babette's) mysterious and sensual French culture and her employers' puritanical and spartan Danish culture. It is a film about food's ability to both define and transcend cultures. Point out specific differences between the two cultures, which are manifested both in the characters and in the cuisines. In what sense does Babette always remain an outsider? What are some of the prejudices of the diners? If "you are what you eat," how should we characterize the dinner guests? the General? Babette? Compare Babette's experiences to Kothari's.

2. Have students form groups to arrange the sections of Kothari's essay according to some specific plan of organization (in order of chronology or importance, for example). Ask the groups to share their revisions. Which plan(s) works best for this essay? Why? How do the changes affect the tone? the thesis? the development?

## GENERATING WRITING

1. Assign a short paper that asks students to describe their family's eating habits and choices and to consider how food defines them. They might want to address the following questions: Do they consider their family cuisine typically American and, if so, what does that mean? What ethnicities fold into their family food and eating traditions? Do they have certain traditions regarding food, such as when and where they eat meals, religious practices associated with eating, a social hierarchy acknowledged at the dinner table, and so on?

**49**

2. Have students research and write a ten-page paper that attempts to define American cuisine. What makes certain foods "American"? What does American food say about who Americans are or perceive themselves to be? Does American cuisine offer the same kind of cultural identity that other cuisines offer? Why or why not? For a shorter paper, you may want to narrow the topic to defining fast food, Southern cooking, Kosher-American food, or college-cafeteria cuisine.

## THE READER'S PRESENCE

1. Kothari worries that not caring about traditional Indian foods as much as her parents do means she is losing part of her identity. She has developed her own tastes based on Americans' love of expedient, cheap, and tasty food and her own stubborn refusal to fulfill others' expectations. Because of her varying food choices, she questions her identity: "I am . . . not Indian. . . . I am not American either" (para. 55). Ultimately Kothari embraces her different tastes as integral to her hybrid identity, and she ceases to view them as flaws. According to her title, she is a hodge-podge of different cultures, having eaten, and at some point craved or identified with, Indian, American, English, and Italian food.

   Kothari concludes that she is after all "my parents' daughter" (para. 65) because of the *way* she treats food, rather than the ethnicity of the cuisine she consumes. She may not like the same dishes as her parents, who also have changing tastes, but she finds similarities that nonetheless link her to them and inform her identity. Like her parents, Kothari finds raw meat strange, can differentiate Indian herbs, and expects her husband to "know what I know, see what I see, without having to tell him" (para. 65). These traits are a stronger bond than liking the same kind of dal or making it the way her parents do.

2. Kothari recognizes that American food is quickly prepared, cheap, predictable, and full of "large quantities of [animal] protein" (para. 63). She enjoys the sense of belonging that it provides, but also fears that acceptance means losing touch with her Indian roots. She tries to retain her heritage by teaching her husband to cook without red meat. Jokingly, she asserts that he will one day leave her for a meat-eater who "doesn't sniff him suspiciously for signs of alimentary infidelity" (para. 51). Because to Kothari food is more than just nourishment, she worries that the different food choices she and her husband make will have repercussions in their relationship.

3. As children, Kothari and Amy Tan ("Mother Tongue," p. 232) are both disappointed with their parents for not helping them "negotiate the world outside" (Kothari, para. 8). To Kothari, this means knowing and eating American food, while for Tan it means not speaking with an accent. However, as they grow older, both women learn to cherish their mothers' (and their own) cultural differences because that is what defines them and makes them unique.

Students should note that Kothari implies that fast food is contributing to the destruction of ethnic cuisine: the first real Indian restaurant in her neighborhood is run out of business by restaurants that "use plastic cutlery and Styrofoam cups" and "do not distinguish between . . . Indian, Pakistani, and Bangladeshi cooking, and their customers do not care" (para. 24). In effect, the distinctive cuisines are assimilated into a poor substitution.

# Nancy Mairs
## ON BEING A CRIPPLE

### APPROACHING THE ESSAY

Nancy Mairs discusses her disability in a somewhat distanced, jaunty style and links her own case to more universal concerns through literary allusions. Students may be put off by this cerebral approach, or they may assume that it is the correct stance to take regarding others' disabilities. The writer's feelings are not readily apparent and at points are emphatically rejected; thus students may not be able to access the piece emotionally. Further, Mairs uses humor to discuss mishaps that others might find painful. You may wish to have students read this essay "against the grain," asking whether Mairs's stated attitude toward disability is wholly convincing or what she might hope to achieve through it.

The writing in this piece may seem at first largely factual and straightforward. On a second reading, students may note a more subjective approach. You might isolate a paragraph or two for closer examination, pointing out Mairs's selection of words and images, and then ask students to do the same. What details does Mairs choose to focus on? Why might these be important? Where does a sensitive insight or image belie the writer's tough-minded determination? How does the form of the narrative shape the reader's impressions of what is said? How do narrative touches augment, compete with, or undermine the primary line of argumentation? What reaction does Mairs wish to provoke? What do students take away from the piece, and why? How may Mairs's words be related to questions of ability and limitation in general? Disabled students, more stigmatized than most minority students, may feel extremely uncomfortable with the piece or with the discussion; you may wish to discuss the essay with them privately beforehand or simply choose a different piece.

### ADDITIONAL ACTIVITY

1. Have students read Tennessee Williams's classic play *The Glass Menagerie*. How is Laura's disability portrayed? How do other characters react to it? How might Laura have been affected by others' perception of her disability? Does

Williams's perspective appear to echo or contrast with that of Laura's family and new friend?

## GENERATING WRITING

1. Have students spend half an hour freewriting their reactions to Mairs's piece. Encourage them to move from intuitive opinion to more sophisticated analysis by looking closely at Mairs's statements and writing techniques—phrasing, rhetoric, use of imagery, and so on. Students should then select the most sophisticated points they have made and develop them into a two- to three-page essay.

2. Have students write three drafts of a one-page essay about a situation in which they felt limited by forces beyond their control—by a physical, emotional, social, or economic "handicap." In each successive draft, have students work on tightening their descriptions and including commentary on larger issues. How might the "just do it" mentality of today's world come into conflict with the reality of most people's lives? What can be learned in this regard from Mairs's piece?

## THE READER'S PRESENCE

1. Although Mairs adopts a matter-of-fact and an offhand attitude in discussing her disability, students should not confuse that with the impression they are meant to take. Mairs resists pity but certainly demands empathy and respect. By letting her readers in on the motives for her defensive postures, Mairs breaks down barriers between herself and her readers, making it easier for them to identify with her. And yet Mairs does not want to deny the differences between herself and her noncrippled reader; a key reason for writing the essay is to examine the pain and knowledge that comes with her special condition (para. 31).

2. Bogan's words in the epigraph may refer to inner, psychological conflicts, where "escape" may be the belief that one is not imprisoned, which would create a feeling of freedom despite literal confines. Yet "escape" can also be understood in the sense of "escapism," or refusing to face conflicts. Students should be encouraged to "feel" Bogan's words out for themselves.

3. Mairs's move from the self-loathing of paragraph 20 to the realization that "what [she] hate[s] is not [her] but a disease" (para. 22) is remarkable in its capacity to evoke at once the specific condition of MS, the more general condition of her gender, and the inclusive condition of human existence. Both Mairs and Alice Walker ("Beauty: When the Other Dancer Is the Self," p. 244) manage the delicate balance between expressing their own struggles with self-acceptance and giving voice to the existential pain most readers have experienced at some point in their lives. Most students can readily relate to this theme.

# Malcolm X
## MY FIRST CONK

### APPROACHING THE ESSAY

Malcolm X's memoir of growing up in racist Boston society intersperses hard truths with humor and even nostalgia. Most American college students today have worked difficult first jobs, faced tensions with authority figures, and tried disastrous new styles of self-presentation. Students should, in this sense, easily relate to Malcolm X's coming-of-age experience. However, the painful subtext of the events related must not be overlooked. Students should be alerted to small, telling details in the narrative that make Malcolm X's self-portrait period-based and specifically African American.

You might ask students to take turns rereading sentences aloud; stop students after every few sentences to discuss their meaning. Where do humor and pain collide in this retelling? Which images seem most vivid or vital to students? How might this scenario be linked to the greater picture of racism at that time? How might the points raised by the piece be seen as valid today? Which aspects of our culture's approach to race have changed since that time? Which aspects have remained the same? How might these formative experiences have led Malcolm X to his radical program and to changing his last name from "Little" to "X" to mark both his unknown African heritage and his rejection of the legacy of slavery?

The "conking" episode can help one discuss prejudice as it is manifested in the aesthetics of personal appearance. The young Malcolm X's conflict with Ella suggests larger issues surrounding the role of minorities in mainstream culture and the struggle for civil rights. Ella and her neighbors believe in bettering their circumstances through conformity to mainstream values, whereas Malcolm X rejects conformity and then, as discussed later in his autobiography, chooses rebellion. You might ask students how Malcolm X's early identification with the poorest of African Americans prefigures his later social program.

To avoid causing discomfort among minority students in a mixed classroom, expand the discussion to one of conformity and rebellion in general. Is it more effective to work from within "the system" to improve social welfare, or to resist the compromises conformity entails? Is it brave or foolish to cling to the courage of one's convictions in a world that may not be ready to embrace them? Malcolm X achieved heroic status; would we read his words differently if he had not succeeded in his goals? You may wish to briefly discuss the opposing teachings of African American leaders Martin Luther King Jr. and Malcolm X in relation to this question, steering the class beyond sensitive racial issues to civil rights in general.

### ADDITIONAL ACTIVITY

1. Have students view Spike Lee's films *Do the Right Thing* and *Malcolm X* and stage a debate around issues of conformity and rebellion. Divide students

randomly into two groups and have them focus on the conflict between the two quotes at the end of *Do the Right Thing*: Martin Luther King Jr. insists on peaceable resistance at all costs, whereas Malcolm X justifies certain types of violence in the cause of freedom. One group must argue from King's perspective and the other from Malcolm X's. Students opposed to the position they have been assigned must rely, as a lawyer might, on argumentative skills rather than personal opinion. Allow time for group consultation, statement of group position, reconsultation, and rebuttal. What have students learned from the debate?

## GENERATING WRITING

1. Have each student write three drafts of a two- to three-page essay exploring a situation in which he or she encountered "the school of hard knocks." What expectations did the student bring to the situation? How did it differ from what was anticipated? what was learned? With each draft, pair students to discuss papers, posing questions — "Can you describe the scene in more detail?" "Was there humor in the situation?" — to deepen the investigation and enhance the piece.
2. Have each student write a two- to three-page position paper based on the young Malcolm X's tensions with Ella: Is it more productive to conform and change society from within, or to rebel and work to influence society from the outside? Steer students away from questions of race to those of social progress in general. Encourage students to reason from concrete or even hypothetical examples rather than simply express an opinion. Have each student present his or her position to the class in a two-minute speech, and then open the floor to discussion.

## THE READER'S PRESENCE

1. By leaving the reflection to the end, Malcolm X keeps his readers in the moment, experiencing the experience as *he* experienced it. It seems as though, among Malcolm X's crowd, the "sharp dressed young cats" of Roxbury, getting one's hair conked was standard procedure, a rite of passage, almost; it was something you had to do if you wanted to be cool. So getting the conk is narrated without question. Malcolm X accepted it without reflection. It wasn't until later in life that he realized it was "ridiculous," that he'd "endured all of that pain, literally burning [his] flesh" just to have his hair "look like a white man's hair" (para. 23). Therefore, he doesn't say anything about the degradation of it in the piece until the deed is done. Students are likely to have a variety of reactions to the piece. You might ask them why Malcolm X came to see having his hair conked as a concession to white racism.
2. This selection is narrated in the past tense, as is common for memoirs. When Malcolm X refers to "today" (para. 27), the attentive reader may recall that the *Autobiography* was published in 1965, *after* Malcolm X's assassination

by one of his former Black Muslim brothers. Ask students if they think that "today" has continuing, contemporary relevance.

3. Henry Louis Gates Jr. ("In the Kitchen," p. 97) seems to have a more compli- cated emotional relationship with hair straightening in the African American community. Although there is the suggestion that he sees the practice as cul- turally and politically problematic, he is not quite as willing (or, perhaps, able) to reject it in the wholesale fashion that Malcolm X does. "In the Kitchen" has a fundamentally different purpose: there is a nostalgia to the way Gates talks about Nat King Cole, for example, that leads one to believe that Gates has a sentimental soft spot for straightened hair, if only to the extent that it reminds him of his past, his youth, and some of the great icons of African American culture. Even his criticism of Sammy Davis Jr. (who, according to Gates, does *not look good* with straight hair) indicates a willingness to con- sider the practice aesthetically, a willingness Malcolm X specifically rejects. Malcolm X objects to hair-straightening practices because they represent, for him, a concession of identity, a concession to racism, which he cannot (or will not) consider in purely aesthetic terms. Gates refers specifically to Malcolm X, so he is clearly familiar with *Autobiography* and, more likely than not, is in some degree of agreement with Malcolm X's conclusions. But he can't bring himself to deny that Nat King Cole, at least, *looked* good.

Daniel Akst ("What Meets the Eye," p. 293), however, seems less interested in race or fashion: he presents scientific evidence that (in his opinion) suggests that the socially or culturally constructed aspect of what we consider "beauti- ful" is limited. He says the results of surveys are surprisingly consistent across cultures. He does, however, indicate that research suggests that norms are changing to embrace more characteristics—fuller lips and narrower eyes, for example—not typically associated with white people. This, he says, indicates that the circle is widening to include Asian, Hispanic, and African features. Although a principle like symmetry may remain consistent, the preference in any given period for features such as straight hair, full lips, or almond-shaped eyes may reflect cultural standards rather than biological ones.

# David Mamet
## THE RAKE: A FEW SCENES FROM MY CHILDHOOD

### APPROACHING THE ESSAY

This memoir describes incidents of chilling insensitivity in a startlingly understated manner. A playwright by vocation, David Mamet avoids much outright interpreta- tion in this text, allowing his parents' actions and words to speak for themselves.

The separation of Mamet's restrained voice from the psychological violence perpetrated in the family creates a dramatic tension that may stun many students. At the same time, the memoir's overall tone is not ambiguous, just implicit.

Ask students to locate where Mamet's voice shapes the presentation of events or reflects on them, even as he seems to withhold judgment. In the scene of the school play, the mother's outrageous behavior is presented with great understatement: she "suggested" that the sister continue eating, that such would be "good form." Students can see from this memoir the effectiveness of the old writing chestnut to show and not tell.

One of the most impressive aspects of this essay's crafting is Mamet's careful and yet seemingly casual arrangement of events. You might ask students to make a time line of events and then to examine how and where Mamet has departed from this order. Events such as the family "joke" and the abuse suffered by Mamet's own mother take on a different tone after having been set up by the parents' abusive behavior. The ease of Mamet's transitions—"And it seems," "We went to the new high school," "We were raking the lawn"—belies the care he has taken to begin and then delay the central story of the rake while providing the context necessary to understand it. Terror of their parents' reaction overrides the usual tendency of quarreling children to assign blame, overrides even their concern about the sister's bleeding mouth. Such a reaction makes a kind of sick sense only in the context of the parents' previously detailed behavior.

The essay's casual structure suggests an almost disinterested teller, and Mamet's understatement contributes to the sense of a distanced narrator. Ask students why they think Mamet may have chosen to convey these events with such a distanced tone. One thing this tone may do is reduce the potential for revelations about the mother's upbringing to read as excuses for her abusive behavior. That is, in a more sentimental text, the abuse the mother suffered might be presented cathartically, as how the narrator comes to terms with her behavior. Mamet's distanced tone, however, allows him to avoid accepting this information as an excuse; it barely conveys explanation, and there is no suggestion that it provides emotional resolution. This distance also allows the story of the joke to be genuinely pathetic. The narrator does not bother to point out the joke's symbolism—that the children are unwanted/unloved. Having spoken with restraint throughout, he can offer up even his enjoyment of the ritual and remain confident that the reader will see its more troubling implications.

With even analysis of the mother's abuse held back, this memoir remains focused on outlining the family dynamics rather than on explaining their origin. Mamet veers somewhat into the area of social criticism, however. The central event takes place while the children are being made to maintain that central suburban accouterment: the lawn. That the family lives in the model home of a new development implies some criticism of the façade of happiness a suburban lifestyle provides. Ask students what Mamet is doing in the last paragraph. Is there a distinction being made between the potential "natural" pleasures and the false pleasures of the model, suburban lifestyle? What kind of hope does the prairie signify? Does such a dichotomy seem justified?

## ADDITIONAL ACTIVITIES

1. Information about the mother's childhood suggests a recurring pattern of family alienation and abuse. Other selections in *The Writer's Presence* propose ideas of how values and behavior are handed down. Ask students to read Raymond Carver's "My Father's Life" (p. 60) and compare the author's description of parent–child relationships with the description presented by Mamet.

2. You might also ask students to compare Mamet's essay with film or television representations of dysfunctional family life that appears normal on the outside—for instance, *American Beauty*. Most popular accounts suggest catharsis or recovery, or use examples of early abuse to explain later abusive behavior. How would students compare these with Mamet's approach?

## GENERATING WRITING

1. In a way, the recurring joke about the car is the closest thing Mamet's family has to a meaningful ritual. Although it demonstrates the horror at the heart of their relationship, it also seems to have been about the only family activity that even hinted at shared intimacy. Have students write about a recurring scenario, joke, or ritual shared by a group to which they belong. What does the activity seem to celebrate, and what might it reveal, if examined more closely, about the group's dynamics?

2. Ask students to write about a time when they collaborated to keep something secret. On what bases were their in-groups and out-groups formed? What did they imagine would be the consequences of revealing the truth? Did the secret come out, and was the result what they expected?

## THE READER'S PRESENCE

1. Mamet's story of his own unhappy childhood is also a meditation on the bankrupt values that underlie the "American dream" of the happy family in their model home. "Being assigned to the beautification of a home that [they] found unbeautiful in all respects" (para. 10), Mamet and his sister are acutely aware of what his parents deny: the sometimes abusive dysfunction of their family.

2. The "joke" of the parents driving away from the children, returning to get them, then driving away again just as they start to climb in—repeated over and over—is about as unfunny as a joke can be, especially as a "cap" to this painful essay. That the family "laugh[ed] in camaraderie" at "what [Mamet believed] was [their] only family joke" (para. 30) may distance the reader further from the parents and deepen the reader's empathy for Mamet and his sister.

3. The rake, like the table, is associated with blood; the two bloody objects frame the essay. Mamet's throwing of the rake at his sister (in anger at his parents)

is a displacement similar to his father's smashing of the table (in anger at his children, that is, at himself). In both cases, the children are blamed and punished for the misdeeds of their parents. In "Shooting an Elephant" (p. 180), George Orwell uses the gun and the elephant as symbols, respectively, of the power and the vulnerability of colonial rule. (The symbolic meanings are much more complex, but for the purposes of this discussion these meanings will suffice.) Similarly, the table and the rake take on symbolic importance by virtue of their centrality to this family's daily routines, but also by virtue of their seeming capacity to draw blood: they bring family members to express the violence inherent in the family. In Mamet's essay, as in Alice Walker's ("Beauty: When the Other Dancer Is the Self," p. 244), siblings lie to their parents to protect one another from their parents. Ask students to compare the situations in these two essays.

# Adam Mayblum
## THE PRICE WE PAY

### APPROACHING THE ESSAY

The firsthand accounts of Adam Mayblum, a survivor of the attack of September 11, 2001, on the World Trade Center and Michihiko Hachiya ("From *Hiroshima Diary*," p. 107), a survivor of the atomic bomb attack on Hiroshima, are examples of writing about extreme experiences. Both men recall considerable detail written soon after the experiences they describe. Both essays benefit and suffer from the fact that they are written by nonprofessional writers. What they may lack in an elegance of style, they gain through their gut-wrenching authenticity. These first-person accounts are recalled in nearly real time. Mayblum's essay especially has a sense of immediacy as he leads us, floor by floor, down the tower stairs to safety. He rarely varies sentence structure, leading to a kind of monotony, and yet his use of sentence fragments vividly conveys a rush to get his ideas down. How do both writers move their narratives forward? What is the relation of sentence to sentence in each piece? Neither man knows what has happened; both must put the pieces together through rumors and observations. Ask students to reread the essays, in search for the pieces of the puzzles that finally lead each author to understand what has happened. Whose understanding is the more difficult for its author to accept? Why?

You may want students to compare the writers' extraordinary descriptions: which one seems more surreal? What vivid observations do the writers recall? Students will no doubt see connections between these observations and familiar, even stock, images found in science-fiction movies. Ask your students to relate the nightmarish scenes to specific sci-fi movies with which they are familiar. How do they explain the apparent lack of panic in both situations? Mayblum is writing from the perspective of a survivor among other survivors. Hachiya, too, is a survivor, but he also writes from the perspective of a doctor working through an incredible medical emergency. How does the doctor's voice (which is also a scientist's voice) differ from the survivors' voices?

Have students comment on any political or patriotic tones they detect. Is one essay more political? Ask students why, they think, each man wrote his recollections? Building on this comparative work, you may have students examine Don DeLillo's tone in his essay, "In the Ruins of the Future: Reflections on Terror, Loss, and Time in the Shadow of September" (p. 355). How does this well-known literary writer handle the immediate description of disaster and confusion? Where do the insights of participants and witnesses overlap? How does DeLillo's purpose for writing affect the tone of his essay differently from the other two?

Finally, you may want your students to discuss the word *terrorist* in terms of these three essays. Can a single word chosen by an author really matter in a big way? Why or why not? Point out to students that both attacks—on the World Trade Center and on Hiroshima—were deliberately directed against civilian populations in part, at least, to instill fear. How do the students feel about this kind of warfare? Is one more justified than the other? Why or why not?

## ADDITIONAL ACTIVITIES

1. Have students do a Web search for other eyewitness accounts of the attacks of September 11, 2001, and bring to class one noteworthy example. Have students read aloud the most vivid paragraph or two—the passage that lends itself most readily to a dramatic reading. Discuss as a group what techniques seem to bring alive the words on the page.
2. Find an event that all students in the class will attend or an experience that all of them are about to share. Have them write a journal-style account as soon after the event or experience as possible. Have them bring it in, unrevised but legible. Organize them in pairs and have them exchange, read, and discuss one another's pieces. Ask them to note where their accounts differ. Have them rewrite their first drafts, retaining the freshness of the account while elaborating on the unexpected details.

## GENERATING WRITING

1. Assign a short, analytical essay in which students compare and contrast two accounts of the same event.
2. Have students rewrite the analytical essay (above), adding one more account of the event, and ask them to interpret the differences among the accounts. This essay should be longer, and it should also be quite different in nature. Whereas the first essay may have been neutral or equivocal—may even have had no particular argument—the second essay must make a claim about the relative strategies or effects of the accounts. (Make sure students incorporate parts of the first essay into the second.)

## THE READER'S PRESENCE

1. As students review the people Mayblum talks with, they will note that the people outside the tower were as important to him as those who were escaping with him. The cell phone was for Mayblum, and for many people, an important means of communication that morning; it allowed him to make contact with some of his family members. Another prominent theme of the morning, however, was the failure of technologies we have come to depend on for basic human contact. Even basic observation failed to supply answers; note how often Mayblum says that he had no idea what was going on. His parents' warnings to get away because "a third plane [was] coming" (para. 6) reminds us how little anyone knew during those first hours of September 11, 2001.

2. Mayblum's account is structured as a countdown; paragraphs 5, 6, and 7 proceed very regularly, as he descends approximately ten floors between paragraphs. Paragraphs 8 and 9 are the most intense: Mayblum and his colleagues hear the rumble of Tower 2 collapsing, though they can't identify it as such, and they finally escape Tower 1. Readers who watched the event from the outside know that Tower 1 was about to collapse as Mayblum and his colleagues emerged. This knowledge increases the suspense that is built into the story. Although we know, of course, that Mayblum survives, the account is sufficiently detailed to bring the reader back to his or her experience of that morning. The tragedy pulled together people who might otherwise never have interacted; there was a distinct feeling of unity following the attack. Mayblum's political conclusions, however, seem out of keeping with the neutral yet personal description of the morning's experience. People working together to help one another through a disaster are not necessarily doing so because of patriotism; some Americans might dispute Mayblum's suggestion that as citizens of a democratic nation we have the constitutional right to go on vacation "when and where we want" (para. 12).

3. Mayblum's story differs from DeLillo's because it is more personal and Mayblum is not a professional writer. He begins with the two most important bits of information he has to offer: "My name is Adam Mayblum. I am alive today." DeLillo, however, is a well-known writer who seeks to convey the tragedies of these events abstractly through figurative language. DeLillo relates to the destruction in a series of narratives and counternarratives, real and imagined, with observers, visitors, victims, survivors, and terrorists. He juxtaposes the "medieval expedience" (para. 55) of the terrorists against the technologies of the future. The "passenger jets that become manned missiles" (para. 64) provide the intersection of the past and the future. Students should not dismiss Mayblum's essay just because it may seem less "writerly" than DeLillo's. His is, perhaps, the more genuinely articulated because of its immediacy and very personal nature.

# Dinaw Mengestu
## HOME AT LAST

### APPROACHING THE ESSAY

In "Home at Last," Mengestu describes an experience more and more common to Americans: how to feel at home in a country that both is and is not one's own. Mengestu writes specifically of the sense of displacement that comes from immigrating at a young age. Told, as a child, to remember that he is Ethiopian (para. 2), Mengestu nonetheless confesses to feeling that "it would be a lie to say [he was] *from* Ethiopia" (para. 1) because he was raised almost entirely in the United States. Mengestu's parents are clearly Ethiopian, but he describes himself as "irrevocably assimilated" (para. 3). Coming as it does before a space break, this observation is heavily weighted, and you might devote some class time to discussing exactly what it means. Depending on the demographics of your classroom, it is likely that at least one of your students will be either a recent immigrant or the son or daughter of recent immigrants. In many parts of the country, the majority of students in a given class might actually have direct experience not unlike Mengestu's own: in this case, it may be quite easy to generate an enthusiastic discussion of what that experience is like. Even when this is not the case, the vast majority of Americans are still the descendents of immigrants, and even the smallest of American towns are likely to have neighborhoods that are historically ethnic. As Mengestu is specifically concerned with finding a *neighborhood* to call home, some discussion of the neighborhoods in the vicinity of your particular school may also be a helpful way to start the discussion.

One thing that makes Mengestu's essay effective is the way he personalizes the experience, providing particulars and details from his own life. In this sense, "Home at Last" provides a good model of an essay that makes an abstract topic (like "the immigrant experience") come alive for the reader. It is also, at the most fundamental level, an ideal model of the traditional sense-of-place essay, providing descriptive details to convey the "feel" of Kensington: what the neighborhood looks, smells, and sounds like, and how the details make the place meaningful for Mengestu. You might lead the students into a discussion of what "makes" a home: how details make a place unique and how the uniqueness of a place might be a defining element of its role in our lives. Why is it important to Mengestu, for example, to memorize the layouts and routines of the neighborhood streets (para. 5)? What does it add to our understanding of his desire to feel as though he has found a home? a place to be "from"? In paragraphs 9 and 10, he describes street scenes that give us a sense of the lives of other immigrants, as well, including those "with a culture and history different from the one I had been born into" (para. 10): these passages, in particular, might serve to illuminate how Mengestu's experience is common to many Americans. But they also lead directly to the conclusion of the essay: Mengestu's desire to feel "attached to something" (para. 11). Call your students' attention to how the physical world of the essay allows Mengestu to connect to it on a more abstract level. Ask them to think about how the particularization of a place endows it with meaning.

## ADDITIONAL ACTIVITIES

1. Mengestu claims he has been "irrevocably assimilated" (para. 3). What does it mean to be assimilated? Consider the idea of America as a "melting pot." Where does the idea originate? What about the phrase itself: "melting pot"? Is America really a melting pot? What are the implications of the metaphor? The idea of America as a melting pot is supposed to be positive, but what are the real implications of melting?

2. Following up on the melting-pot discussion, you might have your students research their family histories. Ask them to prepare brief presentations on their cultural heritage. To what extent has that cultural heritage been subsumed or absorbed by the larger American culture? Has something been lost? What has been gained?

## GENERATING WRITING

1. Much of the success of "Home at Last" depends on its attention to detail. Have your students write an essay using the same degree of attention to detail to convey a sense of place. To provide direction, you might suggest they write about their own homes or neighborhoods. It is important to remember that Mengestu's essay is as much about identity as it is about place, so you will want to have your students write about a place that in some way informs or reflects their identities. How do the details of the place make it home? If you teach at a college where most of your students live in dorm rooms, you might want to steer them away from writing about their dorm rooms. The problem is that, aside from the decorations and articles of furniture that students bring to them, most dorm rooms are alike. You might want to force them to dig deeper. A neighborhood is a perfect subject. Many students will have difficulty finding unique features in their neighborhoods: pre-fab suburban neighborhoods are often regarded as sterile, for example. But this can work to your advantage (and theirs) because it will make them look that much harder to find what is unique. It could also lead into a sort of meditation on how the pre-fab nature of much of the American landscape robs many Americans of a sense of identity associated with home. Mengestu's father tells him never to forget that he is Ethiopian, but Mengestu himself doesn't have any real sense of Ethiopia. He has fully assimilated his American identity. Most Americans have in some way been integrated into the packaged world of pre-fab America, and this could make for an interesting paper topic.

2. Have your students research their family histories. With the exception of Native American students, all of your students come from immigrant

families: it's just a matter of how many generations they have to go back. Have them write a brief family history, followed by some reflection on the extent to which their Irish (or Italian or African or Vietnamese or Dutch) roots shape their sense of themselves in the larger American culture.

## THE READER'S PRESENCE

1. Mengestu likes the sound of the word *Kensington*, first of all, but that isn't his main reason for choosing the neighborhood. He is primarily drawn to the variety of immigrant communities that call Kensington home. He has never really had a sense of "home" because he is at once an immigrant from Ethiopia (a stranger in America) and an average American kid, a kid who grew up in Illinois. He can't really acknowledge that he's from Ethiopia because in a sense it would be dishonest: despite his mother and father's cultural background and national origin, Mengestu himself probably feels (or felt, at the time of writing this essay) that he knows Illinois better than he knows Ethiopia. Your students may or may not feel that he has made Kensington home, and their interpretations of the final paragraph may vary, but much of the discussion will probably depend on defining what Mengestu means by "home." Beyond its literal meaning, what does the word suggest? Ask your students what "home" means to them, and what they think it might mean for Mengestu.

2. Mengestu says that he did not host a Kensington night because he had "established [a] private relationship to the neighborhood" (para. 7) that could not be shared with others in one night. Indeed, the remainder of the paragraph includes a lengthy description of all the sights, sounds, and smells with which he had become intimately familiar: it seems almost as though he is in love with the place. He doesn't want to cheapen it by turning it into a curiosity, a tourist attraction for his friends. But, despite Mengestu's strong feelings for the place, his essay "Home at Last" is essentially about being an outsider. Mengestu is an outsider in America, in his family, and in his community. It would have been much more difficult to convey that feeling if he had introduced a friend: the reader would then see Mengestu not as an outsider but as part of the friendship presented on the page. Leaving his friends and associates off the page makes it much easier to convey the feeling of being an outsider. Writing about standing on the fringes of a conversation taking place in a language that the narrator does not understand accomplishes the desired goal much more effectively.

3. As the children of immigrants, both Mengestu and Geeta Kothari ("If You Are What You Eat, Then What Am I?," p.132) grew up principally in the United States. As a consequence, they find themselves adrift. Mengestu is Ethiopian; Kothari, Indian. Yet they are both American, in some way, as well: assimilated outsiders, with national identities they don't quite feel connected to. Mengestu relies on a sense of place to convey his feelings on the matter, while Kothari explores her relationship with Indian cuisine.

# Manuel Muñoz
## LEAVE YOUR NAME AT THE BORDER

### APPROACHING THE ESSAY

"Leave Your Name at the Border" deals with a common American theme: the loss of cultural identity that accompanies assimilation. Specifically, Muñoz is concerned with the Mexican community in his hometown, Dinuba, California, and the area around Fresno. More specifically, Muñoz is interested in the "Anglicized pronunciation" (para. 4) of Mexican names and, further, how it has become commonplace to meet children of Mexican immigrants who have "American" names: he mentions Brandon and Kaitlyn in particular, paired with "last names like Trujillo or Zepada" (para. 7). The significance of the essay, of course, goes far beyond names, but you might begin the discussion by asking students about how our names broadcast our identities. What assumptions do we make about people based on their names? What assumptions do they make about us? In paragraph 1, Muñoz says, "Around Fresno, identity politics rarely deepen into exacting terms." Many of your students will have extensive experience dealing with identity politics: some of them will have strong opinions. But chances are good that many of your students have not heard the phrase "identity politics" before, even the ones for whom "identity politics" are a daily fact of life. Some of your students will see the word *politics* and tune out. Others will not understand quite what the word *politics* means in this context: they may be thinking that people are either Democrats or Republicans, that those are their political identities. So you may have to begin by defining identity politics, and talking about names and first impressions is an excellent way to do that. In this sense, "Leave Your Name at the Border" can serve as an introduction to the subject of identity politics, a subject many of your students will be very interested in before they are even aware that there's a phrase to describe it. Once you have discussed identity politics and names, it will be easier to branch out into some of the more pervasive aspects of assimilation: the loss of language and culture that Muñoz laments in paragraph 17.

### ADDITIONAL ACTIVITIES

1. You might consider pairing this essay with Dinaw Mengestu's "Home at Last" (p. 170), broadening the discussion of America as a "melting pot" to include Muñoz's view. Mengestu claims he has been "irrevocably assimilated." From the standpoint of his assimilation, his search for a place to feel "at home" demonstrates a clear sense of longing, but it doesn't seem as though Mengestu is particularly concerned about his sense of himself as an Ethiopian. In other words, he doesn't seem to lament his assimilation so much as he simply acknowledges it, factoring it into his way of thinking about the world and his search for a place to feel at home in America.

Muñoz, however, clearly views assimilation as a threat. For him, the Anglicization of names alone constitutes a major loss, never mind the more generalized "assimilation" that Mengestu claims for himself. With this in mind, reconsider the idea of America as a "melting pot." Ask again if your students feel that America is actually a melting pot, and what the implications of the metaphor might be.

2. For all practical purposes, this activity is the same as Additional Activity 2 for the Mengestu essay, only with a slightly different emphasis: this one emphasizes names. Following up on the melting-pot discussion, you might have your students research their family names (surnames). What are their origins? Ask them to prepare brief presentations on their cultural heritage. To what extent has that cultural heritage been subsumed or absorbed by the larger American culture? Has something been lost? What has been gained?

## GENERATING WRITING

1. Have your students research their family histories by way of their surnames. With the exception of Native American students, all of your students come from immigrant families: it's just a matter of how many generations they have to go back. Have them write a brief family history, followed by some reflection on the extent to which their Irish (or African or Spanish or English or Japanese) roots shape their sense of themselves within the larger American culture.

2. Have your students write an essay either advocating or attacking the idea of America as a melting pot. The essay should not only address the question of whether America actually *is* a melting pot but should also address the question of whether a melting pot is something to be desired: Is assimilation a good thing? Why or why not? And to what extent? What does it mean, in other words, to be an American? *Who* is an American? Why?

## THE READER'S PRESENCE

1. At the end of the essay, Muñoz states that he was only able to learn how language could have ruled him (had he allowed it) by leaving the Valley. In that light, it makes sense to think that *returning* to the Valley would lead to the sort of meditation on identity and language that takes up most of the rest of the essay. In particular, Muñoz is concerned with names, so the Anglicized pronunciation of the name Eugenio Reyes over the loudspeaker at the airport is a logical starting point. Throughout the essay, Muñoz seems to feel that this Anglicization is a corruption, even going so far as to say so in more or less direct terms, in paragraph 17, when he considers the "corrosive effect of assimilation." Yet, in the last paragraph, he takes a more humble tone, wondering, "Who was I to imagine" who Eugenio Reyes was, where he was

**65**

from, where he was going, and so on? So, while Muñoz holds fast to the conviction that the Anglicization of Mexican names constitutes a problematic displacement of one culture in favor of another, he also counts himself lucky for having the ability to take that position and, in so doing, withholds any explicit judgment on Mexicans who take Anglican names and, to one extent or another, whites who have spent their whole lives in the Valley and still have difficulty understanding the degree to which their Anglicized pronunciations of Mexican names might represent a sort of racism or sense of cultural superiority that Muñoz is only able to see clearly after spending a few years living away from it.

2. Your students will, of course, have a variety of answers to this question. You may struggle with the pronunciation of some of the names in the essay yourself. For that matter, your name might be Manuel. The point is to explore the issue, opening a dialogue between your students—no matter what their ethnic or national origins are—about the sometimes uncomfortable subject of pronouncing unfamiliar names. As a teacher, you are likely to have a great deal more experience in this particular area than any of your students, but they have all seen teachers struggle to pronounce the names of students on the first day of class, and we all know how embarrassing and uncomfortable those moments can be, both for student and teacher. Muñoz doesn't offer a lot of help, probably because he feels that the burden to learn how to pronounce names properly belongs to the person pronouncing them. How do your students see the division of that burden? How does the dialogue about pronunciation lead to a larger dialogue about identity? Does it? Can a conversation about the pronunciation of names lead to a greater understanding between people of diverse ethnic and national origins? How does the Anglicization of Mexican names *prevent* that dialogue from taking place?

3. Both Muñoz and Mengestu ("Home at Last," p. 170) deal with the idea of assimilation and its effect on identity. Muñoz rejects assimilation, viewing it as a corrupting influence. Mengestu, however, says that he has already been assimilated and, as he struggles for a sense of home, the sense is that he is also struggling for a sense of identity. In a way, it might be said that, by resisting assimilation, Muñoz has avoided the problem that Mengestu now faces. A comparison between Muñoz and Richard Rodriguez ("Aria: A Memoir of a Bilingual Childhood," p.187) yields a somewhat different conflict: Rodriguez doesn't seem to view speaking English as theft of his identity. English was his *public* language, but it didn't rob him of an intimate life (or *private self*), and therefore doesn't seem to rob him of a sense of identity. This comparison might lead to an especially fruitful dialogue, especially if you have ESL students who speak English in public and another language in the home. Do they agree with Muñoz? with Rodriguez? Are Muñoz and Rodriguez talking about the same thing? Or are they dealing with entirely different subject matter? Is there a space in which the writers are both right? wrong? What do your students think?

# George Orwell
## SHOOTING AN ELEPHANT

### APPROACHING THE ESSAY

This is one of George Orwell's most accessible essays; try to make sure students aren't put off by its exotic setting. You may need to explain why Orwell, an Englishman, was a police officer in Burma. Ask the class to think about what preconceptions the Burmese might have had about Orwell. How do the circumstances of British rule over India seem to have contributed to Orwell's personal and political consciousness? Of what kind of government was Orwell a representative? How might he have been perceived by the Burmese?

It might be helpful to introduce the concept of alienation here. Why would a representative of the English government be perceived as an outsider by the Burmese? Does Orwell see himself as connected to the Burmese community? Does he see himself as connected to the other representatives of the British Empire? Have students look closely at paragraph 7, in particular the passage where Orwell says of the white imperialist, "He wears a mask, and his face grows to fit it." What does this sentence mean to the class? In what other contexts, in their experience, can this be true?

Discuss Orwell's style in this essay. How would students describe his tone? What kind of diction does he use? What does his attitude toward himself and his actions seem to be? How is this attitude conveyed? Ask the class to pick out specific passages in which Orwell distinguishes between his attitudes at the time he shot the elephant and his attitudes when writing the essay. How does he create a sense of distance between his current and his former selves?

The structure of this essay is central to the power of its characterization. Have students look closely at its opening sentence: "In Moulmein, in Lower Burma, I was hated by large numbers of people." What is the impact of the word *hated* here? What is the effect of Orwell's focus on the first person? The essay could have opened with a sentence like this: "During the British reign over India, the colonial police were despised." Would its force have been substantially diminished by such a beginning?

Orwell begins by relating various ways in which the Burmese expressed hatred for him and other Europeans. After providing some context, he discusses his conflicting feelings about his job and the people around him (para. 2). How is this paragraph organized? Are Orwell's objections to imperialism expressed clearly? Does the alternation in the opening paragraphs between attacks on the British Empire and disgust with the Burmese people mirror the ambivalence Orwell must have felt when he shot the elephant? Ask the class to talk about the sense of identity Orwell expresses here. Was he comfortable with the role he played in Burma?

You may want to talk about the language and tone Orwell uses in relating the actual episode. Why does he refer to the elephant as *it* rather than *he*? Direct

**67**

students' attention to the phrase "had turned the van over and inflicted violence upon it" (para. 3). Might this be an attempt to reproduce the idiosyncratic English of the Burmese witnesses? How does Orwell's tone change when he discovers the dead man? Does this change in tone reflect a change in attitude toward the elephant? This might be characterized as the rhetorical equivalent of sending for an elephant rifle.

One question you may want to ask students is what, in their opinions, led Orwell to change his mind. What pressures were on him to shoot the elephant? Why could he not resist them? The dilemma he depicts in paragraphs 6 and 7, that he "knew with perfect certainty" he "ought not to shoot him" yet "realized" he would "have to shoot the elephant after all" has an unusual context here, but it is a problem common to us all. The impossibility of reconciling his moral decision with the social pressures around him lead Orwell to understand just how dangerous are the forces that create those social pressures. Ask the class to comment on this issue, and think of analogous situations in the world of today.

Of course, Orwell's moment of understanding is not the end of the essay. What effect does the account of the elephant's death have? What does Orwell's chief preoccupation seem to have been at the time of shooting the elephant? How did his concerns change between the incident itself and the time of writing about it? You may want to read the description of the elephant's death aloud. It is strangely wrenching — why? Ask the class to discuss the irony of the concluding sentence, "I often wondered whether any of the others grasped that I had done it solely to avoid looking a fool" (para. 14). What does this admission tell us about Orwell's isolation from his fellow Europeans and their isolation from one another? How might that alienation contribute to the dangerous state of affairs that Orwell first perceived while facing the crowd and the elephant?

## ADDITIONAL ACTIVITIES

1. Consider this essay in connection with Brent Staples's "Just Walk on By: A Black Man Ponders His Power to Alter Public Space" (p. 217). How does each author depict his behavior as shaped by the expectations of a hostile society in which he is an outsider? How have these outside hostilities shaped each man's self-perception? Ask students to discuss how Orwell's and Staples's responses to their isolation differ.

2. Interested students might want to read Orwell's novel *Burmese Days* (1934), an account of experiences very similar to his own. How are the themes in this essay echoed in the novel? Does the novel genre give Orwell the freedom to present various points of view on the conflict between Burmese culture and British imperialism? Some class members might want to report on Orwell's other works and their treatment of similar themes. Both *Animal Farm* (1945) and *Nineteen Eighty-Four* (1949) trace the ways in which social pressures and preconceptions can come into conflict with individuals' identity and sense of self. Why does Orwell present the freedom to make one's unique moral choices as the ultimate freedom?

## GENERATING WRITING

1. Ask students to recall an incident in their own lives when social pressure drove them to do something they knew to be wrong. What realizations did the event help them to reach? How did their experience parallel Orwell's? How did it differ from his?

2. Have the class write a brief analysis of the ways in which Orwell uses language to convey emotional states. Ask your students to analyze Orwell's style in this essay, with a focus on tone and diction. What kind of imagery is used? What kinds of verbs and sentence structures does he use? How does style help to create the essay's powerful effect?

## THE READER'S PRESENCE

1. Orwell's essay is as much about the consuming ideology of colonialism as it is about one subdivisional police officer named George Orwell. At the beginning of the essay, Orwell admits that he hated British imperialism: "In a job like that you see the dirty work of Empire at close quarters" (para. 2), but he also says that he was passively brought to that dirty work. His hatred was that of an ignorant young man. He felt "an intolerable sense of guilt," but that guilt seems to originate somehow outside of him: it comes with the job. By the end of the essay—after the transformative act of shooting the elephant and watching it die—Orwell displays a bitterness and an irony that is entirely his own, arising from his gut. The basic opinions haven't changed; his ownership of them has changed.

2. Students may point to Orwell's use of place names (Moulmein, Coringhee), his specific details ("an old .44 Winchester" [para. 3], "a rifle and five cartridges" [para. 5]), and his straightforward, journalistic style. Others may focus on the depth of feeling Orwell reveals, arguing that it would be unlikely for him to be so moved by a fictional episode.

3. Both Orwell and Brent Staples ("Just Walk on By: A Black Man Ponders His Power to Alter Public Space," p. 217) exploit for narrative purposes the social situation of acute scrutiny. Putting themselves in the position of those watching them, Orwell and Staples convey to their readers the heightened state of self-consciousness generated in oppressive societies based on hierarchies of race and caste. W. E. B. Du Bois ("Of Our Spiritual Strivings") called this self-consciousness a form of "double consciousness," writing of African American existence at the end of the nineteenth century. Both Orwell and Staples depict themselves playing the fool (have students look up *fool* in the *Oxford English Dictionary*) so that they may go on to see through their foolishness.

# Richard Rodriguez
## ARIA: A MEMOIR OF A BILINGUAL CHILDHOOD

### APPROACHING THE ESSAY

Richard Rodriguez offers an effusive tribute to Spanish, his immigrant family's "private" language, concluding with the declaration that he does not wish this language to be integrated into English-based education. The piece is unusual in combining two essay forms—the memoir and the argument. In addition, students may be puzzled by the apparent conflict between Rodriguez's love of the Spanish language and his opposition to bilingual education. You may wish to make an outline of the essay, listing the general thrust of the information conveyed in each paragraph.

Rodriguez strongly links the personal and the political. You may wish to have students trace the paths by which family experience is rendered as cultural experience, and how Rodriguez in turn attempts to link his individual experience of his culture to policy issues. What images and anecdotes does Rodriguez use to convey a sense of his background and the tensions between that background and his young life in America? By what means is his individual experience made to stand for a more general situation, and to what extent does Rodriguez keep his experience individual?

Students' attention should be directed to the structure of the essay. In what ways do the memoir sections of the essay rely on "showing" rather than "telling" and the power of the unsaid? How do the argumentation sections of the essay differ from the memoir sections? Are the memoir and argument sections mutually reinforcing, or does one dominate or undercut the other? Are students convinced by the argument? Why or why not? How might it be debunked or strengthened?

The issue of bilingual education is a sensitive one; minority students may feel uncomfortable unless class discussion is expanded to larger issues of isolation and assimilation. How does Rodriguez characterize his feelings of belonging to his cultural group? What does he feel is lost when his family becomes "American"? Why then, in seeming contradiction, does he endorse an assimilationist educational policy? How does he later reconnect to his heritage? What is the role of language in his sense of cultural identity? How might language be said to determine culture?

### ADDITIONAL ACTIVITIES

1. The question of bilingual education has been the subject of much debate. Divide students randomly into two groups and have them further research the issue. One group must argue from a pro–bilingual education perspective, and the other from an English-only position. Students opposed to the position they have been assigned must rely, as a lawyer might, on argumentative skills rather than personal opinion. Allow time for group consultation, statement of group position, reconsultation, and rebuttal. What have students learned from the debate?

2. Break students into small groups to discuss their family backgrounds and how their personal experience was linked to greater cultural forces—ethnicity, class, and so forth. Do members of the group find their experience different or similar? Which traits do students classify as belonging to their families or subcultures, and which traits do they classify as mainstream American? Have each group briefly report its findings to the rest of the class as a springboard for discussion of these issues as they are raised in Rodriguez's piece.

## GENERATING WRITING

1. Have each student choose and rewrite a scene from Rodriguez's essay as a three-page "treatment" for a screenplay, writing dialogue based on the scenario described by Rodriguez. How does the scene open? How does it close? Students should describe the set, the mood intended, and the characters' gestures in depth. Afterward have students discuss their artistic choices and what aspects of the essay they hoped to highlight through those choices.
2. Have students spend half an hour free-writing their reactions to Rodriguez's piece. Encourage them to move from intuitive opinion to more sophisticated, better-reasoned analysis by looking closely at his statements and writing techniques—phrasing, rhetoric, use of imagery, and so forth. Students should then select the most sophisticated points they have made and develop them into a two- to three-page essay.

## THE READER'S PRESENCE

1. Rodriguez links Spanish with early family ties, which he places in opposition to the family breakdown occasioned by assimilation. Whereas for some "the personal is political," for Rodriguez the reverse appears more vital. Ending the essay with his grandmother's death allows Rodriguez to express the ambivalent feelings he has about his Mexican relations. On the one hand, he is consumed by the intimacy of his memories of his grandmother and is saddened by the loss of cultural connection that her death represents. And yet the image of her face—which "the mortician had designed with his dubious art" (para. 63)—also reveals to him how even after death one's identity is susceptible to the warping pressures of assimilation. He is alienated from "her public face."
2. Paragraphs 50–55 are an example of Rodriguez in his mode of persuasive argument—in this case, against bilingual education. With paragraph 56 he begins to make the transition to the personal with the notion of "the mystery of intimate utterance." The next paragraph begins "My grandmother!," thereby making the move into autobiography. This exclamation point echoes those used in paragraph 33, when he introduces his mother and father. For Rodriguez they seem to connote the larger-than-life quality of his intimate relations and his inability to reduce them to names in English or Spanish.

3. Walter Benn Michaels ("The Trouble with Diversity," p. 744) would probably agree with Rodriguez's stand. Like Rodriguez, Michaels sees the real issue as ending economic inequality, rather than promoting diversity. He believes that the role of education is to provide a level playing field for all people. Rodriguez sides with those who believe bilingual education will further marginalize Latino populations. Minority students may have particularly strong views on these issues; these should be distinguished from those of students who fear bilingual education will drain national resources. Discussion leaning toward this latter position should be refocused.

# Marjane Satrapi
## MY SPEECH AT WEST POINT

### APPROACHING THE ESSAY

Known for her graphic novels, Marjane Satrapi uses this genre to broach serious subjects like nationality, freedom, and identity and to recount her experiences growing up in a fundamentalist Islamic society. You might want to begin by discussing the graphic-novel genre. Ask students to find examples of cartoons, comics, and graphic novels or essays and to bring them to class. Discuss the differences and similarities among the examples. What kind of issues do these pieces raise? How are certain ones both funny and serious? What value does graphic representation add to the written text? Is anything lost using graphics?

In this short graphic essay, Satrapi presents an anecdote about her speech before cadets at West Point. What is her thesis? What moral does Satrapi's piece offer? How would it work without images? Satrapi's anecdote uses simple graphics and text, yet she marries the two fluidly and conveys a deeper, emotional truth. She uses repetition for both emphasis and humor. Have students break down the structure of the piece: the before and after segments (Satrapi's imaginative exaggeration of what she expects versus what actually happens) and locate the humor: the way she sets up her imagined death or the pizza joke. How does Satrapi allude to grave issues like war, death, and narrow-mindedness through her innocent and funny graphic narration?

Ask students why they suppose Satrapi's graphic memoir, *Persepolis: The Story of a Childhood*, was put on the required reading list at West Point. How do they feel about graphic literature being taught in college? Why?

### ADDITIONAL ACTIVITIES

1. In groups of three or four, have students compose a graphic essay based on an essay in this book. Each group can designate an "artist," but the decisions about the art and text should be collective. How do the essays

students have chosen lend themselves to the visual medium? What decisions must be made when creating a graphic essay? How are their graphic essays translations or adaptations of the original works and how do they stand on their own?

2. Have students read Satrapi's *Persepolis: The Story of a Childhood.* Class discussion might focus on many topics, including rebellion, censorship, feminism, war, religion, and life before and after "the veil."

## GENERATING WRITING

1. Satrapi says, "I know that I don't know anything. That makes my life even more complicated." Have students write a short essay recalling a time when they were faced with a confusing or conflicting viewpoint about an idea, a person, or an action. How did they resolve this complication?

2. Recognized by the Pulitzer Foundation since 1922, political cartoons address current political or social topics and make their point by the use of caricature and visual metaphors or puns. They usually appear in the editorial section of large newspapers. Have students write an eight- to ten-page research paper on a political cartoonist and his or her work, paying close attention to the political references and historical context of the cartoonist's time period.

## THE READER'S PRESENCE

1. Satrapi expects an unfriendly welcome at West Point, but, to her surprise, everyone treats her cordially. Her expectations imply that the military academy trains cadets to be narrow-minded and intolerant. Her views may have been influenced by one-sided books, movies, and newspapers. More likely, her opinion may be an extrapolation from the U.S. military activities in the Middle East. This encounter complicates her point of view: it was much easier to condemn the military before she found out that some of its members are kind and respectful. Students may find it humorous that of all Satrapi's negative expectations, it was the pizza that proved to be worse than she had anticipated.

2. Satrapi's tone is dry, witty, direct, and to the point. She draws sharply contrasted black and white images, resembling an etching or a simple woodcut, with the text appearing overhead or in dialogue bubbles. She reinforces the depiction of herself as an imaginative yet direct and opinionated individual through the stark imagery and precise text. The text and images have a symbiotic relationship—one cannot tell the story without the other.

3. Like Satrapi, Jerald Walker ("Scattered Inconveniences," p. 251) exhibits paranoia and misreads the situation. His wife offers a competing perspective by remaining open-minded. Dissimilarly, Brent Staples's ("Just Walk on By: A Black Man Ponders His Power to Alter Public Space," p. 217) summations of his white "victims" are very often correct: he understands why women fear him on deserted streets or in elevators. However, this understanding does not help the way their actions make him feel.

There is no "real" resolution in the three essays because the writers have not put an end to racism or war. Staples seems to have the least resolution because his narrative is about how he is perceived by others—something he can't do much to alter—while Satrapi and Walker deal with how they view others. In Walker's case, his view of others is affected by how he thinks they view him. Both Walker and Satrapi learn something about themselves, and possibly become more open-minded through their experiences.

# David Sedaris
## ME TALK PRETTY ONE DAY

### APPROACHING THE ESSAY

David Sedaris made his debut as a writer on the air in the late 1990s, on the radio show "This American Life," produced by Ira Glass at WBEZ in Chicago. Sedaris's short personal essays—which fall into the category of both memoir and monologue—grew into collections of short pieces, *Naked* (1997) and *Me Talk Pretty One Day* (2000), both of which sold well. Sedaris is now a sought-after speaker, reading to packed audiences across the country and in Europe. The second collection, from which this essay is the title piece, for the most part describes Sedaris's experiences in Paris.

Anyone who has listened to Sedaris in person or on the radio cannot help but hear his nasal voice and deadpan delivery while reading this essay. Because tapes of his books are readily available (and many of Sedaris's pieces are archived on the Web site of "This American Life"), it may be worthwhile to play one of the essays for students. Ask them how the essay affects them as readers and as listeners.

This essay works on a theme that is as old as comedy itself: the unintentional crimes done to a language by foreign speakers. Some of the most satisfying moments in the essay turn on the abusive communication between the sadistic teacher and her students, and the communication between fellow students as they commiserate. But Sedaris does not rest here. Though the title of the collection is *Me Talk Pretty One Day*, his career has been based on ugly, awkward, inappropriate, or painful talk. This type of talk characterizes Sedaris's actual voice—with its unmusical twang—as well as the voices he adopts in his essays. Through these voices Sedaris confronts his coming-of-age, his homosexuality, his mother's death from cancer, and other serious subjects, and he does so by making his readers laugh almost in spite of themselves.

Sedaris's central insight is that our fumbling attempts at communication reveal more than the trivial exchanges we generally participate in; his essays exploit the tension between our readiness to accept superficial appearances and our hunger for deeper, sometimes more painful truths. Sedaris has established himself as one of the new generation of American writers—at once ironic and earnest, cynical and sentimental.

**74**

## ADDITIONAL ACTIVITIES

1. Play a segment of "This American Life" (available at www.thislife.org) for the class. Discuss as a group how the piece works: How is music incorporated? How is the pacing established? Where does the piece gather momentum? What is the conflict, and how is it resolved? Is the piece fiction or autobiography? How do students evaluate its truth?

2. Have each student bring to class another piece of humor writing—for example, a piece by Mark Twain, Will Rogers, Dave Barry, Barbara Ehrenreich, Michael Chabon, Jonathan Safran Foer, Eudora Welty, James Thurber, Calvin Trillin, or Garrison Keillor (some of these authors are represented in this anthology). Have a few of your students read some of the shorter pieces (or excerpted passages) aloud. Discuss the various ways of making people laugh through writing. How do these techniques differ from those we use when speaking? You might want to show a video segment of a stand-up comedian's performance, by way of contrast.

## GENERATING WRITING

1. Have students listen to a few broadcasts of "This American Life" (available at www.thislife.org). Have them write a four-minute piece (approximately two pages of writing, double-spaced) and practice reading it aloud. Once they have mastered the delivery, have them record their pieces on tape or digital audio.

2. Divide the class into pairs, and have students interview one another. Tell students to conduct their interviews until they hit on something surprising. From this point, they should accumulate enough information (including physical setting, characters, psychological and emotional detail) to form the basis of a three-page piece they will write *in the voice of their interviewee*. Remind them that the persona they create should bear a strong resemblance to—but not remain strictly true to—their partner. Refer them to Sedaris's essay as a model for how exaggeration may be used to convey an experience that is essentially true.

## THE READER'S PRESENCE

1. Much of Sedaris's humor turns on emphasizing the differences between French and English, using literal or nonidiomatic translations of French to show the stilted speech of a beginning student of the language and using the standards of English to poke fun at perfectly correct French. A precise but ridiculous translation appears in paragraph 1, where Sedaris calls himself "a true debutant." This is a translation of a French phrase referring to the author's status as an entering student, but in English the word *debutante* connotes a young woman's entrance into society. Such words are cognates, words that look alike in both languages but have different meanings in each. Sedaris also pokes fun at the fact that every French noun is considered either masculine or feminine when he describes "Lady Crack Pipe or Good Sir Dishrag" (para. 17).

**75**

"Deadpan" humor is humor that does not draw attention to itself, either in anticipation of a punch line or in appreciation of a joke just made. The jokes in deadpan humor are delivered in the same tone as the exposition. The result is that every line becomes equally suspect; every reader will have favorite moments. Students may want to discuss the lines that they found funniest.

2. Many reasonable English words can be substituted for the nonsense words to make the sentences work: Thus, "'Were you always this *palicmkrexis?'"* (para. 16) could be, "'Were you always this *thickheaded*, or *recalcitrant*, or *ignorant*, or *ox-dumb*?'" and so on. The humor works not only on our imagining the sound of the virtually unpronounceable word, and on the fact that Sedaris can't even understand how he is being insulted, but also on the reader's instantaneous, and largely unconscious, working through the list of possible words that could be substituted. We get more words for our money than any single word could give.

3. Sedaris's last line is, again, a precise, word-for-word translation of a simple French sentence. It doesn't tell the reader that he hasn't learned anything, but that he's back for more. George Orwell's essay "Shooting an Elephant" (p. 180) ends with a sentence that is surprising but with a sentiment that has been forecast throughout the essay. In E. B. White's "Once More to the Lake" (p. 260), the last sentence changes the author's lighthearted examination of taking his son to White's childhood vacation spot into a meditation on mortality.

# Brent Staples
## JUST WALK ON BY: A BLACK MAN PONDERS HIS POWER TO ALTER PUBLIC SPACE

### APPROACHING THE ESSAY

This essay begins with an immediate, concrete incident instead of a generalized statement. Students should be aware of such openings and notice how effective they can be in an essay. Too often, introductory students see essays as a string of expository statements that offer very little possibility for narrative or dramatic action. It would be worth the time to work closely with Brent Staples's opening paragraph in class, observing how he sets up a scenario that at first makes it appear that he is in fact a threat (ask students to explain how he achieves this effect).

The opening paragraph also introduces a shift in point of view that is significant in the essay and essential in understanding Staples's attitude. There's a complexity in this essay that could easily be missed. In the middle of the first paragraph Staples suddenly assumes the young woman's viewpoint— "To her, the youngish black man . . ." Students should see that this movement in point of view supplies more than drama; throughout the essay Staples shows a remarkable capacity to see himself as others might see him. Students must be aware that Staples is not blaming the woman for being afraid—in a sense, she really is a "victim." Instead of proclaiming his innocence and wondering why he is frightening to people, Staples himself assumes the burden of making himself "less threatening."

Staples's attitude is complex because of his double awareness: he realizes that the danger women perceive is real, but he also is aware of the alienating power of their fear, which turns him into a suspect, "a fearsome entity" (para. 6). Invite the class to discuss how this double awareness is related to Staples's own background (paras. 7–9). For example, why does Staples not take any satisfaction in his "power to . . . intimidate" (para. 8)? Notice how his images of "manly" intimidation show that he sees this power as infantile.

Staples's double awareness—that he is both victim and victimizer—is not without struggle. Make sure the class sees that Staples has "learned to smother the rage" he feels at being "taken for a criminal" (para. 12). Instead of giving in to this anger and becoming paranoid, he deliberately takes precautions that will relieve the fear and anxiety his presence often produces. All these precautions, your students should know, relate to his behavior in public spaces. The final paragraph invites interesting discussion. You might ask why whistling melodies works so well: What does this "tension-reducing measure" tell us about Staples—and about people's fears? Students should pay close attention to the last sentence. It's a wonderful analogy, and they might discuss how it summarizes the essay.

## ADDITIONAL ACTIVITIES

1. You can link discussion of public space and racial discrimination to several easily available films that students will find both entertaining and instructive. John Sayles's *The Brother from Another Planet* (1984) and Spike Lee's *Do the Right Thing* (1989) both deal with street life and alienation. These films lend themselves directly to a discussion of public and private space, for this issue is vital—both visually and thematically—for both directors. Discussion will be enhanced if students are encouraged to watch either or both of these films, specifically paying attention to the "space" theme.

2. Invite your class to select a specific "territory" on campus—a classroom, hangout, library, cafeteria, vending-machine area, or parking lot—and observe how people handle the necessary adjustments between personal and public space. How close together do people come? What distances are maintained? Who are the dominant groups? How is hostility controlled or heightened? How do individuals and groups "mark" their territory? After careful observation and notetaking, students could write an essay in which they describe the territory and the territorial behavior as objectively as they can.

## GENERATING WRITING

1. Staples's essay is a suitable model for a similar student writing topic. Ask students to ponder their own ability to alter public space. They might consider these questions: In what ways have they achieved such alteration? Have their experiences been negative or positive? Did they ever feel—like

Staples—that they had to assume the burden of behavioral change? Did their ability to alter public space also change their self-perception?

## THE READER'S PRESENCE

1. The "My first victim" opening is, of course, very effective. It gets the reader's attention, and it carries several meanings. The woman imagines herself as his "victim," even though we realize in reading the essay that Staples is not dangerous. In a way, though, the woman is a victim—she is afraid to walk down the street at night. There are other victims in this essay as well: Staples is a victim of prejudice, and the young thugs who learn to love the power they feel at being able to alter public space are victims of a sort as well.
2. The "Approaching the Essay" section of this entry discusses Staples's skillful handling of point of view.
3. The contrasting strategies of the two versions of "Just Walk on By" reflect the ambivalence Staples expresses in both of them. Eight years elapsed between the two versions, between 1986 and 1994. How might students describe and account for the differences between the two versions? Do they ascribe them to greater maturity on the part of the writer? or to a heightened sense of political outrage? In both cases, Staples emerges from his street walks safely, and with his dignity intact. What do students think are the relative costs of these strategies, both personally and for society? Have them imagine alternate scenarios for getting through a tense situation.

   Malcolm X ("My First Conk," p. 153) frames his coming-of-age narrative in terms of racial conformity or assimilation versus rebellion. The mature, adult narrator distances himself from his younger, foolish self by concluding that conked hair is a sign of shame through conformity. Natural hair is the real symbol of rebellion and racial pride. Meanwhile, the conclusion that Staples offers in his ironic essay is of course not a solution at all. On the one hand, by whistling in the street, he attempts to change the misconception that as a black man he is a threatening presence; on the other hand, the need to change his behavior implies that in order for a black man to survive he must give credence to (thus, in a sense, conform to) this racist notion.

# Andrew Sullivan
## THE M-WORD: WHY IT MATTERS TO ME

### APPROACHING THE ESSAY

Reading this essay is an excellent way to broach the controversial subject of homosexual marriage. You may want to begin the class by informally soliciting opinions on gay marriage. You will most likely find students of several different opinions:

those who oppose gay liaisons of any kind, those who accept gay partnerships but not marriages sanctioned by law, and those who see no reason to deny gay couples the legal recognition of marriage. You may also have gay students who are anxious to express their personal opinions.

Try to get your class to define Sullivan's thesis. Is he against civil unions? What does he mean when he says in paragraph 7, "When people talk about 'gay marriage,' they miss the point"? Answering this question will probably help reveal Sullivan's main point.

Why is the institution of marriage so important to Sullivan's identity and its affirmation? Have students look for places in the essay where Sullivan talks about his upbringing and the values his family instilled. Why is family so important and why must family be defined through blood and marriage? Is there any other way to define a family? Sullivan never directly states how his parents reacted when he told them he is gay. Where does he imply how they felt? Why does he compare how they would have acted if he were discussing heterosexual relationships? Ask students to describe his tone.

## ADDITIONAL ACTIVITIES

1. Sullivan starts his essay, "What's in a name?" Students should be familiar with this famous line from William Shakespeare's play *Romeo and Juliet* about two lovers for whom marriage was seemingly impossible because of their feuding families. Why does Sullivan start his essay with this line? How does it bolster his argument? Can students think of a way in which this line might be used as a counterargument for Sullivan's thesis? Is Sullivan arguing the opposite of what the play's line intends—that calling marriage "gay marriage" does matter, it does not smell as sweet?

2. Based on an off-Broadway play, *Boys in the Band* (1970; directed by William Friedin) addresses the conflicts of gay men in a candid and matter-of-fact style. Show this film to your class and discuss its main points. Students should notice the fears and prohibitions associated with homosexuality almost forty years ago. The plot, however, is not too dated; homophobia is treated especially well. Discuss with your class other social and cultural movements of the period. Which movements have made the most progress? the least? Explain.

## GENERATING WRITING

1. In a three- to five-page paper, have students present research on the history of homosexual relationships in some specific culture. What, for instance, were the ancient Greek and Roman attitudes toward homosexuality? When did it become widely prohibited and by whom? How did American Puritans feel about same-sex relationships? How did Native Americans feel? In this paper, students should address the rationale(s) behind these attitudes.

2. Look at the last line of Sullivan's essay: "Only marriage can bring him [an unidentified gay kid who might one day read the essay] home." Have

students write a short paper analyzing this statement. What do they see as the value of marriage in their own lives? In relationship to their other goals, where do they place having a happy marriage? having a family?

## THE READER'S PRESENCE

1. Sullivan calls marriage the "M-Word" to emphasize that society censors the possibility of marriage for gay couples. He implies that heterosexual couples take marriage for granted, while gay couples must fight to be included in this cultural practice. Ask students what word they thought the author was referring to before they read this essay.

2. Sullivan refers to "civil unions" and "domestic partnerships" as euphemisms, or indirect phrases, for marriage (para. 7). Prohibiting gay couples from marrying and calling gay unions something other than marriages creates a barrier between homosexuals and heterosexuals. These actions imply that gay people do not have the same needs and rights as straight people. Sullivan would probably consider the term "same-sex marriage" a euphemism as well. He wants the recognition of marriage without it being distinguished as "gay marriage" or considered a separate category from heterosexual marriage. A gay marriage is, in fact, just a marriage. Sullivan thus seeks acceptance through conformity.

3. Calvin Trillin's essay ("A Traditional Family," p. 581) is humorous and light, but he poses the same question as Sullivan: who defines a family (or marriage)? Trillin suggests that a family should be defined by characteristics like celebrating Christmas with a big meal, losing socks in the wash, and having a father who is easily manipulated by his family.

# Manil Suri
## KEYS TO THE KINGDOM

### APPROACHING THE ESSAY

Manil Suri's essay is perhaps best understood as a piece about the changes adulthood effects on our relationships with our parents. You might begin the discussion by asking the students to look at the way the author's attitude toward Disneyland parallels his perception of his mother. Note the contrast between his desire "to leave (his) naïveté behind" (para. 3) and his mother's uncritical, almost childlike excitement for the famous theme park. Paragraph 6 provides a particularly clear example of this role reversal, comparing Suri's behavior to the behavior of the parents around him: he is the patient (if long-suffering) parent to his mother's child.

But his attitude changes when he photographs her with Goofy. Ask the students to pay particular attention to what he sees through the lens of his camera: "She didn't look like a girl, not quite—her smile was too wistful for a child. I gazed at the longing on her face even after the shutter clicked, as if absorbing it for the first time" (para. 12). Why does longing make her less childlike? What do the students imagine the source of her longing might be? How does Suri's sudden (and, significantly, first) perception of his mother's longing change the way he thinks about their relationship? And how is this change reflected in the way he thinks about Disneyland? Why does the park "[come] alive around [him]" (para. 13) at this point? Why does Suri's sudden (and very adult) perception of his mother's "longing" make it easier for him to embrace Disneyland with a childlike amusement similar to her own?

"Keys to the Kingdom" also provides an opportunity for a somewhat complex discussion of cultural identity: this essay resists common cultural critiques in favor of a greater focus on the individual. In other words, Suri's cultural observations serve mostly to illuminate the differences between his personality and his mother's. Ask the students how Suri's experience as a young Indian living in America affects his view of Disneyland. He says, for example, that his "years in America had trained [him] to peel back every image and look for the commercial motive beneath it" (para. 3). This sentence suggests an attitude critical of American consumerism, and an astute reader might expect it to segue into a larger cultural critique. It is interesting, therefore, that Suri declines to provide such a critique, instead explaining his suspicion of commercial motives as a part of his "eager[ness] to assimilate" (para. 3). It seems, in this case, that his critique of American commercialism is rooted not in a desire to distance himself from Americans but in a desire to join them in being too sophisticated for Disneyland. By contrast, his mother is fascinated by Disneyland's commercial appeal and even asks, "What else is there to see in America?" (para. 2). Later in the essay, she is charmed by the revelation that "even the fruits [in America] had brand names" (para. 7). What does her enthusiasm for brand names say about her way of engaging the world, as opposed to her son's? Again, we see a sort of inversion of our expectations; where we might expect Suri's mother's reaction to brand-name fruit to spark a critique of the American consumer culture, it is instead used only as a way to highlight the joy she is capable of taking in things Suri has come to regard as ordinary.

## ADDITIONAL ACTIVITIES

1. Disneyland plays a pivotal role in this essay, not simply because so much of the story takes place there but because the *idea* of Disneyland has been central to Suri's relationship with his mother, even going as far back as his middle-class childhood in India. Ask students to think about the role consumer culture has played in their own lives: have them talk about how certain brand names (Dole, Coca-Cola, Starbucks) both form and (possibly) cheapen their experience as Americans. Do they identify more with Suri's initial attitude toward Disneyland or with his mother's? How would their opinion change if

someone important to them (a parent or a friend, for example) enthusiastically expressed the opposite view?

2. In paragraph 2, Suri's mother explains her desire to see Disneyland by asking "What else is there to see in America?" Although on one level the question is tongue in cheek, on another level it also seems to capture something universal about tourism, especially international tourism. Ask the students to think about the tourist attractions they associate with other countries. Would they go to France without wanting to see the Eiffel Tower? Would they go to Egypt without seeing the Sphinx or the pyramids? What does this say about the way we view other countries and their cultures? What does it say about the United States and the way other cultures view us when our principal attractions are, to a large extent, primarily commercial, like Disneyland?

## GENERATING WRITING

1. The central event of Suri's essay seems to be the change in his attitude toward his mother that results from photographing her with Goofy. One of the most interesting things about the essay, and indeed part of its point, is that this specific and *apparently* trivial event was the catalyst for a major change of heart. Ask the students to write a personal essay about a similarly specific and (again, apparently) minor event that caused a significant change in their own lives. Remind them to be specific, remembering that Suri's change of heart is occasioned by actually, physically *seeing* his mother in a new way. It might be helpful to have the students focus their essays on a person. Suri's essay seems to be about the first time he saw his mother as a complete person, a person who is more than just his mother. Have the students had similar experiences?

2. Like Walker Percy's "The Loss of the Creature" (p. 539) and Nathaniel Hawthorne's "My Visit to Niagara" (p. 438), Suri's essay deals with a visit to a place that is so famous one cannot arrive there without some preconceived notions. In a way, these notions prevent us from experiencing famous places for ourselves: we have seen too many postcards of the Statue of Liberty, for example, to see the real thing without comparing it to the postcard. Likewise, Suri has been so inundated by the idea of Disneyland that, before he ever arrives, it has become impossible for him to think about the place without being critical of the advertisements calling it "the experience of a lifetime" (para. 3). Using Hawthorne's "My Visit to Niagara" (p. 438) as a model, students should write a personal essay about their own visit to a famous place. Ask them to consider the things they'd heard or seen prior to their visit and how those things (movies, postcards, television shows, or popular songs) might have affected their ability to experience the place for themselves. Did their preconceived notions enhance, or interfere with, their ability to enjoy the visit? Why or why not?

## THE READER'S PRESENCE

1. Suri clearly explains his lack of enthusiasm in paragraph 3, saying that five years in America had trained him to "peel back every image and look for the commercial motive beneath it." He is "eager to assimilate, to be hip, to leave [his] naïveté behind." It is likely that most of his colleagues—doctors, teachers, and medical school students—would view an enthusiasm for Disneyland as a lack of sophistication, and Suri wants to embrace those values. However, on the second day of his visit to Disneyland, his mother hugs Goofy (para. 11), and in paragraph 13 Suri cannot help but begin to see "Disneyland through [his] mother's eyes." At this point, the experience becomes almost magical because he is able to share in her enthusiasm.

2. Concluding the essay at paragraph 15 may have been poignant, but it would have been a little sad, perhaps, and not quite accurate. An important element of Suri's essay is the fact that this visit to Disneyland strengthened his relationship with his mother. If she'd never come back, we wouldn't have the opportunity to see them looking through the photo album together. If he'd left going to see "Cats" out of the essay, the reader wouldn't have a sense of their continuing relationship and of his mother's continuing ability to pull a sense of wonder out of her experience of life in general, and of American kitsch in particular. It is clear from this essay that Suri (like, one might assume, many of his readers) has an eagerness to be "hip," to rid himself of "naïveté," an eagerness that borders on cynicism and, in a way, interferes with his ability to enjoy life. His interaction with his mother exposes this eagerness as a kind of snobbishness, which Suri is presumably able to drop as a consequence of the interactions.

3. Like Hawthorne ("My Visit to Niagara," p. 438), Suri visits a place that is so famous one can hardly form an objective impression of it. There are so many images of Niagara (and there were, even in Hawthorne's time) that virtually every visitor has (or had) probably seen one before he or she ever actually sees the real thing. The same is true of Disneyland. As a consequence, the contrast between one's expectations (whatever they might be) and the reality of the place had become an inescapable part of the experience for every visitor. Hawthorne and Suri are therefore disappointed by their initial impressions, impressions that only give way to more favorable (and, perhaps, authentic) perceptions when the authors are able to find new, and more personal, ways to live the experience for themselves (Suri through his mother's eyes, Hawthorne through *listening to*, rather than *looking at*, the falls).

   A comparison with Ha Jin's "Arrival" (p. 122) is a little more complicated, and discussion of it might best focus on how the writers view America. What, for example, are the similarities and differences between Suri's desire to assimilate and Jin's anxieties about living a meaningful life in his new home?

# Amy Tan
## MOTHER TONGUE

### APPROACHING THE ESSAY

An important issue in American society is the role of language in our national identity. Without advocating bilingualism, Amy Tan presents the possibility that other "Englishes," that is, the versions of English spoken in immigrant communities, might actually enrich rather than debase the standard English taught in most American schools. Though the experience of learning English by native speakers differs greatly from that of people who must learn English as a second language, Tan's essay offers a good starting point for a discussion of the difficulties of learning a language and the ways language shapes our identities.

Tan is the best-selling author of *The Joy Luck Club* (1989), one of the most widely read novels of the late 1980s and early 1990s. Tan was cited for her remarkable storytelling gifts and for her vivid and poignant portrayal of the lives of Chinese women in contemporary America. In order to write this book, Tan had to remain very close to the ways and language of the community whose life she is depicting. Students might find it interesting to obtain a copy of the novel and to read a few random chapters from it after reading Tan's essay. Do they find that Tan writes in the manner she describes in the essay? Is the book's language easy to read for persons who were not raised within the Chinese American community? What difficulties does Tan's style present to the native speaker of English?

How would your students characterize the examples of English that Tan offers in paragraph 3? Are they good examples of standard English? Are they good examples of the way English is usually spoken? Ask your students to describe the factors that might contribute to the way a person speaks. For example, why would someone addressing a large audience speak differently from a person addressing a close friend or family member?

In paragraph 6, Tan offers a long example of her mother's way of speaking. Ask your students to describe the ways in which it differs from the way English is taught in school. Clearly the speech is ungrammatical, but does that fact hinder our understanding of what the speaker is saying? Is there anything in it that strikes the reader as ambiguous? Does Tan's mother get her message across? Ask your students if they agree with the author that her mother's speech is "vivid, direct, full of observation and imagery" (para. 7). To what degree does Tan imply that her mother's speech has advantages over the speech of many native speakers?

Consider Tan's views on the role a parent's language plays in childhood development in paragraph 15. How could she go about proving that the way her parents spoke English affected her performance on the verbal part of the SATs? Ask your students if they agree with Tan that her slightly above average performance in school and on standardized tests was due to her immigrant background. What other factors might have affected these scores? Consider her discussion of the analogies section of these tests. Her failure to score high on this part of the test might not stem, as Tan seems to believe, from her grasp of English but from errors in logical association—analogies test our ability to perceive similarities between relationships. (Note that the SATs no longer include an analogy section.) Is Tan suggesting that imaginative people have a more difficult time with this kind of test than people who are literal-minded? If this is Tan's implication, what does it have to do with her main argument?

## ADDITIONAL ACTIVITY

1. There has been significant debate in the United States concerning whether English should be adopted as the official language of the United States. Tan's essay, however, significantly complicates our notion of what English is. Your students may wish to explore Tan's notion of "Englishes" and its possible challenge to the campaign for English as the official language.

## GENERATING WRITING

1. Tan stresses the importance of imagining her ideal reader. Ask students to try to imagine their ideal reader. Then ask them to write an essay in which they describe that reader, in the manner that he or she would best understand and enjoy.
2. Most of us come from immigrant backgrounds. At some point in your students' family histories it is likely that their ancestors left some other place to settle in North America. Accordingly, there may be someone in their family who has maintained the speech patterns of the old country while using an English vocabulary. Students should write an essay in which they describe this person and his or her background. They should describe the way this person speaks by using numerous examples, and discuss the person's influence on the student's speech and writing.

## THE READER'S PRESENCE

1. The "Englishes" of which Tan writes are the nonstandard forms of English spoken by the Chinese immigrant community in which she grew up. What is odd about the term is that we usually think about English as one language. The language that Tan describes is not, strictly speaking, a dialect, because it is not unique to a particular region or a group of people but belongs uniquely to her mother.
2. The sentence Tan presents as an example of her "mastery" of English is not complex in structure but reflects the author's lack of confidence in choosing the right words (para. 20). *Quandary* and *nascent* are words that appear in a thesaurus but rarely in plain English. The audience for whom this sentence was written probably does not exist. She might have rewritten it more plainly as "That was the problem that has just begun to form in my mind."
3. Tan's "mother tongue" is, quite literally, her mother's version of English: "Her language, as I hear it, is vivid, direct, full of observation and imagery.

That was the language that helped shape the way I saw things, expressed things, made sense of the world" (para. 7). In paragraphs 10 through 14, Tan describes occasions when she would translate her mother's English into "perfect English" (para. 13). As Tan says, these are "the Englishes [she] grew up with" (para. 2). As a writer, Tan is aware of her mother as one of her ideal readers; thus she weeds out sentences that might strike her mother's ear as forced or unlikely. Richard Rodriguez ("Aria: A Memoir of a Bilingual Childhood," p. 187), in contrast, fantasizes that in becoming a writer of English he has effectively ruled out his Spanish-speaking parents as readers. Rodriguez argues that there should be a healthy distance between the intimate language one shares with one's family and the public language one shares with one's audience or readership. Tan works to bridge this distance.

# Robert Vivian
## TOWN

### APPROACHING THE ESSAY

Many teachers find it useful to have first-year writing students compose essays conveying a "sense of place," and in that context "Town" can be a useful teaching tool. One of the most important techniques your students can lift from it will probably be "defamiliarization." Put simply, Vivian loads his essay with figurative language to get the reader to see the grotesque and the sublime in the otherwise unremarkable town of Alma. The underlying idea that Vivian seems to be working against is the idea that the small town is an unremarkable and generic place: most people don't really *look* at small towns. We are impressed by big cities or charming landscapes, but small towns are just small towns: they all look alike, and no one cares. Vivian uses figurative language to get us to see Alma in a new way, as a place full of wonder and "moon vibes" (para. 2). With figurative language, he manages to make familiar things (a visit to the dry cleaner's, for example, in paragraph 10) seem oddly wonderful: almost fantastic. He is in "quiet awe" of the dark-haired girl behind the counter. He will "carry [that] awe forward like the lit end of a Lucky Strike" cigarette. He's grateful for "the tiny flashing doors of her perfect teeth."

The term "defamiliarization" was coined by early twentieth-century Russian writer Viktor Shklovsky; whether that information is useful to your students will, of course, be up to you: it might help generate interest in the idea if you can attach it to a person. However, it might only confuse the students to get too insistent on an obscure Russian critic or even the term "defamiliarization" itself. The hope here is only that this may be useful shorthand for the larger message, which is that when your students compose their own essays, they will need to pay attention to detail and to find ways of using language to make those details seem interesting and new; they need to help their readers see things in ways they may not have seen them before. Otherwise, a description of a town is just a list of street names, sprinkled with clichéd images.

Another element of "Town" that you may find worth discussing is Vivian's interest in what he calls, in paragraph 7, *eternity*: "The radiant, startling truth is that a small town like Alma burns eternity into your soul. . . ." What do your students think Vivian means by this? How does a little town like Alma contain the infinite? How and why does the "heartbreak" that Vivian refers to in paragraph 6 lead him to the idea that eternity can be experienced in Alma? How does "defamiliarization" contribute to the effect? Does seeing the familiar in a new way lead to a sense of the eternal in the ordinary? There is something almost spiritual about the way Vivian regards this apparently dingy, mundane, and polluted town, as though it is at the same time a place of transcendent beauty. Consider paragraphs 11 and 12, in which Vivian accidentally stumbles upon a homosexual encounter between two men in hunting clothes. He finds the intimacy "hushed and heartbreaking" (para. 11). What "eternity was burning" (para. 12) the two men (as well as Vivian) at that moment? In paragraph 12, Vivian suggests that the men had secret lives. One might be inclined to discuss the ways in which homosexuality is forced to the margins in small towns, but there seems to be another aspect to the passage, as well: eternity itself is pushed to the margins, to the dirty banks of a polluted river (para. 11). Consider the passages where the terms *heartbreak* and *eternity* were first introduced, in Bob's Big Boy (paras. 6 and 7). What is heartbreak? What is eternity? In what ways does the ordinariness of life — its *familiarity* — push the eternal aside? And how does that lead to heartbreak?

## ADDITIONAL ACTIVITY

1. Have the students do an in-class writing assignment in which they describe a familiar object in a new way. You might bring a few objects to class from which they may choose: a tennis ball, a stuffed animal, a vase, a shoe. Anything will do. Students can then share their descriptions with the class. This should be a good way to both engage and reward their creativity in preparation for an essay conveying a "sense of place."

## THE READER'S PRESENCE

1. Vivian suggests that he would find another place equally fascinating at a number of points in the essay. In paragraph 8, for example, he says, "I could live here for the rest of my life or leave tomorrow, staying or going not all that important somehow." In paragraph 9, he explains that he's "not the kind of person who chooses where to go, only submits to the place where he is bidden." He lists a few of the places he has lived, ranging from Poland to Nebraska, and says that he feels as though he has "been called to live in this town . . . [to] let its river of dreams run through me in order to offer a report of what it's like." It is almost as though he feels there is some external force (it could be something spiritual, or something as concrete as a job offer)

dictating his movements. He doesn't specify. Again, it doesn't matter. What matters is his apparent sense of purpose, the idea that he somehow has a responsibility as a writer to record what he finds in the places he has been. In this sense, it doesn't matter what the place is. This leads us to the second part of the question: why does he find Alma so appealing, and how does that support the implied conviction that it doesn't matter where he goes? It seems evident that an essential part of the appeal of Alma is the arbitrariness of it: it is apparently a relatively normal small town, but Vivian sees "eternity" in that ordinariness, and the vividness of his descriptions of ordinary things makes them remarkable. Part of this discussion probably has to do with the poignancy of everyday life (Vivian uses the word *heartbreak* several times), suggesting that a place (or a life) need not be extraordinary in order to be meaningful. Much of the conversation also has to do with Vivian's use of language (see the following question).

2. A discussion surrounding this question might present an ideal opportunity to discuss the concept of defamiliarization—how writers use language to get readers to see familiar things in new ways—explored in Approaching the Essay and Additional Activity. Many of us have sat in red-cushioned booths at chain restaurants like Bob's Big Boy, but how many of us have imagined the upholstery as "gruesome ribbons of congealed blood" (para. 6), as Vivian does? In paragraph 4, he compares the fields full of trash behind the local Wal-Mart, juxtaposing them with "the pastel bands of the sun going down" to liken the scene to "the fading twilight of a Tuscan vineyard," calling far more picturesque associations to mind. Vivian hardly lets a sentence or two go by without a similarly evocative bit of language play, so your students should have no difficulty finding further examples. Almost any example will serve to acquaint them with the power of figurative language to defamiliarize the ordinary, and therefore demonstrate how effective (and, indeed, essential) defamiliarization can be in the "sense of place" essay.

3. Dinaw Mengestu ("Home at Last," p. 170) and Vivian have different motivations. Mengestu is actively looking for a place to call home. He doesn't want to be an outsider anymore. Vivian, however, seems to be attracted to the idea of being an outsider. He lets the town get under his skin, lets "its river" flow through him, but only because he happens to be there and only because he seems to feel obliged, as a writer, to record what he sees. Mengestu willfully chose Kensington, for very specific reasons. Both writers explore their surroundings and describe them in vivid detail, but Mengestu is meticulous: he memorizes the layout of the neighborhood, trying to make himself feel as though the neighborhood is *his*. Vivian looks for more transcendent images: he wants to liken what he sees in Alma to something eternal. Vivian looks for beauty in the black polluted river; Mengestu tries the local restaurants and watches the other immigrants hang out on the corner. Vivian makes a point to defamiliarize; Mengestu doesn't have to. Mengestu is a stranger in town, wanting only to make the place so familiar it feels like home. It is likely he would have done the same thing in Alma. And Vivian, for his part,

probably would have made an effort to see in Kensington all the ugliness and beauty and heartbreak, the "continuous outpouring of moon vibes" (para. 2) he detected in Alma.

# Alice Walker

## BEAUTY: WHEN THE OTHER DANCER IS THE SELF

### APPROACHING THE ESSAY

This selection presents a profound and complex problem of identity: How are we to deal with the physical flaws and imperfections that form an essential part of who we are? Alice Walker's childhood injury has left her profoundly marked, both physically and emotionally. How can other, lesser "differences" shape self-perception? Ask students to think back to times in their lives when they felt all eyes on them, judging them. How did they overcome their fears and anxieties about their appearance? Did their process of self-acceptance resemble Walker's?

The essay is rich in literary technique. Reading and rereading this essay will help the students come to an understanding of the ways nonfiction, like poetry and fiction, can weave strands of imagery into a web of meaning. Nearly every image in this essay is mirrored by a parallel image. The Easter-lily poem Walker recites (para. 4) is echoed later in the "lily leaves" her father applies to her injury (para. 12). The tree that appears as the last image her right eye sees (para. 11) will resurface later in her poem about the desert (para. 44). These are only a few parallels; your students will find others.

Some students may be confused by Walker's abrupt shifts in time. The essay presents incidents and reflections from her life, ranging from age two and a half to her late thirties. You might invite speculation about her narrative technique. What advantages do these jumps in time offer her? Ask the class to analyze Walker's use of tense. The present tense is used in all descriptions of events, regardless of when in Walker's life they occurred. Past tense is reserved for Walker's judgments and speculations. What functions do the tenses serve? Certainly, the use of present tense helps Walker establish dramatic immediacy and focus. It also makes the events described seem current and vivid, as though they are constantly being relived. The few moments of past tense, however, give us some insight into the perspective Walker has gained.

Aside from the "accident" to Walker's right eye (you might want to ask why she encloses the word *accident* in quotation marks), the essay is interlaced with references to violence and torture. Ask students to identify some of these incidents. In this way they will see how much detail in the essay reinforces a world of pain and violence: the childhood cowboy-Indian games (para. 8); the penitentiary and electric chair (paras. 16–19); her mother's illness (para. 25); and the shooting death

**89**

of her high-school classmate (para. 32). How do students react to this aspect of Walker's world? Ask them to discuss the role white society plays in this essay. The white people who appear here are violent (the "cowboy" stars, para. 8), exploitative (Miss Mey, para. 2), or cruel (the man who drives away, para. 42). How might these patterns of antagonism be related? Does the prejudice Walker experiences because of her injury mirror the hostilities of racism?

This essay, though, is not only about pain; it is about beauty, as its title indicates, and about seeing. Ask students to pay attention to two quotations: the doctor's warning that "eyes are sympathetic" (para. 12), and Walker's child exclaiming, "Mommy, there's a *world* in your eye" (para. 47). Students should examine the language closely here. Each quotation has both a literal and a figurative meaning. Ask them to explain what each meaning is and to see how Walker uses the figurative meaning of each expression as a source of inspiration.

## ADDITIONAL ACTIVITIES

1. One of the most powerful aspects of this essay is the way it presents the ongoing debate between outer and inner voices of the past and present. Consider Bernard Cooper's "A Clack of Tiny Sparks: Remembrances of a Gay Boyhood" (p. 78). How does Cooper depict the conversation that exists among himself as writer, the self that has lived his life, and the world around him? How does Walker's representation differ? Which do students find more effective?

2. Students who are intrigued by this essay might be encouraged to read Toni Morrison's *The Bluest Eye* (1972). A primary theme of this novel is its protagonist's obsession with white culture and its standards of beauty. How is the eye an important image for Morrison and Walker? Other students may want to read further in Walker's poetry and discuss recurrences of this essay's imagery. Flowers and children appear often in Walker's poems, as do suffering, violence, and shame. Ask the class to discuss the connections Walker makes between beauty and pain.

## GENERATING WRITING

1. Ask your students to consider carefully what Walker means when she says "There *was* a world in my eye" (para. 48). What are the origins of this image? In what ways is the image appropriate? How does Walker transform its meaning? Invite the students to write an essay in which they explain this image in the context of the entire essay. They should describe, too, how the image enables Walker to deal emotionally with her injury.

2. You might take this opportunity to have students write a brief personal essay about their own experience of physical difference and its role in self-definition. They may wish to describe a physical difference of their own and the ways in which they have coped with it; they might discuss an experience in which physically different friends have revealed their feelings about the difficulties of their lives; they may want to analyze a depiction of the physically different on television or in the movies. How do the experiences of the physically

different and persons with disabilities challenge some of society's pet preconceptions? Does the fear inspired by these challenges prompt exclusion
and hostility? How can the targets of this hostility learn to adjust?

## THE READER'S PRESENCE

1. Walker introduces her father's "beautiful eyes" as a foreshadowing of
   the essay's central images of eyes and beauty. Some other images Walker
   includes here are those of her mother as "knocked out," herself as resisting
   the "pressure" of her mother's knuckles, and the gala "beribboning" of her
   hair (para. 1). The pain Walker mentions foreshadows the pain and violence
   that run throughout the essay.
2. Walker's subject is the past, but she uses the present tense. The choice of
   tense makes her past experience seem vivid, continually relived. Rewrite
   the opening paragraph with the class; most students will agree that the past
   tense causes it to lose the power of its immediacy.
3. Aside from the occasional use of italics to indicate emphasis—one of its
   traditional uses—Walker also uses italics to convey a voice from a dream or
   memory: a voice like her own, perhaps even from some part of her, but also
   unnameable. Her poem, also italicized, seems to flow from "the shock of . . .
   possibility" (para. 44) that she might never have seen the desert. In using the
   present tense, Walker creates more limits for her narration than if she had
   used the past tense; the move to italics temporarily allows her to escape the
   confines of the present tense. Similarly, Judith Ortiz Cofer's italicized passages in "Silent Dancing" (p. 68), follow from her switching between the present narration of the home movie and the recollection of scenes from the past.

# Jerald Walker
## SCATTERED INCONVENIENCES

### APPROACHING THE ESSAY

Jerald Walker's essay examines a side of racism that is rarely explored: black prejudice against whites. Driving through Indiana, Walker and his family encounter a
white man in a pick-up truck who appears to be trying to provoke a confrontation.
You may want to discuss the theme of this essay before students have read it. The
ending will be a surprise to most readers. After students have read the essay, call
their attention to Walker's admission that he himself is a "racist." Were students
surprised when they read that? Is a black person who is racist any different from a
white person who is racist? Is a white racist worse? Walker's paranoid reaction is
probably a result of the forces of African American slave history and of the racism

he has experienced firsthand. Have students locate passages in the essay that demonstrate that Walker is being irrational or paranoid. Is racism ever justified?

You may also want to examine the behavior of the white truck driver. What led Walker to think that he was a bigot? What led the reader to believe that the truck driver was a bigot? What is the importance of the cowboy hat and the Chevy truck? Have students offer textual support demonstrating that the truck driver was probably a nice guy. Discuss the passage describing the truck driver after he gets the author's attention: "The man tooted his horn and gave me a thumbs-up, then rode off into the night" (para. 28). How do we feel when we discover that he is not a bigot? Embarrassed? Proud? Hopeful? Ask your class to consider what obligation, if any, the white truck driver owed the black family.

An analysis of this essay would not be complete without looking at the writer's style. Note, for instance, the strong verbs in the first few paragraphs. Words like "barreled" (para. 1), "gripped" (para. 2), "lurched" (para. 10), and "crush" (para. 8) possess an aggressive quality that enlivens the story. What images do these verbs conjure? How does the diction affect the tone of the story? Note, too, the author's use of self-deprecation: calling himself a "fool" (para. 10), a "racist" (para. 12). How does this affect the author's voice in the essay? Is it effectively used and, if so, in what way?

Finally, you may want to discuss two important subplots: Walker's relationship with his wife and his brother. Why is his wife's competing perspective important to the larger story from early on? What is the wife's role in the development of the author's point? Through their interaction, we learn that Walker is prone to exaggeration, when he claims they are driving in the middle of the night ("It's only eight [o'clock]," [para. 5]). Is this an early sign of the narrator's unreliability? How and why does Walker transition to the flashback of growing up in Chicago and his brother, Clyde (paras. 13–16)? Ask students to locate the humor in this passage.

## ADDITIONAL ACTIVITIES

1. How does racism manifest itself today in America? Students may offer good reasons for insisting that racism no longer exists in the United States. This discussion would lend itself to a good class debate. Students may want to buttress their arguments with facts and personal experience.

2. A discussion of rage and racism in America is also a discussion of gender. Encourage students to reread "Scattered Inconveniences," this time focusing on the gender issue of being a black male—or being a white, male Chevy truck driver. If the truck driver had been a woman, how might the scenario have been altered? Are there sex stereotypes that might have played into this second, hypothetical situation?

## GENERATING WRITING

1. Not all prejudice is racial prejudice. Have students write a personal essay about a time they prejudged some person, thing, or incident only to discover they had seriously misread the situation. What role did their cultural

backgrounds and previous experiences play? What lesson, if any, did they learn? What damage, if any, resulted? What was the primary reason for their miscalculation?

2. Assign an eight- to ten-page research paper on affirmative action legislation. Students should approach this essay in order to answer this question: Is affirmative action legislation a manifestation of prejudice? You may want students to also read Stanley Fish's essay, "Reverse Racism, or How the Pot Got to Call the Kettle Black" (which can be found online).

## THE READER'S PRESENCE

1. Walker refers to the minor racial incidents that still plague black Americans as "scattered inconveniences." He first heard the phrase from a "black intellectual" (para. 12) in Iowa. By calling subtle racial incidents "inconveniences," Walker displays a weary tolerance and expectation of such behavior. The incident with the truck driver is clearly not an example of a "scattered inconvenience." However, a lifetime of minor displays of bigotry may have conditioned Walker to read the situation incorrectly.

2. Walker sees himself as a "recovering" racist (like a recovering alcoholic) who must be ever vigilant of a relapse. He is a racist in the sense that he often prejudges white people as racist or antagonistic, as in the case of the helpful truck driver. He is quick to accept stereotypical rumors: "I vaguely remembered hearing [that Indiana] was a breeding ground for racists" (para. 11). He also was part of a culture that believed: "Whites, in some vague and yet indisputable way, made the winos drink and gangbangers kill" (para. 13).

   Clyde is important in this essay because he represents the "Sambo" or the "Uncle Tom." To succeed, he became a staunch conservative who, Walker believed, was a "sell-out." Meanwhile, Walker went another, more socially acceptable, direction: into a "decade of lawlessness" (para. 17). Why does Walker see these two directions as the only ones open to young black men growing up in urban poverty? He, himself, is a third, unmentioned example: the black intellectual. Has his wife "sold out" by working in academia? Has he, as a writer? Does he imply that there are other options?

3. Both essays are concerned with racism but from a decidedly different angle. Having been a victim of white racism in his youth, Walker has found that, as an adult, he is suspicious of whites and, as such, has become racist himself. He is afraid of whites because he expects them to discriminate against him: in "Scattered Inconveniences," he fears that a white man may actually wish him harm, only to discover that the man in the cowboy hat is only trying to help. Staples, however, finds that whites are afraid of him: he is the victim of racism *now* because people sometimes assume that he's a potential mugger. He deals with this racism by trying to find ways to avoid it, to make whites feel more comfortable (by whistling Vivaldi, for example, the idea being that if a black man appears to be a classical music enthusiast, a white person is less likely to fear that he is a mugger). Walker advises writers to focus on telling a story, keeping their meditations on its meaning (its "lesson") to a

minimum. Staples relates a series of incidents, allowing their meaning to make itself clear without much commentary. Both essays begin with narratives, then they move into exposition: Staples talks about the language of fear, reflecting on the anxieties of some of the white writers he's read; Walker reflects on his own past.

# E. B. White
## ONCE MORE TO THE LAKE

### APPROACHING THE ESSAY

This essay is a modern classic, and deservedly so. It is a joy to teach because every detail works to create a coherent whole, demonstrating that equation so dear to the English instructor's heart: form is inseparable from content. Vladimir Nabokov used to tell his students always to value the *how* over the *what*, but never to confuse it with the *so what*. "Once More to the Lake" is an essay with almost no *so what*. We like to begin by challenging our students to identify the smallest points of style imaginable—E. B. White's use of the definite pronoun *the*, for instance, or his use of the conjunction *and*. If they ask themselves why it's "the dragonfly" rather than "a dragonfly" in paragraph 5, or why White prefers parataxis (linking by coordinating conjunctions) over syntaxis (linking by subordinating conjunctions), their answers will always lead them to a more profound understanding of the ideas and emotions in the essay.

Furthermore, analyzing almost any passage in the essay will lead the student eventually to consider everything else in the essay. Take the metaphor with which White opens paragraph 6: "We caught two bass, hauling them in briskly as though they were mackerel." Ask your students to analyze this simile. They might notice that it's unusual in that it yokes two similar entities—it's surprisingly unsurprising, as similes go. Ask them why White might have created such a simile. Someone might mention that whereas these bass are freshwater fish, mackerel live in the sea. This observation could lead to a discussion of the sea versus lake motif that runs through the essay. What does the sea represent to White? to his son? in the context of World War II? What does the lake represent? The surprising lack of surprise might lead someone to mention White's surprise at other unsurprising occurrences; an example from the same paragraph might be, "When we got back for a swim before lunch, the lake was exactly where we had left it," which observation leads White to comment that this "seemed an utterly enchanted sea." Ask students where the sense of enchantment comes from. Do they find other indications of a supernatural feeling of wonder occasioned by contact with the natural world in this essay? This line of thought might lead to a discussion of the religious imagery in the essay, and an attempt to characterize White's spiritual position. Yet another response to the question about the bass-and-mackerel comparison might be to call attention to the analogy's being drawn from the natural world. This clue might lead your class to look at White's other metaphors drawn from nature, to see how they function in the essay. What is the effect of the simile comparing outboard motors to mosquitos (para. 10)? How does that simile help reintegrate the new sound into nature, erasing the difference that White initially claimed for them? This line of questioning might lead students to consider the opposing forces in the essay: change and stasis, a sense of time circling versus a sense of time moving forward. Another student might call the bass-and-mackerel simile redundant—why describe something by comparison to something that's nearly identical? Ask your students to find other examples of redundancy in this essay, on different scales. They might find phrases such as "the years were a mirage and there had been no years" (para. 5) or the pervasive use of repetition. Or they might jump to psychology and point to White's sense of his own redundancy: if his child replaces him, then he has no place. This line of thought will lead to analysis of the final scene, in which generation and death come together in one chilling sensory image. Many students might have felt that this ending comes out of nowhere in this essay about "jollity and peace and goodness" (para. 9). Then lead an exploration into the early signs of White's ambivalence, his anxiety about his own mortality. You might also point out that the Freudian reading prompted by the final scene is supported by the earlier suggestion of a primal scene from White's boyhood at the lake, where "the partitions . . . were thin and did not extend clear to the top of the rooms" (para. 2).

## ADDITIONAL ACTIVITIES

1. White's classic essay raises classic issues about reading and writing that enable us to help students discover a great deal about their own resourcefulness with language and their ability to use it to express the ideas they want or need to express. Yet, in addition to the mastery of language highlighted in the essay, White also explores several important themes that link it with other selections.

2. A fundamental choice that writers routinely make is diction. Have the class consider White's choice of words and describe it in a few paragraphs. What makes White's word choices so effective? Invite students to compare and contrast White's diction with, say, George Orwell's in "Shooting an Elephant" (p. 180). They might choose examples of distinctive diction and then discuss the similarities and differences.

3. You might apply the same basic exercise to other aspects of each writer's prose style, including the syntax and rhythms of their sentences and the devices with which they build unity into their paragraphs. This classroom exercise can be readily extended to any other "classic" essay in this collection. A still more informative exercise would be to do a comparison and contrast of stylistic features in less celebrated essayists. Studying stylistic features in White and less celebrated writers will not only introduce your students to "canon" issues in the first-year composition course but also help demystify these texts.

## GENERATING WRITING

1. Assign an essay in which your students analyze the doubling motif in "Once More to the Lake." How does White's eerie feeling "that he was I, and therefore, by simple transposition, that I was my father" (para. 4) form the core of this essay? How does White reinforce this main theme on other levels of the essay, in style, imagery, rhythm, and so on? What are the larger implications of this eerie sensation?

2. Assign an essay in which your students analyze one comparison from the essay (other than the similes you have already discussed in class), tracing all its implications and connections throughout the essay to their logical conclusions.

3. If any students find the unassailable coherence of "Once More to the Lake" uncongenial, have them write an essay arguing against the value system that places a high premium on artistic coherence and unity. They might want to argue, say, from a cultural perspective that offers other aesthetic values, or from the standpoint of a feminist critic of the male academy. They might want to offer—and analyze—another essay as an alternative to the traditional values demonstrated in White's prose.

## THE READER'S PRESENCE

1. White identifies the associative logic of memory: "You remember one thing, and that suddenly reminds you of another thing" (para. 2). The structure of his essay seems to follow this logic, though the reader knows that as a writer White is fully in command of the chain of associations he records in the essay. In the last two or three paragraphs (have students debate where exactly the shift occurs), White seems to grant more power to his unconscious mind. Details bubble up from darker places than we've seen in the essay thus far. With the final paragraph, White seems to have abdicated his authorial control; with the last sentence, and especially the last phrase, he admits his worst fear.

2. You might want to point to the sights of the lake in paragraphs 5 and 6, the "sleepy sound" of the inboard motors in paragraph 10, the breeze and the delightful sense of weariness in paragraph 11, the thunderstorm in paragraph 12, and of course the wet bathing suit in the final sentence. All these sensory details contribute to White's sense that nothing has changed.

3. The "creepy sensation" White refers to in paragraph 4 is his first sensation of the fear of mortality that surfaces when he experiences the confusion of himself for his father, or his son for himself. This fear catches up with him again at the end of the essay (see question 1 in this section). Raymond Carver, named after his father, experiences a similar blurring of his own and his father's identity. Writing after his father's death in "My Father's Life" (p. 60), Carver examines himself for evidence that he is not only like his father but doomed to repeat his father's life.

# Elie Wiesel
## EIGHT SIMPLE, SHORT WORDS

### APPROACHING THE ESSAY

Wiesel's account of life in a concentration camp during the Holocaust is sparely written, expertly seen, and often very moving. Students will immediately be familiar with the Holocaust, one of the most infamous events of the twentieth century, but they may not have experienced it at ground level, with someone who lived through the event. Wiesel's account here of his family arriving at Auschwitz, ending up in Birkenau, and finally separating from his mother and sisters, while remaining with his father, will bring students into the stark and horrific world of Nazi Germany during World War II. Wiesel's excerpt from *Night* immediately engages readers, by letting them envision how they might act in such a situation, how they could cope with the separation from other family members, and what they might do in the face of the crematoriums.

You will want to direct students to the sparseness of the prose. Why are Wiesel's paragraphs so short? Why are his sentences rather clipped? What does this terse prose do for the reader? It is of note that the entire account of *Night* is only about one hundred and fifty pages—why has Wiesel chosen to write in this minimalist style? The answer should be clear once students understand what they are dealing with. Here, at the beginning of this excerpt, the narrator and other Jewish people are imprisoned in a cattle car; as they arrive at Auschwitz, they remain imprisoned, until they are let out, either to be killed immediately or to live for some time in the death camp itself. No matter where these people step, they are imprisoned. In the same way, *Night*'s prose looks out from behind bars. It mimics the imprisonment that the narrator feels: the cattle cars are dark, and there is not much to see through the barred windows; at the prison camp, soldiers direct people where to go in terse, emotionless commands. Wiesel's prose is meant to be both clear and stark, mimicking the starkness of the world, one that rides the line between life and death and is, as the title of the book indicates, full of darkness. One might almost say it is a black and white world—the Nazis having sucked the color and joy out of it.

As you move forward, ask the students what they think the role of Mrs. Schächter is (paras. 11–45). Students should immediately remember that she is the woman who continually screams, as if in a dream-like state, that she sees a great fire. As the train moves to its destination, she frightens many of the people in the cattle car with her cries. At times, the others in the car even hit her to keep her quiet. Ask students why this violence is significant. What does it show about the situation and the mental state of these people? What has happened to them? Furthermore, when the train finally arrives at the camp and the Jews see "flames rising from a tall chimney into a black sky," what do students make of these flames and Mrs. Schächter's cries now? Is it the fire Mrs. Schächter has been seeing in her mind's eye? And, if so, what of that premonition, that prophecy? Toward the end of the excerpt, Wiesel mentions his faith being consumed by these horrible events; what does Mrs. Schächter's prophecy have to do with truth, vision, faith, and, possibly, God?

## ADDITIONAL ACTIVITIES

1. Show your students part of the movie *Schindler's List*. Do the students notice anything similar in the style of the movie and Wiesel's prose style? Why is the movie shot in black and white and how does this either correlate with or differ from Wiesel's prose style?

2. Ask students to highlight and examine the religious language or religious moments (or both) in the excerpt. For instance, Wiesel notes that one man begins saying the Kaddish, the prayer for the dead. There are other moments where the Jewish religion is shown to be important. Why is Wiesel including these and how do they ironically relate to the end of the excerpt?

## GENERATING WRITING

1. Have students write an essay in which they research two or three articles exploring the atrocities at Auschwitz or other "death camps." They should report the information they find in a two- to three-page paper, informing the audience of the motivation of the Nazis, the resistance of the Jews, and the outcome of these two forces. Alternately, students could research America's rather complicated involvement with the Holocaust. The students may not know, but it took some time for the U.S. government to become fully involved in helping European Jews during World War II. Why was this? Again, students should research two or three articles.

2. Wiesel writes, "Never shall I forget those flames that consumed my faith forever" (para. 134). Have students write an essay describing a moment when their faith or beliefs were tested in some way. Was there ever a moment when they were so disillusioned by the world that they discarded their faith or their moral principles as Wiesel seems to have done by the end of this excerpt? If so, what did they learn from that experience and how do they picture moving forward?

## THE READER'S PRESENCE

1. The other prisoners are trying to warn, albeit harshly, the newly arrived prisoners. Also, they may believe the prisoners came to Auschwitz by choice, which is not the case. Their tone is both full of rage and full of fear. The father and son lie about their age because the older inmate tells them to do that in order to help them avoid the crematorium. The older and younger, he implies, are not fit for work.

2. Wiesel's faith is more than shaken by his experience. He becomes enraged at God and, in so doing, loses his faith. The prayer-like litany at the end of the piece fills in for the prayer for the dead that is spoken during the walk toward the crematoriums, when another inmate begins chanting the Kaddish. Here,

Wiesel replaces the traditional prayer with another type of prayer, one of lost faith and the need for memory, to never forget the Holocaust.

3. Looking at the two essays together can provide an interesting contrast and possibly lead to some useful insights about writing, mostly concerning audience, purpose, and tone. First, though, it is important to remember that the authors are dealing with fundamentally different experiences: Adam Mayblum ("The Price We Pay," p. 164) lived through a horrific incident; Wiesel survived a prolonged ordeal. Mayblum had to flee a burning building; Wiesel was confined in a Nazi death camp. Mayblum was an adult; Wiesel was, if not necessarily a child anymore, still certainly not an adult. It is unlikely that writing about the experience was the first thing that occurred to Wiesel upon his liberation from a Nazi death camp. So, although Wiesel's piece may be equally vivid in its account of what took place, it is still more reflective and less immediate than Mayblum's. As an adult who survived a single, cataclysmic event, Mayblum wanted to provide an account of what he had been through immediately after it happened, to let people know that he had survived and to describe the events. It is also worth noting that he is writing in an electronic age: his account was originally in the form of an e-mail for family and friends, hence the immediacy. Wiesel was writing a book for an anonymous readership, not a letter to friends. His tone is more reflective, then, not only because he had some distance from the original event, but because his audience would have expected it.

# Tobias Wolff
## PROSPECTING

### APPROACHING THE ESSAY

An excerpt from his book-length memoir, Tobias Wolff's "Prospecting" can be read as a short essay about the relationship between a mother and son as they set out to begin a new and (probably) ill-fated life in Utah. One of the most interesting things about the selection is the way that Wolff handles the narration itself: writing as an adult, he naturally has a more sophisticated understanding of his mother's ill-fated decision to move "out West," but as a *character* in the *text* he doesn't seem to know any more than he would have known as a child. He passes no explicit judgments, yet there are subtle markers throughout the essay, giving us, as readers, adult insights into what's happening.

Look, for instance, at the exclamation point in paragraph 13, after the word "friendly," and the next sentence in which he says his mother "just knew she'd get a job out of him" (the man who wrote to tell her he couldn't offer her a job). From the author's tone, we know that his mother is being naïve, even though he never actually *says* it. What other incidents of her naïveté do your students see? In paragraphs 8 and 9, Wolff tells us that, according to his mother, "everything was going to change when we got out West," contrasting their old life with the promise of the new. His mother clearly miscalculated. Do your students find her optimism irresponsible? The young Toby seems to go along for the ride without passing much judgment, but does it seem as though the adult Wolff is more critical? How is this critical perspective represented in the text?

It is also worth noting that, despite its naïveté, there is something lovely in the mother's optimism. How does Wolff counterbalance the implied judgments of his prose? How does the fact, for example, that his mother gave her car to a *stranger* complicate the fact that she just gave it away?

## ADDITIONAL ACTIVITIES

1. You might consider having your students watch the film *This Boy's Life*, starring Robert DeNiro and Leonardo DiCaprio. How do the filmmakers bring Wolff's "characters" to life? Do they capture the naïve optimism of the mother? How is the narrator portrayed? You might even consider having your students read the rest of the book, particularly if you want them to write memoir pieces of their own.

2. Lead the class in a discussion of a comparison between "Prospecting" and Manil Suri's "Keys to the Kingdom" (p. 227). How do the narrators portray their mothers? From a certain point of view, their presentations of their mothers might be considered condescending: why do your students suppose that these narrators view their mothers from a certain height? How is Jamaica Kincaid's representation of her mother ("The Estrangement," p. 129) different? She is more explicitly judgmental but somehow less condescending, viewing her mother as almost god-like. Is that because her mother was less kind than Wolff's or Suri's? Is Kincaid's view of motherhood less romantic? Why? To what extent does the fact that Wolff and Suri are men affect their perspectives?

## GENERATING WRITING

1. Have your students write an essay about a childhood memory involving an adult. As adults (or young adults), your students should be able to think of some memory that they see differently now, in the same way that the adult Wolff sees his mother's decision to move to Utah. Ask them to write about an experience without explicitly judging it. Can they, like Wolff, find ways to convey their adult judgments without directly stating them?

2. Have your students write a brief essay in which they examine the way that Wolff conveys an adult sensibility in "Prospecting." How does he use language to imply a critical perspective without explicitly "breaking character?"

## THE READER'S PRESENCE

1. The opening passage is grim and funny. It's terrible that the truck goes over the edge, presumably killing the driver, but Wolff's honesty is amusing when he uses the emotional aftermath of the event to his advantage: having witnessed the accident, his mother apparently feels a heightened affection for the young Wolff, and Wolff uses that affection to get her to buy him some souvenirs—souvenirs he knows they can't afford. Both of these aspects of the opening sequence color what's to come. There is a sense of foreboding, a less-than-hopeful outlook for the future, almost as though the truck careening off the highway and over the cliff is a metaphor for the ill-fated voyage of the mother and son. But there is also a sort of bonding that takes place between them. After all, even if Wolff uses his mother's vulnerability to his advantage, the two travelers feel affection for one another, much as they do at the end of the selection when, with their dreams at least partially dashed, they approach a new destination together, counting down the mile markers together.

2. Toby's mother is not particularly practical. Her emotional response to the truck going over the ledge leads her to spend more money than they have, but that's only the beginning. The fact that she's driving halfway across the country to follow up on get-rich-quick rumors demonstrates a naïveté that is perhaps not the best quality in a single mother. This is especially clear in paragraph 13: warned against coming to Utah, specifically because there are no jobs, Toby's mother goes anyway, because the "letter was so friendly . . . [she] just knew she'd get a job." She reacts emotionally to situations. She doesn't use her head. But it is important to emphasize that her impracticality tends to err on the side of optimism and, of perhaps equal import, kindness: Wolff demonstrates this not only in the opening passage but again when he tells us, in paragraph 7, that she got so fed up with her car that, finally, she just gave it away.

3. In "Prospecting" and "Keys to the Kingdom" (p. 227), Wolff and Suri, respectively, paint pictures of naïve, emotional creatures. Suri's mother is a simple soul, easily pleased and easily amazed, not just by Disneyland but by trivial things, like fruits with brand names. Wolff's mother is endlessly optimistic: in fact, irresponsibly so. Jamaica Kincaid's mother is not impractical. At least there isn't a lot of evidence to support such an assertion. She *is* emotional, but her emotionalism does not manifest in optimism, affection, or wonder. Instead, she is cold, unkind, judgmental, and unforgiving. She is not cast in a favorable light. The extremes here might lead a reader to wonder if perhaps it is difficult for these writers (or for anyone) to quite *see* their own mothers: it seems unlikely that women who have raised children are indeed the simple creatures with which we are presented here.

# PART 2

# EXPOSITORY WRITING
## Shaping Information

---

# Joan Acocella
## A FEW TOO MANY

### APPROACHING THE ESSAY

Acocella begins by explaining, or at least attempting to explain, what exactly a hangover is: "attempting" because, as Acocella indicates, science doesn't quite have it figured out yet. You might ask your students to talk about their experience (however limited) with drinking and hangovers. For instance, if they get headaches or muscle cramps or both, they're probably experiencing a form of dehydration. If they don't drink, what after-effects do they see other people experiencing the day after? Acocella tells us that if people get the shakes or the sweats, they are going through withdrawal; the alcohol has left their bodies and they want more. Students should note Acocella's strategy here. Here investigation of the hangover—her *research*—is quite thorough: she wants to explain what it is, how it happens, and exactly how alcohol consumption contributes to different factors experienced during a hangover. Although the subject matter may seem lighthearted to students, as, indeed, is Acocella's *treatment* of the subject matter, the point remains: even the most lighthearted essay must be thoroughly researched, and "research" does not necessarily mean "boring." You might use this essay as a way to open the issue of the research paper, to explore the various ways that a research paper can be something other than a dull activity.

Once Acocella has explained to the best of her and science's ability how alcohol consumption leads to a hangover, she switches gears and aims for the ever-elusive hangover cure. Students will probably have some experience with such remedies. One of the more interesting elements of the piece is that Acocella traces the hangover and its cures across cultures. She finds that the word *hangover* means different things in different languages and that the cures for the hangover differ from culture to culture. You might ask your students to think about what this means, what it says about the world. It might get them thinking about their own culture, whether it is "American" culture or Japanese or European culture, for example, or simply campus culture: What are the ideas of leisure and enjoyment and responsibility in a given culture? Which ideas cross cultural lines? Some of your students will likely have religious or cultural backgrounds that promote abstinence from alcohol (Muslims, certain denominations of Christianity, and so on). What are their attitudes toward hangovers? Are hangovers richly *deserved*?

Toward the end of the essay, Acocella addresses those who believe that the best way to avoid a hangover is to avoid drinking; she also suggests that some see drinking as a negative personality trait, bordering on a problem. This should be a valuable lesson to students: not so much about drinking but about audience. Ask students who they believe Acocella is writing to in the beginning of the essay, the middle, and toward the end. Her audience seems to shift throughout, and students should note the importance of directing their writing toward different groups in a single article. What does Acocella think about those who look down on drinkers, who believe the best way to avoid hangovers and avoid trouble is to avoid drinking? How does her tone change while she addresses this different audience?

## ADDITIONAL ACTIVITIES

1. Many of your students are probably underage, but you can safely assume that most of them have, at the very least, had experience in situations where social drinking is occurring: whether at a party or in a dorm room or even while watching a band at a bar. Have them think about how American culture views drinking. When is it okay? When is it unacceptable? Are there any paradoxes or contradictions in what they find?

2. Have students pick two different paragraphs from vastly different parts of the essay (from the beginning, middle, or end), then explore the different audiences that Acocella is addressing. Depending on the point Acocella is making, her audience changes. Why is that, and where do students find solid examples of this?

## GENERATING WRITING

1. Have your students write an essay in which they explore the pros and cons of drinking. They should explore the two main views presented in Acocella's essay: that drinking is an undesirable and problematic social activity and, conversely, that it is a necessary, social, and ultimately life-affirming cultural activity. This should be an exploration paper, but by the end of the paper students should choose one side over the other. This should be a classical-type argument in reverse. Ask students to do some research on these two perspectives and, based on the information they find, come to side with one of the perspectives by the end of the paper. They can think of the paper as an exploration that ends with a stance.

2. Conversely, have the students write a more classical argument, taking a stance right from the beginning. Suggest to students that they argue in one of two ways: either for complete abstinence from alcohol or for moderation in drinking. If they argue for moderation, they should set up the criteria for this on their own. Either way they choose to argue, they should have strong supporting points to propel their argument along.

## THE READER'S PRESENCE

1. Acocella is supporting the idea that drinking is a necessary uninhibitor and allows people to come together, laugh and love, and forget about their troubles for a short time—this is directly stated. She makes the point that life is tragic and people don't always want to be consumed in that tragedy. Social drinking, hangover included, is a way that helps people come together to share and forget. Acocella supports this notion by giving plentiful examples of global cultures that use alcohol; she discusses both their drinking habits and their hangover cures, which implicitly supports her argument that all drink, in some ways, to forget troubles and come together. Acocella also implicitly argues that alcohol consumption, if done responsibly, shouldn't be a problem in anyone's eyes.

2. This technique (writing about alcohol consumption through multiple lenses) is one that is apparent from the start. Acocella explores how science understands the hangover, what the contributing factors are, and how best to counteract those factors, then she explores how different cultures view the hangover and how these cultures try to cope with the effects of a hangover. She even explores the etymology of the word *hangover* and what it means in different cultures, revealing how the culture views the hangover; some see it as a headache; others as more associated with the stomach and vomiting. Either way, Acocella's point here seems to be that drinking spans not only cultures, but generations, and we've been dealing with the problem of the hangover for centuries with no real answer—not that that's a serious problem. The price, Acocella seems to believe, is worth the enjoyment with friends at the time of consumption.

3. In "Consider the Lobster" (p. 839), David Foster Wallace is somewhat careful approaching the moral problems associated with eating lobster. He says he doesn't want to ask too much of his readers—in this case, readers of *Gourmet* magazine—because he himself enjoys eating lobster, and the issue becomes an uncomfortable one for him upon reflection. Acocella, however, is almost dismissive when it comes to the moral question of drinking. She can afford to be. Drinking has had moral problems associated with it for years, problems that have been explored and reiterated and accepted: in popular culture, the moral problems of drinking are often treated as a joke. Eating lobster is not generally considered a moral problem, especially not among readers of *Gourmet* magazine, so Wallace has to approach the question with some degree of seriousness, as well as restraint. If Wallace were to use Acocella's tone, one might assume that his essay is a joke: that he is not genuinely concerned about the moral implications of boiling lobsters alive. If Acocella were to invoke Wallace's tone, her essay might almost be nonsensical: to explore the moral problems of drinking as though they were new, never mind serious, would likely confuse readers. We would be waiting for the punch line, and confused when it never arrived.

# Daniel Akst
## WHAT MEETS THE EYE

### APPROACHING THE ESSAY

Students will probably have a lot to say about this essay. You may want to begin by asking what they think the essay's thesis is. Some observant student will, no doubt, locate it in the first paragraph: "Perhaps it's time to say what we all secretly know, which is that looks do matter, maybe even more than most of us think." Ask students how they feel about so obvious a thesis statement presented so early in the essay. Does this influence their reading of the essay? Does it guide their reading? Does it offer any surprises? Does it conflict with any cultural norms they may hold?

Akst develops his argument through the use of scientific data. Ask the class to go through the essay and find specific examples of the author's use of expert testimony. Are these statements sound? Do any seem to be taken out of context? Does Akst gloss over any inconsistencies that trouble you? Does he extrapolate too much from the studies? Which statements are strong? Which are weak? Do any of the statements seem counterintuitive? Has the author used testimonials and scientific data wisely? Does he create or pose questions that he does not address?

Although Akst presents a lot of support, there might be flaws in his argument. For instance, he maintains that beauty has to do with symmetrical features, from an evolutionary standpoint. However, many of the so-called attractive Hollywood stars have asymmetrical features: Harrison Ford, for instance, admits to having a lopsided nose (note what Camille Paglia has to say about the "great faces" of Diana Vreeland and Lillian Hellman in "The Pitfalls of Plastic Surgery," p. 774). Students might be able to think of other famous people whose features are not symmetrical but who are considered attractive, even sexy, nonetheless.

Weight, specifically obesity, is one of Akst's most examined topics. Ask students to find statements about weight in the essay, such as: "Fully two-thirds of American adults have abandoned conventional ideas of attractiveness by becoming overweight" (para. 6), and rebut some of them in class. Do Americans become overweight to "abandon conventional ideas of attractiveness"? Is Akst's tone here ironic or facetious? To what extent do his claims hold up to the class's experience with weight and weight problems?

What connection does Akst make between weight and clothes? Akst asserts that "America's weight problem is one dimension of what seems to be a broader-based national flight from presentability, a flight that manifests itself unmistakably in the relentless casualness of our attire" (para. 8). Could it not be that styles are simply changing? What is intrinsically presentable about a suit? Does this assertion have some evolutionary evidence? Is wearing a suit a personal preference or a biological imperative? Akst also identifies good looks with an elite that he associates almost exclusively with Hollywood. Does he reconcile Hollywood's "images of beauty" (para. 34) with the stars' sometimes tasteless standards of dress? How does this burden his thesis?

Point out that Akst is not talking exclusively about women. What are the evolutionary necessities, according to Akst, associated with beauty in both women and men? How are they different? Do they suggest any advantage—social, sexual, or otherwise—for one sex over the other?

Make the class aware that Akst uses certain strategies to make his argument convincing. Draw students' attention, for example, to the author's use of diction. What is the effect of such words and phrases as "everyone knows" (para. 1), "in all likelihood" (para. 2), "which is obvious" (para. 10), and "people know instinctively" (para. 13)?

## ADDITIONAL ACTIVITIES

1. Akst intentionally uses clichés to debunk or expose some of the disingenuous truisms about appearances. Scanning the essay again, students should search for these clichés and decide how Akst uses them to advance his argument. Does he agree or disagree with the cliché? Are clichés generally useful in an argument? Why or why not? Does this essay suggest any clichés that Akst has not used? Discuss in class.

2. This essay contains many points that are excellent topics for debate. Ask the class to suggest points from the essay, perhaps a quote or statistic, that are arguable and then divide students into groups. After the groups have developed an argument about some specific point, have them debate it in front of the class. For this assignment, you will want to decide whether students will be assigned to a team (and proposition) or choose a team themselves. Sometimes students learn a great deal from having to defend a proposition with which they initially disagree. Keep the number of students in each group to three or four for each of the sides. The essay is meaty: there should be enough points to argue so that each student will eventually get a chance to be on a team.

## GENERATING WRITING

1. Several essays in this book address issues of body image and self-esteem. In a five-page paper, have students research eating disorders. To arrive at a workable thesis, they will need to narrow the topic. A few of the many possibilities include how and why teenagers are susceptible to obesity, bulimia, and anorexia; the history of eating disorders; and the treatment of eating disorders.

2. Have students write a short personal narrative about a specific celebrity they admire. Some questions this essay might address include the following: Why does the student like this celebrity? What influence, if any, has this person had on the student's life, fashion and music choices, and philosophic outlook?

How has this person influenced the student's personal goals or attitudes or opinions about the opposite sex or about gender identity?

## THE READER'S PRESENCE

1. People, especially Americans, do not want to believe in privilege; we believe beauty to be "a natural endowment, and as a people we dislike endowments" (para. 19). As a result, we insist that looks are literally superficial ("skin-deep"); it is "impolitic, if not immature, to admit giving too much weight to a factor as shallow as looks" (para. 1). Inconsistency results from the fact that good looks probably have, according to the author, evolutionary origins: they speak to us of "health, reproductive fitness, agreeableness, social standing, and intelligence" (para. 4). Consequently, we don't have much choice but to respond to good looks favorably. Student responses to this explanation will vary.

2. Akst draws from disciplines that include evolutionary biology ("it makes sense that men should care more about the way women look than vice versa" [para. 34]), evolutionary psychology ("the evolutionary environment . . . made it worthwhile . . . for mothers to invest themselves" in "better-looking babies" [para. 23]), plastic surgery, dentistry, and economics ("better-looking people make more money" [para. 27]). Students' responses to these reports will vary. Some of Akst's points could be disputed by pointing out that the studies are conducted in specific contexts, yet he uses the results to support generalizations.

3. Like Akst, Camille Paglia ("The Pitfalls of Plastic Surgery," p. 774) feels that the human attraction to beauty is unstoppable. Akst does not seem to judge the idea: he says, essentially, "This is the way it is." It is instinctual. Paglia, however, describes "the drive of the human species toward beauty . . . one of our deepest and finest instincts" (para. 4). In other words, she *does* judge the idea: although she likes it, she is bothered by the socially constructed aspect of beauty norms. At the end of his essay, Akst says those norms are becoming more inclusive. Paglia says they emphasize a sort of youth and innocence that is degrading to women. She is not concerned by the desire to be beautiful—the social pressure. She says "maximizing one's attractiveness and desirability is a justifiable aim in any society" (para. 10), but she feels that plastic surgeons draw "from too limited a repertoire" (para. 12). Personality is being wiped out by conformity, and the image women conform to is juvenile.

# Akhil Reed Amar
## SECOND THOUGHTS: WHAT THE RIGHT TO BEAR ARMS REALLY MEANS

### APPROACHING THE ESSAY

Is this essay about gun control or is Akhil Reed Amar saying something more? What effect does his scholarly expertise have on this essay? Amar provides a close reading of the Second Amendment, but he is also careful to examine the wording of the Constitution as a whole. By looking at the social milieu into which the document was born, he is able to glean an accurate interpretation from its historical context. Amar has said that "text without context is empty." You might want to come back to this quote and ask your class if it transcends constitutional interpretations. Can we use this idea in our understanding of other texts? of literature and poetry, for instance?

Amar writes an engaging and a unique essay about the constitutionality of gun control. Most "libertarian" gun owners invariably call up the Second Amendment to the Constitution as justification for their right to keep and use weapons of all kinds and for all purposes. Discuss with your class the meaning of "libertarian," which is someone who believes in freedom of thought and action without government intervention. Rather than dismiss the libertarian argument, Amar carefully approaches it and the counterargument used by "gun controllers" who maintain that the Founders meant only that the government could keep and bear arms for the defense of the nation.

Ask students what they believe to be Amar's personal opinion about gun ownership. Be sure that they use textual support to make their arguments. Some of Amar's feelings do creep into this otherwise objective approach. What does he mean when he says that "the Framers envisioned Minutemen bearing guns, not Daniel Boone gunning bears" (para. 9)? Why is he using humor here?

The basis of Amar's analysis rests on an analogy between the people's militia and the jury system. Have students scan the essay and locate the similarities between the two. After making his analogy, Amar states that "the legal and social structure on which the [Second] amendment is built no longer exists" (para. 11). What is the problem with using the jury/militia analogy today? What problem does this create for Amar's insistence that text must be studied always in context? Another issue raised in this essay is the problem of today's guns. How do they differ in ways that the Founders probably never imagined? What does the author mean when he says that "single-fire muskets had certain . . . democratic properties" (para. 13)?

Although the libertarian argument usually rests on the Second Amendment, Amar suggests that "the best constitutional arguments for [the libertarian] view come not from the Founding but from the Reconstruction some fourscore years later" (para. 20). To what arguments is he referring? Why does he use the term "fourscore" instead of eighty? To what is "fourscore" an allusion?

**109**

Finally, Amar considers a broad reading that would "try to stay true to the vision of the Founders' Second Amendment while also making modern sense" (para. 19). What would this mean, according to the author, in terms of who has the responsibility and right to serve in the armed services? What does this mean for women? for gays? How does the Nineteenth Amendment alter the Second Amendment?

## ADDITIONAL ACTIVITIES

1. Amar speaks specifically of the Fourteenth and Nineteenth amendments and their influence on the interpretation of the Second Amendment. Hand out copies of these two important amendments and have students read them in class. Discuss the implications of these amendments and their influence on our interpretation of laws and in our daily lives. How did our culture change after the adoption of each of these amendments?

2. In paragraph 1, Amar says: "Then came Littleton." A brief summary of the tragedy at Columbine High School, April 1999, is in order. Amar believes that Columbine changed the discussion of gun control in America. Most students will have a good memory of the images and news of that tragic event. Lead them in a discussion of their memories of Columbine and what it felt like to be a student at that time. What were their concerns? How did they feel going back to their own schools? Did they know students who they thought might have been capable of this kind of violence? What do they remember about the argument against gun control that peaked at that time? What do they believe to be the lasting results, if any, of the shootings?

## GENERATING WRITING

1. If, as Amar asserts, "Text without context is empty," what can be said about scripture and perhaps other books of the world's religions? Assign a ten- to twelve-page research paper that explores the interpretation of scripture and the role of context in this interpretation.

2. Have students write a three- to four-page personal essay expressing their own feelings about gun control. Following are some questions they may want to answer: Should *any* private citizen (this would exclude the armed services and the various police forces) be allowed to own a gun for personal protection? Does outlawing guns make the average, law-abiding citizen more vulnerable to shootings because criminals, by definition, do not obey the law? Should certain kinds of guns be controlled and others not? What about other kinds of weapons? How do students feel about registration of guns? licensing of guns (based on adequate demonstration of capability and mental soundness)? Even if it is legal, is gun ownership immoral? Why or why not?

## THE READER'S PRESENCE

1. Amar sees two readings that must be reconciled. First, he addresses the "statists," those who read the Second Amendment as a mandate for the right

of a militia (confusing the word to mean "government military") to keep and bear arms. This reading is identified today with "gun controllers." Second, he addresses the "libertarians," those who read the amendment as approval for individuals to own guns. This group is identified with "gun owners and their supporters." Each group latches on to one of the two clauses of the opening statement: "A well-regulated militia being necessary to the security of a free state" (statist), "the right of the people to keep and bear arms shall not be infringed" (libertarian). Amar says that both readings are wrong (and right, to some extent). The militia of the Founders was nothing like the National Guard or a SWAT team. Every voter was included in the militia; every voter had the right and responsibility to serve. Furthermore, "people" was always used by the Founders as a collective term: it did not mean individual persons. The jury-militia analogy is appropriate: every citizen is expected to answer the call to serve on a jury. Twelve individuals getting together on their own to decide guilt or innocence is not a jury. As Amar puts it: Both the jury and the militia were "local bod[ies] . . . summoned by the government but standing outside it, representing the people, collectively" (para. 8). Other similarities include the following: participation in both was a right and a duty; both were composed of amateurs "designed to check . . . permanent and professional government officials (judges and prosecutors [and] a standing army)" (para. 8); and the goal of each was a collective, not private, pursuit.

2. The syntax in paragraph 1 is choppy, using primarily sentence fragments, sounding almost conversational. The tone is definite and assured but colloquial. The pivotal sentence is the last sentence: "Properly construed, the Second Amendment means quite a lot, but not what the NRA thinks." After this sentence, the essay is written, for the most part, in complete sentences. The tone becomes analytical at this point; the reader senses in the author's voice an authority, and the essay seems almost instructive. Amar moves in the direction of consensus, pointing out that neither reading is correct (or completely incorrect). In a sense, he uses a comparison-contrast analysis of the two clauses of the Second Amendment to discuss the different meaning of "people" and "persons" and the "statist" versus the "libertarian" interpretations.

3. Answers to this question will vary. Amar and Stephen Jay Gould ("Sex, Drugs, Disasters, and the Extinction of Dinosaurs," p. 430) both make a case for why certain interpretations work and others do not. Amar strongly argues for a historical interpretation of the Second Amendment by examining the context of what certain words and phrases meant at the time of its conception. Similarly, Gould points out that a hypothesis must be testable and rooted in empirical evidence. The first two theories for the extinction of the dinosaurs cannot be tested and therefore remain mere speculation. The third hypothesis, however, is rooted in evidence—high levels of iridium—rather than speculation. Gould meticulously distinguishes between "testable proposals" (para. 4), "intriguing idea" (para. 5), and "useless speculation" (para. 5). He also engages his reader through humor; even his title is outrageous and funny.

# Dave Barry
## BEAUTY AND THE BEAST

### APPROACHING THE ESSAY

On the surface, "Beauty and the Beast" is a fairly straightforward humor piece about the differences between men and women and how they think about their appearances. Some students will find it amusing. Some may be offended. Although Barry goes out of his way to say that he does not mean to suggest that men are superior (para. 9) and even says that men are idiots (para. 11), it is still easy to see how some readers are likely to be bothered by what they see as sexist generalizations or condescending remarks (para. 12, "the average woman spends 5,000 hours per year worrying about her fingernails"). But on another level, the essay is critical of the popular culture's attitude toward women, and this essay might serve as an entry point for a larger discussion of how women are portrayed in the popular media. You might want to begin by focusing on paragraph 7, where Barry brings up Barbie. His idea is a fairly simple one, and most of your students have heard it before: Barbie sets an impossible standard for beauty, a standard which in turn has a profound effect on women's self-esteem. Ask the students if they think there are different standards of beauty for men and women, and why they think this. Is the pressure to be physically attractive greater for women? Why? Where does that pressure come from? And does Barry's criticism of that pressure negate the sometimes condescending tone of his humor? *Does* the average woman actually spend 5,000 hours per year worrying about her fingernails? And if so, is it funny?

### ADDITIONAL ACTIVITIES

1. Ask the students if they feel the emphasis on Barbie is correct. Is it too limited? Or is Barbie simply emblematic of a larger trend in popular media? Where else do your students see impossible standards set for feminine beauty? You might ask them to bring in copies of fashion magazines or to cut out photographs from other magazines where standards are set for feminine beauty. The media that your students bring to class should be directed toward women, particularly young women and girls. You may even want to limit the exercise to "all things Barbie," though the discussion will probably open up in a profitable way if you widen the net a bit. What other toys are marketed to girls? How do those toys reinforce or challenge the link between self-esteem and physical beauty for girls? How do popular culture and media continue to reinforce that link into adolescence and adulthood?
2. You might find it fruitful to engage the students in a similar discussion of the standards set for males. If girls are taught that they must be pretty, what can be said of boys? What sorts of toys are they given to play with? How do those toys nurture or complicate the development of self-esteem in men? Have the standards for boys and girls changed in recent decades? For example, we

see more female action heroes in cinema than we used to. Has this effected a change?

## GENERATING WRITING

1. Have the students write a response to Barry's essay, challenging or affirming his conclusions and drawing on more in-depth research to support their positions. In other words, have them approach the topic from a serious, academic perspective. Does Barry's assertion hold water? Why or why not? Is his tone appropriate?
2. Have your students write a whimsical essay in which they take another children's toy and use it to explain some problem aspect of adult life. For instance, do G.I. Joe action figures lead to violence and war? Could world peace be achieved by getting rid of toy soldiers? Do chemistry sets lead to meth labs?

## THE READER'S PRESENCE

1. From the beginning of this essay, Barry makes generalizations: women are obsessed with their appearance; women spend hours doing their nails, and so on. Some students might be offended by these generalizations from the outset, turning off altogether. Barry won't persuade them of anything. It is interesting to note, however, that the humor of the piece depends almost entirely on these generalizations. It seems apparent, therefore, that Barry is aware of them. One of the central claims of the essay is that the blame for all of this business lies with Barbie. This particular claim might usefully illuminate the way that Barry uses generalization. First, it isn't entirely true: beauty and self-esteem are connected in all kinds of ways, for young girls as well as for grown women, and Barbie is only one element of the larger media assault reinforcing the link. Indeed, Barbie probably dominates the scene less now than at any point in the past fifty years (the line was launched in 1959). But Barbie is emblematic. She is an easily recognizable manifestation of a larger cultural trend. Barry uses Barbie as shorthand for a much more complicated, and many-faceted principle. In one sense, he's reductive. In another, he's making a joke. Because of that, he might at times seem sexist. But ultimately, he's discussing (and decrying) an issue that many feminists take very seriously, and Barry's view is essentially the same as theirs: socially constructed norms for beauty—which are often quite unnatural—have adverse effects on the self-esteem of women, starting at a very young age. It will be important to make sure that students can see past the humor and identify the real argument. After that, they will be in a better position to judge Barry's rhetorical strategy. It may be that, in spite of his quasi-feminist ideological position, his approach to the problem belies a reductive attitude that your students will still find condescending to women.
2. Students will have a variety of answers to the second part of this question. For the first part (how would it read straight?), it might be interesting to

note that Barry's point is actually very simple: socially constructed norms for beauty—which are often quite unnatural—have adverse effects on the self-esteem of women, starting at a very young age (see above). Barry is a humor columnist, and it seems that, without the humor, he doesn't have much to say. The lesson here is not necessarily "shame on Dave Barry," but it does say something about some kinds of humor writing. You might consider pairing the essay with Augusten Burroughs's "Absolutely Fabulous" (p. 57). Burroughs is also a humorist, but it could be argued that he makes a more complicated point. The idea of audience and purpose might be a nice center point for your discussion of Barry's essay.

3. Numerous examples of this kind of rhetoric appear in both essays. Barry's major generalizations are that (1) women are overly concerned with their appearance, and (2) it's because of Barbie. In paragraph 3 of "Will Women Still Need Men?" (p. 650), Ehrenreich says that women would be "fat and happy" without men, and that men would spend their evenings "staging belching competitions" if it were not for women. But that is only the beginning: you could spend an entire class period delineating Ehrenreich's generalizations.

Both Barry and Ehrenreich rely on generalizations—exaggerations, really—to (1) lend humor to their arguments and (2) get those arguments across quickly in terms that are easy to understand. When Barry says that women spend 5,000 hours a year doing their nails, for example, it is probably meant as an amusing shorthand for a much larger idea (i.e., that the average woman is almost obsessively concerned with her appearance). When he blames this phenomenon on Barbie, Barry is probably talking about popular media in general. Barry's essay criticizes the socially reinforced link between women's self-esteem and the absurd standards of feminine beauty promoted by popular media. Ehrenreich makes a number of generalizations in order to highlight the differences between men and women, ultimately attacking the idea that marriage is or should be the norm for male/female relationships and arguing instead that there is nothing natural about it: that by treating marriage as the norm, we "base our entire society on wavering sexual connection[s]" (para. 14). Both authors are critical of societal norms and expectations, and both authors use humor to make fun of those norms.

There is, however, a difference in their approaches. Although both authors position themselves as social critics, Ehrenreich seems to be attacking cultural assumptions that limit the character of the *relationships* between men and women. Barry is attacking the way media works on women, so he must therefore level his criticisms not only at media but at women in general. Ehrenreich does seem, at times, to be particularly critical of men, but she is not directly concerned with problems that are unique to men. So there is a subtle difference between the rhetoric the two authors use: Ehrenreich's essay deals with both men and women, whereas Barry's "Beauty and the Beast," written as it is by a man, deals explicitly with the *other*. As such, Barry's rhetoric might seem problematic, by comparison.

# Michael Bérubé
## ANALYZE, DON'T SUMMARIZE

### APPROACHING THE ESSAY

Michael Bérubé writes from the perspective of an experienced college professor (and paper grader). First, lead the class in a discussion of the title: what is the difference between analysis and summary? According to Bérubé, "Students seem to understand this principle perfectly well when it comes to music, sports, and popular culture" (para. 21). You may want to ask students to provide anecdotal evidence that demonstrates their knowledge of this difference. Ask for examples of both a summary statement and an analytical statement about a song or a game. Strive to demonstrate that students, in fact, do know the difference between analysis and summary. You may want to solicit several responses from the class.

Then examine with your students the content and organization of Bérubé's essay. You may find that students disagree on the thesis. Have them reread the essay, this time looking for a thesis statement. What does the title suggest about the thesis? What effect does the lack of transition between paragraphs 3 and 4 produce? How does paragraph 7 serve as a transition for the essay? Is Bérubé's analogy between grading and sports commentary surprising? Point out that some of his paragraphs consist of concise, "rapid-fire" (para. 5) fragments, much like TV sports commentary.

### ADDITIONAL ACTIVITIES

1. A senior professor advises Bérubé to tell his students: "Your paper was not born with an A. Your paper was born with a 'nothing'" (para. 2). Later in the essay, Bérubé states, "My students . . . are often suspicious of what they regard as an idiosyncratic and a subjective enterprise [grading] that varies from English professor to English professor" (para. 22). Open the class up for a discussion of these quotes. After students have had an opportunity to express their feelings, ask them what changes, if any, they would suggest to make the grading system more responsive to student concerns. What would be the effects of abolishing grading altogether? Would it impact some students more than others? How else could student progress be evaluated, or is such evaluation even necessary? What does grading measure? What is the feasibility of changing the grading process? Why? Stress that while it is important to recognize problems, it is also important to offer solutions.

2. Distribute the analyses assigned in Generating Writing question 1 to your class so that everyone gets someone else's essay. Instruct students to grade the essay, which should include extensive marginalia. This task should be taken seriously; student comments should be included to help classmates understand the grader's "visceral" response to the paper. The grader should

comment on form and content, paying attention to such areas as spelling and grammar as well as thesis, development, and organization. More important, the grader should be able to offer a cogent explanation for his or her responses and be able to "justify" the suggested grade.

## GENERATING WRITING

1. Have students write two five-paragraph papers. The first should *summarize* a movie, a sports event, or an anecdote; the second should offer analysis. Then ask the students to compare the differences in a third, short paper. Which essay was more challenging? more satisfying to complete? Which took longer to finish? Why?

2. Have students find and read an article supporting or condemning the American educational system of grading. The students should then write a four- to six-page critical paper on this article. Encourage them to reread the article and apply Bérubé's three criteria for a good analysis.

## THE READER'S PRESENCE

1. Both the writer and the sports commentator must produce an analysis, which is more than a summary. The rules for a good analysis, regardless of the medium, include "mastery of the material" (para. 20), "cogency of supporting evidence" (para. 20), and "ability to imagine and rebut salient counterarguments" (para. 20). Writers should provide their own personal interpretation of the book, just as sports commentators offer their own views on a game, which can be challenged by others who disagree. Both the sports commentator and the writer have little time or space to make their points. As in the sports game show, points are added if the critique is "compelling and unusual" (para. 18); furthermore, points are subtracted if the claims contradict the observation (of the literary text or of the sport). Some students may point out that the analogy is not complete: the author himself admits that the mute button and the elimination of players have no counterpart in paper-grading. Are home viewers comparable to the grader? Or is the emcee of the show the counterpart of the grader?

2. Student answers will vary. Bérubé's claim is rooted in the idea that when students enjoy something or do it of their own accord (like pursuing a hobby or listening to favorite music), they are able to analyze it without realizing that that is what they are doing. However, when they are compelled to write a paper, they do not approach it in the same way. By likening grading to sports commentary, the author is at least hoping to re-engage students' interest in paper-writing through an innovative analogy.

3. The author's tone toward grading papers is tentative; he feels less than sure of himself. However, he is fairly critical of sports commentary, suggesting that the "endless metacommentary" (para. 6) has too little to do with the sport. In fact, the sport is simply "gainful employment" (para. 6) for these unnecessary parasites. The author uses very specific and strong adjectives

and verbs: "nonplused" (para. 1), "intimidated" (para. 1), "embellished" (para. 2), "sublime" (a particularly clever, and unusual, modifier for "rant") (para. 2), "dorky" (para. 4), "confuses" (para. 14), "rebut" (para. 20), and "salient" (para. 20). He feels that the marginalia are useful: "They're the record of my responses to your argument" (para. 2). He suspects, however, that he has not been able to transmit a "visceral idea of what goes through" (para. 3) his head when he grades. A sport as an opportunity for "metacommentary" implies that the sport becomes the occasion for the commentator to express himself or herself; the focus is on the comment more than the event. The word "entourage" is an excellent choice; it suggests a host of supportive personnel moving around, especially useful when identified with "chattering parasites" (para. 6). Answers to the last parts of this question will vary. All three of Bérubé's rules hold: He is an experienced teacher, his mastery of grading has matured beyond the "nonplused" graduate student's, and he has used supporting evidence from two scholars who corroborate his own thesis. Furthermore, he creatively imagines his students' replies to several of his points and intuits their suspicion of the professors' idiosyncratic grading systems.

4. George Orwell's list ("Politics and the English Language," p. 527, para. 18) primarily focuses on good style: avoid overused figures of speech, use the shortest word possible, omit unnecessary words, use active voice when possible, and avoid specialized diction (jargon, scientific and foreign phrases, and so on) when possible. Essentially, Orwell's rules encourage succinctness and clarity. Bérubé's rules encourage mastery of the material, cogency of supporting evidence, and the ability to anticipate and rebut counterarguments, that is, the content of the argument itself. Both style and content work together to produce a well-developed thesis. Both rely on the author's creativity and knowledge. Analyzing style and content separately distorts the essay unnaturally and unnecessarily. It is probably hard for anyone to match Orwell's prose — or to fault it. According to his own standards, Orwell's piece holds up very well. For example, the following sentence is typical of Orwell's craft: "Political language . . . is designed to make lies sound truthful and murder respectable, and to give an appearance of solidity to pure wind" (para. 19). The figure of speech — "to give an appearance of *solidity to pure wind"* — is original and effective. In this case, it is not the vividness of the image that dazzles but rather the total lack of substance with which the metaphor is imbued. And is this not exactly what Orwell hopes to accomplish with this statement? The sentence also shocks but shocks succinctly: political language, he says, makes "lies sound truthful [we know this and accept this] and *murder respectable."* Orwell's simple adjective, "respectable," is right on target: it makes the "politician" a fiend and us, fools for not seeing it. Not only does Orwell's essay hold up under his own scrutiny, it holds up under Bérubé's rules as well. Bérubé would probably agree with Orwell's advice: "What is above all needed [in good prose] is to let the meaning choose the word, and not the other way about" (para. 18).

# Charles Bowden
## OUR WALL

### APPROACHING THE ESSAY

Although "Our Wall" is clearly focused on the wall between Mexico and the United States, and even more specifically on the border town of Naco, which is divided by that wall, discussion of Bowden's essay will most likely (and is, indeed, intended to) lead to a broader discussion of the subject of immigration, illegal immigration, and U.S. immigration policy, specifically in regard to Mexico. In some classrooms, this will be a politically charged discussion. It may even provoke strong emotional responses from some of your students. This is certainly as it should be: Bowden no doubt intends to provoke a politically and emotionally charged response. However, this sort of discussion will easily lead away from a thoughtful examination of the essay as a piece of writing. It might therefore be helpful to stay as close to the text as possible, reining in the larger political discussion the essay is meant to provoke so that you can focus on the writing strategies Bowden uses to provoke it. "Our Wall" is, after all, an excellent example of how a writer can use trivia to generate interest and history to illuminate current events and criticize current politics. Bowden writes descriptively about the wall itself, making it real for the reader, even a reader who may live far from the border, and he interviews people who live near the wall, adding a personal dimension to the essay that would be missing from a straightforward political, historical, or economic analysis of the issues surrounding the wall. You might ask the students how those details shape their attitudes toward the essay and the problem of immigration. For example, in paragraph 18, we meet Rodolfo Santos Esquer, editor of a weekly newspaper in the Mexican town of Naco, who describes the wall as ugly and racist. How does the fact that we know who he is and what he does change the way we view what he has to say about the wall? How does it add weight to the historical discussion of the Great Wall of China and the Berlin Wall that takes place in paragraph 14? How does paragraph 14 color what Esquer says in paragraph 18? How does the juxtaposition of these elements of the essay—the historical discussion and the direct quote from a contemporary source—generate meaning? How does it add to the persuasive influence of the essay? Ask the students to imagine the essay without the historical background, and again without the direct quote from the Mexican newspaper publisher. In paragraph 25, Bowden introduces Jesús Gastelum Ramírez, saying that Ramírez "understands a reality forgotten by most U.S. lawmakers." Living near the wall obviously sheds light on aspects of the issue that might not be understood by those living elsewhere. By introducing local color, Bowden keeps the essay—the *writing*—close to the wall, as well, using description and personalization to illuminate the more abstract parts of his argument for the reader in much the same way that living near the wall might illuminate the political argument for the hypothetical politician.

## ADDITIONAL ACTIVITIES

1. Although the Berlin Wall was meant to keep people *in*, Bowden's comparison suggests a correlation between the United States and the repressive communist regime of the former East Germany. Consider the idea put forth in paragraph 13, that a border wall violates the American sense of self, and ask the students if a comparison between East Germany and the United States seems in any way accurate. Bring (or have your students bring) images of the Berlin Wall to class. Ask them to focus on the descriptive details of the essay (in paragraph 5, for example) and consider the comparison again.

2. Divide the students into groups and have each group research a different aspect of the current controversy surrounding immigration (the Arizona law, for example). You might consider organizing a debate in which different teams advocate different reforms to immigration law. Make sure they factor the North American Free Trade Agreement (NAFTA) into their thinking about the subject. Bowden has sharply criticized NAFTA. Why? Does NAFTA contribute to the problems along the U.S.–Mexican border? If so, how?

## GENERATING WRITING

1. Have the students read Robert Frost's "Mending Wall"—easily found—and write a paper explaining how it serves to support the point of view espoused in Bowden's essay.

2. Have the students write a research paper on the controversy surrounding immigration and immigration reform. As in Additional Activity 2, make sure your students take NAFTA into consideration.

## THE READER'S PRESENCE

1. In order to write about the wall, Bowden must, to one degree or another, deal with what's on either side of it. Part of the point of the essay is that the Mexican side of the border gets the short end of the stick. This would not be clear unless the reader had some sense of what the other end, the "long" end of the stick, looked like, nor would it have any particular intellectual or emotional resonance for the reader. Another important element of Bowden's argument is that the division between the two towns is artificial. Naco is in fact one town, divided by a wall. Viewed in this way, it becomes clear that the wall between the United States and Mexico serves less to separate Americans from Mexicans than to separate the "haves" from the "have-nots."

2. This question is discussed briefly in the Approaching the Essay section of this entry, but the main idea of mentioning other famous walls from history seems to be to provide a sort of background against which *our* wall stands out more clearly. America touts itself as a land of opportunity, a melting pot of many cultures, and a beacon of freedom and justice in the world. Yet we've built this wall, and it looks just like the Berlin Wall, built by communists,

who—according to American political rhetoric—were a force for oppression and tyranny. Bowden seems to ask: what is the difference?

3. In Bowden's essay, "our wall" is the wall between the United States and Mexico, erected by the United States. "Our," in this case, refers to Americans. David Brooks ("People Like Us," p. 330) uses the word "us" more loosely. It could be anyone, as long as that person belongs to a certain demographic. He claims that most Americans try to group themselves with people who are "basically like themselves" (para. 1). Your students might suppose that this is what is happening in Naco: Americans on one side, Mexicans on the other. However, Bowden seems to be arguing that the wall is artificial—unnatural—while Brooks seems to maintain that it is natural for people to group themselves into homogeneous units. You might introduce this idea and see what your students do with it. Ask them how wealth and poverty affect these groupings. Does it change anything? The "haves" might group themselves together, but do the "have-nots" choose to stick together? Or are they thrust together by their circumstances, based on the principle of "having-not"?

# David Brooks
## PEOPLE LIKE US

### APPROACHING THE ESSAY

David Brooks, a columnist for the *New York Times*, begins his essay on diversity with an admission: "We don't really care about diversity all that much in America." He goes on to discuss how people naturally congregate with people similar to themselves, for the sake of either comfort or support. We also make extremely small distinctions between values in order to find people as similar to ourselves as possible and, in doing so, create communities that are so homogeneous as to become almost parodies of themselves. Brooks claims that this is human nature and that we find security in surrounding ourselves with like-minded people. In the end, he concludes that "it's probably better to think about diverse lives, not diverse institutions" (para. 18). More Americans should venture out of their churches, neighborhoods, and towns to experience what life is like for people unlike themselves.

Ask students to analyze how Brooks builds his argument. What statement or idea does he begin with? What examples does he offer, and what part of his argument do they support? What is his tone throughout the piece? Does he offer any nods to other arguments on the subject? What evidence does Brooks ignore or omit? What are the greatest challenges to his argument? Ask students what they think Brooks's position is in the end. In what ways is he encouraging us to break out of our comfortable patterns, and in what ways does he believe that homogeneity has its merits?

Have students brainstorm the meaning of *diversity*. They will likely first think of racial diversity at the expense of class, sexuality, gender, political beliefs, and religion. Discussing their own institution will offer a common ground for looking at homogeneity and diversity. In what ways is your school diverse? In what ways is it homogeneous? Do diverse groups mingle with each other, or do they tend to remain isolated by certain characteristics? What are the benefits of diversity—and of homogeneity—in higher education?

Unless you instructed them to look at the headnote, your students may not read Brooks's essay as politically biased. If you choose to discuss Brooks's political leanings, you may want to save that point for the end of the discussion and then ask students whether they saw his essay as politically motivated. If they did not, ask them how knowing Brooks's political background might change the way they read the piece. How important do they think that information is? Is there anything within the essay itself that suggests his political beliefs? To what extent has diversity become a political issue in the United States?

## ADDITIONAL ACTIVITIES

1. Have students survey their neighborhoods. What kinds of cars are parked on the street? What kinds of housing are available? What defines the neighborhood or community? What are the main appeals of living there? What are the characteristics of the average resident? Are any people present who differ significantly from the average resident? Are they an accepted part of the community?

2. In Brooks's opening paragraph, he pictures the unrealistic neighborhood where "a black Pentecostal minister lives next to a white anti-globalization activist, who lives next to an Asian short-order cook, who lives next to a professional golfer," and so on. Beyond race and political interests, however, many neighborhoods' housing makes it difficult for people of different classes to live next to each other—for example, middle-class homes next to apartment buildings, condos, subsidized housing, or upper-class mansions. Have students research situations where disputes have erupted over the introduction of housing for the homeless or subsidized housing. What are these neighborhoods' arguments for keeping alternative housing options out of their communities? What fears or concerns drive these disputes? Do these situations support or refute Brooks's argument?

## GENERATING WRITING

1. Have students write a personal analysis in which they examine diversity in their own lives. When do they tend to associate with people similar to themselves? In what areas of their lives do they move in more diverse circles? Where do they feel they have benefited from diversity? Where do they feel that homogeneous groups have merit?

2. Students should write a position paper in which they choose one relatively homogeneous institution or social situation and argue for the benefits of

increasing diversity in that institution. Encourage them to think both about encouraging traditions and supportiveness and about challenging assumptions and misconceptions.

## THE READER'S PRESENCE

1. Brooks may gain credibility with his initial honesty, as well as with his claim that across the board Americans don't care about diversity. His frankness also acts as an enticing hook, encouraging readers to continue, regardless of whether they initially agree with him. Some students, however, might find it a risky tactic for Brooks to speak for his readers in this way. He provides many examples of how people with similar interests and backgrounds group together, as well as how institutions such as higher education represent a very narrow part of the population. However, students may want to look closely at Brooks's assertion that Americans don't actually *care* about diversity. These students might consider reasons other than apathy that contribute to our national homogeneity. Finally, have students look at the particular suggestions Brooks offers for countering homogeneity. What do these suggestions reveal about Brooks's own presumptions about diversity in America?

2. "Make no mistake," writes Brooks, "we are increasing our happiness by segmenting off so rigorously" (para. 4). One advantage of homogeneous institutions and neighborhoods is the comfort and support that people with similar interests or backgrounds can find in each other. This, argues Brooks, is "called community" (para. 14). If America were truly diversified, for example, would a Democratic professor from Brown really want to live next door to a pro-life member of the NRA, and vice versa? And yet Brooks argues that Americans do not know each other and have fewer opportunities to challenge their misconceptions about each other if they do not regularly interact with different people. "Within their little validating communities," writes Brooks about political segregation, "liberals and conservatives circulate half-truths about the supposed awfulness of the other side" (para. 16). This argument could certainly be extended to include misconceptions that can occur when people are segregated by religion, class, race, ethnicity, profession, or sexuality.

3. Brooks describes our desire to group ourselves homogeneously as "human nature," an instinct we have for seeking out support and comfort from those most like ourselves (para. 14). In E. B. White's "Once More to the Lake" (p. 260), White shows us a community of like-minded people that seems to change very little with the passage of time. He finds comfort not only in the farmers and waitresses who have not changed but also in the seeming stasis of the lake and the woods. This homogeneous environment allows White to share his childhood experiences with his young son. How would Brooks feel about this lack of diversity?

   Brooks argues that homogeneous groupings are a matter of choice: "People want to be around others who are roughly like themselves" (para. 14). However, Walter Benn Michaels ("The Trouble with Diversity," p. 744) sees class as a key factor in the formation of communities. Michaels also believes that focusing on promoting diversity distracts us from the real issue of economic inequality. In contrast, Brooks values an effort toward exposing oneself to diverse thoughts and people. However, he believes it cannot be achieved at a community level because what we believe to be diverse communities are in fact homogeneous ones.

# Stephen L. Carter
## THE INSUFFICIENCY OF HONESTY

### APPROACHING THE ESSAY

Stephen L. Carter's essay is exciting in the way the author engages a moral subject with a mixture of seriousness and good humor. Students will recognize that he is trying to identify—and in so doing, promote—ethical behavior, but they will not feel preached at or talked down to. Carter provides a model for the rigorous yet expansive exploration of a moral subject, and he gives students a nonpartisan means for judging the behavior of public figures, making possible the kind of reasoned debate that is too often absent from American political discourse.

Ask students what cultural trends may have prompted Carter's suggestions. As a lawyer, he may be thinking about the increasingly litigious environment surrounding issues of responsibility in America. As lawsuits spring up in response to every perceived inconvenience, companies become ever more reluctant to own up to their obligations, as responsibility so often becomes liability. Carter's argument is directed at reintroducing the notion of doing the best you can think of, not just the minimum you can be held accountable for.

Carter's elevation of responsibility above simple honesty is part of a larger replacement of self-interest with communitarian values. Students may recognize parts of his philosophy from their upbringings, or from elementary school civics lessons: Tell the whole truth, put yourself in the other person's shoes, stand up for what you believe. Because these are all easily *namable* American values, ask students why they think Carter's essay has become necessary: Why don't people seem to live up to these standards? If these values seem idealistic in the most public of realms, do people feel compelled to hold to them in more private relationships?

Actually, private relationships seem to be what Carter is most interested in. Although his argument may stem from a larger, public trend, his examples all depict private individuals weighing the responsibilities of their actions. Ask students to examine what metaphor of relationship seems to guide most of the "before" examples. In many cases, it seems that the individuals have reduced a sense of connectedness to a sense of contractual relations. In the example of the man fathering a child (para. 21), Carter suggests that this sense of only being responsible for one's conscious intentions is uniquely Western, and problematic. It is on this basis, too, that Carter questions the "I did my best" defense. Unless you have worked hard enough for the "best" to actually be good, Carter suggests, you may still be acting without integrity.

## ADDITIONAL ACTIVITIES

1. Two essays that raise similar issues to this one are George Orwell's "Shooting an Elephant" (p. 180) and Brent Staples's "Just Walk on By: A Black Man Ponders His Power to Alter Public Space" (p. 217). Have students read one or both of these essays and evaluate the protagonist's behavior by the standards Carter sets for ethical action. Because Orwell makes his moral compromise the subject of the essay, it may be easy to determine that he acts without integrity. By explaining the overwhelmingly powerful cultural context, however, Orwell raises questions about an element of Carter's premise—whether behavior can be seen as the result of individual decisions. Given Staples's frank and engaging tone, students may be reluctant to see him as acting without integrity. But if Carter requires us to announce the beliefs we act on, does Staples's nonconfrontational style avoid ethical responsibility?

2. Acting with integrity is the subplot of nearly every third episode of any given sitcom, and nearly all children's programming. You might view such a program with your students and ask them to evaluate how the problem is framed, using Carter's criteria.

## GENERATING WRITING

1. Ask students to write an essay about an ethical dilemma they have faced or have witnessed in someone close to them. Ask them to write not moral fables with happy resolutions but analyses that probe the difficulties of acting with integrity in a setting where others may take advantage of you for it. How much murkier is the situation than Carter makes it out to be?

2. Have students write an essay in which they evaluate a current political scandal or situation, using Carter's standards to analyze the actions of everyone involved. Are these actions motivated by integrity? Is it possible to claim that the ends justify the means while still maintaining integrity?

## THE READER'S PRESENCE

1. All honesty requires is not to lie. If all one is attempting to do is not lie, then passivity, ignorance, and silence are possible. Carter leads with honesty in the title because it names the level of virtue to which we are usually held. Desiring a greater sense of civic, and communitarian, responsibility, Carter tries to outline a position of higher ethical value. He wants us to work harder to know we are right, to act on what we know, and to proclaim our allegiance to the truth.

2. One part of the definition of *integrity* that may have added to Carter's idea is its connotation of "soundness" or "completeness"; in this way it is often applied to mean physical sturdiness, as in the question of a substance's "structural integrity." By suggesting that honesty, relative to integrity, is insufficient, Carter partakes of the sense of "completeness" in this element of integrity. The definition of *integrity* also includes a "code of values." Carter clearly defines it this way in practice. To define the terms explicitly may have worked against his effort to replace honesty with integrity. Rather than only point out their differences, by reference to definitions, he wants to show that the one we usually hold up as an ethical principle is deficient. By using Sissela Bok's discussion of honesty, Carter does essentially define it, but because Bok is a sociologist, Carter places the initial definition solidly in social terms (para. 3). This supports his larger effort to locate ethical decision making in a community setting.

3. Because, according to Amy Cunningham ("Why Women Smile," p. 347), women smile in order not to show what they are really thinking—presumably thoughts that would not result in a genuine smile—they are presenting the kind of "intentionally deceptive message" that Carter would probably accept as a lie (para. 3), even though the message of the smile is not explicitly stated. Carter defines *integrity* as "discerning what is right and what is wrong; acting on what you have discerned, even at personal cost; and saying openly that you are acting on your understanding of right and wrong" (para. 4). By this definition, Cunningham's attempt to quit smiling when she does not really feel like it shows much more integrity than the deceptive smile. She argues that "self-deprecating grins and ritual displays of deference" (para. 23) make women appear less competent, which she sees as wrong; Cunningham also notes that women who do not smile face personal costs (they are perceived as less friendly and more threatening, characteristics not commonly seen as positive in women). Finally, her essay says openly that her attempt to stop smiling is in response to ethical considerations.

# Michael Chabon
## FAKING IT

### APPROACHING THE ESSAY

"Faking It" hits on some fundamental stereotypes about fathers that will be immediately familiar to your students: the father as fixer, the father as all-knowing, the father as endlessly competent, completely cool under trying circumstances. Chabon argues that none of these stereotypes touches anything like the truth about fathers. Most of the time, he decided, fathers fake it in an attempt to fit the stereotype.

He begins with an anecdote about installing towel racks in his bathroom. He's got his tools, a nice heavy-duty drill, and the racks themselves. He's set to do his work. And yet, as he begins his task, he knows there's a good chance he won't exactly know how to proceed. When his wife questions whether he'll be able to put up the racks, he responds that it's no big deal, despite his doubts, which leads to a main point: "This is an essential element of being a man: to flood everyone around you in a great radiant arc of bullshit, one whose source and object of greatest intensity is yourself" (para. 7). He makes the claim that what men do, generally, despite self-doubt and failures and possible failures, is attempt, like Rudyard Kipling says, "To keep [their] head." Students should be able to relate to these notions of fathers and men and it would work well in having them relate to the piece to have them find such notions in their own lives.

Chabon's point becomes all the more pertinent when he begins discussing his own father. Here, you should have students notice Chabon's main tactic in the piece: he moves from a smallish personal experience (with the towel rack) to a larger one (growing up with his father). He describes how his father's own well-formed "front" against the world helped Chabon create the type of father he is. He says that he consciously has tried not to be that stereotypical all-knowing father figure who actually doesn't know squat. He has tried to stop and ask for directions, rather than adhering to cliché. Yet, Chabon remarks, "Sometimes I waver in my resolve. My sense of myself as a father, my sense of fathers, is so deeply caught up with some kind of primal longing (which I think we all share) for inerrancy, for the word of God" (para. 12). And so we come to the crux of Chabon's argument: that sometimes fathers need to fake it, to be the "rock and redeemer" for their kids and their wives, even for themselves. What will students think of this? Will they sympathize? Sometimes, with enough luck, Chabon suggests, faking it turns into not faking, but actually doing, as Chabon elaborates in the blizzard story at the end of the piece.

This is a highly anecdotal essay. Chabon moves from personal story to personal story, highlighting stereotypes and clichés along the way, showing where those stereotypes break down in his life, and also revealing that sometimes those stereotypes about fathers are necessary for the loved ones around him. It's a charming piece with a lot of character, and it can be used to show students how to incorporate personal anecdotes into larger arguments. Also, it will be important for students to see the character that Chabon makes of himself on the page—his character here is probably more complete and more fully formed than any other classical argument piece they've read thus far.

## ADDITIONAL ACTIVITIES

1. "Faking It" is mainly focused on masculine and, more precisely, fatherly stereotypes. A good activity may be to broaden the gender horizon. You could ask students, what are some popular female, or motherly, stereotypes? When are these stereotypes, male and female, accurate and helpful, if ever, and when are they inaccurate and unhelpful, even harmful? What students should find is that no stereotype ever truly holds, but there are aspects of

some that are accurate—why is this? The discussion could move on to ideas of gender in our popular culture.

2. Have students think about an instance where they had to "fake" something. Have them write a couple paragraphs about this experience. When they faked it, did they end up with positive results or negative results? What did they learn from faking? Did they find they were being untruthful to themselves, or did they experience the faking in the same way Chabon did, as eventually not fake at all? This could lead to further discussion of what exactly authentic experience is really about.

## GENERATING WRITING

1. Have students write a personal narrative about their memories of their father or their mother or both. In Chabon's piece, he shows that the way his father behaved when he was a child shaped his own ideas of what a father should be. Have students tie their essay to this idea. How have their parents shaped their lives? In what ways have they tried to be like their parents and in what ways have they tried to do something differently from their parents? Instruct them to model their paper on Chabon's "Faking It," using personal anecdotes to support their ideas. The focus of the paper will be twofold: (1) writing good, clear scenes to fully explore these anecdotes, and (2) trying to create a unique persona/character, like Chabon has here, on the page. It's a challenging task but one that students should be enthused about. Tread lightly: some students might be adopted or have complicated family situations, and in this case you can fill in "father/mother figure" for parents.

2. Have students interview two fathers (their own or someone else's). Have them prepare a set of six or seven questions related to Chabon's essay. They should be asking the interviewees whether they feel the same about fatherhood as Chabon does. Do they feel this is an honor (to be seen as all-knowing and ever-competent) or do they feel it as a burden? Do they ever fake or affect an appearance in order to seem stronger, more confident, or more knowledgeable? After interviewing the two father figures, have them write a two-page "journalist report" on their findings and whether those findings fit with Chabon's main ideas.

## THE READER'S PRESENCE

1. Chabon is clearly using personal anecdotes about masculine behavior to highlight problems of patriarchal society. Possibly he's referring to the incompetence of male world leaders to understand their own incompetency in regard to some of the world's largest problems. However, this is generally implied, and most of Chabon's examples, such as the towel rack, the discussion of his father, and the drive through the snowy mountains, are meant to highlight all males' needs to feel in control at all times.

2. Both stories illustrate the idea that fathers (and men in general) often are aware of their incompetence to complete particular tasks. Yet being aware

of this incompetence is not enough to keep most men from "faking it" and trying to complete the task, no matter how ill-prepared they are. In the story about the towel rack, Chabon knows there's a good chance he's going to screw up putting the rack together; however, there's not much risk and so he fakes it and completes the task. The drive through the mountains is the same thing: Chabon is aware that it's dangerous, he might not be the best driver, and he's scared; yet, despite the risk here, he fakes it and again, thankfully, completes the task. Both stories highlight the idea that, in some cases, feigning the idea of control actually helps one achieve that control.

3. Both Chabon and Dave Barry ("Beauty and the Beast," p. 315) use generalizations to augment and highlight their humor. The primary difference seems to be that Chabon's humor is in a sense self-deprecating: he's making fun of the stereotypes, but in order to do that he has to make fun of himself. He is not supremely competent, never mind *confident*. Barry, on the other hand, only makes superficial—one might even argue *disingenuous*—gestures toward self-criticism. For the most part, his jokes are about *women*. How this will affect your students' readings of the essays will vary from student to student, but it seems less likely that Chabon's piece will alienate female readers, in spite of Barry's quasi-feminist ideological position. For more on Barry's tone, see Reader's Presence Question 1 in the entry on "Beauty and the Beast" (p. 113).

# Amy Cunningham
## WHY WOMEN SMILE

### APPROACHING THE ESSAY

Amy Cunningham's essay is particularly interesting because its focus is both sociological and personal. It can manage both of these perspectives precisely because the author assumes and successfully argues that social values shape our conduct, even our facial expressions. While reading this essay, your students should pay close attention to those points where Cunningham makes a transition from the sociological to the personal, and vice versa.

In paragraph 2, Cunningham's husband tells her that her smile inspires people to like her "in a fuzzy way." Ask your students what he means by this and why Cunningham takes this as a signal to stop smiling for the wrong reasons. What, according to Cunningham, are the wrong reasons?

Consider with your students the author's interesting remark that "the women's movement might be measured by the sincerity—and lack of it—in our smiles" (para. 3). In what way does this sentence sum up the central purpose of the essay?

Ask your students why they think Cunningham chose the practice of smiling as a means to gauge the success of women's efforts for social equality. Would Cunningham say that these efforts have been largely successful?

Many male students and even some female students might reject the author's analysis of smiling as too exclusive. Even Cunningham would agree that the urge to smile to win affection and attention begins in infancy in female *and* male children. Ask your students to locate another point in the essay where the author seems to be referring to both genders. Does Cunningham make it clear at what moment in human development females begin to smile for different reasons than males?

In paragraphs 5 and 6, Cunningham explains why it is often difficult to trace the difference between men and women with regard to smiling. She notes that cultural conditioning may be equally as or more important than animal instinct in determining such differences. Ask your class which of these two factors is more influential; they could design an experiment to determine whether instinct or cultural influence is predominant in such behaviors. In paragraph 14, Cunningham remarks that "the social laws" governing women's smiles have reversed over a 2,000-year period. Ask your students what might account for this change. Does this reversal seem to argue for the dominance of cultural influence over natural instincts?

Midpoint in her essay, Cunningham discusses studying women's portraits to discover their ways of smiling at different points in history. Ask the class if they think that studying painted portraits is a good way to trace actual historical developments. What are the advantages and dangers of this approach?

Some students may feel that Cunningham undermines her own argument by including an analysis of smiling in American culture as a whole and in the African American community. Ask your class what kinds of distinctions the author draws between women's smiles and those of the other groups. Do they regard these distinctions as significant? What similarities does she attempt to draw between these groups?

## ADDITIONAL ACTIVITIES

1. Have your students collect ads from contemporary magazines or newspapers in which women are featured. They might even be able to locate older ads printed during the last twenty-five years. Most libraries stock past issues of major magazines going back several decades. As a class, analyze the way that women are depicted in these ads, using what was learned in Cunningham's essay. Does the depiction differ significantly depending on whether the ads are directed toward men or toward women?

2. Students especially interested in learning more about the depiction of women in art and advertising as a reflection of social attitudes may want to look at John Berger's *Ways of Seeing*, a book first published in 1972. In Chapter 3 of that book, Berger traces the history of the relationship between the male gaze and the female body. Ask your students if they agree with Berger that the essential ways in which men see women have not changed.

## GENERATING WRITING

1. Ask students to select an ad from a magazine or newspaper that features a woman and to "read" it in the way that Cunningham herself might. Ask them to examine the relationship implied between the woman in the ad and the audience. How would they describe the intended audience of the ad? They should then write an essay in which they record their findings and argue whether the ad promotes an image of women that is at variance with that of actual women.

2. Most students, both male and female, will have cultivated behaviors that they would now like to abandon in response to changing social conditions. Have them write an essay in which they describe the behavior and explain why it came about in the first place. They should also describe what circumstances have led them to cease acting in this manner.

## THE READER'S PRESENCE

1. One of Cunningham's most effective strategies is her blending of the elements of a scholarly essay with those of a personal essay. The strength of this approach lies in the essayist's ability to substantiate her personal impressions and opinions with factual knowledge. However, her personal tone prevents the presentation of factual information from becoming dull or merely instructional.

2. From the outset of the essay, the author examines gender by isolating one behavioral pattern of women—smiling. She then moves beyond gender into a discussion of race and the behaviors of African Americans (paras. 15–18). By examining the practice of smiling in African American culture, she indirectly establishes a link between the oppression of black people and women of all races.

3. Cunningham's essay refers to psychological studies, but the bulk of her evidence is drawn from casual social observation and artistic representations of smiling. The title of her essay is somewhat misleading—or perhaps it reveals what the essay was originally meant to be about. If one reads the essay expecting to discover either *how* gender difference is expressed in human smiling or *why* such differences exist, one will be disappointed. Cunningham's essay moves across cultural moments, places, and time periods to provide a sweeping survey of how some people have smiled at various times: it's a sampling of facial gestures. Look at paragraph 12 for a good example of how loose her argument is in respect to social or historical particulars: Are all women in all cultures at all moments "expected to smile"? Does the whole world want a woman's "willing deference" proven by her smile? What, exactly, is the cause-and-effect relation between Hollywood films and their social and cultural contexts? Are films the primary cause of the male sexism Cunningham characterizes in the last sentence of the paragraph? The answers to these questions suggest that Cunningham's aim is less to persuade or provoke than to entertain her reader with "light" facts. Do your

students agree with this interpretation of the essay? In "Sex, Drugs, Disasters, and the Extinction of Dinosaurs" (p. 430), Stephen Jay Gould takes issue with precisely this type of approach. He argues against declarative statements and generalizations that are not based in empirical facts. In discussing three hypotheses of the extinction of dinosaurs, he repudiates restrictive and irrefutable hypotheses as unscientific. He grounds his argument in historical evidence. He may even place Cunningham's argument in the same category as the theories of the scientists he derides for seducing the general public with inaccurate but "popular presentations of science" (para. 2).

# Don DeLillo

## IN THE RUINS OF THE FUTURE: REFLECTIONS ON TERROR, LOSS, AND TIME IN THE SHADOW OF SEPTEMBER

### APPROACHING THE ESSAY

With this essay, Don DeLillo takes up one of the most difficult challenges for a writer: to express what is not only inexpressible, but as yet—DeLillo published the piece in December 2001—incomprehensible. He poses the problem directly: "The writer wants to understand what this day has done to us. Is it too soon?" (section VI, para. 68). This was a common refrain in the immediate aftermath of September 11, 2001. With the exception of members of the news media, who are effectively licensed to display human suffering as it occurs, the depiction of true terror remains off limits until enough time has passed for the disaster to assume coherent form. But DeLillo justifies his efforts and gives us his method: an often jarring mix of the observed and the imagined, of small moments and grand, interpretive explanations. It's useful here to recall that the original meaning of the word *essay* is *to attempt*. DeLillo's piece is a courageous effort to understand what for many Americans remains still inchoate.

For the purposes of discussion, it may be useful to evaluate the overall effect of the essay before moving into a more analytical consideration. At the end of section VI, DeLillo claims that "the writer tries to give memory, tenderness, and meaning to all that howling space" (para. 69). Do the students think he succeeds at this attempt?

A good way to return to close, textual analysis—especially if students' emotions have been excited in the process of collectively remembering the event—is to study the structure of the essay. Its divisions make its components clear; what is not always clear is the relation between these sections and their disparate styles and subjects. A quick summary (which you might ask students themselves to generate): sections I and II frame the "catastrophic event" (para. 3) in the context of the rise of terrorism; sections III and IV move in close to the details of the day; section V considers the immediate aftermath; section VI returns to the problem of the event's "singularity," reexamining it in the context of the media's distorting coverage of the Gulf War; section VII considers the philosophical implications of the event; section VIII contrasts the "clamor" of Canal Street in the first week after September 11 with a memory of "the old jostle and stir" of that street a month before the event (para. 78), culminating in an image of an Islamic woman praying at sunset, facing east, "toward Mecca" (para. 79).

Schematically, the essay moves between sections given over to abstraction and sections that dwell in detail. The use of descriptive detail is familiar to most students, but many will have trouble defining the "abstract"; this essay is a great occasion to discuss how DeLillo's naming of the concepts *fear*, *dread*, *heroism*, *astonishment*, *danger*, and *rage* differs from their instantiations. "Ideas evolve and de-evolve, and history is turned on end," he writes at the end of section VII (para. 76); "technology is our fate, our truth," begins section V (para. 54); and, in section II, "there is no logic in apocalypse" (para. 11).

When a novelist, whose stock in trade is necessarily the minutiae of life, uses such terms, readers should take note. DeLillo, admittedly, has traveled the terrain of modern apocalypse and terrorism in his fiction (*White Noise* [1985] and *Mao II* [1991], for example), but this essay represents an entirely different sort of writing. Why might he be shifting gears or changing modes? This may be a good place to discuss prose style, reinforcing the point that while writers can never control how their texts will be read, they are very much in control of which words end up on the page.

You might begin this part of the discussion by drawing students' attention to section IV, which begins in a style that suggests fiction by its omniscient point of view. But just as the reader has begun to accept that the writer is in perfect control of the unfolding story, DeLillo writes, "When the second tower fell, my heart fell with it" (para. 43). This sentence jolts the reader. Whose heart is this? And what is this person's relation to what has just been described in an almost disembodied voice? "I called Marc, who is my nephew, on his cordless," DeLillo writes, as if in answer. And the reader realizes that this is not fiction, but fact—that DeLillo is not an impersonal authorial voice but a person with only one degree of separation from the crashing towers.

To tell the real story, DeLillo has to draw on his imagination, piecing accounts together and supplying narrative to fill the gaps. He makes things up, that is, to get all of us closer to reality. Have students examine the essay for those details that must have been imagined by DeLillo in the retelling.

On the subject of terrorism, DeLillo is eloquent; on the subject of the terrorists themselves, he is circumspect. He discusses fundamentalism and mentions Islam several times, including the powerful image at the essay's end. (He mentions Islam relatively late in the essay; have students locate the first instance.) But he is less interested in assigning blame to individuals, nations, or sects than he is in naming the transnational conditions that have given rise to the new terrorism.

DeLillo gives considerable attention to narrative and what he calls "counter-narrative[s]," which include "shadow history," "rumor, fantasy, and mystical reverberation" (paras. 22–23). What stories will we tell about this moment when we look back on it? he wonders. "Today, again, the world narrative belongs to terrorists" (para. 2). DeLillo's interest in time complements his interest in narrative. "The terrorists of September 11 want to bring back the past," he writes at the end of section I; they are reacting against the future-oriented juggernaut of the American-backed global economy, and those who protest that "momentum," "trying to slow things down, even things out, hold off the white-hot future" (para. 4). Ask students to define these different narratives that appear in DeLillo's essay. Where does he come down?

The problem of narrative returns us to DeLillo's central purpose here: to give a meaningful shape to the chaotic mess of events and emotions—not to put them to rest, but to name them and, in naming, to begin the process of recovery.

## ADDITIONAL ACTIVITIES

1. Have students read Adam Mayblum's essay ("The Price We Pay," p. 164). Discuss how his account accords with and diverges from that in DeLillo's essay.
2. The end of DeLillo's essay may be read as an oblique prayer of mourning: he ends with the image of the woman praying toward Mecca, in the middle of the bustle of Canal Street a month before the attacks. The living and the dead, DeLillo writes, are "a union of souls" (para. 81). What do students imagine is a fitting memorial for those who died on September 11?

## GENERATING WRITING

1. Section VIII of DeLillo's essay is a description of the scene on Canal Street "before and after" the attacks of September 11, 2001. Have students follow DeLillo's model and write a similar short essay in which they describe a place before and after it was radically transformed.
2. DeLillo's shift of mode and register is hard to pull off, but it is worth imitating if only to gain a fuller understanding of his essay. Have students describe an event from two extremely different points of view: one firsthand and personal, the other somewhat objective and explanatory. (Edgar Allan Poe's short story "The Imp of the Perverse" is another good example of this technique.)

## THE READER'S PRESENCE

1. This subject is discussed in "Approaching the Essay." Time is central in part because DeLillo wants to understand the intimate details as well as the largest meanings and implications of the event. The former takes him into the immediate past (the use of the present tense brings that past even closer, as though the passage of time has been held up); the latter puts him on a narrative trajectory that includes ancient religious beliefs and "the white-hot future" (para. 4) of new global economics.
2. Islam is mentioned sparingly throughout the essay; clearly DeLillo is trying to avoid the racism and hate mongering that was rampant immediately after

**133**

the attacks. But the last section of the essay comes into close focus on a woman praying; have students consider this image: Why a woman? Why praying? Why the emphasis on the design of the prayer rug? Why, especially, does DeLillo end with bilingual praise of Allah?

3. In some sense, DeLillo is as reliant on his informants (his nephew and others) as Barbara Tuchman ("'This Is the End of the World': The Black Death," p. 584) is on her documentary evidence. Tuchman is known for her ability to bring distant historical actors alive in the complex retelling of massive events. The two writers in this instance are more alike than different. For extended discussions of the relative advantages and disadvantages of writing about fresh experiences, see the Approaching the Essay discussions in this manual for Michihiko Hachiya (p. 35), and Adam Mayblum (p. 58).

# Joan Didion
## ON MORALITY

### APPROACHING THE ESSAY

This essay is about the dangers of abstraction. Didion begins by expressing her reservations about writing on the subject of morality in abstract terms. She explains those reservations, using some examples to illustrate her point. She begins with an anecdote about a couple who refused to leave a dead body on the side of the road. The woman whose husband stayed with the body overnight said, "You can't just leave a body on the highway. . . . It's immoral" (para. 2). Didion uses this example to illustrate her interpretation of the concept of "wagon-train morality," that morality which is most simple, concerned with survival and, in some sense, loyalty. This seems to be the only kind of "morality" that Didion trusts. She doesn't spend a lot of time connecting the incidents she relates to any abstract concept of morality, rather saying that "it means nothing manageable" (para. 7). By the end of the essay, Didion seems to conclude that the word is ultimately unreliable, as it can be bent to any purpose.

This may or may not be an easy point for your students to understand. It might be best to simply move through the piece from front to back. After a discussion of paragraph 1 and the idea of being "drawn to particulars," you might linger on paragraph 4 and the idea of "wagon-train morality." You might draw the students' attention to paragraph 5, where Didion deals with possible objections to her approach: the idea that this sort of morality is too "primitive." But paragraphs 7 and 9 will be essential to getting her point across: there are plenty of examples of people who did very immoral things under the banner of morality, and ultimately Didion's point seems to be that any abstract definition of the word lends itself too easily to misuse. Ask the students if they can think of some examples. Hitler is an easy starting point: it might be facile, but he's become the reference point and emblem for everything evil in popular culture. Yet he surely *believed* that he was doing the right thing. How often does "morality" serve as a justification for suspicious endeavors?

## ADDITIONAL ACTIVITIES

1. In keeping with the Hitler example in the Approaching the Essay section in this entry, have students scour the news or the Internet for examples of the use of morality as a justification for actions that might not be, strictly speaking, "moral." How is one person's morality another's oppression? Politics and religion might provide particularly useful examples. The terrorists of 9/11 certainly felt that they were acting out God's will, as did certain members of the Catholic church during the Spanish Inquisition, or the Holy Crusades. The Soviets who killed the czar and his family also seemed to believe they were acting righteously. You can achieve two goals with this activity. First, you can get the students involved with research. Second, you can help them understand Didion's point. Make sure they can explain how the subjects of their research evoked an abstract sense of morality to justify a specific action, a *particular*, which would otherwise be indefensible. The word *communism* invokes the idea of community. As an ideology, it takes its moral authority from the idea of equality. Most Americans view equality as a moral imperative. Yet certain Soviet leaders, in Russia, used communism as a justification for starving the rural population and murdering dissenters. The U.S. government has, at times, used the ideas of democracy and freedom to justify military actions that some would see as immoral. How is the *idea* of morality distorted to justify such actions? The Salem witch trials might also prove a useful breeding ground for discussion.

## GENERATING WRITING

1. Have your students write a paper exploring their own ideas about morality. Tell them to stay as close to "the particular" as possible, avoiding abstraction. You might have them focus on a particular event (telling a "little white lie," for example), when they had to make a personal choice and when the abstract idea of morality, or a "moral code" to which they had previously subscribed, proved to be of little use or to lack concrete meaning. Be careful here: Some students will be hesitant to share this kind of personal information. Others will be all too eager to tell you about their private lives. It might be prudent to establish some parameters, asking them, for example, to refrain from writing about certain subjects: sex, for example, or drug use might be inappropriate topics for a paper of this kind.

2. Have the students write research papers stemming from Additional Activity 1. Ask them to research a particular person or event and analyze the way the abstract concept of morality served as justification for behavior that your students find less than moral.

## THE READER'S PRESENCE

1. Didion probably distrusts the word *morality* because it could mean any number of things to any number of people and because those definitions seem all too likely to shift in varying circumstances. In paragraph 4, Didion says "wagon-train morality" is the only kind that doesn't seem to her to have a "potentially mendacious meaning." In other words, any other moral code is probably dishonest: such codes would break down in circumstances like those that the Donner party encountered, and moral codes that break down under difficult circumstances aren't *codes* at all. Therefore, they are lies. At the most basic level, only wagon-train morality seems consistent. Those who violate wagon-train morality are those who have "somewhere abdicated their responsibilities . . . [and/or] breached their primary loyalties" (para. 4). Hence, one does not leave a dead body to be eaten by coyotes. This could be taken literally or figuratively, as it has to do with holding human life (and death) sacred. It seems as though, at its core, wagon-train morality has to do with the primacy of one's immediate circle (the people in your caravan, so to speak) and, beyond that, the primacy of the species: human beings. It is, she says, a "primitive [morality] . . . its point only survival" (para. 5). Yet, at the same time, it is the only moral code that she finds honest. What do your students think?

2. Didion doesn't spend a lot of time on the abstract. When she does, it is mainly to ask, "How many madmen have said it [I did what I thought was right] and meant it? How many murderers?" (para. 7). The idea seems to be that the abstract definition is not reliable because it can be bent to serve any purpose. Didion spends most of her time on particulars, returning to the abstract only to demonstrate its inadequacy or impossibility. In the last section of the essay, she considers the ideas of good, evil, and conscience, and she says, "There is something facile going on, some self-indulgence at work" (para. 9). The danger in using the word *morality*, then, and one reason why she distrusts it, is that we can "start deceiving ourselves" (para. 9) into believing that what we *want* is "a *moral imperative*" (para. 9), regardless of whether we need it or whom it hurts.

3. Stephen L. Carter ("The Insufficiency of Honesty," p. 337) finds the word *honesty* suspicious in more or less the same way that Didion distrusts *morality*. Honesty can mean telling the truth or it can mean *not* telling a lie. One can avoid telling a lie and still lack integrity, because integrity "requires a degree of moral reflectiveness" (Carter, para. 4). One can be honest without ever really engaging in hard work or being responsible. One can be honest and hurt someone's feelings, essentially without reason. Your students are likely to draw any number of lines separating morality from ethics. A discussion of these distinctions alone could easily fill a class period.

# Annie Dillard
## THE DEATH OF A MOTH

### APPROACHING THE ESSAY

"The Death of a Moth" might be a difficult essay to approach in the classroom set-ting. It's easy enough to read—a pleasure, even—but its meaning is difficult to pin down. It is obviously a response to Virginia Woolf's essay, "The Death of the Moth" (p. 625), so it seems logical to begin with a comparison, but what does such a com-parison yield? For Woolf, the moth's death had a certain significance. Through the course of her essay, the moth seems to become a metaphor for all of us: it is a bead of life, and its struggle mirrors our own. Dillard's use of the indefinite article sug-gests that she makes less of the moth than Woolf, or that, perhaps, she makes less of life. Early in the essay, Dillard describes the insect carcasses behind her toilet, victims of the spider who has spread its web there. Their deaths are not particularly significant. What's more interesting is that Dillard has not bothered to clean them up, possibly because she lives alone. In fact, the first sentence of her essay begins, "I live alone."

It may be helpful to have some background on Virginia Woolf. In Woolf's famous long essay, "A Room of One's Own," she posited that a woman—and, more specifi-cally, a woman who aspires to be a writer—needed a room of her own, a private space in which to work. Annie Dillard has that space. She also finds herself in a sort of crisis. Does she still want to be a writer? Although she does not ask the ques-tion specifically in the essay, she does say that the reason she goes camping is to reread the book that made her want to become a writer in the first place "hoping that it would do it again" (para. 6). From this we can assume that she is tired of the literary life, or that she at least is questioning it. Part of this life, for her, could be living alone. The end of the essay reinforces this interpretation. If her vivid written account of the moth's death is any indication, she has regained her desire to write. Because, at the end of the essay, she says that she doesn't mind living alone, we might suppose that living alone and writing are somehow connected.

Even if your students have read Woolf, this interpretation of Dillard's essay might be difficult for them to pick up on. You might explain it from the outset or try to elicit it with questions. You might also just ask the students what they think. Why does the essay begin and end with living alone? Why does Dillard think "it is pretty funny" (para.12) that she lives alone? What does this mean, given that she really only wishes she lived with someone else when she found something funny? It seems to be a contradiction: if she didn't live alone, it wouldn't be funny that she lived alone, and there would be nothing to laugh at. Hence, she wouldn't need someone to live with anymore. The essay seems, at times, to deliberately resist interpretation. Why? What is the advantage of writing a personal essay that resists interpretation? The meaning of Woolf's essay is relatively plain. Does that suggest that her view of life is simpler—perhaps because it can be expressed and under-stood simply?

Dillard's essay, in part, is about her attempt to reconnect with her writing, with her *desire* to write. Because the essay begins and ends with a brief meditation on living alone, it seems evident that living alone is part of her writing life: that writing and living alone are in some way connected. In his Nobel Prize acceptance speech, Ernest Hemingway said, "Writing, at its best, is a lonely life . . . for he [the writer] does his work alone, and if he is a good enough writer he must face eternity, or the lack of it, each day." Does this attitude appear in Annie Dillard's essay? What about Virginia Woolf's? It is clear enough why the writer *writes* alone, but in what way does he or she "face eternity, or the lack of it"? How do Dillard's and Woolf's concerns with life and death relate to Hemingway's assertion?

## ADDITIONAL ACTIVITIES

1. Because the title of Dillard's essay is an obvious reference to Virginia Woolf's "The Death of the Moth" (p. 625), you should probably have students read the two essays together. Both essays are relatively short, so this is easily accomplished. You might want to put the students in groups and have them compare notes. You could even give them some specific directions: For example, what sorts of descriptive words do the authors use for their respective moths? How are their tones different? How are they alike? They should be able to cite specific examples from the texts to back up their points.

2. If time permits, you might have students read "A Room of One's Own," or some selections from that essay, to give them a sense of the kind of writer that Woolf was and what her concerns were, particularly her concerns about being a writer and being a woman. Does Dillard share her concerns? She certainly doesn't have to fight for personal space, sharing it only with two cats and a spider. In what ways are her concerns similar to or different from those of Woolf?

## GENERATING WRITING

1. Have the students write a short description of a thing observed. It could be something from nature—the activity around an anthill, for example—or something associated with human affairs: a train arriving at the station or a baseball game. Annie Dillard describes the death of a moth. Your students should describe a similarly finite event: something that *happens*, something with a *beginning* and an *end*. This need not be a long essay. In fact, the shorter is it, the better: a paragraph or two, at most. The idea is to describe the event with as much precision as possible.

2. Have your students write an essay about something that they like doing, something that they care about, and how it affects their lives. For Dillard and Hemingway, it is writing, and they end up alone. Are your students passionate about anything? For example, a student who is interested in a particular kind of music might only socialize with other people who like that music. A student who spends hours and hours perfecting a skateboarding trick might not have time for his or her schoolwork. A student who practices

violin six hours a day might not have time for a social life. Have your students write about an interest that they have and the sacrifices they have to make to pursue that interest. If they can't think of one, ask them why not. What *do* they do? Many times, when given an assignment of this nature, students do not believe that their *actual* interests will serve as appropriate material for a paper. It might be useful to explain to them that Hemingway wasn't writing for *school*: that *any* interest will do. Even a student who spends hours playing video games has something to write about, simply because they spend time and money on video games, time that could be spent in other ways. The important thing will be to get them to pick *something* they care about. After that, the challenge is to get them to think (and write) about the sacrifices they make for that interest, rather than the interest itself: you don't want to read a five-page paper about Dungeons and Dragons, but a paper about not being able to get a date because of it might be interesting. Students should note that Dillard seems, by implication, to conclude that the sacrifice she makes is worth it. Do your students feel the same way about the sacrifices they make to follow their passions? When Dillard goes camping, it is because she hopes to regain her desire to be a writer. Have your students had similar crises? How did they deal with these experiences, if they've had them?

## THE READER'S PRESENCE

1. The imagery is vivid, sometimes lovely. The burning moth's wings are compared, for example, to "angels' wings" (para. 8). However, when the insect's legs are described, later in the same paragraph, they curl and blacken. Dillard seems to be willfully choosing language that creates cognitive dissonance: the burning moth is both beautiful *and* horrific. Because the essay is, in a way, about writing (Dillard's camping so she can reread the book that made her want to be a writer), it also makes sense that the essay would be invested in figurative language and other "writerly" devices.

2. The end of the essay is about living alone. Given that the essay begins with the words "I live alone," the end provides a sort of mirror, an echo that seems to open up the middle, giving the piece an emotional resonance it might otherwise lack (see the Approaching the Essay section of this entry). If the essay had ended two paragraphs earlier, we would not have been reminded that the speaker (Dillard) lives alone, and the connection between her writing and living alone might not have been suggested quite so clearly.

3. Dillard's essay responds to Woolf's first by changing the definite article to the indefinite—not *the* moth, but *a* moth—but the anonymity of the moth doesn't seem to be the primary concern of Dillard's essay. She seems, rather, to be concerned with the writing life. For her feminist writings, Woolf is often considered emblematic for women writers, particularly based on her essay "A Room of One's Own." Dillard's tone is both lighter and more morbid: the essay is interspersed with humor, and the moth is not quite so profound; at the same time, though, the death of Dillard's moth is quite grizzly by comparison.

# Brian Doyle
## THE GREATEST NATURE ESSAY *EVER*

### APPROACHING THE ESSAY

"The Greatest Nature Essay *Ever*" is both an instruction manual for the would-be nature writer and a commentary on current trends in environmental writing and politics. One way to approach the piece is to look at Doyle's suggestions for the would-be essayist, using them as a way to discuss both the writing instruction and the implied political message. Doyle maps the beginning, middle, and end of the hypothetical "greatest nature essay" but deals with nature itself only in nonspecific terms, suggesting a "startling and lovely and wondrous" image (para. 1), or some "explosive Conclusions" (para. 3), without telling us what, exactly, those conclusions should be. He has very specific things to say, however, about the structure and the writing of the hypothetical essay: the lovely image should open the essay, followed by a "small story" (para. 2). About halfway through the essay, the sentences should get shorter, "more staccato" (para. 3), and at this point, Doyle's sentences become staccato, too. Ask the students to look at the essay as a bit of writing instruction. What kind of writing does Doyle want to see in a nature essay? What kind of writing does he want nature writers to avoid? This particular point can serve as an entry to the larger cultural and political argument of the piece. Doyle says the essay should lack "opinion or commentary . . . shouting . . . persuasion . . . accusations . . . sermons [and] homilies" (para. 3). Why do the students think he feels that way? Why does he insist that there should be "no call to arms . . . no website to which you are directed, no hint that you, yes you, should be ashamed of how much water you use or the car you drive" (para. 5)? Ask the students why a call to arms might be a bad thing. What does Doyle seem to be saying about environmentalism or, more specifically, about the rhetoric of environmental politics? This can tie nicely back to the writing instruction with which the discussion began: ask the students why Doyle suggests that, upon finishing the hypothetical "greatest nature essay *ever*," the reader would be "changed" (para. 5). What kind of change do they imagine he means? Is it the same kind of change "a call to arms" is intended to elicit? Why would an essay without a sermon be more likely to effect change? It might be particularly useful, at this point, to return to the first and second paragraphs and look at what Doyle has to say about the power of image and story and about why we read nature writing to begin with.

### ADDITIONAL ACTIVITIES

1. Doyle wants nature writers to avoid sermonizing, but he also wants nature writing to provoke a change of heart, a change presumably similar to the one called for by the rhetoric he discourages. In other words, he wants people to *care* about the environment, but he doesn't think lecturing them is going to make them do it. Ask the students to suggest other ways to get people to

change. Is it as easy as Doyle makes it sound? What does the discussion suggest about the potential power of writing?

2. Many magazines devoted to nature writing have radically different audiences and objectives. Ask the students to compare an article from *Field & Stream*, for example, to an article from an explicitly conservationist periodical, like *National Wildlife* magazine. While identifying the separate audiences and objectives of the essays, students should be mindful of the *similarities* they see in the approaches and attitudes of the authors, as well. We generally expect writers who publish in conservationist magazines to perceive (or present) themselves as defenders of the environment. But, based on what the students read, can it be said that a hunter or someone who fishes for recreation writing for *Field & Stream* is the same type of nature lover as the environmental activist? What is the difference, then, between a nature lover and an environmentalist? And where do the students imagine Doyle falls in that spectrum?

## GENERATING WRITING

1. Have the students write a short essay describing a perfect piece of writing. Point out that much of Doyle's essay describes how his hypothetical nature essay would affect the reader. Similarly, ask the students to focus on how *their* ideal piece of writing would affect the reader: for example, the greatest sports essay ever would be unlikely to leave the reader "near tears" (para. 5), as Doyle's ideal nature essay would. But what feelings would a sports essay elicit? Would it elicit excitement? pride in the home team? You might even consider following this assignment with another, asking the students to actually write the essay they've just described.

2. Have the students browse popular nature magazines (*National Geographic, Nature, Smithsonian*) for examples of nature writing. Have them write an essay evaluating one of the pieces they find by the standards set in "The Greatest Nature Essay *Ever*." How does it measure up? Does it sermonize? Does it direct them to a Web site? Does it begin with an image? Is it self-indulgent? Does it change the way they think or feel about its subject matter?

## THE READER'S PRESENCE

1. Your students will obviously have different ideas about the effect achieved by the opening paragraph of the essay, but if they can point to examples of figurative language, you will be off to a good start. You may have to help them along by giving them a few examples, yourself. As to the specific example, it's interesting to note that it is not an image from nature: it is, rather, the image of the reader, looking through the mail, stopping because his or her attention is attracted by a particular article. This is the whole essay, in a nutshell: Doyle writes not about any specific natural wonder but, rather, about the experience of reading.

2. Again, your students are likely to have different ideas about the answer to this question, but some of Doyle's criteria, at least, should be reasonably clear. He wants to avoid sermonizing. He wants to arrest the readers' attention with images. Whether he is successful depends on the reader. It is perhaps interesting to note that the piece *does* sermonize, in a sense, about *not* sermonizing. It *lacks* imagery, in another sense, because there aren't too many images from nature. However, it is full of natural imagery: it's just that the images are being used to describe the *writing*, or the *experience of reading*, rather than nature itself (sentences are like mountain ranges, for example).

3. You might want to have students give presentations to the class in answer to this question. Put them into groups, assign each group one essay, and have each group report its conclusions. You'll get students working together. The ones who find this sort of thing easy can help the ones for whom it is more difficult, and you can get them thinking critically, both as individuals and as a group, about what makes a piece of writing effective or ineffective.

# Lars Eighner
## ON DUMPSTER DIVING

### APPROACHING THE ESSAY

Though your students will certainly be aware that homelessness is one of America's most pressing social problems, it is unlikely that many of them have gained insight into the day-to-day trials facing the homeless. Lars Eighner's essay can serve as one means of bringing your students closer to the actual experience of homelessness even as it tests their assumptions and preconceptions about the people who find themselves in a daily fight for survival. Although the tone of the essay often seems detached and at times even lighthearted, its subject matter prevents the reader from taking a complacent attitude toward homelessness.

One characteristic of Eighner's essay is its close attention to language, especially language pertaining to the state of being homeless. In fact, Eighner spends his first five paragraphs reflecting on the origins of the word *Dumpster*. The author's pronounced interest in word origins might seem incongruous to students who believe that much of the homeless population is made up of people who are illiterate. Ask your students if they find it surprising that someone with such an acute awareness of language is also homeless. Ask them to describe the distinctions the author makes between the synonyms *Dumpster diving*, *scavenging*, *scrounging*, and *foraging*. Ask them to name the terms that possess a strongly negative connotation. Which terms do they think are the least negative? You might conclude these initial reflections on language in the essay by asking students what role Eighner's imaginative use of words plays in his struggle to survive under the harshest conditions. Does his verbal play ever obscure the real dangers that he faces each day as he makes his rounds looking for food?

Notice that Eighner does not consider himself infallible with regard to "scavenging"—there is clearly a good deal of uncertainty that goes with retrieving foodstuffs from the trash (paras. 15–16). Self-reliance and sound judgment are required in making decisions about what to eat. He says as much in paragraph 73, echoing the title of Ralph Waldo Emerson's famous essay. Ask your students whether Eighner extends this individualistic philosophy to other aspects of his existence. They should consider as well whether a person needs to be homeless or in another extreme situation to share such a view of the world. To what degree do they think that Eighner's assumptions about the world were in place even before he became destitute?

The question "Why was this discarded?" appears several times in the essay, and it is literally the test to which each found food is subjected before being eaten. Discuss with your class whether this question applies to more than food scavenging. How, for example, might this statement be seen as a comment on homelessness in general? Seen in this light, the question might be expanded as "Why did our society come to see certain individuals as no longer deserving of food, shelter, and clothing?" This is but one example of how, as promised by Eighner in paragraph 7, the essay moves from concrete to abstract considerations of the art of staying alive.

At many points in the essay Eighner provides insights into his own moral and emotional character. He insists in paragraph 23 that he never placed a "bogus" pizza order himself, even though he is aware that this practice might result in more fresh food. Ask your students how their opinion of the author is affected by such statements and why they think Eighner needs to offer these assurances. Discuss whether Eighner views his ethical standards as those belonging to a typical homeless person or whether he wishes to separate himself from the rest of the homeless population by asserting a kind of moral superiority over them. Consider Eighner's attitude toward the "can scroungers" of paragraphs 50 through 52 or toward persons who rummage through individual garbage cans in paragraph 58. Why does he consider the latter practice an invasion of privacy? Ask your students what other "rules" the author would like to see upheld by the homeless community. Rules and courtesies like those described by Eighner are certainly instrumental in shaping a sense of community. How might we view the "scavengers" as a community; of what might "scavenger ethics" consist? Ask your students why Eighner thinks that most people would find such a conception "too funny for words" (para. 59). Do they tend to view homeless people as more or less moral than people with a place to live and enough food to eat?

Another important point to consider is the psychological changes that a person undergoes when first learning to scavenge. These are described by the author in paragraphs 38 through 43. What, according to Eighner, causes the initial sense of disgust to dissipate? Does Eighner place any limits on "Dumpster diving," that is, does he ever feel that "diving" can go too far? Note that despite his relative success in keeping himself nourished, he is not convinced that this unorthodox practice will always provide him with enough food to eat. What does his lack of faith in a method he claims to have perfected say about the conditions of even the most resourceful homeless persons?

The lessons Eighner has learned from his scavenging experiences are recounted in paragraphs 74 through 77. The first lesson is that "there is no value in the abstract" (para. 74); in other words, there is no point in keeping what you cannot use. The second lesson is that of "the transience of material being" (para. 76). Eighner learned this lesson through constant reminders that all material goods ultimately end up on the trash heap. The dualism he speaks of is a philosophical model in which the real and the ideal constitute two separate realms, though only the ideal is eternal; material things by their very nature must fade. This attitude seems to comfort the author, who possesses nothing himself. He can place himself above the consumer society for whom objects possess genuine value. Your students might want to discuss the shared values of consumer society. Do they find Eighner's criticism of this society valid? Students should be able to offer their own views about the society to which most of them belong and its value system.

## ADDITIONAL ACTIVITIES

1. Have your students make a list of the kinds of food items they throw away regularly. How many items on their list do they think Eighner might be able to use? What other kinds of items do they throw out that might still have value for others? Does the fact that someone in Eighner's situation might look at their kitchen garbage or other refuse as a source of nourishment and usable items make them feel wasteful?
2. At several points in his essay, Eighner speaks of an ethics of scavenging. As a class, try to reconstruct the moral guidelines Eighner has set forth throughout his essay. Could these principles be extended effectively to serve as ethical guidelines for society at large? What modifications would need to be introduced to make them applicable to people other than the homeless?

## GENERATING WRITING

1. Have your students think about their own attitudes toward Eighner's way of life and that of homeless people in general. Then ask them to write a personal essay in which they recount their attitudes toward homeless people before they read Eighner's essay. They should explain whether these attitudes were shaped primarily by firsthand experiences with the homeless or by television, the movies, and other media. Finally, they might address whether Eighner's essay confirmed or challenged their previous assumptions about homeless people.
2. At several points in the essay Eighner rejects the materialist values of mainstream consumer society. On a very practical level, however, everyone alive must be a "materialist" in some sense. Human beings depend on food and water for survival and cannot completely ignore these material needs. Ask your students to develop an essay in which they analyze the extent to which such values continue to inform Eighner's views. To what extent has

he succeeded in freeing himself from the brand of materialism that characterizes American society? They should support their findings with examples from the essay and pay close attention to the author's language, which is often rich in irony and understatement.

## THE READER'S PRESENCE

1. Eighner's process of self-education is re-created by examples throughout the essay, though rarely in strict chronological fashion. For example, though we do not know at what point Eighner decided that rummaging through individual trash cans was unethical, we can imagine that he came to this decision after experience had shown him how much about people's private lives could be reconstructed from what they throw away. The author's self-education may also be traced by imagining how he began to make distinctions among the terms *scavenging*, *scrounging*, and *collecting*.

2. Eighner's tone changes depending on the kinds of information he is attempting to convey. While describing the activity of Dumpster diving or food categorization, his tone is usually lighthearted and somewhat detached as though he does not wish to evoke the sympathy of his readers. At other times, as when he describes the difference between himself and the can scroungers, he adopts a tone verging on outrage and righteousness. At still other times, as in the essay's final consideration of values, his tone becomes meditative, even philosophical. Student responses to Eighner may run the gamut from contempt for his efforts to survive on the refuse of others to respect for his resourcefulness and positive, though sometimes wary, outlook.

3. Insofar as Eighner no longer sees himself as a member of consumer society, he differs from most readers of his essay. Even if some students bristle at being thought of as "consumers," most will have a difficult time proving that they are not subject to consumerism. However, Eighner's easygoing tone and his attempts to distinguish himself from other homeless persons may be an effort to identify with his readers. Though it is not entirely clear whether the author expects his readers to be familiar with the information he supplies, he presents it in a manner that evokes neither pity nor indifference.

4. Both Eighner and Jonathan Swift ("A Modest Proposal," p. 831)—spanning a gap of two and a half centuries—draw readers' attention to the perennial effects of poverty and the immorality of those who ignore it. Swift's proposal is no more outrageous, as he makes us see, than allowing thousands to go hungry while the rich thrive. In effect, Swift holds a mirror up to society's face and makes it look at its inhumanity. Lacking satire, Eighner's essay has an earnest tone, congruent with the seriousness of survival. His essay is moving because he gives us his personal, firsthand account. As readers, we are immediately propelled into his difficult life through how-to instructions on Dumpster diving. His essay does not allow for distance through abstract theories on homelessness and impersonal statistics.

   Peter Singer ("The Singer Solution to World Poverty," p. 814)—who is sincere in his compassion for the poor—would, ironically, put Eighner out of work! Initially, Singer's utilitarian solution finds much agreement in Eighner's occupation: both seek not to waste. However, if Singer's philosophy were adopted on a large scale, no one would be filling those Dumpsters with good food and usable castoffs. Singer instructs: "Whatever money you're spending on luxuries, not necessities, should be given away" (para. 22).

# Joseph Epstein
## THE PERPETUAL ADOLESCENT

### APPROACHING THE ESSAY

Joseph Epstein's essay argues that our national obsession with youth has contributed to the downfall of culture and limited the benefits of a mature adulthood. Although youth culture has "triumphed" since the 1960s, American culture has suffered from this immaturity and refusal to embrace adulthood. The strength of Epstein's argument comes from the many examples of how culture has shifted since the 1950s, from styles of dress to the demeanor of presidents. His argument, however, hinges on the idea that the American obsession with youthfulness has had a negative effect on national culture and that "maturity" (para. 36) has its own benefits. Of course, Epstein's job is doubly tricky because his readers—or, at least, those under age sixty—have been immersed in youth culture for decades now and are likely to see "adulthood" (para. 34) and "maturity" (para. 37) in a negative light.

Some might argue that the triumph of youth culture is not the slippery slope that Epstein describes, but rather part of a cycle that has grown out of a period of relative prosperity and peace since World War II. Epstein does mention that the generation that lived through the Depression and both world wars was pressured to grow up quickly because of these national events. However, Epstein spends little time addressing opposition viewpoints, preferring to hold closely to his own thesis. Ask students to consider what Epstein suggests is lost in the triumph of youth culture. What would be different if maturity were more valued? You might list on the board the various areas of life that Epstein uses as examples and have students imagine what each would be like if adulthood were prized instead of adolescence.

Students will likely agree that Americans today value youthfulness and shun maturity. They may, however, question Epstein's assertion that the triumph of youth culture has negatively affected our quality of life. Ask students to analyze Epstein's examples for the values he implicitly promotes. What values does he associate with maturity and adulthood? Do students agree with this association? Do they agree that the values Epstein prizes are good qualities? What values does he associate with youth? How important are these values to your students? Do they seem more or less important than the values of maturity? Does Epstein omit anything that might contradict his thesis?

## ADDITIONAL ACTIVITIES

1. Put the words *adolescent* and *adult* on the board, and ask students to spend ten minutes brainstorming words or terms they associate with each. Then copy onto the board all the words your students come up with, and discuss them as a class. What patterns of associations did students come up with? How many words have negative connotations? How many have positive connotations? You could also ask students to free-associate on the word *youth* and compare the responses to those for *adolescent*. Which word seems more positive?

2. Tape-record fifteen to twenty minutes of commercials and watch the tape in class. Have students examine the commercials for examples of what Epstein calls "the exaltation of the young" (para. 10). How are youthfulness, maturity, adulthood, parenting, and aging depicted? What general fears or concerns do the commercials appeal to? What seems to be the age range of the intended audience? How do stylistic choices represent either maturity or youthfulness in the commercials?

3. Although Epstein focuses on how adolescence has invaded adult culture, many cultural critics have commented in the last decade on how adolescence has invaded childhood as well. Ask students to consider how the divisions between different stages of life have been blurred. In what ways are children being introduced to young-adult life at a much younger age? What are the benefits or drawbacks of this trend?

## GENERATING WRITING

1. Assign students a reflective essay in which they discuss what they believe being an adult means today. How have their ideas about adulthood changed since they were children? What aspects of adulthood do they characterize as negative? as positive? How does their conception of adulthood differ from Epstein's?

2. Have students write a five-page paper analyzing the strengths and weaknesses of Epstein's argument. Remind them to consider Epstein's intended audience and purpose when evaluating his success. How do his methods—tone, examples, nods to the opposition, word choice, use of expert testimony, and rhetorical questions—add to or detract from his argument?

## THE READER'S PRESENCE

1. Epstein believes that the shift to youth culture began following World War II, after *Catcher in the Rye*, with its disparaging view of adulthood, was published. Epstein suggests a shift between those growing up with the Depression and world wars and those baby boomers who experienced relative peace

and prosperity in the 1950s and later. The election of John F. Kennedy—the youngest president elected to date—was a turning point for the triumph of youth over adulthood, and soon afterward the student movements of the 1960s glorified the young and cautioned against trusting adults. Epstein also points to iconic youth heroes, such as Elvis Presley and James Dean, as support for his position.

2. Epstein argues that youth culture in business has resulted in a general lack of responsibility from corporate leaders; he cites Enron and other corporate scandals as examples. Adolescent tastes have lessened the quality of television and movies, as exemplified in "potty humor" and profanity. Advertisers sell youthfulness to all age groups. The media market toward shorter attention spans. News outlets value clever, sarcastic, or ironic style over formal, serious journalism and allow pop culture, sports, fashion, and gossip to creep onto the front pages. Many of Epstein's examples suggest that he values serious culture and responsibility, with distinct life stages offering unique benefits and responsibilities.

3. In "Against School" (p. 665), John Taylor Gatto argues that compulsory schooling was envisioned as a way of making eternal children out of our youth in order to keep them highly susceptible to the powers of marketing. Capitalism sees children as the ultimate consumer, and schooling staves off critical thinking that might lessen the effects of marketing. Epstein says that the market reinforces adolescent culture and that up to 95 percent of advertising offers appeals to youthfulness, suggesting to adults that purchasing such products is the only way to remain young—and suggesting that remaining young is desirable.

# James Fallows
## THROWING LIKE A GIRL

### APPROACHING THE ESSAY

Following Hillary Clinton's less-than-stellar performance throwing out the first ball at a Chicago Cubs baseball game in 1994, James Fallows examines the phenomenon of "throwing like a girl": Why do feminists resist the phrase? Is it accurate? What does "throwing like a girl" actually consist of? How does "proper" pitching differ? Can it be learned? Fallows's piece is part argumentative essay, part investigation, part how-to essay.

Male and female students alike should have strong reactions to the piece, though not always along gender lines. Encourage students to argue through reason rather than through ridicule or prejudice. To what extent does Fallows's position disempower women through its insistence that only "male" athletic practices are correct, and to what extent does Fallows attempt to empower women by challenging stereotypes about bodily differences and rendering a traditionally male skill more accessible to women? How do Fallows's line of argumentation and specific word choices either perpetuate or repudiate stereotypes? What is Fallows's stated motivation in writing the article? Are students convinced by it? Why or why not? Are students more convinced by Fallows's or the standard feminist argument? Why?

## ADDITIONAL ACTIVITIES

1. Have students list common activities on the board in columns headed "Male" and "Female" for discussion. Which activities are traditionally associated with men, and which with women? What associations do students maintain with "gendered" activities? Which gendered activities do they enjoy? Are men or women naturally suited to certain activities? If so, does it matter? To what extent do stereotypes determine estimation of ability? To what extent do these stereotypes limit and determine the courses of our lives? You might also offer military service, sports, and stay-at-home child care as activities whose gender basis has recently been hotly debated.

2. Take students outside or to the gymnasium with balls and have them attempt to follow Fallows's suggestions—throwing with the wrong hand and using the guidelines he suggests. Are his guidelines easy or difficult to follow? Do students experience the results he has described? Would they change his instructions? If so, how? Do students, male and female, feel less satisfied with their performances when throwing with the wrong hand? more satisfied when following Fallows's guidelines? Why or why not? How many enjoy the game less, or more, with these modifications? How many attach importance to athletic prowess? What reasons do they give?

## GENERATING WRITING

1. Have students free-write about a difficult learning process they experienced—for instance, how to shop for a used car or study for a test—and work the free-write into a two- to three-page essay that includes descriptions of failures and successes along the way and step-by-step instructions for others duplicating what they learned. Recirculate papers with names removed for class discussion. What was learned about the subject through the process of articulating it to others?

2. Have students write three drafts of a two- to three-page position paper supporting Fallows's or the traditional feminist argument. After the first draft, pair students taking the same position to discuss and strengthen their positions. After the second draft, pair students taking opposite positions to strengthen their positions through counterargumentation and rebuttal. Have students discuss what they learned from each stage of the process.

## THE READER'S PRESENCE

1. Two examples of activities traditionally associated with men are manual labor and sports; two activities associated with women are cooking and child care. In general, activities traditionally linked to men garner greater cultural respect. Fallows apparently feels that certain activities may simply be performed better; there is little evidence that Fallows fails to respect women's activities or performance in general.

2. Fallows's lighthearted approach to the subject is indicated, for instance, where he admits with exaggerated seriousness that he needs his wife to play ball with him, and where he mockingly indicts himself with possibly "dancing like a white man" (para. 4). The writer is better able to win his audience's attention and agreement through a light approach to the subject matter.

3. The kinetic chain involved in throwing is a complicated series of actions that takes place very quickly. The pace of the essay slows down, with good reason, when Fallows describes it: many parts of the body are involved, and that is the point. Therefore, Fallows *has* to slow down, otherwise one would not be able to conceptualize the kinetic chain he's writing about. It's like filming a throw, then playing it back in slow motion to break it down. In "The Death of a Moth" (p. 371), Annie Dillard's purpose is different, but the idea is basically the same. She wants the reader to really think about that moth, trapped in the flame, so she slows down, spends some time describing it. It might be useful to express the principle to the students like this: one way to get your reader to focus on a particular thing is to slow down and spend a paragraph or two describing that thing in detail.

# Daniel Gilbert
## NEXT TO NOTHING

### APPROACHING THE ESSAY

This might prove to be a very interesting essay for students: many of them will probably enjoy thinking about the apparent contradictions in human behavior, particularly when it comes to money. Gilbert's humorous approach to his subject matter might also appeal to students, which will make it easier to conduct a group discussion of the issues raised by "Next to Nothing." There may be some initial resistance to Gilbert's argument, of course. Look at the first bit of research: your students are likely to feel, at least initially, that it always makes sense to take *more*, rather than *less*, money. Therefore, logically speaking, most of them will argue for taking the job with the decreasing pay, since that job pays more over a period of time. But the purpose of this essay is to get the reader to think about what is wanted on a more nuanced—and more realistic—level. According to Gilbert's research, the truth is that most people would prefer to take less money, total, provided the amount went up over three years, instead of going down. A raise provides the *perception* of more money, though, a perception that is always preferable, even if it is an illusion.

The idea of the essay is that we make our decisions based on comparisons. The brain makes *relative* judgments rather than absolute ones. Gilbert feels that this is a mistake, because—logically—less is less and more is more. Paragraphs 4 and 5 are particularly important. Here Gilbert puts forth the idea that what we should do, when considering our options, is compare with the *possible*, rather than with the past. He says that, because we find it difficult to "generate new possibilities" (para. 5), we often make decisions without considering our options. There are several iterations of the basic theme: the vacation packages and the $20 concert ticket in paragraph 6, for example. You might ask the students what they would do, particularly regarding the concert ticket. Once you have spent some time discussing these examples, go back to the beginning of the essay: contextualized thus, the preference for the lower paying job might be easier to understand.

## ADDITIONAL ACTIVITIES

1. You might try coming up with a fictional assignment. If it is a Friday, assign one hundred pages of reading or a five-page paper. Better yet, assign one hundred pages of reading and a five-page paper. Then, after they've complained and protested and said, "That's not fair," give them the real assignment. Make sure it's more reading or writing than you assigned the weekend before. Chances are, they will still feel as though the assignment is pretty easy. Point this out to them.

2. Bring some catalogs to class or have the students bring catalogs from home and instruct the class to compare prices and products. An interesting exercise might be to divide the students into groups and play something like a version of "The Price Is Right," based on comparisons between pictures taken from separate catalogs. If, for example, you (or one of your students) were to show the class a picture of a couch from a Pottery Barn catalog, then a lower quality picture of a more expensive couch—a picture off Craigslist, for example—you might have fun proving Gilbert's point.

## GENERATING WRITING

1. Have your students conduct interviews or surveys of their own, asking a predetermined number of people a set of questions similar to those Gilbert asks in "Next to Nothing." Students can then report their findings in short papers, drawing conclusions that either confirm or refute Gilbert's point about how people make decisions. This assignment would be an ideal way to introduce

students to writing from nontraditional, or at least nonwritten, sources. It will provide a sort of brush with experiential learning, allowing students to get directly involved in their research.

2. Ask the students to write a short essay about an experience they've had with the principles Gilbert discusses. Have they ever made purchasing (or employment) decisions that later seemed illogical? What were those decisions? Why were they illogical?

## THE READER'S PRESENCE

1. Gilbert's hypothetical example—an employee asking for a 15 percent pay cut (but willing to settle for 10)—is meant to highlight the absurdity of the way that we make decisions. As Gilbert points out, "people *hate* pay cuts" (para. 1). No one would *ask* for one: indeed, Gilbert jokes that asking for a pay cut would be a good way to "get into *Guinness World Records*" (para. 1). One would be inclined to imagine that the reason for hating pay cuts is the desire to make more, rather than less, money. Yet Gilbert's research indicates that most people would take less money over a period of time, just to avoid taking the pay cut. Many of your students will probably find this surprising, arguing that it makes no sense at all. Others will probably find it easier to understand. A raise *feels* good. A pay cut doesn't. Gilbert argues that we make most of our decisions based on comparison, so it follows that the "absolute" amount is not of paramount importance, whether it "makes sense" or not.

2. The idea seems to be that the perception—even the illusion—of getting more for less is always desirable, regardless of absolute value. Your students can decide for themselves whether it is irrational, but ultimately Gilbert's studies seem to confirm that it is true. You might even argue that it *is* rational: if one is concerned with *feeling* good, then doing the thing that makes you feel good is the rational choice, regardless of its material value. For the example of the pay raise, consider how bad it would feel to have one's pay decreased. Furthermore, having to adjust to decreased pay might be more difficult than living off less to begin with.

3. Steven D. Levitt and Stephen J. Dubner ("What Should You Worry About?" [p. 475]) and Gilbert use statistics and probability to shed light on behavior. They observe patterns. In that sense, Gilbert's research in sociology resembles economics not only because he is interested in financial decisions but also because both essays are interested in numbers and what those numbers reveal about the underlying motivations behind human behavior.

# Malcolm Gladwell
## SMALL CHANGE: WHY THE REVOLUTION WILL NOT BE TWEETED

### APPROACHING THE ESSAY

You might start by pairing Gladwell's essay with Nicholas Carr's "Is Google Making Us Stupid?" (p. 633). They both deal with how Web-related technology has affected the world: unfortunately, both are rather negative about the role of Web technology in modern life, but they are comparable essays and should generate good "real life" connections for students. Students may agree that Gladwell's essay probably makes a more convincing argument, however, in the long run. It might be overly easy for students to bash the Google essay; they will have a harder time trying to stave off Gladwell's attack on Twitter as a useful tool for social change. The essay should get your students thinking: what is all this technology really useful for besides social networking? When they begin discussing social revolution (specifically the civil rights movement depicted in "Small Change") they may be hesitant at first to really engage with the problem that Gladwell is depicting; the Web is their world, after all. After careful consideration of Gladwell's comparison of real protests versus online protests, however, it should be glaringly obvious that Twitter and Facebook as tools for revolution and protest are lacking. Discussing why this is so will lead to further and more important points that Gladwell outlines, such as the strong-tie versus the weak-tie relationship.

Essentially, Gladwell is arguing that revolution and even helpful social protest are ineffective through Web-related social media because the ties between people are too weak in those media. It might be easy to donate a few bucks to help the victims in Darfur, Gladwell suggests, but clicking a few buttons doesn't get you over to Darfur, physically helping out. The relationship between the online donor and the victims in Darfur is a weak tie; there is nothing at stake for the donor. Gladwell highlights this point by showing what a real protest looks like: the Greensboro sit-ins during the civil rights movement. Gladwell contrasts the two worlds: (1) the online, weak-tie world, where any person at a computer can become a protester, and (2) the world of real, live protest, in which people put their bodies on the line. Gladwell suggests that the sit-ins in Greensboro were more effective because they were based on strong-tie relationships—that is, people who knew one another in nonvirtual, physical life and were able to spread the word. These sit-ins affected businesses, daily life, and society in general. A donation to Darfur, relayed by a friend of a friend, goes almost (though not quite) unnoticed. Students should be learning the importance of comparing and contrasting here, for this is almost Gladwell's entire rhetorical strategy.

## ADDITIONAL ACTIVITIES

1. Much of Gladwell's essay focuses on the idea that social-networking sites are not very good vehicles to create real social and political change. Gladwell gives his "weak-tie" argument as the main reason for this. Now have students try to pinpoint other reasons Gladwell might take this stance. Encourage them to discuss ways in which the Internet might be better used to help create social change and come up with specific examples of social change occurring in the present day and associated with the Internet—Egypt's government, for instance, blocked access to the Internet in response to the protests about Hosni Mubarak. What does this say about the power of the Internet?

2. Put students into groups and have each group outline a rhetorical strategy contained in each section of the essay. For instance, students should be noting why Gladwell doesn't mention anything about social networking until six paragraphs in. Also, they will find it interesting and worthwhile to explore Gladwell's prose when he describes the Greensboro sit-ins versus his prose when he describes the cell-phone incident. In one, Gladwell's prose moves slowly and patiently and creates a visual picture; in the other, Gladwell's sentences are combined with semicolons and move fairly quickly. Why?

## GENERATING WRITING

1. Have students create a mini-essay in which they describe an injustice or a problem they have experienced in everyday life, describing in detail the injustice or problem and the eventual resolution. Then, have them write another essay, this time focusing on an injustice or problem they experienced in a virtual medium. Again, they should describe the details and eventual resolution. In the conclusion of the mini-essay, they should describe how these two situations were resolved differently. How were the problems different? How were confrontations handled differently, and were there any miscommunications?

2. Have students write an essay in which they defend the Web and social-networking sites as viable forms of social change. They will have to argue against Gladwell's points and thus must be able to represent all his claims clearly. They might have to make concessions on some points, but this should be a good exercise in learning that no matter how convincing the argument, there is always another stance to take, if well thought through.

## THE READER'S PRESENCE

1. Gladwell's essay will clearly focus on social change, and the civil rights story of protest at the beginning serves as an example. Gladwell repeats the words *protest* and *sit-in* several times, while emphasizing the physicality of the situation: all these people coming together physically, literally embodying protest. He doesn't mention anything about social media in order to show that social media isn't necessary (or very helpful) for real social change.

2. Notice that Gladwell is more patient with the Greensboro account. He lets details accumulate and uses prose that highlights the slowly mounting tension of the situation. Also, the prose is politically charged: words like *protest*, *sit-in*, and *civil rights* are frequent. In the account of the New Yorker who lost her phone, Gladwell breezes through the losing and finding of the phone, subtly emphasizing the fact that the story has almost no historical or political significance. The Sidekick anecdote is one of small injustice; the lunch-counter account is one of great social injustice; one is no revolution at all, while the other is one of the most important social revolutions in U.S. history.

3. Nicholas Carr's essay ("Is Google Making Us Stupid?" [p. 633]) differs from Gladwell's in that Carr is concerned with how the Internet is changing the way we think. Carr believes the Internet has made us all skimmers, essentially with shorter attention spans. Gladwell is more concerned with the Web's inability to create real social change; it isn't a good tool for revolutions. So, although their arguments are very different, both are attacking Internet technology in one way or another. Greatly generalized, one could say that both see the Internet as a technology that creates surface-level interest in things but nothing greater than that. Gladwell uses historical civil rights moments to highlight the incapability of the Internet for such purposes; Carr uses history, specifically Nietzsche using a typewriter, to show how the mind reacts to new technologies. Carr's historical facts help support his main point that the Internet is making us all attention deprived; Gladwell's use of history is to contrast how historical moments play out online.

# Cynthia Gorney
## THE URGE TO MERGE

### APPROACHING THE ESSAY

Cynthia Gorney's "The Urge to Merge" is an informative and amusing essay about a common but little commented-upon phenomenon. Most of your students have probably had experience merging in heavy traffic and, as Gorney points out, most drivers have strong opinions on the subject when the subject comes up. But it doesn't come up very often in conversation, and chances are none of your students have ever read an article about it, either. The article is interesting in that capacity. Everyone can relate to it, and no one has written much about it, at least not in mainstream media, which leads us to another point: the article is well researched. Gorney manages to dig up a textbook called *Traffic Flow Fundamentals* and actually meets the author of another book, *Traffic: Why We Drive the Way We Do (and What It Says About Us)*. Gorney makes a point to consult a variety of sources as she explores her subject matter, and the variety makes the article persuasive. Nothing is overlooked. She includes her own observations (two-thirds of us are lineuppers, para. 5), as well as mathematical formulas like the algebraic equation at the end of paragraph 11. She interviews a highway patrolman, Sam Morgan, dominating the last part of the essay (paras. 22–30). The variety of sources also keeps the article lively: Gorney doesn't get bogged down in the math. She makes sure there's plenty of anecdotal action to keep readers entertained.

Gorney also laces her prose with ironic humor: her description of Morgan as "a big-shouldered guy" who has "maybe transcended the tendency many of us have toward driving around in a state of constant micronegotiation with the world" (para. 24), for example. You might spend some time discussing various examples of similar humor. Look at almost any paragraph and you are likely to find a sentence loaded with five- and seven-syllable words or phrases that seem oddly technical for their context: "culturally mandated compulsive queuing" (para. 12) or "this anti-aristocratic all-men-are-created-equal narrative we pretend to cherish while simultaneously celebrating the individual's right to do whatever advances his own interests without technically breaking the law" (para. 9). Gorney mixes high diction and low diction to achieve this effect, which is a common element of humor writing that your students might benefit from understanding, as many of them probably use the strategy quite frequently themselves, without being aware of how it works or why they do it.

Finally, what is most interesting about Gorney's essay is probably the fact that the conclusions she comes to are markedly different from the conclusions she might have preferred. As a lineupper, a driver Bill Beaty would put in the "Vigilante" category (para. 15), Gorney would have liked to believe that sidezoomers—Beaty's "Cheaters"—slowed traffic: that sidezoomers were the problem. She says "with some reluctance" (para. 16) that it is not their fault that traffic slows when lanes merge. Gorney's resistance to her own conclusions is a valuable teaching tool, especially because so many students are either unwilling or unable to understand that their research can—and, indeed, *should*—be able to lead them to unwelcome or at the very least unexpected conclusions. As novice writers, many of your students will believe that they have to come up with their thesis statements *before* they begin their research or write their papers. Novice writers often do not understand that this actually makes their work much more difficult, not to mention that it limits their intellectual growth. For all its humor and the apparent triviality of its subject matter, Gorney's essay might in fact serve as a powerful way to motivate students to become more flexible and sophisticated writers.

## ADDITIONAL ACTIVITY

1. Ask your students to go to a place where there is heavy traffic. It doesn't have to be automobile traffic but traffic of some kind: it could be a crosswalk in a busy part of town when people are on their lunch breaks, or it could be a hallway in your school between classes. Ask your students to observe the way people negotiate the traffic. Can they identify certain types? Sometimes, for example, there is a clear line at the deli counter in the grocery

store. Other times, people just crowd around, waiting for their turn. In most cases, the deli attendant can keep track of who showed up first, second, and so on. In other cases, it is less clear. Do some people hang back while others are quick to assert themselves? What generalizations, if any, can you make about these people? If you can manage to isolate a few spots where these behaviors manifest themselves in your community, places all of your students will be familiar with, you might manage to provoke an argument, hopefully civil, but otherwise similar to the ones Gorney describes in her essay. You might try picking a particular place that the students will be familiar with, having the discussion, then sending them out to observe on their own. They can report their findings during the next class. Were their original opinions confirmed? refuted?

## GENERATING WRITING

1. One of the most interesting things about Gorney's essay is that her academic conclusion (sidezoomers and lineuppers are equally culpable for the reduced speed of traffic around merging lanes) is a notable departure from her personal opinion (sidezoomers are scum). This demonstrates that open-minded research has the potential to change one's opinion. Most of your students are likely to have limited experience with open-minded research. They're used to coming up with a thesis statement and then conducting selective research to support it. Ask them to write a research paper that begins not with a thesis statement but with a question. They can choose the topic themselves, within any limits you'd like to establish, so long as—in your judgment—there will be enough research materials available to build an informative paper. Topics might include premarital cohabitation—does it improve the chances that the marriage will be successful?—or vegetarianism—is it good for your health? Does hand sanitizer prevent disease? Does videogame violence contribute to actual violence?

## THE READER'S PRESENCE

1. Drawing on multiple sources tends to make the reading both more interesting and more persuasive. If, for example, Gorney had only provided her point of view and anecdotal evidence to support her opinion, the bias would have been clear and the article might not have persuaded anyone of anything. If, however, she had drawn exclusively on academic sources, the article would have been dry, and as such substantially less entertaining. In addition to adding personality and humor, Gorney's personal take on her subject matter also provides an interesting foil for her findings, because the conclusion that she is forced to come to—that "sidezoomers" are no more to blame for slow traffic than "lineuppers"—is one she would not have agreed with when she began to research the piece. The article *has* to be convincing, then, simply because Gorney presents herself as the last person on Earth who would *want* to be convinced.

2. Gorney's tone is, for the most part, humorous. Students will have a variety of opinions about her approach, but it seems likely that she exaggerates specifically because we *do* tend to overreact where driving is concerned (hence, road rage). Gorney mixes high diction and low diction to achieve this effect (see the Approaching the Essay section in this entry). She also makes occasional use of one-sentence paragraphs, as in paragraph 8 ("Not in front of me, though"), where the sentence itself seems to momentarily stop the traffic of the prose as Gorney blocks a sidezoomer from entering her lane.

3. Joan Acocella ("A Few Too Many," p. 283) doesn't do much to illuminate her personal experience. She doesn't write scenes like the one Gorney gives us, with Sam Morgan, watching traffic from the overpass. Acocella's research is based more in what she has been able to *read* about her subject matter. Gorney's readings are only a part of her essay. Both authors take a light-hearted approach to their subject matter, though. The intended effect seems to be to keep the writing entertaining and to avoid making too big a deal of hangovers. In the grand scheme of things, hangovers are not that important, and traffic—while it often provokes strong feelings—is for most people a matter that seems inconsequential compared to other sorts of "moral" transgressions. As angry as a "sidezoomer" might make us, we have to concede that he is not a murderer and that the proper object of our outrage—if there is one, for traffic problems like the one Gorney describes—is probably more properly located somewhere in government bureaucracy than in the car next to ours.

# Stephen Jay Gould
## SEX, DRUGS, DISASTERS, AND THE EXTINCTION OF DINOSAURS

### APPROACHING THE ESSAY

Someone is likely to protest here that this is an English class, and these students shouldn't be expected to know about the experiments that showed light to be both particle and wave. If no one does voice this protest, you can be sure that some are thinking it but are too polite or politic to mention it. If they don't voice it, maybe you should—and let *them* argue against *you*. Stephen Jay Gould, they may say, would blame the writers of "popular presentations of science" for our ignorance. Isn't it possible that science has really so progressed that lay people couldn't understand the implications of scientific experiments even if they were explained, and that without the work of such popularizers the public would have no access to scientific knowledge at all?

Gould, of course, has structured his essay so as to refute such a position. He proves, by briefly emulating their technique, that the popularizers put their readers in a position where it is impossible for them to make up their own minds: it's not that lay readers cannot think about these questions, but rather that they have been trained not to. Have your students turn to his summaries of the three proposals on the extinction of dinosaurs. Ask them to characterize these summaries. Do they notice the bald, declarative sentences giving the kinds of conclusions that Gould deplores? Do the summaries themselves show any evidence by which we as readers can judge which of the statements are predicated on mere speculation and which on falsifiable evidence?

Some students will probably have the scientific knowledge necessary to know, for example, that livers and testes do not fossilize. But nothing in the summaries suggests this limitation. These summaries resemble the mysteries solved in contemporary popular crime or mystery novels: the vital case clue is always withheld from the audience so that the viewer cannot figure out for himself or herself who committed the murder. Of course, people have figured out how to solve those mysteries by structural means: they have found that it's always the least conspicuous character, or the character whom the camera picks up at a precise moment in the courtroom scene. Similarly, most people familiar with stories such as "Cinderella," "The Three Billy Goats Gruff," and any fairy tale involving three brothers, three sisters, or three tests is likely to know by "intuition" that Gould's third option is the correct one. But any mystery fan will tell you that a story that does not provide all the clues necessary for its solution is not a good mystery. And Gould himself as much as admits that his withholding the vital clue was unfair: "much of the popular commentary has missed this essential distinction by focusing on the impact and its attendant results, and forgetting what really matters to a scientist—the iridium" (para. 24).

## ADDITIONAL ACTIVITY

1. Gould's essay, by explaining how the three hypotheses evolved, lets us see which are mere speculation and which is properly falsifiable and expansive, thus meeting his criteria for good science. Because he describes the "mode of inquiry" and not just the "enticing conclusions" (para. 1), Gould's essay meets his own expectations. After your class has examined his thesis and argument, you might want to direct your students' attention to his language. What, for example, is the status of such words as *titillating, enticing,* and *primally fascinating*? Is Gould using these words to imply a criticism of the press for playing upon the reader's baser emotions to seduce their interest in scientific theory? If he is, then where would Gould's essay stand in relation to the articles he judges in this way? After all, his essay has a titillating title. Or look at his use of the word *intriguing* (para. 5 and throughout). He obviously finds science intriguing, but at the same time he considers "intriguing ideas" not "good science." Similarly, you might ask if Gould would consider *fertile imaginations* and *speculates* (para. 15) good or bad. If your students protest, with some reason, that "good and bad" are value judgments, with no place

in a discussion of science, then point to any of Gould's many uses of that dichotomy (for example, "Good science is self-corrective," para. 16). Does "good and bad" imply a moral judgment in this context? Why does Gould refer to his own argument as "preaching" (para. 5)?

## GENERATING WRITING

1. Have students go to the library and find back issues of *Discover*, *Omni*, or other journals that provide popular accounts of scientific advances. Instruct them to use Gould's criteria to judge the essays they have chosen from these journals. They may choose two essays covering the same breakthrough to analyze their relative merits. Or they may choose to compare and contrast an essay from a popular science journal (or from the science section of the *New York Times*, for example) with one of Gould's other essays from any of his books on science written for a lay audience. Does Gould's own writing live up to his criteria? How, if at all, does it differ from the other essay your student has chosen?

2. Assign an essay in which students examine Gould's tone in this essay. When does he use the diction and syntax of the serious scientist, and where does he become more colloquial? How, if at all, does Gould's silliness differ from the silliness he criticizes in Siegel's statement that "elephants drink, perhaps, to forget . . ." (para. 14)? What is the effect of Gould's shifts in tone? What might be the intention behind the stylistic choices that create those shifts?

## THE READER'S PRESENCE

1. Gould lays out his thesis in his very first sentence: "Science, in its most fundamental definition, is a fruitful mode of inquiry, not a list of enticing conclusions." It's a fairly controversial thesis, at least to the lay reader. You might illustrate its measure of controversy in class by asking your students what scientists have been doing in the last hundred years. How many mention "enticing conclusions," such as superstring theory or that light is both a particle and a wave or superconductors? How many can identify the "mode of inquiry" that led to these discoveries?

2. You might point to the colloquial paragraph 3 ("titillating," "sex, drugs, and violence," "silly"), the more scientific list of theories ("Cretaceous" [para. 13], "angiosperms" [para. 21], "psychoactive" [para. 15]), and the now-familiar, now-scientific paragraph 10 ("rectal thermometry," "Well, let's face it," "high ratios of surface to volume").

3. "Testable proposals" (para. 4) are hypotheses that have withstood enough scientific scrutiny to be accepted provisionally. "Useless speculation" (which is usually reduced to an "intriguing idea") describes claims that may be either true or false but that offer "no material for affirmation or rejection" (para. 5). Useless speculation, in other words, is useless for science. It gives us nothing

to do beyond baselessly agreeing or disagreeing. (A common mistake for beginning writers is to formulate an argument that *makes no claim, one that may be neither disputed nor proven.* Such an argument gives the writer, and the reader, nothing with which to engage.) Gould focuses on a particular set of hypotheses about dinosaur extinction to prove his point about the usefulness of scientific inquiry (and to teach his reader a bit about dinosaurs and geochemistry along the way); in "Small Change: Why the Revolution Will Not Be Tweeted" (p. 411), Malcolm Gladwell attacks the increasingly popular perception that technological innovations associated with the Internet constitute a force for social change. Both writers model critical, scientific thinking for their lay readers, but Gould conveys more hard information. Gladwell uses more anecdotal evidence. Both writers use humor to engage their readers in serious subjects, giving their essays lighthearted titles and incorporating examples designed to make the audience smile — if only at the folly of fellow human beliefs and actions.

# Nathaniel Hawthorne
## MY VISIT TO NIAGARA

### APPROACHING THE ESSAY

The most obvious difficulty most of your students will have with Hawthorne is that he is Hawthorne: originally published in 1835, much of the language in "My Visit to Niagara" is antiquated. For some of your students, Hawthorne's syntax will make his sentences seem incomprehensible at first glance. Although in most cases this is a matter of habit rather than reading comprehension (students seeing the name "Hawthorne" and shrinking in fear, not even trying to make sense of it), overcoming the obstacle will still take a fair amount of class time. You might consider introducing the students to the essay and going through the first couple of paragraphs with them before you send them off to read the rest of the essay on their own: it might prove beneficial to break down the second paragraph sentence by sentence. If students are made to understand the irony of Hawthorne's situation, the "deathlike slumber" (para. 2) of his enthusiasm upon approaching a thing long desired, they may be able to relate to it. With luck, you might be able to raise their interest based on this identification.

In fact, much of the appeal of Hawthorne's essay is probably that most people can, in one way or another, relate to his initial disappointment upon encountering, after much anticipation, the "real thing." Draw your students' attention to the opening of paragraph 6: "Oh, that I had never heard of Niagara till I beheld it." Ask them to think of experiences they have had with looking forward to something that ultimately let them down. It could be something as simple as a hyped movie that turned out to be a disappointment. How does expectation diminish (or enhance) our ability to enjoy things that we have looked forward to? More specifically, how does expectation factor into our ability to *see* things that we have heard a lot about, like Niagara Falls, when we encounter them in reality? Hawthorne begins to overcome his disappointment when he listens to the sound of the falls late at night. Ask the students how listening might differ from seeing: how does expectation factor into the relative effects of the two experiences? How many of your students, when considering pictures of the falls like the ones included with the essay (or others like it) or even hearing the words *Niagara Falls*, consider what such a massive waterfall might *sound* like? You might ask them, again, to recall experiences that they looked forward to: What parts of those experiences were unexpected? Did the unexpected aspects of the experience make it more memorable? If so, in what way?

Hawthorne's essay is primarily a narrative, describing the experience, so he doesn't make a lot of explicit intellectual connections between his observations and subsequent emotions; it is interesting to note, however, that in the two somewhat long paragraphs (10 and 11) near the end of the essay he describes in detail his observations of other people seeing the falls for the first time. You might ask the students how watching other people react to an experience can make an experience more meaningful. For example, we often enjoy watching children react to things that adults take for granted. How does watching a child react to, say, animals at the zoo, make the experience of going to the zoo new for us? In paragraph 10, Hawthorne describes two "adventurers" emerging from behind the waterfall as "children of the mist." What implications does such a metaphor make about our relationship with nature? At its basic level, "My Visit to Niagara" is an essay about expectation and experience, anticipation and perception. Seen in this light, students may be able to view the essay as something new and learn to appreciate Hawthorne in much the same way Hawthorne learns to appreciate the falls.

## ADDITIONAL ACTIVITIES

1. This essay can be paired with Walker Percy's "The Loss of the Creature" (p. 539). You might discuss Percy's idea of the "preformed complex" (para. 5) as a way of understanding Hawthorne's impressions of Niagara. Just as with the Percy essay, you might have your students collect advertisements from travel brochures and bring them to class for discussion. How are wonders of the natural world marketed? How does such marketing affect the way we experience tourist destinations?

2. You might also pair "My Visit to Niagara" with Manil Suri's "Keys to the Kingdom" (p. 227). Percy and Hawthorne write explicitly about wonders of the *natural* world (Niagara Falls in Hawthorne's case, the Grand Canyon in Percy's). Is it different when the tourist destination is not a natural wonder? If so, how is it different? It seems, at first glance, that Suri has simply "outgrown" Disneyland by the time he gets there, but if we note the way his mother's enjoyment of the theme park enables his own, we might discover parallels to the other texts.

## GENERATING WRITING

1. Have the students write a personal essay about their own visit to a famous place. Ask them to consider the things they'd heard or seen prior to their visit and how those things (movies, postcards, television shows, or popular songs) might have affected their ability to experience the place for themselves. Did their preconceived notions enhance, or interfere with, their ability to enjoy the visit? In what ways?

2. Have the students write an essay describing a place. Ask them to select a location to visit—a park or a department store, any place will do—where they can spend a few hours simply *observing*, taking notes on what they see, hear, and smell. They should use "My Visit to Niagara" (particularly the last part of the essay) as a model. Hawthorne picks a particular vantage point from which to view the falls, remaining there for much of the day. Your students should do the same, recording what they see and using their observations to produce an essay that re-creates the feeling of being in a particular place at a particular time.

## THE READER'S PRESENCE

1. In paragraph 10, Hawthorne uses words like *adventurers* and *children* to describe humans in the midst of nature. This suggests that we should view nature with a sense of humility and wonder: we should marvel at its splendor, aware of our insignificance and its beauty. He also suggests, by *hearing* the falls, that we should attempt to apprehend the things we encounter with all of our senses, not merely with our sense of sight. Most of us have a tendency toward the primacy of vision: Hawthorne seems to suggest that this is probably a mistake.

2. At the beginning of paragraph 2, Hawthorne says that he is "quite ashamed of [him]self." The idea seems to be that the reader will expect Hawthorne to be ashamed of himself for losing his composure—for being overly enthusiastic and running "like a madman, to the falls" (para. 2). However, Hawthorne seems to establish this expectation only to dash it, by saying that his enthusiasm was, in fact, "in a deathlike slumber" (para. 2). It may be that Hawthorne is attempting to build and dash the expectations of the reader in the same way that his own expectations were built up and then dashed, because what he is actually ashamed of is not losing his composure but, rather, maintaining it: he is, in fact, ashamed of his *lack* of enthusiasm. One should marvel at the majesty of nature. Hawthorne seems to yawn, and he is disappointed not only in the falls but in himself, when that is his response. Hawthorne overcomes his disappointment during the night, listening to the falls, and that changes his attitude toward the natural world as well as toward himself. He does not pretend to have the enthusiasm of some other "more fortunate spectators" (para. 8), but he does realize that it is possible to experience a sense of wonder at the place upon reflection.

3. Hawthorne relates the experience of seeing Niagara Falls for the first time by narrating his own experience: we see Niagara for the first time because he's seeing it for the first time. Percy, however, talks somewhat dispassionately about the experience of seeing the Grand Canyon: he talks about how one *might* experience it, or fail to experience it, without talking very much about his personal experience. Your students will have a variety of reactions: they will probably struggle with both essays. Which one they will find more informative and memorable is anybody's guess. The difficulty of this particular question is augmented by its structure: informative *and* memorable. In this case, students may find Percy's essay more informative because it appears to be more concerned with being strictly informative; Hawthorne's essay, though, is loaded with imagery and narration, which students might find more memorable.

# Siri Hustvedt
## EIGHT DAYS IN A CORSET

### APPROACHING THE ESSAY

Draw your students' attention to the fact that the author has cleverly framed this essay with images of mirrors: mirrors begin the essay and mirrors conclude the essay. "Framing" is a rhetorical strategy that imposes a cohesive structure on an essay by containing it. A mirror is doubly useful here because it is, in itself, a kind of framing device. It frames a reflected image much in the same way that this essay frames images.

As we come to learn from the series of anecdotes, Siri Hustvedt assumes a number of personae that are influenced and even created by her clothing: Jamesian heroine, movie star lover, the "manly" character at Halloween, defiled transvestite, elegant lady, and stooped scholar. Examine these roles in depth with your class. You may want to compare and contrast some of them. For instance, Hustvedt assumes two roles as a cross-dresser: wearing high heels and a red jumpsuit, she is mistaken for a male transvestite, and, at a Halloween party, she intentionally dresses as a man. Compare the reactions—by the man who thinks she is a transvestite and by the author herself—to these identities. What do these reactions suggest? Why is a "man" dressed as a woman so violently debased, while a woman dressed as a man feels confident and attracts a positive reaction?

A close look at paragraph 6 reveals a great deal about how the clothes women wear often suggest class and class expectations. The author describes the somewhat pleasing transformation as a result of wearing the corset. The corset, however, is only part of the Victorian package: what are some of the other items of the

Victorian female package and how does the author feel about the total uniform? What, too, is the role of class in the Victorian milieu of Henry James's *Washington Square*? What does the author mean when she says, "No one can scrub floors in a hoop" (para. 7)? How did class "bind" rich women? What does Hustvedt mean when she says "[the hoop's] restriction meant luxury" (para. 7)? How did the extras that were cast as maids dress and what seem to be their attitudes? In general, do style changes affect the wealthy or the poor to a greater degree?

You may want to discuss the author's voice in this essay: What is her attitude toward clothing, especially women's clothing? Look specifically at paragraph 5 (at the Buddhist monastery and nunnery) and paragraphs 11 and 12. In paragraph 11, Hustvedt says, the experience of being mistaken for a male transvestite, "gave me a sudden insight into . . . the often hazy line between femininity and its parodic double." What does Hustvedt imply about gender, especially for women?

## ADDITIONAL ACTIVITIES

1. Hustvedt says of her daughter: "My daughter dresses up. . . . She is always somebody else" (para. 14). Encourage students to share their personal memories of dressing up when they were children. Why did they try on other people's clothes? Whose clothes did they try on? Discuss who felt more restricted, men or women, when they were children playing dress-up? At what age did they become aware of gender restrictions? Which is the more pejorative term, "tomboy" or "sissy"? Why? Does this pejoration suggest sexual denigration? If it does, is it against males or females?

2. Language, like dress, imposes cultural roles in many subtle ways. Ask students for definitions—both denotative and connotative—for the following pairs of terms: major/majorette; governor/governess; master/mistress; tailor/seamstress; chef/cook; gentleman/lady. What are the cultural expectations for each role? How is the relationship between words and dress similar? different? What are the restrictions imposed by both?

## GENERATING WRITING

1. At the end of her essay, Hustvedt says, "Wearing clothes is an act of the imagination, an invention of self, a fiction" (para. 15). Have students write a three- to five-page personal narrative on what their clothes say about them. Through their choices of clothing, what self have they invented? They should approach this assignment using specific examples to define their style. What does their style say about them?

2. Henry James often wrote about the cultural mores, passions, and repressions of the American aristocracy of the nineteenth century. Have students research the clothing for both men and women of this time period and class structure and write an essay that suggests how costume might reflect or shape the zeitgeist of that period, or both. (The Internet has many interesting sites that look at the relationship between culture and dress in different milieus.)

## THE READER'S PRESENCE

1. The second paragraph of the Approaching the Essay section of this entry discusses Hustvedt's transformations.

2. A mirror allows Hustvedt to see her reflection; it is literally an image into which the real person can check her appearance for things like "blemishes and dirty hair" (para. 3). Figuratively speaking, however, the mirror suggests "a ghost double" (para. 3): it is not real, it is noncorporeal and yet it is there, staring her in the face. It reminds her of herself (we don't see ourselves most of the time). It also reminds her of her mortality (her "ghost").

    Surprisingly, Hustvedt finds the corset slightly erotic, like an "embrace" (para. 4). It is feminine and allows her to feel like the heroines she has read about. She does understand, however, that the corset is part of the uniform of femininity that kept women in submission to men. It ruined their bodies by crippling women and even causing them to lose consciousness at times. It exaggerated the shape of a woman, perpetuating her sexual objectification. Hustvedt notes, "The cultural trappings of sex are overwhelming. We make them and live them and are them" (para. 5), yet she "fell prey to [the corset's] charms" (para. 4) because it "catapulted [her] into another time and another aesthetic" (para. 3). The author addresses our ability to transform ourselves through the imagination, the realization that others know what we look like more than we do, and that clothes articulate not who we are but who we want to be. Her personal examples address these issues successfully; we identify with her observations.

3. Hustvedt brings life to her story by personifying corsets and discussing mirrors as places or "sites," rather than objects. She avoids tired clichés and instead offers interesting similes and metaphors: a corset is like "a permanent embrace" (para. 4), while hoopskirts are "our private balloons" (para. 7). Like her "ghost double" (para. 3) in the mirror, Hustvedt's similes and metaphors have a duality about them. An embrace can be both restraining and loving. A balloon suggests both restriction (living in a bubble) and freedom (flying in a hot air balloon or children playing with balloons). This playfulness and flight of fancy is what Hustvedt discovers in the transformative power of clothes.

4. Dave Barry ("Beauty and the Beast," p. 315) is not concerned so much with clothing, specifically, but his argument is similar to Hustvedt's in that—despite arguing that the pressure on women comes from external cultural forces, like Barbie—according to Barry, women are concerned with their appearance and put themselves through all manner of hell in order to look good. Hustvedt similarly acknowledges that, although the corset is vilified by modern feminists, women of the nineteenth century were in favor of the use of corsets, even though physicians (mostly men, at the time) were against them for all sorts of health reasons. Hustvedt even likes the corset, to a certain extent. Therefore, in a way, both Barry and Hustvedt agree that—despite all arguments to the contrary—much of the pressure on any

given woman to look a certain way comes from the woman herself. Hustvedt is more comprehensive in her exploration of social expectation, though, exploring some of the ways in which, for women, clothing is a costume, almost as though it's part of some kind of cultural role-playing game: a woman in a certain outfit might look beautiful or terrible, but never does a man say, "You look like yourself" (para. 10). Dressed as a man, Hustvedt felt more confident and powerful (para. 11). Mistaken for a male transvestite, though, she was insulted by a man she walked past on the street, giving her an insight into "the venom" that appearances can produce. You might ask the students why they think it's okay, in some people's minds, as well as in the fashion world, for a woman to wear masculine clothes, but a man in women's clothing is practically regarded as vermin.

Your students are likely to have different opinions about which author makes the more engaging and convincing argument about the relationship among looks, cultural expectations, and identity. Chances are that many of them will prefer Barry's article, because it's shorter and it's funny. But when compared to Hustvedt's piece, Barry's argument is a bit simple. Hustvedt has clearly put more thought into the issue. That doesn't necessarily mean that she's right and Barry's wrong, but your students should be able, at least, to see that her argument is much more complex: her interpretation of the relationship among appearance and gender roles and social expectations is, in this case, much more nuanced than Barry's. Much of this has to do with audience. Barry is not *trying* to make a nuanced argument. His piece was a humor column for the newspaper. It is meant to be thought provoking but on a limited scale: its primary purposes are to get a laugh and to persuade the reader that Barbie—and the popular culture at large—has a negative impact on women's self-esteem, and that this probably is not such a good thing. Hustvedt is writing a much more sophisticated piece for an audience that expects a more sophisticated argument. "Eight Days in a Corset" would be out of place in a newspaper, particularly if it ran as a humor column. Similarly, "Beauty and the Beast" would probably strike Hustvedt's readers as a bit of low-brow humor, rather than authentic *thought*. In a sense, Barry's attitude toward women and appearance—that women worry too much about their looks, probably because of Barbie—exemplifies the kind of thinking that strikes Hustvedt as comic and sad, precisely because it is too simple.

# Stephen King
## EVERYTHING YOU NEED TO KNOW ABOUT WRITING SUCCESSFULLY — IN TEN MINUTES

### APPROACHING THE ESSAY

Stephen King's essay is light but entertaining. "Everything You Need to Know About Writing Successfully" is both a riff on and an instance of a resolutely practical American attitude toward the world, as expressed in self-help books, in how-to manuals, and on matchbook covers that promise to teach you how-to-draw-in-only-eight-lessons! To be sure, King is having fun with these corny claims; but he also borrows this popular form to demystify writing, to insist that writing is a form of communication that can be successfully taught.

The form of the essay is also an indirect response to critics disturbed by King's chosen genres or by his phenomenal commercial success. Plain-spoken King refuses to believe that "entertaining fiction and serious ideas do not overlap," an idea he attributes to "pernicious critics" (item 7, para. 28). Instead, King sidesteps metaphysics ("We're not talking about good or bad here. I'm . . . telling you how to get your stuff published"; item 1, para. 20), insisting that reading and writing are *communal* activities that can be judged by their success or failure in the world. Not right away, perhaps; but if every reader agrees that a particular plot device doesn't work, or a character isn't believable, "change it." Alternatively, if particular writers consistently meet with commercial success, it is, for King at least, evidence that "they are clearly reaching a great many someones who want what they have" (item 1, para 20).

It's an argument that is hard to deny, just as the deceptive simplicity of King's form goes hand in hand with his unerring sense of drama and rising action. This sense is evident even here, in the way King gives his essay quick dramatic pressure by insisting—and then successfully demonstrating—that he can beat the clock, revealing his secrets within the strict time limit imposed by his title.

### ADDITIONAL ACTIVITIES

1. According to King, if a number of readers agree in their criticism, writers ought to change whatever isn't working, but if no two readers agree in their criticism, writers may safely ignore all suggestions. Distribute sample pages from two or three student papers or stories to each member of the class, with instructions to suggest changes. How much agreement is there among members of the class? Is there sufficient consensus to give the writer confident directions for making changes?

2. "Remove every extraneous word" (item 4). Does King's dictum hold up when applied to successful, even classic American writers? Again, distribute to students unidentified sample pages from stories by writers as different, say, as Edgar Allan Poe, Eudora Welty, Raymond Carver, and Alice Munro,

along with directions to eliminate all extraneous words. Compare the texts that result with the originals. Do students agree that the texts have been improved? What kinds of writing were judged extraneous, and why?

## GENERATING WRITING

1. Hand back to the class students' first drafts of a story or an essay. Direct half the class to expand their drafts by 300 words; direct the other half to shorten their drafts by an equal amount. Compare the results.
2. Peer review: have pairs of students edit drafts of each other's essays. Each student should then revise his or her own essay in the light of the peer review, submitting both the marked-up draft and final revision to the teacher. Grades for the essays should take into account both the caliber of students' peer reviews, as well as their revisions of their own essays.

## THE READER'S PRESENCE

1. King justifies his inclusion of sections I through III in paragraph 17: "And I told you the story above not to make myself sound like a character out of a Horatio Alger novel but to make a point: I saw, I listened, and I learned." In these sections, he models the way he wants his reader to take his advice. The only rule of his own that he breaks in this piece is number 4, "Remove every extraneous word." Multiple introductions to an essay are hardly necessary. King flaunts the authority, the celebrity, and the wealth he has earned from his writing; he does this not out of arrogance but to prove that number 8 is most important to him at this stage of his life: "Ask yourself frequently, 'Am I having fun?'"
2. King can't help but play on his reader's fears. Almost everyone who reads an essay that promises to teach writing—successfully or unsuccessfully—in ten minutes is harboring a secret hope that his or her inner writer will emerge. One of the ways King taunts his reader is to ask rhetorical questions that sound foolish when stripped down to their simplest meaning: "You want to get up on a soapbox and preach? Fine" (para. 25); "You want to write a story? Fine" (para. 26). He also ridicules someone who is like the reader, but is not the reader: the "dimwit" who sends out the wrong kinds of stories to the wrong kinds of magazines, in "ignorant fashion" (item 6, para. 27). One of the basic human fears is the fear of being found out as a fraud. King plays on the edge of encouraging aspiring writers and exposing them as pretenders.
3. The answer to this question will depend on the writers the students choose to evaluate. All works in this anthology—all works of literature, in fact—are guilty of the occasional infelicity or outright error; the trick is to make such errors in the cause of the greater whole. In successful writing, mistakes usually go unnoticed, or, if detected, are quickly understood and forgiven.
4. In "George Orwell on the Four Reasons for Writing" (p. 538), Orwell's "desire to share an experience which one feels is valuable" (para. 3) could, in King's estimation, lead to "publication and money"—that is, if Orwell wrote about

**169**

the experience in a way that would entertain his readers. King would probably advise Orwell that in order to sell, "serious fiction" needs to be entertaining, and that writing for "political purposes" should be avoided unless political ideas are put forth in a way that "serve[s] your story, not the other way around" (para. 28).

# Maxine Hong Kingston
## NO NAME WOMAN

### APPROACHING THE ESSAY

"No Name Woman" blends fact and fantasy in a way that can be dizzying to the reader encountering Maxine Hong Kingston's prose for the first time. For this reason, it works best to start by making sure that students understand the essay's overall structure. Have them tell you where Kingston's mother's story ends and Kingston's versions start. Also see if they can identify the versions of her aunt's story that Kingston considers in her attempt to understand the truth.

The truth, always problematic in such autobiographical narratives, is especially tricky in "No Name Woman." Make sure your students don't make the mistake of referring to the mother's account as "the truth" and Kingston's account as "fantasy," just because Kingston is open about the speculativeness of her contributions to this family story. Encourage students to question the mother's veracity. It might be easiest if they start by recalling the doubts that Kingston raises about her mother's story. Then, if they can't think of further doubts to raise, you might lead them to think about the mother's motive for telling this story. Because she tells Kingston the family secret as a cautionary tale, timed to coincide with Kingston's first menses, she may have altered the story to make its cautionary effect more powerful. And a tale whose moral is the consequences of one's actions works best when the consequences follow directly upon the actions. How else could one explain these improbable lines, spoken by the mother and unblinkingly accepted by Kingston: "The village had also been counting. On the night the baby was to be born the villagers raided our house" (para. 4)? (You might point out—or one of your students may notice—the similarity between the mother's technique and the villagers': both can be charged with speeding up the circling of events to make their message clearer.)

Alternatively, students may consider the mother's story more suspect than Kingston's versions. After all, the mother has an ulterior motive for the tale she tells, whereas Kingston seems to be genuinely searching for the truth, using every bit of data on Chinese culture she can find to help her reconstruct what really happened. And Kingston characterizes the two generations—her mother's and her own—in this way: "They must try to confuse their offspring as well, who, I suppose, threaten them in similar ways—always trying to get things straight, always trying to name the unspeakable" (para. 11). Still, it's not accurate to draw a sharp line between Kingston's mother, as an inscrutable, superstitious Chinese woman, and Kingston, as the American-born child who sheds the objective light of truth on her mother's confusing stories. Kingston is neither Chinese nor American, but rather Chinese American, and both traditions have shaped her identity and outlook. You might have your students identify elements in her stories that non-Chinese people might consider superstitions but that Kingston doesn't question. In short, do everything you can during class discussion to make sure that your students don't construct neat little boxes for their ideas about this complex and rewarding text.

## ADDITIONAL ACTIVITIES

1. During class discussion you might find it useful to ask what Kingston means when she writes that her mother's stories "tested our strength to establish realities" (para. 10). Ask students how her mother would have meant that statement, if, indeed, one can attribute its sentiment to her. Then ask what else it might mean, in the context of the story she tells in "No Name Woman." How else does that story function for Kingston? for her mother? in general? How closely would their explanations of the function of stories coincide? On what points would they disagree?
2. Gender is a primary motif in "No Name Woman." Judging from the evidence in this piece, how would your students characterize Chinese expectations of men? of women? How much do these gender stereotypes determine the events of the story about Kingston's aunt? Have students describe the double bind that these stereotypes create for Kingston. Have them describe the double bind that Kingston imagines them to create for her aunt.

## GENERATING WRITING

1. Call your students' attention to the opening line of "No Name Woman": "'You must not tell anyone,' my mother said, 'what I am about to tell you.'" Help them unfold the implications of that tantalizing opening. Among all the other observations and inferences they might mention upon reading that sentence, they should notice that it sets up two doubles for Kingston: her aunt, whose act of rebellion is mirrored in the disobedience necessary to writing "No Name Woman"; and her mother, who, like Kingston, gives voice to the family secret. Have your students write an essay in which they pursue this doubling motif throughout the essay.
2. Kingston identifies her aunt's sin as that of individuality: "Children and lovers have no singularity here, but my aunt used a secret voice, a separate attentiveness" (para. 31). Have students write an essay exploring the tension between the individual and the community, also figured as a tension between individualism and duty to one's family, in Kingston's piece. Among the many passages to which you'll want to direct attention on this issue is the birth scene.

171

## THE READER'S PRESENCE

1. & 2.  These questions are meant to help students puzzle out "the truth" in this intricate and fantastic story. Some students will want to accept the mother's account as "the truth" and the narrator's account as fantasy; others will suspect that the mother made up her version or embellished it. For a full discussion of ways to handle this issue in class, see the Approaching the Essay section of this entry.

3.  The narrator of "No Name Woman" (a mixture of fiction and memoir) sets forth the problem of intergenerational communication in the first sentence: "'You must not tell anyone . . . what I am about to tell you.'" The story that follows is told under the prohibition of speech, a theme that recurs in the story of the nameless aunt and in the framing story of the niece's uneasy relationship with her immigrant parents. The narrator hungers for the story of her aunt; she needs to know what happened to the woman she will never meet. In the story of her aunt's horrible death, the narrator learns (or imagines) what her parents left behind when they came to America—the ghosts and the crimes and the losses—and what they brought with them: her aunt's "weeping ghost . . . waits silently by the water to pull down a substitute" (para. 49), taking form in Kingston's writing. For N. Scott Momaday ("The Way to Rainy Mountain," p. 504), as for Kingston, there is an undeniable—if at times undeniably difficult—bond between the generations of one family, regardless of the mutations of language over time and place. Richard Rodriguez ("Aria: A Memoir of a Bilingual Childhood," p. 187), in contrast, feels himself losing his parents as he masters English and loses Spanish; he wants to retain his use of Spanish as the intimate language of family. Rodriguez has a romantic view of the purity or immediacy of his first language; Kingston sees the language she learns from her parents as already tainted by the very process of transference.

# Dan Koeppel
## How to Fall 35,000 Feet — And Survive

### APPROACHING THE ESSAY

Although the ostensible purpose of Dan Koeppel's "How to Fall 35,000 Feet—And Survive" is to provide instructions for surviving a free fall from 35,000 feet, it is primarily an entertainment piece: few people will ever have—or want—the opportunity to act out the instructions he provides, and even fewer would be likely to remember those instructions were the opportunity to arise. That said, the how-to format of the article is an interesting way to approach unusual subject matter, and thus "How to Fall 35,000 Feet—And Survive" provides an excellent model for both the how-to article and the research paper. By choosing unusual subject matter, Koeppel demonstrates that research writing doesn't have to be dull. By delivering the results of his research as a set of instructions, he demonstrates that instructions don't have to be dull, either. For this, "How to Fall 35,000 Feet—And Survive" could just as accurately be called "How to Write a Research Paper or a Set of Instructions—And Stay Awake."

There are a few essential points to go over with your students. One is the decision to write the article in second person. In general, instructions are written in the imperative: recipes, for example (marinate 10 oz. fish filet five to seven hours, preheat oven to 350 degrees, bake 20 minutes). Koeppel opts to include the "you," making the essay more readable, more lively, and less formal than a simple set of instructions. Use of second person also tends to make the prose feel more immediate: it puts the reader in the text. It's a particularly effective device for an essay of this kind because the subject matter is exciting. The reader is immediately involved, and the suspense keeps you reading. The immediacy and suspense are further heightened by the decision to write the article in present tense, as if the reader were falling as he or she reads. In paragraph 8, Koeppel informs us that, were we to fall from the average commercial airliner's cruising altitude (35,000 feet), we would almost have time to read the entire article.

The article is split into four sections, each one headed with a time and corresponding height: 6:59:00 a.m., 35,000 feet; 7:00:20 a.m.; and so on. Koeppel begins each section with a description of the circumstances the reader would find him- or herself in: section three, 7:02:19 a.m., 1,000 feet, begins "Given your starting altitude, you'll be just about ready to hit the ground as you begin this section" (para. 17). After establishing the situation, Koeppel proceeds with the instructions themselves. Then he transitions to his research, providing information about studies that have been done (para. 16), stories of fall survivors (paras. 5 and 6, para. 21, and so on), and other assorted trivia associated with surviving falls (in paragraph 14, we learn that the world's tallest bridge, in France, is 891 feet tall).

## ADDITIONAL ACTIVITY

1. The transitions from narrative to research are nicely done and might provide a useful model for students. It will not readily occur to them that what they are reading is, in fact, "research," simply because most of them have probably come to associate the mere word *research* with boredom. You might spend some time talking about the transitions, as well as the research itself. If you can get the students excited talking about the information in the article, you may be able to make a step (if only a tiny one) toward disabusing them of the notion that research must be boring. Ask them what topics they might *choose* to research if left to their own devices. Surely they've been curious about something—anything—that had nothing to do with school, something they researched on their own, if only by Googling it. Every now and again, you might be able to glean some ideas for research papers based on what they say in response to this question.

## GENERATING WRITING

1. Have the students write a set of instructions that is also entertaining. They can choose to write about something they enjoy doing or something they've never done, as long as it is something one *does*, for which there is a procedure. It could even be something invented or something one would not typically do, such as alligator wrestling. This will probably require them to do some research, although not necessarily: you might have a student, for example, who knows how to quilt and who will write instructions for making a quilt. If you want to make research an integral component of the assignment, you might need to generate a pool of topics from which students can choose.

2. Have the students write a research paper on an unusual topic. In keeping with Koeppel's essay, you might pick survival stories: people who have been set adrift and lived to tell the tale, like Captain Bligh, or people who have survived dangerous situations in the wild, like Aron Ralston, the subject of the film, *127 Hours*. In addition to researching anecdotal evidence, you might encourage your students to consult survival guides. If they'd like to take a more whimsical approach, Max Brooks's *Zombie Survival Guide* might be an interesting alternative to explore. The point is only to find some fun or fascinating way to get the students engaged in research. Use the assignment to teach them how to write from sources. Have them cite their sources in MLA format. They're unlikely to find that part of the assignment *fun*, but they might be more receptive to learning citation if it is in service of something unusual: something they're not generally used to associating with "homework."

## THE READER'S PRESENCE

1. It is unlikely that Koeppel sincerely intends to provide instructions for surviving a fall from 35,000 feet. More likely, his aim is to write an unusual piece about an interesting bit of trivia. Addressing the reader directly makes the piece feel immediate: it draws the reader in, builds suspense, and makes the reading feel urgent. This, in turn, makes for a very readable and entertaining piece. Candidly speaking, Koeppel writes for money. One way to write work that sells is to make reading it feel urgent and fun.

2. Koeppel's research is interspersed within the larger narrative of the imagined fall. He weaves the two threads together by using his historical facts and research as anecdotal evidence in support of the various survival strategies he recommends. This makes the essay more persuasive and gives the reader something to think about between the specific times that he uses to head each of the four sections of the essay.

3. Joan Acocella's essay ("A Few Too Many," p. 283) is a leisurely read. Koeppel's is more urgent. To convey this sense of urgency, Koeppel often relies on shorter sentences or even sentence fragments. His diction is straightforward and easy to understand. If there is a term that is not commonplace,

he explains it. Again, this has much to do with audience. Acocella's writing for the *New Yorker*. She's addressing a literate audience that is interested in good writing and open to a variety of subjects. Koeppel's article was published in *Popular Mechanics*, a magazine whose readers are interested in a specific type of subject matter ("mechanics," and all the things that might mean). Those readers are attracted to the magazine for the information it is likely to contain. They're not necessarily reading exclusively for leisure, so an entertainment piece has to grab their attention and keep it and it has to be full of the kinds of information they are likely to be interested in. Acocella's readers didn't pick up the magazine to find out about hangovers: they picked it up simply for the pleasure of reading it. So Acocella can play a little more, take her time, throw in any type of information she wants, as long as the article is reasonably well written.

# Steven D. Levitt and Stephen J. Dubner
## WHAT SHOULD YOU WORRY ABOUT?

### APPROACHING THE ESSAY

Levitt is known for applying economic theory to subjects that are not traditionally the focus of economic study, and one of the first things you might have to do is explain that when Dubner and Levitt say "economics," they do not necessarily mean the study of the economy. Although the authors make some effort to get this idea across in the second paragraph, when they say that most people hear the word *economics* and think of "incomprehensible charts," it still may not be entirely clear to your students that the "huge piles of data" to which the authors refer do not have to be piles of *economic* data. Levitt and Dubner are only talking about using the principles of economics to study *any* statistical information. Some, if not most, of your students will understand this intuitively, but it might be worth making sure it is understood explicitly before you proceed. After that, the discussion is likely to be centered on the subject of cultural anxieties: the fear and handwringing that Dubner and Levitt discuss later in the essay. "What Should You Worry About?" is an optimistic piece: indeed, it never really directly answers its own question, instead suggesting that trends like global warming, while real and perhaps dangerous, are not the apocalyptic problems that popular culture makes of them. Ask the students how Levitt and Dubner put global warming (and shark attacks) in perspective. How do statistics illuminate risk? How does comparing disparate sets of data (like horse manure in turn-of-the-century New York City and global warming now, or the number of shark attacks versus the number of elephant attacks in any given year) put our fears in perspective?

## ADDITIONAL ACTIVITIES

1. Statistics can be misleading. For example, let us assume that Levitt and Dubner's figures regarding shark-attack and elephant-attack fatalities are correct. Does that really mean that one has a greater chance of being killed by an elephant than by a shark? If we take the total of all the humans currently living on Earth, perhaps. But, in the United States, at least, many more people live near coastlines (and swim in waters with dense shark populations) than interact with free-moving elephants. It stands to reason, then, that many more Americans risk shark attack than elephant attack. To say that one has more to fear from elephants than from sharks is therefore a misrepresentation of the facts. A person who swims at the beach once or twice a year might never interact with an elephant in a way that could get him or her killed. Even if such a swimmer only has a one in a billion chance of being attacked by a shark, he or she is still a million times more likely to be attacked by a shark than an elephant when he or she never goes anywhere near elephants. Statistics can be presented in ways that are misleading: it might be worth spending some class time discussing how and why.

2. You might want to spend some time discussing the issue of global warming as compared with the problem of horse manure in Levitt and Dubner's essay. Does the comparison between a problem that affected a single city and its surrounding area at a particular point in time and global climate change make sense? Cars and public transportation may have done something to ameliorate the first problem: What sorts of technological developments might ameliorate the second? How is the issue complicated by the fact that it is a global, rather than a metropolitan, one? Given the evidence of global warming and the difficulties of reaching international agreements on alternative energies and limits on greenhouse emissions, does Levitt and Dubner's optimism seem a bit too rosy?

## GENERATING WRITING

1. Have the students research statistics surrounding some common fears—car accidents or plane crashes, for example—and write a report summarizing their findings.

2. Drawing on the discussions that spring from Additional Activity questions 1 and 2, ask the students to write a critical essay evaluating Levitt and Dubner's conclusions. How might their statistics be misleading? There is certainly room for comparison between New York's late nineteenth- and early twentieth-century manure problem and our current anxieties concerning climate change: On one level, new technologies could potentially improve the situation. But on many other levels, the comparison is a tenuous one. Ask your students to explain why the comparison is tenuous and to draw some conclusions of their own about whether the comparison is valid. Some students may feel that, despite the difficulties that may arise (the difficulties of coordinating international efforts to combat the problem, for example),

Levitt and Dubner are essentially correct: human ingenuity can and—in times of crisis—most likely will find a solution. Others may be skeptical. Ask the students to justify their opinions in a short critical essay.

3. You might consider having the students write a longer research assignment, exploring possible solutions to global warming. You could ask them to keep their essay grounded, like Levitt and Dubner's, in statistics and hard data. It will be a useful exercise for future research assignments and argumentative papers, where the use of statistics is often the key to a successfully supported thesis. You might also ask the students to consider more nuanced aspects of the problem: for example, a student might come upon statistics suggesting that hydroelectric power could efficiently provide energy for the entire world. Upon discovering such data, it is unlikely that the average First Year Writing student will intuitively follow up by looking into how much money would have to be invested in developing hydroelectric plants, or where those plants would be, or how the political situations in those areas might impact development and production. Many students will also be unlikely to factor in the degree to which the current global economy is dependent on oil and oil products: the number of people who would lose their jobs if we suddenly stopped drilling for oil probably isn't a concern that will readily occur to them. The idea of this sort of research assignment would not necessarily be to yield well-organized, well-argued papers. It might be more productive if, each time your students come back to you with something like a packaged solution based on a set of statistical data, you suggest another direction they might explore or an aspect of the problem they have overlooked. The point is to complicate the ideas for them so that they can learn the infinite variety of ways that statistics can be manipulated or selectively chosen to make an argument.

## THE READER'S PRESENCE

1. Levitt and Dubner use shark attacks as an example because everyone is afraid of them, yet shark attacks are incredibly rare. When someone is attacked by a shark, it's all over the news, and the threat is exaggerated simply because shark attacks provoke a very visceral sort of fear. The kinds of statistical analysis common to economics reveal that the risk is actually very low: more people are killed by elephants every year. The numbers are convincing as far as they go, but it's worth noting that not everyone lives near wild elephants or works with elephants at the zoo. So statistically elephants are much more likely to attack humans than sharks are, and those attacks are much more likely to be fatal. However, the average American doesn't come into contact with elephants, so the statistics are perhaps misleading when taken at face value.

2. There was a time, in New York City, when the horse-manure problem seemed insurmountable. The invention of the automobile eliminated that problem. Levitt and Dubner argue that humans have a way of overcoming adversity,

suggesting that technological advances that will eliminate global warming (or at least reduce the risk of catastrophe) are probably on the way.

3. Michael Lewis ("The Mansion: A Subprime Parable," p. 479) argues that the housing crisis was a consequence of Americans' desire to elevate themselves: people bought houses that were out of their price range because they wanted to be — or at least appear to be — wealthy. When the market crashed, it quickly became clear that only the wealthy could afford to live as the wealthy do. Therefore, according to Lewis, Americans underestimated the risk: they felt comfortable when the economy was booming and acted without considering the possibility that it would not *always* be. Lewis is offering a critique of cultural attitudes that gets to the heart of the American obsession with upward mobility at the heart of the American Dream. He might be right, in a sense, too. But he's not that interested in numbers. Levitt and Dubner would be more likely to look at statistics, to match columns of numbers listing people's incomes and the prices of their houses, before they made any assumptions about underlying cultural attitudes. By the same token, they would probably line up the numbers to rate the risk of a person purchasing a home that was out of his or her price range. They probably wouldn't be alarmist about the housing crisis, either: throughout history, it was not the economic catastrophe that many people thought it to be. Compared to the Soviet famine of 1932–33, perhaps it was not a crisis at all.

# Michael Lewis
## THE MANSION: A SUBPRIME PARABLE

### APPROACHING THE ESSAY

In "The Mansion: A Subprime Parable," Michael Lewis begins by sharing his personal experience with mortgage and housing trouble and from there extrapolates his story to the housing problem across the country, locating the problems in some unlikely places.

Early in the article, Lewis states that "middle-class people have homes; upper-class people have monuments" (para. 8). He goes on to explain that the reason he wanted to live in a big house was that he wanted to live as an upper-class member of society. He always *perceived* himself as upper middle class, but when viewing a mansion he realizes that he has never been "upper" anything. He's always been middle. So begins his quest to class climb; in order to get to that elite upper class, he rents an enormous home in New Orleans that's selling for around ten million dollars. Needless to say, it's out of his price range. Yet, for Lewis, this need for a bigger house is a uniquely American need. He believes that Americans, just before the housing crisis, bought houses they couldn't afford for two reasons: (1)

to appear that they had more money and were more successful than they really were, and (2) because they could sell the house for more money and make some cash. According to Lewis, it was ironic that when the housing market crashed, Americans didn't blame themselves. He writes, "However terrible the sins of the financial markets, they're merely a reflection of a cultural predisposition. To blame the people who lent the money for the real estate boom is like blaming the crack dealers for creating addicts" (para. 24). Of course, many people do blame drug dealers for drug addicts, and even those who don't would generally concede that the drug dealers are at least partially to blame for the drug problem in the United States. Does this analogy seem a convincing one to your students? Why or why not? Lewis argues that if people hadn't lusted after bigger homes, they wouldn't have been dealing with corrupt mortgage brokers in the first place. In a sense, he is fair and even-tempered, spreading the blame around, instead of railing against the corporate powers. You might ask your students what the overall effect is: who is typically blamed for the housing situation? What does Lewis show us about these typical claims?

Lewis ends his article with his own story of renting a mansion far outside his price range (paying nearly $13,000 a month). By the end of the piece, the mansion has taken on a life of its own. It shuts off the air-conditioning when it wants; it traps Lewis's child in an elevator; it calls the police, signaling a break-in. All of this Lewis conveys with a modest humor, yet at the core of his argument is the idea that the house doesn't want him there; Lewis and his family are not the type of people who should be living in a mansion. They're not wealthy. They don't belong. Of course, Lewis is projecting here, personifying the mansion and endowing it with his own feelings, but the projection makes sense. Lewis and his family don't "fit," and therefore it feels like they are strangers in the house, alien to it: they need to get out. This, Lewis implicitly argues, is what hundreds of thousands of Americans have done as well: they bought themselves up a class, tried to be something they were not, and in the end got booted back to where they came from. This section of the article gives a thorough treatment of personification and should show students how to use figurative language even in a nonfiction piece (where they normally believe figurative language to be the grounds of creative writing alone).

When Lewis ends the article, he and his family are leaving the mansion for smaller, more reasonable, and more affordable housing. Students, especially those who may have experienced some familial problems during the housing crisis, will be interested in these issues; others may find it difficult to engage (because they most likely don't own homes), but really the piece is about responsibility, and with that theme in mind, they should easily be interested.

## ADDITIONAL ACTIVITIES

1. Ask students to interview a parent or someone else who owns a home. You might ask them to interview at least three people, possibly even from different classes (upper, middle, working). Students should find out how the housing market and its problems over the last three or so years have affected these people. They should report back with a page or two of written interview.

2. At several points, Lewis considers how his children are handling the situation. At first, the children are giddy; after some time in the house, they don't react the same way and they don't seem to feel that they fit in the house. Why is this? Ask students to come up with a definition of class in America. Is it how much money one makes? what type of job one does? a more complex feeling?

## GENERATING WRITING

1. Ask students to write a three- to four-page essay in which they research the housing crisis and find out what led to it. The goal of this assignment is for students to understand that many elements led to the housing problems and loan difficulties faced by many Americans. They should be writing a paper that approaches the housing crisis from different angles. Require at least five different sources for such an essay.

2. Have the students write an essay in which they give a personal narrative of the housing crisis. They can either create this narrative from interviews they may have completed or use their own family's trials with loans and over-large mortgages. Do they find anything similar to what Michael Lewis experienced? If their own family has had a similar experience, what different factors were involved when buying out of their price range? How was their family's decision similar to or different from Lewis's decisions?

## THE READER'S PRESENCE

1. A parable is a story that typically tries to teach its audience something. Often, parables have somewhat fantastical things occurring, so it's no surprise here that the house takes on human qualities. How the notion of parable informs the essay is by warning people: don't spend out of your price range, don't buy a house you can't afford, and don't be so concerned with looking "upper class."

2. Lewis believes Americans are drawn to big homes because those homes help project an air of success, are markers for upper-class living, and often are the envy of those with smaller homes. For Lewis, part of the housing crisis was caused by people buying large homes they could not afford, causing them to default on loans. Lewis believes that, at least in part, this need to appear wealthy and upper class drove the housing crisis.

3. N. Scott Momaday ("The Way to Rainy Mountain," p. 504) deals with a social world wherein spiritualism and the land are linked. Lewis deals with a world that is artificially constructed: a world of big houses, of class differences, and money. Momaday is concerned with tradition and culture. For Lewis, American culture is explicitly linked to social constructs of wealth and class.

# Abraham Lincoln
## GETTYSBURG ADDRESS

### APPROACHING THE ESSAY

The Gettysburg Address is one of President Abraham Lincoln's best-known speeches, written for the consecration of the Gettysburg battleground. The Battle of Gettysburg, a turning point in the Civil War, marked the beginning of the end of the Confederacy. Lincoln's speech is brief but powerful. He admits that words cannot add any importance to the site of the battle, saying, "The brave men, living and dead, who struggled here, have consecrated it, far above our poor power to add or detract" (para. 3). The speech also acknowledges that despite the great losses that Americans suffered, there is still much fighting ahead of them. He works to inspire his audience to forge ahead at this "great task" and gather their resolve so that "these dead shall not have died in vain" (para. 3).

Have students examine the way that Lincoln uses language throughout the speech. The Gettysburg Address is almost devoid of religious sentiment. Instead, he invokes the language of the Declaration of Independence (p. 695). Have students read the Declaration of Independence and highlight all of the instances where Lincoln uses Jefferson's language in the Gettysburg Address. Why does he use this language? Who is his audience, and what is the larger purpose of his speech? Why might this language particularly appeal to his audience?

### ADDITIONAL ACTIVITIES

1. If you have computer access in your classroom, either present or have students read the Gettysburg Address PowerPoint Presentation (www.norvig.com/Gettysburg/). Have them compare the language of the speech and the PowerPoint presentation. How has technology changed the way we communicate information to one another and the way that language is used? This would be a good opportunity to discuss the effectiveness and power of descriptive language.

2. In class, show a portion of Ken Burns's PBS documentary *The Civil War* to give students a historical context for Lincoln's speech. Episode Five, "The Universe of Battle," begins with a detailed recounting of the battle at Gettysburg and goes on to describe subsequent battles as well as the social upheaval in Northern states. More information on the documentary, as well as classroom activities and images from the Civil War, can be found at (www.pbs.org/civilwar/).

### GENERATING WRITING

1. Have students write an essay in which they compare the tone, audience, and language in the Gettysburg Address and in Lincoln's Second Inaugural

Address. Ask them to research the major events of the Civil War and place each speech in its historical context. Who is Lincoln addressing in each speech? What emotional appeals does he make in each address, and why—given the events of the war and his intended audience—might these be different in each speech?

2. Have students research other presidential speeches in which the American people are asked to make sacrifices in a time of war and to support ongoing conflicts. Then have them write an essay that analyzes the rhetoric of some of those speeches. How have other presidents appealed to the American people? What kind of language do they use, and how does it compare to Lincoln's? Do students notice a shift in the sacrifices that are being asked of Americans? How has presidential rhetoric changed? What tone does each speech take with its audience?

## THE READER'S PRESENCE

1. Lincoln refers at the beginning and end of the speech to the founding of the United States of America, using language from the Declaration of Independence to underscore his point. He emphasizes the nation's founding—and the new form of government "of the people, by the people, for the people" (para. 3) that came into being with the nation—in order to stress what is at stake in the Civil War: the existence of the United States itself. The nation and its unique democracy are the ideals for which "the brave men . . . who struggled here" (para. 3) have died, so Lincoln both begins and ends the address consecrating the battlefield with this reference.

2. The word most often repeated in the Gettysburg Address is *dedicated.* Lincoln uses it first to refer to the ideal—"that all men are created equal" (para. 1)—to which the United States was dedicated when it was founded. In paragraph 2, he repeats that usage and then repeats the word in reference to the dedication of the battlefield cemetery, the purpose of his speech. In paragraph 3, he says that "we can not dedicate . . . this ground" (because the dead have already dedicated, consecrated, and hallowed it) and closes with two parallel sentences that propose another meaning of "dedication": "It is for us the living, rather, to be dedicated here to the unfinished work . . ." and "It is rather for us to be here dedicated to the great task remaining before us."

   Students may notice the way Lincoln repeats key words and phrases from the previous sentence throughout the text of the speech. In paragraph 2, particularly, every sentence contains a key noun or verb that has appeared in the previous sentence. This technique keeps the language moving inexorably forward while it also anchors it in the past—a technique that is also a metaphor for what the speech itself says about the United States. Ask students to read the speech aloud and discuss the effect of speaking the text versus reading it.

3. There's no way of guessing which writer your students will find more successful, but the chances are good that the decision will ultimately be a

political one. Most students think of Abraham Lincoln as the president who freed the slaves. Thomas Jefferson was a slave owner, and the Declaration of Independence describes Native Americans as "savages." It is unlikely this will generate a great deal of sympathy for Jefferson in the modern reader.

# James McBride
## HIP-HOP PLANET

### APPROACHING THE ESSAY

Hip-hop has been controversial almost since it originated. You may want to begin your discussion by asking students to express what hip-hop music means to them. Can they offer examples of other multiethnic contributions—arts, fads, identities, foods, language, dress, or even philosophies—that have been acculturated and adapted into the American mainstream? What exactly does "assimilation" mean? Call your students' attention to the fact that culture is dynamic: ask them what this means and to provide examples. Many of the essays in *The Writer's Presence* deal with this kind of cultural give and take. See, for instance, Henry Louis Gates Jr.'s "In the Kitchen" (p. 97) and Geeta Kothari's "If You Are What You Eat, Then What Am I?" (p. 132).

You may want to look at the author's "nightmare" that begins the essay. Why does James McBride call this scenario a "nightmare" (para. 1)? Does it suggest prejudice on his part? Is this simply the prejudice of any father who has a daughter? Of what is he afraid? For whom is he afraid? Is this a universal fear or is it specific to fathers whose daughters marry rappers? Explain.

At the end of the first section, McBride says, "Hip-hop remains an enigma, a clarion call, a cry of 'I am' from the youth of the world" (para. 8). Make sure your students understand what the author means by "an enigma" and "a clarion call." In what sense is the cry "I am" a universal cry? In what sense is it existential? (Query your class on the meaning of existentialism.) Draw your students' attention to the situation that the journalist McBride found in Senegal. In what sense has hip-hop become a cry of "I am" for the people of that country? In what sense has it been a cry for blacks in urban America? for Henry Rosenkranz, the white, working-class kid who mops floors? What about the "white 16-year-old hollering rap lyrics . . . from the driver's seat of his dad's late-model Lexus" (para. 21)?

Be sure that students notice the single-sentence paragraph near the beginning of the essay: "In doing so [that is, high-stepping away from the music], I missed the most important cultural event of my lifetime" (para. 6). The author, of course, has afforded this statement its own paragraph to emphasize its importance. Ask your students if they think this strategy is necessary and useful. Is it merely exaggeration? Does it reflect the author's prejudices as a black man? With what examples could they contest or respond to McBride's bold assertion?

Draw the class's attention to the important, penultimate paragraph. Paradoxically, it is both the most lyrical and most empirical paragraph of the essay. Discuss with your students the strategy involved in it: why does the author wait until the end of the essay to offer most of his statistics? How has he managed to include in this same statistics-laden paragraph lyrical sentences such as "The music is calling" and "The drums are pounding out a warning" (para. 40)? In what sense does the success of McBride's argument rest on this paragraph? Is he successful?

## ADDITIONAL ACTIVITIES

1. Examine the relationship of rap to poetry and jazz. Have students research (beyond the dictionary) the term "dialectics." In class, discuss how rap is dialectical. What is the role of thesis and antithesis, or give and take, in the creation of hip-hop?

2. Two very important black American poets are mentioned in McBride's essay: Nikki Giovanni (para. 15) and Amiri Baraka (para. 16). Both influenced the development of rap music with their spoken word form. Have students read Giovanni's "Ego Tripping" and Baraka's "Who Will Survive America?" online. Then ask them to search for the poets reciting these works on sites like www.youtube.com. In class, discuss the rhythm and music of their poetry. How did students experience the poems differently when they heard them recited? Discuss the important themes the poets raise. What are the similarities to the music and lyrics of rap artists? Another important poet—a contemporary of Giovanni and Baraka—is Allen Ginsberg, the white poet most often associated as the leader of the beat movement (para. 16). The works of all three of these poets lend themselves to public recitation and performance art.

## GENERATING WRITING

1. McBride credits Baraka, a black poet of the beat generation, with laying the foundation for rap as we know it today. In an eight- to twelve-page paper, have students research and report on the beat generation of the 1950s and 1960s and its contributions. This paper should not be a history of the beats, but rather an analysis of their wide-ranging influence on American culture. What aspects of our culture do we owe to the beats? What was the zeitgeist of the beats? What was its influence, for instance, on the hippie generation of the late 1960s and early 1970s? What aspects of this generation do we still see and how has this generation manifested itself in the post-millennium culture of today?

2. In a personal-response paper, have students write their opinion of rap music. Encourage them to be very specific: theme, sound, language, purpose, status, morality, sexism, violence, prejudice—all play very important parts in the controversy surrounding rap. Although this is a personal essay, it certainly might be enhanced by some research into rap's controversy.

## THE READER'S PRESENCE

1. The historical analysis of hip-hop's beginnings and the investigative nature of the essay display McBride's journalistic approach. However, he smoothly interweaves his personal story with the overarching story of hip-hop and the people and places it touches. His research in Senegal, for example, seems to transform him as he discovers that hip-hop is still the music of revolution and rage—only now it belongs to poor and oppressed people everywhere. Near the end of his essay, in true journalistic fashion, McBride offers statistics and current events to show the continuing evidence of racism. But in the penultimate paragraph, it is the very personal voice of the author *combined* with the voice of the journalist that we hear: "Hip-hop culture is not mine. Yet I own it. . . . This music that once made visible the inner culture of America's greatest social problem . . . has taken the dream deferred to global scale. . . . Over the years, the instruments change, but the message is the same." He comes to accept the importance of hip-hop—which is important to him personally, as well as to writing this article.

2. McBride did not like hip-hop when he was younger "because it held everything I wanted to leave behind" (para. 5). It is "music seemingly without melody, sensibility, instruments, verse, or harmony, music with no beginning, end, or middle" (para. 1). However, he comes to admire its universal truthfulness, the fact that it speaks the same rage in Harlem that it speaks in Senegal. McBride confesses that he still does not like the violence of hip-hop. He sees today's commercialization of hip-hop as a sellout to the glamour of violence and money, which has been appropriated by the white mainstream. It may have some value as the voice of poor white kids, but for the wealthy whites, it is just something else to be consumed. Answers will vary to this last question, but some students may argue that if the music has a message, it is important for everyone to hear it, even wealthy kids. Maybe they will learn something—if they are really listening. The argument can be made, too, that art has the world as its audience, not some segment of the world.

3. Students will have to generate their own lists in response to this question, and their perspectives on which of the two writers is more convincing will naturally vary. You might have the students present their findings to the class. Alternatively, you might make a class activity of it, writing the lists of agreements and disagreements on the board. It is important to make sure that the students can examine and explain the reasons for their opinions.

# N. Scott Momaday
## THE WAY TO RAINY MOUNTAIN

### APPROACHING THE ESSAY

In this essay, N. Scott Momaday uses a rich and loving language to describe the landscape once inhabited by the Kiowa and its association with their culture. Focusing on how his grandmother's sense of herself was composed of equal parts pride and grief about the world of her ancestors, Momaday also makes a strong, implicit argument about how a people's (and a person's) destiny are shaped by their land.

The essay proceeds through a complex interweaving of various narratives. Ask students to outline the essay, identifying the subject of each paragraph. They will find that Momaday continually moves back and forth among the recent history of the Kiowa, their deep history in legend, and his grandmother's individual story. In fact, these items are often discussed simultaneously, demonstrating how each level of the story depends on and shapes the others. At the core of these woven narratives is the land itself—the subject of Momaday's literal journey and the foundation of Kiowa beliefs and practices. Ask students to characterize Momaday's feelings about this land and to trace how these feelings flow into his descriptions of the people. For instance, in discussing gatherings at his grandmother's home, Momaday sketches the neighboring houses, worn and washed out by the weather, and the "lean and leather" visitors (para. 12), similarly weather-stained by the sun, wind, and rain.

In Momaday's interpretation, attention to the land and religious worship are inseparable. The Kiowa changed their gods as they moved across the landscape, and the most fully developed Kiowa myth Momaday relates describes the birth of one of the land's features: Devil's Tower. Ask students to compare the description of this relationship between land and spirit with Momaday's description of his grandmother's actual prayer sessions. Like the blurring of land and spirit, his grandmother's voice seems to emanate from, or travel to, a place between human and divine agency. Alert them, too, to the physical beauty and grace that Momaday recognizes in her; like the land, her face is beautiful because of, rather than in spite of, what experience has traced on it.

That the grandmother maintains her Kiowa praying (which will end with her—Momaday does not understand her words) reveals the importance she attaches to religious practice, not just her reverence of the land. The most explicitly political aspect of the essay is Momaday's report of the U.S. government's prohibition against the Kiowa Sun Dance. Despite the putative protection of religious freedom established by the First Amendment, preventing certain forms of worship was a common tactic to control the actions of Native Americans in the West. Students may be surprised by both the occurrence and effect of this prohibition. You might ask them to imagine why, in the context of Momaday's description of them, such an action would have so wounded the Kiowa. Given the strength the Kiowa draw from the land, in Momaday's depiction, it is not surprising that separation from its worship marks the end of their viability as a people. As Momaday implies, it is difficult to imagine a people living on after the death of their gods.

You might also ask students if they see any potentially religious purpose in Momaday's essay. That is, although he clearly has expository purposes—exploring the connections among Kiowa beliefs, land, and individual lives—is Momaday working through his essay to reenact what was lost? In a way, telling stories of the Kiowa allows Momaday to practice his grandmother's religion. His essay continues the blending of myth and land. By naming his grandmother's grave as "the end," he does not seem to imagine himself continuing the traditions. Perhaps this essay is like his grandmother's prayers, a deep-felt paean to a worship whose active life has ended. Ask students if Momaday's voice in the essay sounds at all like his grandmother's: "of something that is, and is not, like urgency in the human voice" (para. 10).

## ADDITIONAL ACTIVITIES

1. Momaday was one of the principal narrators of the 1996 PBS series *The West*, produced by Ken Burns. If you have access to this series, show portions of it to students so that they can think about Momaday's claim, cited in the biographical note to this essay (p. 504), that he works to put his speaking voice into his writing. In the first installment of the series, in fact, Momaday tells the myth of Devil's Tower. What do students notice in the oral version that they cannot hear in the written?

2. Several other selections in *The Writer's Presence* suggest a relationship between a family, a people, or individuals and the places they inhabit. Have students read David Mamet's "The Rake: A Few Scenes from My Childhood" (p. 158) and compare Mamet's idea of people and place with Momaday's.

## GENERATING WRITING

1. Have students write about the place in which they grew up or, if they know about it, where their parents and ancestors are from. In what ways is their family's history tied to their location? They might also approach the relationship between geography and destiny from another angle: ask them to relate family legends or stories and to read these stories in the light of their geographic setting.

2. Distribute to students the lyrics to "America, the Beautiful" and ask them to read the description of America's beauty the way Momaday reads the story of the Kiowa. If the story of Devil's Tower explains something about the Kiowa to themselves, what myth is constructed in "America, the Beautiful"?

## THE READER'S PRESENCE

1. By overlapping the historical account of the Kiowa, their legendary account of themselves, the story of his grandmother, and the story of his journey, Momaday manages to suggest that all take place in the same time frame, the

eternal present of myth and legend. The grandmother's death is introduced in the context of the land's timeless description; the recent history of the Kiowa is introduced with a reference to the grandmother's childhood; and the Kiowa's deeper history is linked directly to the story about the grandmother's name. By moving among these different stories, Momaday weaves them into one. Although there are several indications that the Kiowa story is over, by including his own journey Momaday manages to connect himself to this deeper story. If he offers no strong hope that the story lives on through him, neither is he completely cut off from it. This blending of legend and historical narrative mirrors the Kiowa way of making sense of their past. As Momaday relates it, the Kiowa tie their destiny to that of the land in the legend of Devil's Tower, a story that suggests a link between their final resting place and an animal brutality at the heart of their lifestyle. Momaday's relaying of his grandmother's story serves the same function—to connect his life with the land from which she came, to make sense of her losses and strength in the context of a much deeper story.

2. Momaday wants to understand how his grandmother's spirit was shaped by stories of a land she had never seen, one her ancestors had left years before. As the Kiowa move from the heights to the plains, they alter their religious practices, adopting a sun god where they had not worshipped one before. In Momaday's interpretation, such a transformation makes sense: the Kiowa spirit is closely tied to the character of the land they inhabit; as that land changes, their essential nature—and how they celebrate it in worship—must also change. His grandmother has a better sense of this land, despite having seen less of it than Momaday, because at the beginning of her life the Kiowa culture still included practices that enacted the spirit of this land. Momaday has only seen it with his eyes; his grandmother has lived the land in her spiritual devotion. This is why his grandmother's grave lies at the end of Kiowa history—literally at the eastern edge of their migration, but figuratively on the point in history when they will no longer continue to evolve as a viable culture.

3. By examining just the first paragraph closely, students can detect a number of literary devices at work. Alliteration and assonance abound, as Momaday describes the grass, "brittle and brown," full of "great green and yellow grasshoppers." Winter "brings blizzards," in contrast to the steaming foliage of August, which seems almost to "writhe in fire." These features give the language a poetic feel and rhythm, which is augmented by Momaday's use of such storytelling phrases as "plenty of time" (para. 1), suggesting a mythic scope to the tortoise's activity. The heightened effect is aided by Momaday's spareness in other sentences; when invoking the sound of oral language, less is sometimes more. This sentence is a model of economy and power: "All things in the plain are isolate; there is no confusion of objects in the eye, but *one* hill or *one* tree or *one* man" (para. 1). Even substituting *but* for the expected *only* elevates the language beyond the ordinary, transforming a landscape description into the evocation of a timeless place of legend,

a place that makes you ponder the location of Creation. In "A Traditional Family" (p. 581), Calvin Trillin avoids the language of spiritual connection, opting for a much more commonsensical, ironic tone: "I just found out that our family is no longer what the Census Bureau calls a traditional American family, and I want everyone to know that this is not our fault" (para. 1).

# Azar Nafisi
## *FROM* READING LOLITA IN TEHRAN

### APPROACHING THE ESSAY

This essay is an excerpt from Azar Nafisi's book-length memoir recounting her experiences teaching an underground literature class for female Iranian students in the mid-1990s. Nafisi is a literature professor by trade, and the strength of her writing lies in her ability to articulate the purpose and power of literature. In the relative safety of Nafisi's home, her female students remove their veils and robes. Nafisi describes the young women as coming alive, revealing, along with painted nails and dyed hair, their hopes and fears about their futures in the Islamic Republic. Nafisi grew up in Iran before the revolution and is well aware that, unlike her, these girls have never experienced life under anything but the Islamic regime: "My generation complained of a loss, the void in our lives that was created when our past was stolen from us, making us exiles in our own country" (para. 40). In running this class, she seems, in part, to want to instill the same sense of loss and desire for freedom in her students.

Nafisi relates each of the books the class reads to their lives in the Islamic Republic but is careful to say that these connections do not constitute direct indictments of Iran: "*Lolita* was not a critique of the Islamic Republic, but it went against the grain of all totalitarian perspectives" (para. 30). In one sense, Nafisi is helping her students see their lives as part of a larger history of struggle, a story that she hopes will be inspirational to them. Vladimir Nabokov's *Invitation to a Beheading* re-creates one man's existence with the continuous threat of death hanging over his head. At the end of the novel, Nabokov's protagonist is saved by repeating the mantra "by myself" and literally "tak[ing] his head in his hands" and walking away (para. 44). Nafisi hopes her own students may escape the worst of the regime's persecutions by reading and writing and thereby creating another world for themselves.

Nafisi's essay will remind Americans of the many freedoms afforded to those living in the United States. Ask students to consider how their educations would have been different if what they were taught were severely constrained to a single ideology or religious belief. How does literature enable us to see other perspectives, to relate to others in the world, or to better understand our own situations?

## ADDITIONAL ACTIVITIES

1. Have students read Nafisi's book of the same name. Afterward, ask small groups of students to present information about one of the four literary works that mark the four sections of her book. When was each written, and where? What is the plot of each book? Why do they think Nafisi chose these books for her class? How do Nafisi's students read and appreciate the novels differently from Western readers?

2. Have students research the Islamic Revolution in Iran, which marked its twenty-fifth anniversary in 2003. What values, beliefs, and institutions were overturned? What was the revolution a reaction against? Who were the revolution's supporters? What, in particular, were the revolution's effects on women and education?

## GENERATING WRITING

1. Ask students to contemplate the meaning and purpose of literature in their own lives. To begin, you might have them brainstorm all the reasons why they have read fiction or poetry. Expand the idea of literature by discussing how other kinds of storytelling—from religious texts, origin tales, and myths to films, novels, music, and television—also constitute literature. What do we get out of engaging in literature? Have the students write a short paper examining how literature has affected them personally.

2. Have students write a research paper on a case of censorship involving literature, such as Mark Twain's *Huckleberry Finn* (1884) or Maya Angelou's *I Know Why the Caged Bird Sings* (1969). What were the prominent arguments for removing the book from circulation or curricula? What was the political, social, religious, or historical context for the censorship? How and why have justifications for censorship in the United States changed over the years?

## THE READER'S PRESENCE

1. Reading Western literature represents an intellectual freedom that is strictly curtailed in Iran. The students come to Nafisi's home because the universities have censored or severely limited the way literature can be taught there, and Nafisi herself has resigned because of rigid control over her teaching. Because they have only known the oppression of the Islamic Republic, Nafisi's students tend to have a more personal, intimate connection to themes of freedom, persecution, individualism, and totalitarianism. In *Invitation to a Beheading*, they find a particularly relevant description of life within a totalitarian state and "the nightmarish quality of living in an atmosphere of perpetual dread" (para. 11). Nafisi describes Cincinnatus as "passive . . . a hero without knowing or acknowledging it" (para. 11), similar to her female students who partake in small acts of bravery in their desire for education.

2. Nafisi describes Cincinnatus's dance with his executioner as one done in circles, going nowhere, and she explains to her students that as long as

Cincinnatus dances with his jailers he will be accepting the world they create for him. She relates a citizen's willing participation in a totalitarian regime to "dancing with [her] jailer" (para. 41). Cincinnatus, at his execution, preserves his individuality by repeating the mantra "by myself." In this way he lets go, in a sense, of the dance with the executioner: "This constant reminder of his uniqueness, and his attempts to write, to articulate and create a language different from the one imposed upon him by his jailers, saves him at the last moment" (para. 44). Nafisi hopes her students will take their lives and dreams into their own hands, just as Cincinnatus literally takes his head in his hands.

3. Nafisi describes a regime that desires to keep women out of sight and carefully segregated from men, according to a fundamentalist interpretation of Muslim law. The education that Nafisi represents is considered Western and immoral in that she encourages her female students to act and think independently. In "The Joy of Reading and Writing: Superman and Me" (p. 27), Sherman Alexie describes his prodigious talents at reading and writing as threatening to many people: "A smart Indian is a dangerous person, widely feared and ridiculed by Indians and non-Indians alike" (para. 6). Alexie also says that Indians are expected to fail in the non-Indian world. Both Alexie and Nafisi suggest that education is a challenge to powerlessness, while withholding education is a way for a privileged few to control many others.

# Danielle Ofri
## SAT

### APPROACHING THE ESSAY

Danielle Ofri is a doctor at Bellevue Hospital, the oldest public hospital in the country, as well as a writer and an editor. Her essays focus on her experiences as a physician, and many of them elucidate the problems of health care in America through the personal stories of her patients. In "SAT," Ofri describes the connection among poverty, poor health, and educational level. A young man who comes into her office reminds Ofri of a striking scene from her days as a medical student. At a morgue, Ofri saw a young man who, unlike the other corpses in the room, appeared completely untouched except for a tiny bullet hole that had pierced his heart. In her current patient, Nemesio Rios, Ofri sees someone who she believes can be rescued from the threats of poverty through education. She convinces Nemesio that he should attend college and agrees to tutor him for the SAT.

Though this essay seems to take the shape of an inspirational narrative, Ofri ends it ambiguously. After a few SAT prep classes, she loses touch with Nemesio.

She writes, "Many days I thought about him, wondering how things turned out. If this were a movie, he'd score a perfect 1600 and be off to Princeton on full scholarship. But Harlem isn't Hollywood, and the challenges in real life are infinitely more complex" (para. 88). The essay argues powerfully for a broader conception of preventative health care for the poor; Ofri raises education to the level of an antidote to poverty, saying that "for Nemesio, his health depended on it" (para. 79). Ask students to analyze the way in which Ofri makes her argument. Rather than relaying a "success story" or relying on statistics, Ofri actually attempts to persuade her reader with what might even be a failed experiment. Ask students if they find her method effective. Do students read this piece as persuasive? Does it implicitly attack the health-care system? Does her conclusion seem to present a possible solution to the problems of poverty she sees in the hospital?

Unlike many expository pieces of writing, this one uses dialogue. Invite your students to consider the effect of reading the conversation between doctor and patient. Why does Ofri allow Nemesio to speak directly for himself throughout the piece? How does this technique emphasize Ofri's overall message?

## ADDITIONAL ACTIVITIES

1. In groups, have students brainstorm possible outcomes for Nemesio after Ofri lost touch with him and write a paragraph describing the outcome of his brief encounter with the doctor. Make sure they ground their hypothesis in the personality traits that Ofri offers about Nemesio. Have them point out parts of the text that helped them "finish" the story.

2. Students interested in reading more on Ofri's experiences as a doctor at Bellevue Hospital may be interested in her two essay collections, *Singular Intimacies* (2003) and *Incidental Findings: Lessons from My Patients in the Art of Medicine* (2005).

## GENERATING WRITING

1. Have students research statistics that indicate how health status relates to socioeconomic status and write an argument essay proposing a way to address the problem. In groups of three or four, have students read their essays and compare them to Ofri's. Which is most persuasive? What do the research papers include that make them more or less powerful than Ofri's narrative?

2. Have students write a personal narrative that describes how another person helped them understand a social problem—such as poverty, racism, or gender discrimination—and advocates for a solution to the problem.

3. Ofri's essay is rich in details that could be used to turn this essay into a movie. Have students write a scene of a movie featuring Nemesio Rios as the main character. You might refer students to Howard Zinn's "Stories Hollywood Never Tells" (p. 860) and challenge them to write the scene not as a Hollywood screenwriter would but rather as Zinn would like such stories to be portrayed on screen.

## THE READER'S PRESENCE

1. By using her patient's own words throughout the essay, Ofri is able to paint a more authentic portrait of him than she would through a description alone. Because he is reserved in his early conversations with the doctor, Nemesio's occasional outbursts and revelations ("That stuff about peer pressure is a bunch of crap") are particularly compelling (para. 30). The reader can also chart the growth of the relationship between doctor and patient by examining the deepening exchanges between them.

2. Although Ofri does not find out any particulars about the death of the boy in the morgue, he haunts her because he represents all the tragedy and injustice of a wasted young life. She writes: "I stared at that hole. That ignominious hole. That hole that stole this boy's life. I wanted to rewind the tape, to give him a chance to dodge six inches to the right. That's all he'd need—just six inches" (para. 61). In a sense, her SAT tutoring is an attempt to provide Rios with the "six inches" he needs to dodge his own potential tragedy. Although Ofri develops the character of Rios enough that students might want to learn his fate, her choice not to reveal it supports her assertion that "Harlem isn't Hollywood, and the challenges in real life are infinitely more complex" (para. 88).

3. John Taylor Gatto's argument in "Against School" (p. 665) is not against education at all but rather against the "deadly routine" (para. 6) of compulsory schooling. Though Gatto offers a compelling argument for the ways in which our national school system "dumb[s] people down" (para. 15), he does not offer many specific solutions in this particular essay. He does make reference to "two million happy homeschoolers," but this is likely not an option for Nemesio Rios. Some students may argue that Gatto's dim assessment of public schools is itself "elitist" and does not take into account the reality of poor, immigrant families struggling to provide their children with any education at all. Others will point out that Rios's predicament supports Gatto's assertion that "mandatory education serves children only incidentally; its real purpose is to turn them into servants" (para. 20).

# George Orwell
## POLITICS AND THE ENGLISH LANGUAGE

### APPROACHING THE ESSAY

This essay is long and rather demanding; be sure students have read it carefully and understood George Orwell's argument. You might want to break the argument down, in class discussion, into its two main branches: (1) Orwell's articulation of what was wrong with political writing in his day, and his identification of some potential abuses of political jargon and doctrine, and (2) his recommendations for avoiding these abuses in one's own writing and thought. To which aspect of his argument does Orwell give more attention? Which does the class find more interesting and relevant?

Paragraphs 1 and 2 of the essay hold the heart of Orwell's argument, that the decline of the English language is caused by social factors in the English-speaking world, but that by succumbing to the tendency toward confusion and obfuscation in political thought, writers and thinkers allow these detrimental trends to continue and gain momentum. He says, "An effect can become a cause, reinforcing the original cause and producing the same effect in an intensified form, and so on indefinitely" (para. 2). What do students make of this vicious-circle hypothesis? How can public acceptance of what should be unacceptable—confusing language used to express confused ideas—lead to dangerous precedents and bad habits that require a great deal of effort to break?

One example in our own time is the trend toward negative political campaigning. One side may not want to make direct personal attacks on the other side's candidate, but unless some action is taken, that side will wind up having to respond to the opponent's antagonistic rhetoric. In the next campaign, the second party may seize the offensive, hoping to avoid an attack, which might spur the first party on to even greater efforts to discredit the opposition. The cycle will eventually be so firmly established that drastic steps will be necessary to end it. Doesn't this sequence support Orwell's claim that it is vital to think our assertions through, carefully, word by word? How might a resolve to do this work affect the current state of our public rhetoric?

Ask the class to read Orwell's five examples of bad English carefully; they might read them aloud. How do students respond to the passages of bad prose? Ask if any remind them of writing or speech they might encounter today. What do they think of Orwell's assertion, "This mixture of vagueness and sheer incompetence is the most marked characteristic of modern English prose, and especially of any kind of political writing" (para. 4)? How accurate is it as a description of these passages? How accurate is it as a description of writing in America in the late twentieth century and early twenty-first century?

Orwell identifies the major problem as reliance on clichés in discussing any potentially sensitive political issue. Do our politicians, writers, and thinkers act thus today? Ask the class for some examples of "dying metaphors" in our society. We have seen the merciful demise of the Iron Curtain as a political metaphor, but the "war on drugs" is still with us. Some of the metaphors in our political arena are incomprehensible but refuse to die, such as George H. W. Bush's famous "thousand points of light." The "verbal false limb" is inescapable in our public and private discourse, which sprouts as many of these appendages as a Hindu god. *At this point in time* for the simple *now* is one example that should be familiar to all students; *the fact that* has spread even further in the decades since Orwell wrote the essay. His "pretentious diction" category is still with us, as is the class of "meaningless words." What does the word *progressive* mean when it is used by a Republican? by a Democrat? by a Socialist or Communist? How could one word have meanings so varied? Have the class think of other buzzwords with no fixed meaning, and discuss their political uses. What are some of the pitfalls in accepting a statement using some buzzword (or word with a private meaning) at its face value?

What do students make of Orwell's attack on political speech as a "defense of the indefensible" (para. 13)? How likely is it that obfuscatory speech is being used to cover up some outrage, offense, or outright crime? The Reagan administration's official response to findings about illegal dealings with Iran was that "mistakes were made." Is this kind of abuse of language an abuse of the public trust? Our nation's Department of Defense (which, until a few decades ago, was called the "War Department") is renowned for this kind of circumlocution. Ask students to bring in "official government statements" (as given to newspapers and magazines) and analyze them according to Orwell's guide. What is their response?

## ADDITIONAL ACTIVITIES

1. Some students may want to read Orwell's *Nineteen Eighty-Four* (1949) and give the class a presentation on Newspeak. Is Orwell's literary invention of a repressive government's repressive language motivated by the same ideals as this essay? What parallels to Newspeak do we see in our society today?

2. Ask students to bring in short political articles from newspapers and magazines. (Editorials are an ideal length and style for this exercise.) Have them evaluate these articles using Orwell's criteria. How are the authors, or the language they use, confusing or misleading? What might their motivation be? How might their political opponents state the same issue differently?

## GENERATING WRITING

1. Have your students examine Orwell's "translation" of the passage from *Ecclesiastes* into bad English (para. 9). Ask them to "translate" some well-known piece of straightforward writing into bad contemporary American English. Choose a short poem (Robert Frost's "Fire and Ice" is an excellent example) or perhaps a few proverbs ("Look before you leap"; "Don't count your chickens before they're hatched"). Have students read their "translation" aloud. (The results will be ridiculous, but emphasize that they illustrate a very serious problem.)

2. Ask students to write a brief essay on their response to Orwell's six rules of writing (para. 18). Do they agree with these rules? Might they use them in their own work? Do they consider valid his claim that adherence to these rules will help writers avoid stale thought and imagery?

## THE READER'S PRESENCE

1. Some examples of questionable prose include "he is almost indifferent as to whether his words mean anything or not" (para. 4) and "the passive voice is wherever possible used in preference to the active" (para. 6). Why do students suppose that Orwell uses constructions like these? Prime examples of Orwell's good writing include "chokes him like tea leaves blocking a sink"

**195**

(para. 11) and "the light catches the speaker's spectacles and turns them into blank discs which seem to have no eyes behind them" (para. 12).

2. Some passages that give away Orwell's political leanings include "the sordid processes of international politics" (para. 7); his discussion of the words "democracy, socialism, freedom, patriotic, realistic, and justice" (para. 8); and his discussion of political writing and orthodoxy (para. 12).

3. Orwell is being facetious when he tells us "to put off using words as long as possible and get one's meaning as clear as one can through pictures or sensations" (para. 18). How can one think about writing without resorting to words? But Orwell's point is that bad writing often has its source in the desire to *wield words*, rather than to convey meaningful ideas. Both Orwell and Langston Hughes ("How to Be a Bad Writer [in Ten Easy Lessons]," p. 121) argue forcefully for the already political nature of language — power moves through language. But Hughes wants to convey meaning through a very particular political problem. "This piece is for colored writers" (para. 11), he writes; his list of bad tendencies forms a portrait of the African American writer who struggles for acceptance by the white audience, exaggerating the familiar and making outlandish guesses about the unknown.

# Walker Percy
## THE LOSS OF THE CREATURE

### APPROACHING THE ESSAY

"The Loss of the Creature" is a difficult essay for most students: Percy makes a complicated argument and the intellectual attitudes he objects to will not be obvious to them. Begin the discussion by talking about the idea of judging the Grand Canyon based on "the degree to which [it] conforms to the preformed complex" (para. 5). The phrase "preformed complex" might seem an intimidating bit of jargon to some students, so you may have to be explicit, connecting the dots between the idea of the complex and the more simple articulation of it in the next sentence: "it looks just like the postcard" (para. 5). Ask the students if they have ever been to (or wanted to visit) a place that "looks just like the postcard." Ask them if they have ever considered it strange that, in a way, the postcard takes priority over the scene: why is a visit to a stretch of beach or a monument (like the Statue of Liberty) validated not by the place itself but by whether it looks the way we expect it to look, the way it has been packaged for us in tourism brochures, on television, or (as in Percy's example) in postcards?

This is essentially the key to the essay. It is about the way our experiences are prepackaged and preformulated by art, education, cultural expectations, and other media. Though Percy uses sightseeing and the Grand Canyon as examples of how some experiences can become inauthentic, his essay is really about experience itself (and, for ambitious instructors, could profitably be paired with Emerson's essay, "Experience," or Hawthorne's "My Visit to Niagara," p. 438). As Percy says, it is almost impossible to see the Grand Canyon today because "the thing as it is . . . has been appropriated by the symbolic complex which has already been formed in the sightseer's mind" (para. 5). By seeing such sights "under approved circumstances," he argues, we lose them. Percy's objection to most education is connected to this phenomenon of loss: most of what we learn in school is also learned "under approved circumstances" and is therefore inauthentic.

Percy's terminology is frequently that of existentialist philosophy, and it is likely that most of your students will be put off by it. Try to get them to grasp the ideas first through their own experiences. Surely they have confronted things for the first time in a context of educational or cultural expectations. Once they've realized how common this experience is, they can begin to understand the meaning of *appropriation*, *authenticity*, *expropriate*, and *concreteness*.

To stimulate discussion, you might ask the class to examine Percy's opening paragraphs. Notice that exploration and discovery are key images throughout. Percy begins by citing Cardenas's discovery of the Grand Canyon, and uses that moment as the criteria by which to judge other experiences of the site, suggesting that the experience is somehow degraded with every subsequent visitor (he even whimsically offers a mathematical formula for this phenomenon). Percy wants to restore the individual's "sovereignty" in knowledge. In other words, he wants us to experience things as they are, to us, rather than as we are told they are supposed to be. Although Cardenas was not, obviously, the first person to see the Grand Canyon, he was the first *European* to see it, and therefore he did not have pictures or travel brochures to feed his expectations or predetermine his response. He was therefore able to perceive the thing as *he* saw it. He was able to see it in a way that few (if any) subsequent travelers have. He had "sovereignty" over his first impression. We do not.

## ADDITIONAL ACTIVITIES

1. Once your students understand Percy's point about how we surrender our "sovereignty" to others, you can introduce the second part of the essay, which deals with the process of education. You might point out how this part, too, begins with references to discovery. Invite your students to discuss Percy's point about the dogfish and the sonnet. In paragraph 53, he suggests "that at irregular intervals, poetry students should find dogfishes on their desks and biology students should find Shakespeare sonnets on their dissection boards." Why? What do your students think? Does it make sense to them? How does changing the instructional context of the dogfish and the sonnet grow out of Percy's earlier attitudes toward discovery and recovery? And what have his examples to do with our attitudes toward the humanities and the sciences?

2. To further pursue Percy's observations about tourism and sightseeing, invite your class to find travel advertisements or brochures for vacation spots. This

kind of material is easy to find in magazines or newspapers, as well as online or at any travel agent's office. Have your students bring the ads to class and discuss them in the context of Percy's attitude toward seeing: how many ads, for example, invite the tourist to "discover" X or Y? What would Percy say about that notion of "discovery"? What other kinds of "prepackaged" attitudes can students find in the advertisements?

## GENERATING WRITING

1. To test Percy's ideas, students might try their own thought experiment. Have them write an essay in which they consider if it is possible, as Percy suggests, "to come face to face with an authentic sight" (para. 23). Does that necessarily mean seeing something for the first time? Or do they think it is possible, say, to visit a famous tourist destination such as the Eiffel Tower in Paris and truly see it? How would Percy define that kind of authentic seeing? In their essays, your students should consider a significant site they have visited.

2. Nathaniel Hawthorne's essay, "My Visit to Niagara" (p. 438), deals with Hawthorne's initial disappointment on his first visit to Niagara Falls. It goes on to discuss the manner in which he was able to "see" past his disappointment and truly apprehend the beauty of the falls: his change of heart begins not with seeing, but with *listening* to the falls from his hotel room that night. The next day he visits the falls again and sees them as though they are new. You might have your students write an essay in which they explain how Hawthorne's experience can be likened to the approach to the world that Percy advocates. Does Hawthorne gain "sovereignty" over his perceptions? How? You might ask them to consider Percy's approach to education, in particular: can *listening* to the falls be related to *dissecting* a sonnet?

## THE READER'S PRESENCE

1. The symbolic complex refers to the set of preconceived notions that almost every visitor to the Grand Canyon *must* have, simply as a consequence of existing in a culture where media have bombarded us with images and ideas about the site. Seeing the canyon under approved circumstances might include taking a tour of the site, looking at it from one of the predetermined overlooks, or viewing it in any way that conforms to the postcard. These circumstances make the encounter with the canyon seem artificial. In the education system, students encounter the world in the artificially constructed context of the classroom, preventing them from authentic learning in the same way postcards and tour groups prevent an authentic experience of the Grand Canyon.

2. Percy is primarily concerned with recovering authentic experience. This he states in the first paragraph, and to this degree he states his purpose immediately. But in order to explain *how* one recovers authentic experience—the true encounter with the world—Percy has to explain what he means by

"recovered." In other words, his purpose is obvious in the first paragraph if you have already read the essay and you know what's coming. If you haven't, you're not entirely sure what Percy is talking about at all until you've read on. His diction is academic and political, his point a complex one about our ownership of our perceptions. His tone is intelligent and patient but ultimately elitist: it is optimistic in the sense that he feels authentic experience can be recovered, less so in that he feels it has been lost, and it takes an advanced intellect to recover it. It doesn't become clear until the second part of the essay that Percy is leading up to a critique of education. Many of your students may (not entirely incorrectly) locate Percy's statement of purpose there.

3. The first part of the essay deals with the Grand Canyon, with sightseeing. Percy moves on to education, retaining the idea of authentic experience, using it to criticize traditional modes of education. The example of the sonnet in the science class might be a particularly useful one, as is the dogfish in poetry class.

4. Hawthorne anticipates Percy most clearly in paragraph 6 of "My Visit to Niagara," when he wishes that he had not heard of the falls until he beheld them. Your students are likely to struggle with both essays: Hawthorne wrote more than a hundred years ago; for this reason, his diction and syntax will be difficult for students. Percy makes a very complicated and sophisticated argument, which many will find difficult to understand. Which essay your students will find more engaging and memorable is anybody's guess. Percy's argument is more clearly delineated, and its critique of education, as well as its twentieth-century sensibility, may be more resonant for most students. By the same token, its complexity and sophistication might puzzle and frustrate them, and Hawthorne's essay, loaded as it is with imagery and first-person narration, might be much more memorable and engaging for students interested in a more personal approach.

# Katha Pollitt
## WHY BOYS DON'T PLAY WITH DOLLS

### APPROACHING THE ESSAY

In this short essay, Katha Pollitt argues that, in the world of Barbie and Street Fighter, no scientific studies are necessary to prove that gender differences are social and cultural constructs.

Students can learn much from this essay's simple, effective rhetorical devices. In many places Pollitt reveals her tone directly: italics in paragraphs 5 and 12, the list of rhetorical questions in paragraph 9. Ask students, however, to trace the tone of the first sentence of each paragraph. The "True" that opens paragraph 2 may be easy evidence for them, revealing itself as a temporary concession—that Pollitt believes that what follows is not, in fact, all that true. But they may need help to recognize in the essay's first sentence an ironic paraphrase of other people's criticisms of feminism. Pollitt is suggesting here that to pretend that feminism's less-than-complete success is evidence of its irrelevance is just plain ornery, or dull. Her tone warns us to be wary, in the second sentence, of what "we are told" about gender difference, when, in fact, the truth is right in front of us.

In the late 1980s and early 1990s, college-age women began distancing themselves from feminism, arguing in the abstract that it had fulfilled its promises or gone too far. Asked, however, if they supported equal protection for men and women, they overwhelmingly assented, as they agreed that such equality was not yet achieved in all realms. It is in this social landscape that Pollitt's essay is launched, and it may be necessary to hear students out on their associations with feminism. Reversing a trend of the 1990s, Pollitt is absolutely unapologetic, criticizing parents who embrace feminism only "tentatively" while desiring privileges for their daughters. Ask students to define feminism, based on what Pollitt values, and ask them then if they see any reason for controversy.

In two places in the essay, Pollitt appeals to the authority of what "the kids" know. You may want to call students' attention to these passages, asking them both to recognize and to evaluate Pollitt's maneuvers. In the first instance, Pollitt admits with a hardened edge that kids will demand the truth of the world even against their parents' hope that obfuscation will be for their own good. Ask students if they have experienced this "do as I say, not as I do" attitude, and how they responded to it. In the second example, near the end of the essay, Pollitt invokes this same authority to argue that the next generation has already advanced in their attitudes beyond their parents. Ask students if they agree with this claim. If so, perhaps they can explain why Pollitt still feels the need to exhort parents with her last sentence. If the parents are behind the children in their feminist attitudes, why, then, do they need to worry about what messages they send? Is Pollitt actually appealing here to vanity, hoping to encourage children to progress past their parents and to scare the parents into not being left behind politically?

## ADDITIONAL ACTIVITY

1. Pollitt might consider children's television for evidence of how it shapes gender behavior. Have students examine the representation of children in adult television and movies and evaluate Pollitt's claim that adults want to see in children evidence that their own behavior is valid and natural.

## GENERATING WRITING

1. Ask students to write an essay comparing their own gender education to that which Pollitt describes. Encourage them to begin by describing particular habits, games, and toys that they were encouraged to enjoy—or dissuaded

from enjoying — and how the effects of these articles and habits of play seem present in their current lives. How do these lives correspond to the differences Pollitt describes?

2. Have students do research on the postfeminist essentialism to which Pollitt refers and then write their own essay examining how these studies reframe gender difference as natural. They should conclude their essay by stating which approach seems more persuasive.

## THE READER'S PRESENCE

1. One competing theory is that differences between men and women are cognitively based; Pollitt alludes to a study suggesting that men orient themselves by an internal sense of spatial relations and women by reference to landmarks (but does this really explain why men won't ask for directions?). According to Pollitt, even if such findings prove conclusive (which she doubts), their authors have for the most part distanced themselves from efforts to generalize from them an entire theory of natural difference. Pollitt does not so much reject these studies in her essay as sidestep them, demonstrating that the direct education toward gender difference in how we treat children is obvious enough to require little scientific investigation about the origins of most of the dichotomy.

2. Students will respond to this question differently, depending on their individual experience with the media. Pollitt seems to blame the mainstream press for latching onto the smallest, most tentative discoveries of gender research and using them to make pronouncements on the verities of sex differences. That the drive for "news" and "scoops" encourages the press to create drama from the smallest crumbs is certain. Whether the media is particularly irresponsible about gender is another question.

3. Pollitt seems to grant parents a grudging sympathy. She recognizes that childrearing is endless work, that parents already shoulder the blame for too much of the outcome of their children's lives, and that they are responsible both for communicating to their children the truth of the world (for example, that looks matter for women's success) and for trying, simultaneously, to better that landscape. A comparison of Bernard Cooper's essay ("A Clack of Tiny Sparks: Remembrances of a Gay Boyhood," p. 78) and Pollitt's reveals the difference from one generation to the next. Cooper's parents unconsciously denied his developing sexuality, pushing him toward heterosexual desires he didn't feel; many of the parents described in Pollitt's article seem to "know better" than Cooper's parents about the need to resist the rigid gender stereotypes encouraged by our culture. And yet Pollitt also suggests that the generations' different styles of parenting may, finally, be negligible. Note the detail of the mother who lets her daughter give a friend a Barbie doll but apologizes to the girl's mother (para. 5). Have your students consider whether bad-faith parenting is better for children than unrepentant authoritarianism.

# Eric Schlosser
## WHY MCDONALD'S FRIES TASTE SO GOOD

### APPROACHING THE ESSAY

Eric Schlosser, author of the best-selling *Fast Food Nation* (2001), from which this piece is excerpted, spent years investigating the American fast-food industry and its effect on aspects of American culture, ranging from suburban sprawl and after-school jobs to meat safety. In "Why McDonald's Fries Taste So Good," he reviews the history of the McDonald's fry, explains what natural and artificial flavors are and why they are added to foods, visits New Jersey's "flavor corridor" (para. 6), and encounters a flavorist for a "taste test" in which he tastes nothing (para. 31).

Schlosser's piece introduces a good deal of surprising information. Although students may have heard that McDonald's once fried its potatoes in beef tallow, adding "more saturated beef fat per ounce than a McDonald's hamburger" (para. 2) to the supposedly vegetarian side dish, they may not know how McDonald's dealt with the need to reproduce the beef-tallow flavor in fries cooked in vegetable oil. The answer is "natural flavor," a phrase that nearly everyone has seen on food labels but that few people really understand. Schlosser's piece is an attempt to educate consumers about these ubiquitous substances.

To find out more, Schlosser visits the "flavor corridor" of New Jersey, a destination that few readers are likely to have heard of. He mentions important flavor companies, whose names are unlikely to be familiar in spite of their dominance of the industry. Schlosser is allowed to enter IFF, "the world's largest flavor company" (para. 6). His whimsical description—it "remind[s him] of Willy Wonka's chocolate factory" (para. 7)—will likely form a beguiling frame of reference for students: the hallways smell delicious, the workers are cheerful and neat, the products seem like magic potions, and the place has a slightly paranoid air of secrecy.

The essay explains the difference between "natural" and "artificial" flavors (the short answer: not much—both are derived from identical chemicals, and "natural" flavors are not necessarily safer or healthier, although they are much more expensive) and considers what the "human craving for flavor" (para. 13) has driven people throughout history to do. Schlosser covers the history of the flavoring industry and notes that humans find food appetizing only when it has appropriate color and "mouth feel." His discussion does return to the McDonald's fries question in paragraph 28, but because corporations guard their flavor secrets closely, Schlosser can only speculate that McDonald's "most likely drew on these advances [in the creation of natural and artificial meat flavors] when it eliminated beef tallow from its french fries. The company will not reveal the exact origin of the natural flavor added to its fries" (para. 28).

Schlosser's method in this essay involves investigation and explanation with little overt attempt at persuasion. Ask students what they think Schlosser is arguing. Does he object to the use of natural and artificial flavors in processed foods? Does he admire the flavorists' ingenuity? Does he find the process peculiar? What do your students feel after reading this essay? Does the fact that apparently familiar foods are filled with odd ingredients make them feel differently about eating such items as McDonald's fries? You might want to point out places in the essay where Schlosser juxtaposes the familiar with the peculiar or distasteful. For example, in paragraph 17 he notes, "Food coloring serves many of the same decorative purposes as lipstick, eye shadow, mascara—and is often made from the same pigments." Schlosser makes us think about eating makeup in this sentence, and the effect is disquieting. You might also point out the description of "carmine" in paragraph 30, where Schlosser observes without comment that this pigment—made from crushed insects—is used to color "Dannon strawberry yogurt . . . many frozen fruit bars, candies, and fruit fillings, and Ocean Spray pink-grapefruit juice drink."

## ADDITIONAL ACTIVITIES

1. Schlosser's essay is unusual in offering critical and analytic discussion of food. Have students bring in two contrasting (and far more typical) forms of writing about taste, such as a magazine advertisement, newspaper food column, or health-food label. Then have them consider the following questions: In what ways does Schlosser's essay resemble these pieces, and in what ways does it differ? What, in Schlosser's opinion, is the relation between our emotional connection to food and our intellectual understanding of its properties and place in our lives?

2. Students may be interested in reading Schlosser's book *Fast Food Nation* in its entirety. Ask them if the excerpt here is typical of Schlosser's argumentative style throughout or whether parts of the book have a more polemical tone. If he changes his style in parts of the book, what seems to effect the change? If he remains objective throughout while presenting discomforting facts, what effect does this stance have on the reader?

3. Show the class Morgan Spurlock's film *Supersize Me*, in which Spurlock spends thirty days eating only at McDonald's. Then have the class consider how Spurlock has been influenced by Schlosser. What views of McDonald's do the two men seem to share? How does each approach the subject of fast food? What seems to motivate each of them?

## GENERATING WRITING

1. As Schlosser acknowledges, our tastes in food are set in early childhood, when they become linked to our experience of nation, family, home, and self. Marcella Hazan, a famous Italian cook, quotes a Chinese saying, "Patriotism is the love of the food we eat as children." Have students explore the narrative potential of writing about food. Assign a two- to three-page essay about food that is also an exploration of another issue, which is never explicitly named.

2. Ask students to research how McDonald's policies on the sources of its raw materials and on the specific foods it serves have changed since Schlosser's

book came out. Then ask them to write a paper discussing their findings. What caused McDonald's policies to change? What effect do your students think the changes will have?

## THE READER'S PRESENCE

1. McDonald's French fries are the favorite food of countless Americans; Schlosser knows that by featuring them prominently he virtually guarantees his readers' attention (if not their appetite).

2. Schlosser is ultimately opposed to unnecessary additives in food, but his essay maintains a fairly neutral analysis of the state of food technology. His final anecdote in the laboratory is ambiguous: On the one hand, he is suspicious of International Flavors & Fragrances' "policy of secrecy and discretion" (para. 31) in that the companies use their flavors without publicly admitting that they use them; on the other hand, Schlosser is disarmed by the flavorist Grainger's genius. Schlosser conveys considerable delight at Grainger's sleight of hand (or should we say nose?) and at the fickle nature of his appetites.

3. James Fallows ("Throwing Like a Girl," p. 400) and Amy Cunningham ("Why Women Smile," p. 347) both use research in their pieces to some extent. Fallows uses sources including a newspaper description of Hillary Clinton throwing a pitch, interviews with softball and tennis coaches and with actors who have played the role of athletes, and handbooks about pitching to answer a question about why so many women throw "like girls." Cunningham talks to psychologists, reads about babies, looks at Dutch art and nineteenth-century advertising, and interviews a media coach to determine why women smile so much more often, and for more different reasons, than men do. Although neither piece includes notes or bibliographical references, some of the materials these authors have consulted could be tracked down on the basis of information given in the essays. Schlosser relies on personal interviews and (apparently) on research into the history of French fries and artificial flavorings, but he does not identify his sources in this excerpt. You might ask students whether the lack of identifiable, traceable research makes any of these essays less convincing than it would otherwise be. What assurance do they have that the authors are not inventing the material? Why are students generally required to document research so carefully when these authors are not?

# James Shreeve
## THE GREATEST JOURNEY

### APPROACHING THE ESSAY

The information contained in this essay may or may not be new to your students. Some of them will know a lot about prehistoric humans, others next to nothing. Most of them have probably heard that humans originated in Africa. One piece of information that might come as news is included in the discussions of mtDNA (paras. 6 and 7) and mitochondrial Adam and Eve (paras. 8 and 9). Using DNA evidence and the fossil record, Shreeve traces the migration of our species out of Africa and our colonization of the rest of the world.

He conceives of the history of the human race as a story and, after the introductory material, relates it as such, in a more or less linear narrative. One interesting element of the essay is that much of it is conjectural: no one can know, completely, what actually happened. We can make some solid assumptions based on the evidence, and there are a few things we can actually know, but much of what Shreeve reports is purely speculative. See, for example, paragraph 15: "The wanderers had reached southeastern Australia by 45,000 years ago, when a man was buried at a site called Lake Mungo. Artifact-bearing soil layers beneath the burial could be as old as 50,000 years—the earliest evidence of modern humans far from Africa." We know that a man was buried in southeastern Australia 45,000 years ago, but what does the following sentence mean? It means, essentially, that humans *might* have been there 5,000 years earlier because the soil where the artifacts were found was 5,000 years older. In the next paragraph, Shreeve says, "No physical trace of these people has been found along the 8,000 miles from Africa to Australia—all may have vanished as the sea rose after the Ice Age." So there's no real fossil evidence that these people came from Africa at all. We can only guess, based on the DNA evidence and the patterns of human migration that we *can* verify with fossil evidence from elsewhere in the world. In paragraph 19, Shreeve candidly admits that we have no idea how Neanderthals and modern humans interacted: we only know that we have no DNA evidence of interbreeding.

Point out to your students that Shreeve does not intend to be dishonest: He makes no false claims. He only fills in the blanks with speculation, as those who study prehistoric life must. He is careful to use phrases like "may have" and words like *perhaps* to signal bits of information for which verification is scant. But the less advanced readers might miss the signposts. An interesting exercise for your class might be to identify them, thus separating fact from conjecture (see Reader's Presence Question 2).

### ADDITIONAL ACTIVITIES

1. Have the class watch *Quest for Fire*, *Clan of the Cave Bear*, or both. To what extent do these representations of prehistoric humanity reinforce or contradict

the speculations in Shreeve's article? Both films show humans and Neanderthals interacting and even interbreeding. How much of it seems realistic? How much of it seems like utter nonsense?

2. Have the students look through old copies of *National Geographic* and other magazines for articles about human evolution and early humans. How has speculation changed over the years? Are there ideas about early humanity that seemed certain at one time and have now changed? In what ways have they changed? What do they tell us about the people who had them? If we look at, for example, an article about stone-age humans that was printed in the 1950s, how much do we learn about stone-age humans? How much do we learn about the 1950s? What kinds of cultural assumptions are reflected in theories about the past? What kinds of cultural assumptions might be reflected in Shreeve's essay? How does the current cultural trend toward tolerance and diversity make itself apparent in Shreeve's essay?

## GENERATING WRITING

1. In keeping with Additional Activity 2, assign the students a research paper tracing the evolution of ideas about ancient humans, or even about evolution itself. The paper might be called "The Evolution of Evolution." Like Shreeve, students will frame their reports as stories. But instead of telling the story of humanity's movements out of Africa, they would tell the story of our ideas about prehistoric humans, beginning with the earliest caricatures of club-wielding cavemen to contemporary conceptions of early human life.

2. Have the students conduct their own research on early human life, using Shreeve as only one of four or five sources. They should look up the people he cites: for example, Alison Brooks of George Washington University (para. 11) and Spencer Wells (para. 14). Who are these people? What have they written? What arguments have they made about early human life? When asked to write a research paper, many students say they don't know where to start. Identifying Shreeve's sources and investigating them will be a useful way for students to learn how to follow up. It will also, in all likelihood, introduce them to more sophisticated kinds of writing. Shreeve's article isn't dumbed down, exactly, but it's intended to be accessible for a mainstream audience. Investigating his sources might lead students to some much more in-depth work, intended for experts in specialized fields of scientific, archeological, or anthropological research. Exposure to these sources can only improve students' reading skills, serving the simultaneous purpose of raising awareness of just how sophisticated authentic, reliable research can (and, indeed, must) be.

## THE READER'S PRESENCE

1. The history of humankind is a story insofar as it unfolds chronologically. The comparison is perhaps less adequate when we consider that the traditional story has rising action, a climax, then a resolution. In other words, the traditional story conforms to an artificial structure that does not necessarily

reflect reality. But that might be a more analytical answer than students are prepared to give. However, it is also useful to note that much of what we "know" about early humans is conjecture: we look at archeological evidence and make up a story that seems to fit the facts.

2. The last two paragraphs of the Approaching the Essay section of this entry explore this question. There are examples of conjecture in almost every paragraph, from paragraph 11 forward. Shreeve is reasonably careful to indicate when he is dealing with fact and when he is dealing with speculation. It will be interesting to find out how your students react: some might be dismissive when they realize how much of what they are dealing with is based on guesswork. Others will be unfazed, taking it for granted that this kind of work requires speculation.

3. One way to approach this question with your class will be to look at paragraph 19: Shreeve doesn't know how Neanderthals and modern humans reacted, and in that sense his findings neither confirm nor refute David Brooks's assertions in "People Like Us" (p. 330). However, paragraphs 21 forward deal with the isolation of different lines of descent from our common ancestors and how that isolation affected us, particularly in the peopling of the Americas. When discussing theories about the first Americans and where they came from, Shreeve mentions the specious claims of one theory, saying it has a "political agenda" (para. 22). The mere existence of such a theory seems to suggest that Brooks is onto something. But the fact that we all share a common ancestor makes the whole concept of people *like us* questionable, as we are *all* "us." In this context, the very notion of ethnic and racial identities becomes almost as specious as the theories meant to promote one of those identities over another.

# Charles Simic
## THE LIFE OF IMAGES

### APPROACHING THE ESSAY

Charles Simic takes a nostalgic tour through the New York City of his youth aided by Berenice Abbott's photographs of the city. He weaves together personal stories that illustrate how the city has changed over the course of thirty years. Abbott's photographs offer Simic an opportunity to improvise stories of New York life that, although not strictly true, capture the essence of his memories of the city. Historic photographs such as Abbott's allow viewers infinite clues with which to conjure up a story and to reconstruct a city's past. Simic compares his musings on the photographs with the single images people often glimpse on the street in large cities.

Simic tells several anecdotes in which a face or a line of dialogue was enough to catapult him into imagining a whole story for someone: "No sooner has one seen an interesting face . . . than one gives it a biography" (para. 8). Each one of us, then, is a camera, and our minds are storehouses for limitless images and their stories. He ends by emphasizing how ephemeral individual lives are even when captured on film, saying that in one Abbott photo "one befuddled old fellow . . . has stopped and is looking over his shoulder at what we cannot see, but where, we suspect, we ourselves will be coming into view someday" (para. 10).

Although your students may not directly relate to the nostalgia in this essay, they will all be able to relate to the meaning of photographs in our lives and how, when viewing a photograph, we imagine a whole world beyond the frame. Ask your students to analyze one of Simic's descriptions of an Abbott photograph. How much is objective description of the photograph and how much is wholly imagined from the scene? What meaning does Simic take from the photograph?

Many of your students, having grown up with television and the Internet, will be more adept at analyzing and describing images than at critical reading of written text. This presents a good opportunity to bring attention to how students naturally analyze images and ask them to apply the same techniques to text. Bring in some photographs and have the class analyze them. What are the different elements that make up each photograph? What meaning do your students take from the separate elements? How do these meanings add up to an overall message? What are alternative ways to "read" each photograph?

## ADDITIONAL ACTIVITIES

1. As a class, discuss how Simic creates a fictional narrative from Abbott's photographs. What visual clues does he draw on? Display one historical photograph for the class and ask students to write a paragraph creating a scene or character inspired by the image. In small groups, have students read their paragraphs aloud and discuss the similarities and differences among their narratives. What details have they drawn on? What does this say about the way we perceive images?

2. Several narratives in this book are accompanied by photographs, including Henry Louis Gates Jr.'s "In the Kitchen" (p. 97), Nora Ephron's "The Boston Photographs" (p. 655), and Errol Morris's "Liar, Liar, Pants on Fire" (p. 753). Ask students to compare and contrast how each writer uses the photograph as a writing device. What is the meaning of the photograph or of photography's ability to capture a moment? To what extent can each essay be read without the accompanying photo? What does the photograph add to a reading of each essay?

## GENERATING WRITING

1. Ask students to bring in one photograph—either personal or professional—to class. Collect them all and then distribute them randomly so that each student has someone else's. Ask students to write a narrative that explains the photograph in front of them and describes it in detail. In groups of three or

four, have students exchange photographs and write another narrative on a different photograph. They should then compare the two narratives that came from each photograph. How do the narratives compare? What elements of the photographs influenced each writer's narrative? How well does each writer use descriptive language?

2. Students interested in photography should be encouraged to collect or take their own photographs of where they live and incorporate them into a photographic essay about place. This type of essay combines image with descriptive or reflective writing to explore an idea, question, or concern. They might concentrate on a single aspect of the place they live, such as the neighborhood, a religious or an ethnic community, a controversy, or the architecture. Ask them to include the photograph in their essay as well as describing it in their own words.

## THE READER'S PRESENCE

1. Simic usually focuses on small details in a photograph and uses them as a springboard to speculate on character or setting. In the case of the "shadowy couple under the El" (para. 3), for instance, the very way they are standing together suggests to Simic that they are more than casual acquaintances. He often creates a narrative involving the subjects of a photograph that takes them beyond the frame of the picture. He also likes to imagine a musical composition from the time period to accompany the scene. Simic reflects that the magic of photography is its ability to capture "an ordinary scene full of innuendoes" that "partakes of the infinite" (para. 3). Simic exemplifies how the power of one's imagination can transform any of those "innuendoes" into a story.

2. Simic opens by discussing Abbott's photography, and then he transitions into his present life in New York, a city "rich with such visual delights" (para. 2). Abbott's photographs bring New York City's past into the present, but Simic's reading of photographs parallels how he reads the daily images that New York City produces: "No sooner has one seen an interesting face in the street than one gives it a biography" (para. 8). Simic also reminds us that just as we observe others as a camera captures a photograph, we are likely being observed in the same way. We are thus always a potential camera as well as a potential subject.

3. Simic's perspective is clearly that of a poet. Photographs afford him imaginative possibilities. He can make sense of an ambiguous caption or "experience nostalgia for a time and place [he] did not know" (para. 5). Nora Ephron's perspective ("The Boston Photographs," p. 655), however, is that of a journalist. She is interested in the reality that pictures represent: what they disclose about the real lives of the people they portray, rather than their potential for the imagination. Abbott's pictures were taken to preserve a bit of Americana and serve an archeological purpose. Forman's pictures are examples of the power of photojournalism.

# Calvin Trillin
## A TRADITIONAL FAMILY

### APPROACHING THE ESSAY

This short essay is part of the tradition of the good-natured neurotic, reflecting on a minor worry in a way that points, gently, to irrationalities in the larger system of which this worry is a part. Students should enjoy Calvin Trillin's mock-paranoid fantasies of contending with government bureaucracy and his concerns about the effects of external definitions on his sense of family identity.

Students will appreciate and understand how Trillin is working if they identify the values playfully invoked in his skewering of the idea of tradition. Ask them, first, to list all the activities Trillin identifies as traditional. A simple way to start this process is to highlight all of the uses of forms of this word and to examine their referents. Having generated a list, students can begin asking questions of each item. Do they recognize this as a tradition? What are the values underlying that tradition in its usual form? Is Trillin invoking that form, or a reversal of it? In many cases, Trillin's humor works through calling "traditional" something that, while common or even usual, in fact contradicts our unconscious assumptions of tradition. For instance, in two places Trillin describes his own subservience to his wife or children as traditional. While certainly plausible, such a power arrangement is in fact contradictory to our expectations of the father's role in a family. If the claim was unbelievable, or if Trillin merely described an accepted truth, then the reversal would not be funny. It is his tweaking of our expectations that makes this element provocative. Can students detect this pattern in other instances of humor in the essay?

### ADDITIONAL ACTIVITIES

1. As a prewriting activity, it might be valuable to have students write their associations with the title of Trillin's piece. What are their expectations for an essay about "A Traditional Family"? After an initial period of writing, you might have them read the headnote for this essay and write again on the same question. Because Trillin's essay only discusses tradition implicitly, and ironically, it will be valuable for students to identify explicitly some of what they believe about the family before reading Trillin's satiric suggestions concerning it.

2. It might be worthwhile to have students read Trillin's essay in conjunction with a piece in *The Writer's Presence* that deals with similar issues less humorously. Scott Russell Sanders's "The Men We Carry in Our Minds" (p. 793) plays off our images of "traditional families." If you have students read this text, you might ask them how the author refers to similar traditional images of the family, and to evaluate the effectiveness of his method for prompting a reader's further reflection and engaging his or her interest.

## GENERATING WRITING

1. Have students examine materials pertaining to the census, either the official report released by the U.S. Census Bureau (available in most public or college libraries in the government-documents section) or news reports published soon after the census was released. Ask them to look for trends other than the one discussed by Trillin and to write an essay discussing what effect they believe one or more of these trends has had on their lives or on that of someone they know, or how they see these trends reflected in popular culture.

2. Have students write an essay about the extent to which their own family is traditional or untraditional. Does it fit the official definition? What "traditional" aspects of their family are not captured in this description, and what "untraditional" aspects are left out? Do they think that their parents have striven to fit inside or outside whatever mold the phrase "a traditional family" seems to offer?

## THE READER'S PRESENCE

1. The U.S. Census Bureau's definition of "a traditional American family" requires two parents living with a child under age eighteen. Trillin reads the definition in a news story about the slowing rate of decline of such families, and his family is disqualified because his youngest daughter is nineteen. Having finally accepted that his children will grow older, he still imagines asking for an exception from the Census Bureau, by suggesting that his children do or will continue to live with him and his wife.

2. Trillin suggests that his family's observance of holidays, and his status as a victim of their bossing, qualify them as traditional. Throughout the text, an elevated diction is used to create a humorous space between the language and the subject, as Trillin uses somewhat passive ("find ourselves included" [para. 2], "have been assured" [para. 8]) and impersonal ("renewed," "surfaced," "acknowledge") verbs to describe the changes in his family. To similar effect, he also uses official terms such as "easement" and unofficial political jargon such as "approach" to convey a bureaucratic and an impersonal relationship to the government. The gap between the formality of the language and the casual subject might qualify as irony, which depends on incongruity or a play against expectation, but Trillin's insouciant terminology might be considered simple wit. One clearer example of irony is Trillin's assertion that "we have been assured by more experienced parents that we can absolutely count on their return" (para. 8). "Assured" and "absolutely count on" imply a positive desire when the event—adult children returning home—might also be viewed as unwelcome.

3. Trillin's essay avoids distinguishing between gender roles in the family: again and again, he uses the first-person plural or the passive voice to describe the family's activities. "The dishes are done and the garbage is taken out regularly"; "We lose a lot of socks in the wash" (para. 4). The only outright expression of gender roles is a stereotype: "We make family decisions in the traditional

American family way, which is to say the father is manipulated by the wife and the children" (para. 4). By the time this statement comes, the reader is likely to laugh. There is no laughter elicited by David Mamet's essay ("The Rake: A Few Scenes from My Childhood," p. 158). Despite the fact that Mamet is often a very funny writer, the story he tells of his family doesn't seem conducive to a humorous retelling. Trillin's piece could be more melancholy because it is really about a father's sense of losing his daughter to adulthood.

# Barbara Tuchman
## "THIS IS THE END OF THE WORLD": THE BLACK DEATH

### APPROACHING THE ESSAY

Barbara Tuchman relates the history of the plague that killed indiscriminately throughout Asia, Europe, and North Africa in the fourteenth century. She provides a sweeping account of its effect on Europe and also focuses on its impact on one area and one family. She recounts the tale in objective terms but also provides a great deal of description and supposition.

You might ask students to consider to what extent history is a science and to what extent it is an art like storytelling. Isolate a paragraph for students to consider in depth, highlighting particularly resonant words and phrases. How much of Tuchman's account seems based on fact? How much seems a fiction? How does Tuchman make history come alive through storytelling techniques? What would be lost or gained if the story were told in a more straightforward manner?

### ADDITIONAL ACTIVITIES

1. Have the students compare this piece to James Shreeve's "The Greatest Journey" (p. 569). In what ways do the pieces resemble one another? In what ways do they differ? How might the notion of history as a "story" be evident in each?
2. Show the students Ingmar Bergman's film *The Seventh Seal*, in which a knight is returning from the war in the midst of the Black Death. In what ways does Bergman's highly symbolic and allegorical film capture or fail to capture the mood of the time, which Tuchman tries to convey?

### GENERATING WRITING

1. Have students research the facts of a historical case for a two- to three-page research paper. The paper should include a discussion of the process of

writing history. How did the students decide between conflicting accounts? In what ways does the history shape itself as a tale?

## THE READER'S PRESENCE

1. Tuchman's narrative relates mainly fact and attempts to be objective. Her perspective is revealed by her inclusion and exclusion of certain elements in the story. For instance, she emphasizes that the poor were more affected by the plague, in general, than the rich, which is both factual and implies a judgment of the class system.

2. Readers will likely recognize human qualities—for instance, selflessness and cowardice—common to both today and the time of the plague. Students may wish to compare the plague to the AIDS epidemic or to reports about the likely consequences of an outbreak of avian flu.

3. Tuchman treats the plague from an international perspective—citing, for example, death statistics for Europe at large—and from a personal perspective—for instance, noting the effects of the plague on one Picardy family. She provides a more complete story, encompassing both the "macro" and "micro" levels, by discussing history both in aggregate and in particular examples. The reader can thus imagine both the widespread devastation of Europe and the experience of facing the plague as an individual.

4. Tuchman's statement refers to the fact that neither the cause of the plague nor the extent of its reach across countries and over time were understood at the time. The terror of the plague was deepened by the people's awareness of their ignorance. Michihiko Hachiya's personal response to the bombing of Hiroshima ("From *Hiroshima Diary*," p. 107) is absolutely absorbed in the immediate, inexplicable set of events; he cannot yet begin to contemplate the causes or effects of the bombing. Don DeLillo's essay about the attacks of September 11, 2001 ("In the Ruins of the Future: Reflections on Terror, Loss, and Time in the Shadow of September," p. 355) is slightly more removed from the event's sources and implications. The more precise comparison might be Hachiya and DeLillo to the fourteenth-century chroniclers upon whom Tuchman's history depends.

# Sherry Turkle
## HOW COMPUTERS CHANGE THE WAY WE THINK

### APPROACHING THE ESSAY

Sherry Turkle sums up the rationale behind her argument in the very first line: "The tools we use to think change the ways in which we think." Turkle's priority is thinking about these changes not in terms of technology and its uses but in terms of the social, political, and moral consequences of those uses.

Turkle builds her credibility by outlining her career studying technology at MIT and explaining the ways in which technology has changed in the last two decades. She examines how computers have changed the way we prioritize aesthetics over content, think about privacy, play with identity, and process text information. Turkle's tone makes it clear that she wants to educate us, and she does not condemn these changes out of hand. Her argument, in the end, rests on an appeal for technology literacy and open dialogue about where technology may be taking us. "Information technology is identity technology," she writes. "Embedding it in a culture that supports democracy, freedom of expression, tolerance, diversity, and complexity of opinion is one of the next decade's greatest challenges. We cannot afford to fail" (para. 32).

Ask students to analyze the tone of the essay. What kind of audience is it meant for? How does audience affect the choices that Turkle makes? You might ask students to compare this essay with Nicholas Carr's "Is Google Making Us Stupid?" (p. 633). What anxieties do the authors share? How do the authors differ?

## ADDITIONAL ACTIVITIES

1. Give students a generic free-writing prompt, such as "Describe the most important thing you did today" or "Discuss one thing you learned today." Ask them one day to handwrite the assignment. The next day, ask them to type directly on the computer. In class, have students compare the process they went through in writing by hand versus typing on the computer. Did they end up revising more the essay composed on the computer? Did their ideas have a different structure when they had to write them by hand? How much do they agree that handwriting and word processing on a computer change the way we write? Do they find themselves making different errors when handwriting than they do when typing?

2. Turkle's essay spans four decades of technological developments. As a class, make a time line of those innovations from the 1970s to the present. Which do students feel they have made use of in their lives today? How many of your students remember life before personal computers and the Internet? Which of these developments do they think have been the most important in our culture?

## GENERATING WRITING

1. Have students investigate your institution's curriculum for media or technology literacy. In what classes have issues of technology literacy been addressed? How long have these objectives been in place? Who at the university is involved in the dialogue? What are plans for future development of technology literacy? Have your students write an essay that not only summarizes their findings but evaluates whether the curriculum is sufficient to

address the issues that Turkle presents. Would she approve of this curriculum? How could the school better address technology literacy?

2. If your school does not have formal ideas outlined for technology literacy, assign students an argumentative essay in which they argue for teaching undergraduates a select curriculum to enhance their technology literacy. What skills do they think are most important in academia and the workplace today? Ask them to draw on Turkle's essay to determine what questions faculty and students should ask about how we use technology and how it may change us.

## THE READER'S PRESENCE

1. The young woman in Turkle's class uses her knowledge of computer processing to demonstrate how the human brain can make a mistake in processing information. Although Freud's theory relies on ideas about the conscious and the subconscious, the young woman here characterizes the human brain as being more like a computer. Some might argue that she has ignored the many complexities of the human brain in categorizing it simply as an information processing system. Turkle points out that this tendency toward the superficial is actually a legacy of our computer age: "Today's college students are already used to taking things at (inter)face value; their successors in 2014 will be even less accustomed to probing below the surface" (para. 24).

2. As a professor of the social sciences at MIT, Turkle is concerned with the nontechnical effects of our current technological era. Socially, she worries that online venues such as chat rooms provide people with the "illusion of companionship without the demands of friendship" (para. 13). Children have the potential to grow up without the ability to share real feelings or understand their "authentic selves" (para. 13). She is also troubled by the tendency of the current "sociotechnical culture" to represent moral dilemmas as overly simplistic battles between Good and Evil (para. 31). Even more disturbing, according to Turkle, is the fact that young Americans are complacent about the potential violations of privacy that the Web engenders. Unlike older generations, who grew up with the concept of privacy as a democratic right, students today are accustomed to the notion that they are under constant electronic surveillance (para. 10).

3. Both writers argue that technology is changing the way people think. Carr argues that the Internet has shortened our attention spans. He also says that our brains begin to behave like the machines that we use. In this respect, Turkle's argument is quite similar to Carr's. Take, for example, her account, early in the essay, of concerns voiced by faculty members in MIT's Department of Engineering: as students sacrificed the slide rule in favor of the calculator, they lost their physical sense of scale. Similarly, word processing has made the "idea of thinking ahead . . . exotic" (para. 22) because a writer can quickly fill a page. According to Turkle, this can make bad writers worse. In her discussion of PowerPoint software, Turkle cites research indicating that,

although it may teach students to organize their thoughts, it fails to teach them how to begin a discussion or construct a narrative. Throughout the essay, her argument seems to be that, for all the good it does us, technology fails to engender—and may even disable—our ability to develop critical-thinking skills and creativity. Carr and Turkle are both, therefore, suspicious of technology and its effects on the human mind. The primary difference between them seems to be that Carr is more pessimistic and more willing to lay the blame squarely on the technology. Turkle is careful to stress, in paragraph 16, that "the software cannot be blamed for lower intellectual standards."

# William Speed Weed
## 106 SCIENCE CLAIMS AND A TRUCKFUL OF BALONEY

### APPROACHING THE ESSAY

Too much advertising is a subject that touches everyone in the twenty-first century. How many times have we, as consumers who are bombarded with ads, thought about the intensity and the disingenuousness of advertising? Furthermore, with the mystifying advancements in technology over the last several decades, science has taken a central place in our daily lives. Unfortunately, as William Speed Weed points out in his essay, most of us are woefully handicapped when it comes to science. Although we are all interested in it, most of us have no idea about the scientific method or the scientific claim. Consequently, Weed's thesis asserts, we are easy targets for the hard sell—"two suckers born every three minutes" (para. 3). In a world of "promiscuous science claims, . . . 'How do we know?' is a demand for fundamental evidence" (para. 10) that most Americans simply cannot recognize or evaluate.

### ADDITIONAL ACTIVITIES

1. As a class project, have students watch television ads for a week or two at different times of the day. Ask the class to make a list of products, the time periods they are aired (hours for TV watching might be assigned to different students), and the shows that they sponsor. How many of these ads make scientific claims? How are the ads different (sophisticated, comical, serious) for different programs and time slots and presumably audiences? Who is narrating the ad? At what demographic does the ad seem to be addressed? Are ads that are specifically aimed at children (weekend morning television, for instance) also scientific? What kind of ads dominate the evening news?

Sunday morning news programs? late night variety shows? What scientific claims do they make? Are some ads more subtle than others?

2. Have groups of three or four students select a product (one not mentioned in Weed's essay) and write an ad for it that makes genuine scientific claims. Each group should present its ad to the whole class. Objectives of this assignment include truth in advertising, consideration of the demographics of their (imagined) audience, and the "marketing imperative" (para. 5). Groups should strive to create a factual, interesting, and yet convincing ad. This assignment requires research and preparation.

3. Discuss with your class the nature and process of the scientific method. How does it differ from what passes for science in popular culture? What are the paradigms within which true scientific investigation works? What is a theory? How are theories tested and proven?

## GENERATING WRITING

1. According to Weed, Americans "are easy prey to the pseudoscientific, and the National Science Board . . . blames education and the media for this" (para. 3). In "People Like Us" (p. 330), David Brooks refers to precision marketing firms that break down America into "psycho-demographic clusters" (para. 8). According to Brooks, "Looking through the market research, one can sometimes be amazed by how efficiently people cluster—and by how predictable we all are" (para. 9). In a three- to five-page paper, have students investigate their own demographic "cluster" for evidence of susceptibility to precision marketing that uses pseudoscience. What role does the media play in this manipulation? What is the role of education?

2. Assign a paper that investigates the sales history of an established product (something that has been around for at least ten years). Ask students to trace the development of the product, which should include changes that its ads have undergone in response to changes in national demographics and cultural diversification.

## THE READER'S PRESENCE

1. The disadvantages include having to interrupt that part of the essay to which each note refers, in most instances. However, footnotes provide the opportunity to read the essay in at least two ways: one might initially read the text and ignore the notes or read the notes as they appear in the text. The text without the notes is a different text: it is less detailed, less analytical, less evaluative, and more reportorial and straightforward. Note, too, that the text is written in journal form, which gives it a sense of immediacy, almost in real time; the notes seem to have come later, when the author reflected on his observations. Had the author weaved the notes into the heart of his essay, it might have seemed unduly ponderous, even boring. The notes give us the option to read or not to read (and how many and which ones to read).

2. The tone of Weed's essay is quite skeptical and remains consistent throughout. He is often frustrated by bogus claims. By the middle of the essay, he is
also frustrated with the public that "learns" its science by "aping" bogus science (para. 30). The tone of the footnotes consistently provides factual, indisputable evidence, unlike the pseudoscientific claims. Relatively neutral, the
tone of the footnotes is not as passionately presented as the main text. Also
the author has provided evaluative categories for each claim, such as "true,"
"false," "unproven," and "bogus."

3. Weed explains that the scientific language and claims seem magical to the
uninformed. According to him, "We generally believe science is good for us"
(para. 14), and therefore take the ads' claims at face value. Weed uses metaphors drawn mostly from food and nutrition: the grocery store is a "feast for a
science-claim junkie" (para. 12). He questions how "nutritious" (para. 4) the
"truck[ful] of baloney" (para. 14) is that Americans are "fed" (para. 4) daily.

4. Eric Schlosser ("Why McDonald's Fries Taste So Good," p. 558) does his own
fieldwork and interviews experts in the field. He provides us with a wealth
of details and statistics. Weed's investigative techniques also involve a kind
of fieldwork: he observes and makes note of the scientific claims in his own
environment. Schlosser's reporting seems more scientific and credible than
Weed's: we don't always know where Weed gets his facts. James Fallows's
piece ("Throwing Like a Girl," p. 400) is light and not well-documented.
Amy Cunningham ("Why Women Smile," p. 347) presents a broad outline
that draws tenuously and generally from psychological, physiological, sociological, scientific, and especially historical points of view. Like Weed, she
uses herself as the investigator. Unlike Weed, she is also the subject of her
investigation. Her references are nonspecific and of the four essays, hers is
certainly the most subjective, making no pretense to be "scientific."

# Tom Wolfe
## HOOKING UP

### APPROACHING THE ESSAY

Using Robert Lacey and Danny Danziger's *The Year 1000* (1999) as a model,
Tom Wolfe, writing as though he were a social theorist from the future, describes
American culture in the year 2000. If the year 1000 was "an Englishman's world,"
as Lacey and Danziger's subtitle proclaims, then 2000 is an American's world,
as Wolfe clearly illustrates. Wolfe uses humor to satirize how far our culture has
"progressed." He takes a far-removed, scholarly tone to describe intellectuals, the
progress of the working class, the power of the United States, the Internet, and
the "sexual revolution." Wolfe spends some time describing the sexual behavior

of today's teenagers and the casual attitude with which today's youth regard sex. Here Wolfe implicitly expresses his judgment of modern American sexual mores: "At puberty the dams, if any were left, burst" (para. 9). Wolfe explores the practice of "hooking up" like an anthropologist or animal behaviorist would, describing terminology, ritual, and rules. Wolfe uses historical comparisons to contextualize the changes in our culture. He compares the old terminology of "first base" to the new milestones of sexual behavior, claims that the old fear of looking poor has been replaced by a fear of looking old, and compares the new West Coast billionaires with old East Coast money.

Ask students to consider to what extent Wolfe is exaggerating his claims for the purpose of satire and critique. What aspects of his portrayal do students find accurate? What do they find misleading or poorly informed? What is Wolfe's purpose in portraying contemporary U.S. culture in this light? Why do students think that Wolfe chooses a scholarly tone to satirize American culture? Is it effective? What other styles could he have used to make the same point?

## ADDITIONAL ACTIVITIES

1. Students may want to read more of Wolfe's essays from *Hooking Up* (2000), for which this essay served as the preface. In it, Wolfe skewers journalism, science, the sexual mores of today's youth, the computer industry, and more.
2. In small groups, have students outline Wolfe's examples, along with a description of the change each exemplifies. Then, as a class, discuss what judgments Wolfe seems to be making about these changes. What is he saying about shifts in our cultural values? What seems to be motivating these changes? What other examples can students come up with about how our culture's values are changing?

## GENERATING WRITING

1. Ask students to imitate Wolfe's style and project by picking a cultural, political, or social institution—such as higher education, the electoral process, religion, public schools, or major league sports—and portray its position in a historical context. Students will need to research some history and may even want to interview older family members for an additional perspective on how things have changed.
2. Ask students to find three reviews of Wolfe's book *Hooking Up*. Have them write a short essay comparing the reviews and using illustrations from the essay to support or refute the reviewers' claims. Ask them to come to their own conclusions about the strengths and weaknesses in Wolfe's style and argument.

## THE READER'S PRESENCE

1. Wolfe opens his essay by saying that the terms *proletariat* and *working class* are dead in 2000, suggesting that this population no longer distinguishes

itself from the comfortable middle class. The language of sex is radically changed in 2000. There is no use for *perversion* and *pornography* (now *adult material*), meaning that indecency is no longer a concern. *Dating* is a defunct term and *virgin* now holds a stigma. Wolfe notes that young women use the term *scoring* to demonstrate that they have adopted a formerly male perspective about casual sex. Several of the terms Wolfe mentions, such as *hooking up* and *crash*, designate the influence of computers on our society.

2. Wolfe uses a tongue-in-cheek tone to satirize the cultural and moral condition of the United States in 2000. To emphasize how Americans no longer look to Europe for guidance, Wolfe describes an American working man's disregard for European science: "He considered European hygiene so primitive that to receive an injection in a European clinic voluntarily was sheer madness" (para. 2). Wolfe also uses exaggeration in his description of the sexual mores of Americans, from teenagers to grandmothers. He does not seriously suggest that all expectant mothers are having their bellybuttons pierced to avoid feeling old or that all junior high school girls are performing fellatio in the school corridors or that all middle-aged men are spending entire days surfing "adult material" on the Internet. He uses hyperbole for comic effect and to paint a general picture of modern America and its sexual and moral decadence.

3. Wolfe uses satire and hyperbole to implicitly critique his subject. He presents his cultural observations from a distance and without explicit commentary. Purposefully using colloquial language, he thus calls attention to the cultural changes he is discussing. Lauren Slater's tone in "The Trouble with Self-Esteem" (p. 822) is sincere, rather than satirical, so students will probably find her more objective. She also establishes objective credentials through her use of expertise. Both authors are concerned with trends they see in American culture, particularly those toward self-centeredness and away from self-control. Slater and Wolfe reinforce each others' arguments: the sexual carnival that Wolfe describes after the year 2000 is peopled by Slater's undisciplined citizens.

# Virginia Woolf
## THE DEATH OF THE MOTH

### APPROACHING THE ESSAY

From the standpoint of description, Virginia Woolf's essay stands as one of the finest in the genre. This description of a dying moth, however, is not merely a writer's exercise. Woolf is brought closer to her subject by her use of detail and as a result achieves insight into the forces that control life.

One way that your students might begin to think about the essay's structure is to consider the unfolding of emotion on the part of the writer. The primary emotion Woolf refers to is pity. In paragraph 2, Woolf pities the moth because its frame of existence, the window pane, is so limited when compared to the larger view Woolf has from her place behind the window. Then, in paragraph 3, she extends her pity to the moth on the grounds of its insignificance in the scheme of things. In paragraph 4, a third wave of pity comes over the author as it dawns on her that the moth is dying. Ask your students how pity differs from compassion. To what extent might Woolf's expression of compassion instead of pity point to a recognition that the properties that apply to the moth also apply to her? Do they think that she has deliberately avoided such a recognition?

The moth's struggle against death also provides Woolf with an insight into the nature of artistic activity and especially that of writing. The act of writing, signified by the pencil she thinks of using to help the moth right itself, itself becomes an assertion of the human will against death. Ask your students to identify moments in the essay where Woolf seems as concerned with her own mortality as with that of the moth. Was it Woolf's intention to construct correspondences between the moth's limited existence and our own? What does she consider to be the place of the human being in the scheme of nature? Would she say that our lives are more significant than those of moths and other creatures?

## ADDITIONAL ACTIVITIES

1. Ask your class what the essay might have been like if it had been written as a purely objective description of the dying moth. Then have students attempt to rewrite a paragraph from the essay in this mode. What kinds of details are lost? What happens to the role of the writer in this kind of description?
2. Ask your students to consider the extent to which Woolf internalizes the experiences of the dying moth. Discuss whether Woolf seems more affected emotionally or intellectually by the death. Students should support their views with direct reference to individual passages.

## GENERATING WRITING

1. Woolf spends most of her essay describing the moth; she says very little directly about the place of the writer. Ask your students to write an essay in which they consider the role of the narrator-writer and how the essay indirectly explores the process of writing itself.
2. Once observed, small events like the death of a moth can have a profound effect on the way the observer thinks about the world. Ask your students to think about a minor occurrence that they observed, which later had just this sort of effect on them. They should then write an essay in which they describe this experience, making its importance known to the reader through description only. They should try to avoid direct comment on the incident.

## THE READER'S PRESENCE

1. By using the article *the* instead of *a* in her title, Woolf generalizes the experience she has witnessed. A moth becomes the type of all moths, and all moths in turn point to all living things, including Woolf herself. The essay thus becomes a meditation on the struggles of the living in the face of death.

2. The pencil, because it is the tool used by the writer, becomes the symbol of Woolf herself. Thus Woolf's desire to use a pencil to help the moth right itself may symbolize the writer's desire to intervene in the flow of experience by capturing and even arresting its moments in writing.

3. Lists of similarities and differences between the essays by Woolf and by Annie Dillard ("The Death of a Moth," p. 371) could go on and on, so you'll want to be careful to focus your students' attention on the elaborations of the questions that follow the list suggestion: have them compare and contrast tone, specifically, as well as diction, metaphor, and irony. For Woolf, "the moth" becomes a metaphor for life itself, and so for all of us. Dillard's treatment of "a moth" is also, in some ways, metaphorical, but her attitude is much less grave, even though the death she witnesses is much more grotesque. Dillard doesn't make so much of her moth, but she doesn't make so much of *herself*, either. Her essay is funnier in this respect, but also more depressing. Woolf takes life and death seriously, and taking them seriously validates them. Dillard's refusal to take them quite so seriously, when juxtaposed with the horrible burning death that she witnesses, makes her piece more disturbing because it suggests not only that life is suffering, but that our suffering is ultimately trivial and insignificant. There's nothing lofty about it. Hence, Dillard's loneliness is funny, and for being funny, all the more sad.

# PART 3

# ARGUMENTATIVE WRITING
## Contending with Issues

---

# Nicholas Carr
## IS GOOGLE MAKING US STUPID?

### APPROACHING THE ESSAY

Carr's general argument is that the Internet shortens its users' attention spans. He writes, "What the Net seems to be doing is chipping away at my capacity for concentration and contemplation. My mind now expects to take in information the way the Net distributes it: in a swiftly moving stream of particles" (para. 4).

Students should be excited about this topic. If there's anything they know well, it's the Web. They should be immediately attracted to a debate about whether Carr's argument is sound. Some of them may feel Carr is right on point, while others may think his reasoning is faulty or only true in some cases. Either way, the essay should make for a lively class debate.

Direct students to the way Carr supports his major claim: the Web is shortening our attention spans. Carr begins by giving other examples of people who have also experienced this attention-span loss. He notes that a pathologist named Bruce Friedman has found the same about his attention span. At the same time, Carr says that anecdotes don't prove much and that "long-term neurological and psychological" studies need to be done (para 7). His strongest evidence for the claim that the Web is changing how we think is his explanation of how Friedrich Nietzsche's writing changed as a result of the invention of the typewriter. Carr writes, "[Nietzsche's] already terse prose had become even tighter, more telegraphic" (para. 11). Carr uses this example to show that the human brain is "infinitely malleable" (para. 13) and will adapt to the technology that it has to use. Here students should find Carr's most interesting point: our brains don't simply adapt, they actually begin to act like the technology they use. Thus, in the quick-moving world of the Web, in which it's so easy to jump from article to video to comic strip, our brains learn to read in that same, jumpy, skimming way.

Students should note what other historical technological advances Carr uses as examples, besides Nietzsche. A group exercise for this essay would be an effective method to show students how Carr supports his major claim. He uses so many different examples and pieces of evidence, students should be able to generate a long list. Have students decide which pieces of evidence are most effective and why. Learning how one supports an argument is crucial to understanding how to create a stance and, if for nothing else, that is why this essay will make a good teaching tool. Finally, it is important to note how Carr addresses detractors to his argument. It's easy to see how Carr supports his claim, but it may not be as clear to students how he addresses those who might disagree with the negative effects of Web life.

## ADDITIONAL ACTIVITIES

1. Ask students to do an experiment. Ask them to do research without using a computer whatsoever: no Google, no Ask.com, no databases. They have to go to the library and do research on any subject they choose. Ask them to find two books or two scholarly articles and to report back both their findings on the subject and how difficult or easy it was to find the information without the aid of a computer or the Web. Also, did they find the research any more compelling? When they read the articles, were they more or less immersed? Ask them to contemplate the positives of such hands-on research versus searching online.

2. Ask students to form small groups. As best they can, have them outline Carr's argument. What are his claims and what are some types of evidence he uses to support those claims? Is all his evidence similar or different? Students should find that Carr's evidence is highly varied. This might be a good way to help demonstrate the importance of considering rhetorical strategies like ethos, pathos, and logos.

## GENERATING WRITING

1. Have students construct a refutation essay in which they research Carr's subject and attempt to find positions that either disagree entirely or disagree in part with Carr's claims. Then they should construct a refutation paper in which they attempt to either discredit entirely or discredit in part Carr's claim. In doing so, students should be aware that they are constructing their own argument, one that is against Carr's but that also is their own. They could model their essay on Carr's, using different types of evidence to support their claim.

2. Have students create a mini-essay that agrees with Carr's and, like Carr's, draws on personal anecdotes for support. The idea is that they're furthering Carr's argument with their own personal experience. They could bring in their own direct experience with the Web; they could use family members or friends as examples. It might be a good idea to have them map out their Internet use in an hour, tracking each site and how much time they spend on each site as a way to construct some valid and interesting evidence to support their claim.

## THE READER'S PRESENCE

1. Carr's use of personal experience is a rhetorical strategy, working on the reader's identification with his observation. We've all, like Carr, experienced

that feeling of trolling through the vast lands of the Internet and skimming articles and blogs here and there after small bits of information. Readers will recognize in themselves the same kind of skimming techniques that Carr speaks of and will in turn be immediately more likely to agree with his claim that the Internet does not encourage deep reading, contemplation, or extended attention. Coupling this technique of personal anecdote with more scientific and historical pieces of evidence makes for a highly successful argument.

2. Carr's support begins with personal anecdote, his own personal experience with the Web and it's attention-shortening effects; then he references a study by University College London, which examined online research habits, he discusses a developmental psychologist's idea of how the Web will affect thinking, and finally he presents historical anecdotes of famous thinkers who encountered new technologies, as with Nietzsche and the typewriter. Carr's essay successfully vacillates among many different fields and types of sources, all the while transitioning smoothly between these different sources, almost as though each is a simple click away.

3. The structures of Carr's and Pico Iyer's ("The Inner Climate," p. 693) arguments are completely different. Carr relies on numerous sources to make his argument truly convincing. His is a complex and research-filled article. Iyer, however, makes a possibly more elegant argument. Although Carr's essay is effective and convincing, Iyer uses only a brief personal anecdote to highlight the point that we all need to look within before looking without for answers to the global climate problem. Settle oneself, Iyer believes, and the world will have a better chance at settling itself. Both arguments focus on the need for reflection and contemplation, but Iyer's argument is certainly more Zen-like, more Buddhist, and more focused on, not moving forward, but the cycles of change. Iyer's essay is simple and precise and more focused on the individual. Although shorter than Carr's, it also asks more of the reader: it asks the reader to sit still and contemplate without any interference from the TV or newspaper or cell phone or Web.

# Jared Diamond
## THE ENDS OF THE WORLD AS WE KNOW THEM

### APPROACHING THE ESSAY

This essay comes from Jared Diamond's book, *Collapse* (2004), which explores how and why many ancient civilizations fell apart, and which also compliments his Pulitzer Prize–winning *Guns, Germs, and Steel* (1997), an exploration of the cultural and environmental reasons why certain civilizations have thrived. Diamond's books are compelling in part because his research encompasses so much territory in such depth and in part because he puts modern questions of our survival into a broad historical and cultural context.

Diamond poses his argument in the context of New Year's Day, asking his audience to take the time to think of both the future of our culture and its place in a much wider context of thousands of years of civilization. Instead of thinking about the future of the country in the next year, he urges us to think about the long-term future of our society. Diamond outlines five factors that he has seen play a role in the collapse of societies: environmental damage; climate change; war; changes in trade; and the society's political, economic, and social responses to these changes. He then puts the idea of societal collapse into a historical context by outlining the cases of the Mayan and Polynesian settlers on Pitcairn Island. Diamond also uses examples of long-term successes, such as the Japanese, northern Europeans, and New Guinean Highlanders as prototypes of how to deal successfully with crises.

The lesson Diamond draws from these histories is that we must take environmental issues seriously because our survival may depend on doing so. He also makes the point that our world is much more interrelated now and that one society's collapse may result in disaster for many others. Diamond outlines two characteristics shared by societies headed for collapse: (1) the elite are sheltered from the destructive decisions they make, and (2) the people fail to adapt or to change longstanding values or habits even though clinging to old habits limits the chance of survival. He connects bad decisions made by elite Americans to parallel situations in ancient civilizations. Diamond also cites the Norwegians who settled in Greenland as an example of a society whose insistence on maintaining their traditions led to their downfall. Ask students if they can think of more examples of Diamond's collapse-threatening characteristics in our society or in other societies with which they may be familiar.

Discuss with your class the differences between this general-audience essay and the academic excerpt that follows it. Point out the different structures and stylistic choices. Which piece is more easily outlined? Why? You may ask students to outline paragraphs 20 through 31 in "The Ends of the World as We Know Them." Note the clear transitions, the organized paragraphs with clear examples and support, and the use of comparison and contrast. How does this organization compare to that in the academic piece? Draw your students' attention to the use of simple imperative and declarative sentences in the first piece compared to the complexity of sentence structure in the academic piece. What assumptions does Diamond make about his academic audience and where can students locate these assumptions? Why does the general-audience piece seem to have more detail than the academic piece? Why does Diamond include textual references (para. 2) in the academic piece but not in the preceding essay? Finally, ask students to isolate vocabulary in each essay that suggests the level of expertise of the two audiences.

## ADDITIONAL ACTIVITIES

1. Diamond's accessible research and clear style make this essay a good model for how to present an argument. Ask students to work in small groups to

outline Diamond's thesis, claims, evidence, and proposal. What are his strongest examples? What are his weakest? Does he anticipate an opposition that might claim that environmental concerns are not pressing? How could his argument be strengthened?

2. The Kyoto Treaty has been designed as a cooperative global attempt to address the problems of global warming. Ask students to do some online research about the arguments for and against the Kyoto Treaty. Why did the United States decide not to sign it? What are the major arguments in the United States for and against ratifying the treaty? What do students think Diamond's position on U.S. involvement is, and why?

## GENERATING WRITING

1. Ask students to choose one of the many historical examples Diamond gives in his essay and research it further for a five-page essay that addresses these questions: How did the culture evolve? What were its major political and cultural beliefs? When did its downfall begin? Which of the five factors led most to its destruction? How can we apply these lessons to our own culture's survival?

2. Assign students a short argumentative editorial on the subject of how your community might take environmental problems more seriously and create a more sustainable community. You might want to present several examples of editorials in class and discuss style and argumentative techniques. Also discuss how to write toward a specific audience, depending on how reluctant readers might be to adopt the writer's proposal. You might also want to encourage students to submit their editorials for publication in a local or campus paper to further stress the practical application of their writing.

3. Many writers and journalists have explored the idea that the United States is at the peak of its power and that our culture is showing signs of strain that might presage the end of the American empire. Some students may be interested in exploring this idea in the realm of politics, the military, and the economy. Ask them to research several writers' views on the subject and then write a paper that presents and debates these claims. How seriously should we take these predictions? Do the writers offer solutions or merely present the case as inevitable? How does Diamond's essay compare to other writers' views?

## THE READER'S PRESENCE

1. By putting the question of our society's survival in a historical context, Diamond compares our society's behaviors objectively with those of many others and allows us to analyze our behavior without the political commentary that often guides these conversations. Diamond's broad historical study of successful and unsuccessful societies suggests that our own society's survival depends on exactly the same factors as that of a culture three centuries ago. Some might argue that Diamond's broad historical context ignores many

modern developments that may make other factors in our survival more important than environmental ones.

2. Diamond makes a number of connections between America's current fiscal, environmental, and foreign policies and those of several now-defunct past cultures. Diamond points to our own American elite classes, who live in gated communities, send their children to private schools, and rely on private pensions, as dangerously alienated from the civic issues that contribute to a society's long-term stability. In addition, Americans must face their "unrestrained consumerism" (para. 26), which is no longer practical in our world of dwindling resources. Finally, Diamond argues that we must reappraise our tendency toward shortsighted militaristic responses to foreign threats. Instead, we should focus on "the underlying problems of public health, population and environment that ultimately cause threats to us to emerge in poor countries" (para. 29). Students might want to address additional potential cultural threats treated in other essays in this compilation, such as racism, religious extremism, and "moral" deterioration. How might these issues contribute to America's long-term survival?

3. Diamond is concerned with the way a growing population draws on shrinking resources. He points out that, in the past, civilizations have collapsed abruptly and unexpectedly for more or less the same reasons: too many people, not enough resources. Michael Pollan's essay ("What's Eating America," p. 781) is more focused. Pollan is concerned about the global environment, but he's focused on the United States and the way we grow corn. Both writers make compelling arguments, so students are likely to have mixed reactions. Because Pollan is so specific, he is convincing. He draws on science and history in a more apparently academic way than Diamond. But Diamond's essay takes a big-picture approach, which is also very persuasive. Students may not be as concerned about what happened in Iceland a thousand years ago as they are with what happens in America now, but the picture Diamond paints is grim enough to raise some antennae.

# Barbara Ehrenreich
## WILL WOMEN STILL NEED MEN?

### APPROACHING THE ESSAY

Barbara Ehrenreich speculates about whether, given the advances in bio-research and cloning, women will still need men in the future. The question is certainly facetious on at least two levels: one is that Ehrenreich doesn't seem to believe particularly that women *need* men now, never mind in the future (she does not, in any case, believe that they need husbands); the other is that, despite the hypothetical futures that she predicts, she does not seem to believe sincerely that men and women will stop being attracted to one another, getting involved with one another, living together, getting married, or having (and raising) children together. In paragraph 3, for example, Ehrenreich predicts that men and women will designate a "Mason-Dixon Line and sort themselves out accordingly." The irony is clear, simply because the prediction is absurd, and students should be able to recognize that the article is tongue-in-cheek: they will probably even be able to understand that Ehrenreich is using irony to make a larger argument.

But you might find that students have difficulty recognizing just how radical the argument is. This is probably because most first-year writing students have been exposed to the argument that women can get along just fine without men, that women don't *need* husbands. Students are less likely to have been exposed to the idea that the institutions of marriage, family, and monogamy are artificial and harmful social constructs. Among friends, they may have said themselves that they don't want to get married or that marriage is just a piece of paper. They may have even thought, at one time or another, that monogamy is unnatural. But they probably haven't heard it in English class, and—despite conversations they've had among friends—many of them will feel threatened when they see the argument in print, in school. They don't mind telling each other that marriage is nonsense, but they don't want their *teacher* to tell them that the social constructs they grew up with are nonsense, their boyfriends or girlfriends will eventually move on, and their mothers and fathers are the victims of a hoax.

Your students might get a laugh out of the essay, though, particularly through the beginning, and you can use that to get them engaged in the discussion. After you go through the essay and have a few laughs, rest a minute on paragraph 14, where Ehrenreich argues that "the real paradigm shift will come when we stop trying to base our entire society on the wavering sexual connection between individuals." Ask the students what the sentence means. What is the current paradigm? In what ways is "our entire society" based "on the wavering sexual connection"? And how will the paradigm shift when we stop basing our society on such a connection?

## ADDITIONAL ACTIVITIES

1. Compare Ehrenreich's essay to Dave Barry's "Beauty and the Beast" (p. 315). Both authors use irony to make arguments about problematic cultural constructs. Which argument is more compelling? Why? In what ways would Barry and Ehrenreich agree about the differences between men and women? In what ways would they disagree?

2. Your students are probably familiar with the standard arguments for and against gay marriage, but it is unlikely that many of them, in a first-year writing course, have been exposed to Queer Theory critiques. You might have them read Susan Thompson's "Speak Now or Forever Hold Your Peace? Why We Need Queer Critiques of Gay Marriage." It is easy to find online, and it serves as a good introduction to some of the basic ideas. How do the ideas Thompson discusses resonate with Ehrenreich's? Although Thompson's article is primarily concerned with gay marriage in Canada, advocates of gay

marriage are generally seen, in both the United States and Canada, as politically and socially liberal: in the United States, that means that Democrats, rather than Republicans, are more likely to advocate licensure for same-sex unions. Feminists (such as Ehrenreich) also generally fall into the liberal camp. It might challenge your students, therefore, to learn that some thinkers who would otherwise be considered liberal are in fact suspicious of gay marriage, and asking your students to disentangle the web of arguments surrounding the issue might be a useful way to help them develop sharper critical-thinking skills. How does the Queer critique of gay marriage affect your students' perception of the debate on gay marriage?

## GENERATING WRITING

1. Using Ehrenreich's rhetorical strategies—irony, exaggeration, and humor— have the students write an essay called "Will Men Still Need Women?"

2. Have the students write a research paper responding to the Queer critique of gay marriage. Insist that they avoid the standard arguments for and against licensure: for this assignment, their job is not to say that marriage is by definition between a man and a woman or that marriage is a civil right. Rather, they should respond to the notion that marriage itself is the problem, that gay marriage would only reinforce the normalization of an institution that is by its very nature problematic. One way of engaging the argument would be to research feminist critiques of marriage, as well.

3. Have the students write a response to the critique of marriage, in general. Does marriage force people into boxes? Does it work in service of capitalism? Is it bad for women? for society in general? Is it the artificial and flimsy social construct that Ehrenreich seems to suggest?

## THE READER'S PRESENCE

1. Throughout the essay, Ehrenreich introduces hypotheticals and hyperboles, jokes that she later explores in more serious terms, using facts to support her arguments. This essay seems to be intended to make an otherwise unsettling argument about the structure of society and to be humorous and easy to read. For example, it is unlikely—absurd, even—that men and women will separate geographically, but Ehrenreich is quick to point out that people like Charlotte Perkins Gilman, a famous feminist and author, have postulated such a separation as a possible utopia (para. 4). Ehrenreich provides statistical evidence for men and women wanting to separate, as well, in the form of divorce statistics. But when she moves on to suggest that one day divorce might be illegalized, she is almost certainly being facetious: it is unlikely that divorce will be outlawed in the United States, if only because divorce is so common here. Ehrenreich leads almost every piece of her argument with a joke before elaborating with facts and logic.

2. Ehrenreich seems to believe that monogamous relationships—and marriage (in particular, the family as traditionally imagined)—are flimsy as foundations

for society. She also seems to believe that the institution of marriage is a little too much "institution" and not quite enough love. She seems to think that the traditional constructs are too limiting and that a truly enlightened humanity would accept all sorts of unions, gay and straight, temporary and long term, as equally valid. By likening this sort of tolerance to growing up, Ehrenreich suggests that intolerance is infantile, as are cultural constructs like marriage. In other words, to disagree with Ehrenreich is infantile. You might ask your students if they feel that this is an effective rhetorical strategy and to explain why or why not.

3. Michael Chabon's authority ("Faking It," p. 343) comes from experience. Ehrenreich draws on sources other than her own experience. They both use humor, but Ehrenreich is more interested in making an argument of social significance, while the social significance of Chabon's essay is more implicit than explicit: he jokes that many social ills can be blamed on "faking it," but he's talking about what it's like to *be* a man, personally; Ehrenreich addresses her subject matter as a sociopolitical issue, and only a personal one for the reason that we all have some personal stake in it. She deals with ideas and arguments. He deals with his own life. One is inclined to go along with Chabon, because—again—he's talking about what it's like to be a man. Because he is a man, he doesn't need any additional qualifications. Some readers—men in particular—might be more resistant to Ehrenreich's argument because from time to time she seems to be criticizing men, specifically.

# Nora Ephron
## THE BOSTON PHOTOGRAPHS

### APPROACHING THE ESSAY

For the first half of the essay, Nora Ephron presents a relatively objective summary of how the public and the media reacted to three photographs depicting a deadly fire-escape collapse in Boston. She opens with the words of the photographer himself, alluding to his intent to capture the scene but also his horror when the woman and child fell from the fire escape: "I realized what was going on and I completely turned around, because I didn't want to see her hit" (para. 1). Ephron describes the photographs, assuming some audience familiarity with them, and details how the photographs were taken and where they were distributed in the media. "The photographs are indeed sensational," she states (para. 4), before moving on to summarize the public's typical reaction to the inclusion of the photographs in daily newspapers. It is not until Ephron presents both the public's reaction, in the form of letters to the editor, and the *Washington Post* ombudsman's written justification that her argument is revealed. She calls the readers' objections censorship and labels them "puritanical" (para. 11). The argument for the privacy of death is hypocritical, she argues, given that we intrude on funerals or morgues and feel free to print photographs of accident scenes where people have lost their lives. "Death," Ephron writes, "happens to be one of life's main events" (para. 12). She sees the media not only as the purveyor of news but also as a documenter of the human experience.

Ephron never argues that the photographs are not sensational or that some media might publish them only for the shock value. She does, however, question the logic behind the newspapers' justification, arguing that the real purpose of publishing the Boston photographs was not really to educate the public on fire-escape safety or to depict a scene of "slum life" (she questions whether the neighborhood can be labeled a "ghetto") or to present a newsworthy event. "They deserve to be printed because they are great pictures, breathtaking pictures of something that happened," she concludes. "That they disturb readers is exactly as it should be: that's why photojournalism is often more powerful than written journalism" (para. 13).

By remaining objective in the first half of the essay, Ephron structures her argument so that readers have an opportunity to form their own opinion and to accept the justifications that she quickly refutes in the second half of the essay. Ask students if they think it is a successful strategy for Ephron to keep her own opinion silent for so long. Why does she present the information without editorializing? What opinion have students reached before they come to Ephron's argument? It might be helpful to have students examine the photographs Ephron discusses, which are reproduced with the essay, before they read her article, and ask them to write a paragraph in which they decide whether the photographs should have been published. Does Ephron's argument change their minds?

## ADDITIONAL ACTIVITIES

1. Break students into groups of three or four, and have each group research one sensational photograph or video clip that incited a discussion of sensationalism or censorship in the media. You might brainstorm as a class to get started. Possible topics include Janet Jackson's Superbowl clip, restrictions on broadcast coverage of military coffins during the Iraq war, or video footage of hostages being executed. Ask students to apply Ephron's standards to their case and debate her argument.

2. Have students research the rules governing what can and cannot be published or broadcast by American media. How well do these standards protect the public from "the sensational"? To what degree do your students think the rules restrict media freedom? How important do they think media freedom is?

## GENERATING WRITING

1. Have the class consider how Ephron's standards for photojournalism might apply to sensational video footage played on the nightly news. Discuss the public's reaction to the footage of assaults on Americans in Iraq or any other

sensational news coverage. What might Ephron say about networks' decisions to play these sensational clips? How might she react to incidents when news networks decided not to play video footage or show photographs that are arguably newsworthy? Where is the line between informing the public and protecting the privacy of individuals?

2. Several essays in *The Writer's Presence* discuss the way images have power to influence our understanding of human experience. Have students choose one of the following essays with accompanying photograph(s): Charles Simic, "The Life of Images" (p. 575) or Errol Morris, "Liar, Liar, Pants on Fire" (p. 753). Assign students an analytical essay that examines how the inclusion of the image(s) enhances the text. Would the essay be less successful if the photograph(s) were omitted? What is the role of the image in the essay?

## THE READER'S PRESENCE

1. Ephron initially describes the photographs for her readers without any accompanying editorial commentary, and she goes on to present the *Washington Post*'s ombudsman's defense of their publication without much commentary. Readers may fall easily for either of these two arguments, which makes the emergence of Ephron's own argument more striking. Ephron's essay takes a turn in paragraph 10. Here, she points out that the arguments on both sides hinge on the fact that the woman in the photographs died: "The questions Seib raises are worth discussing—though not exactly for the reasons he mentions" (para. 11). Ephron thus argues that the press should reconsider how and why we censor death in the press, and why our standing rules against printing photographs of the dead go unquestioned. Ephron's argument stands out because she questions the basis for the argument that both sides are coming from: that death should be kept out of the press. The way she structures the essay is highly successful because it brings attention to how little we, as Americans, question our "Puritan" ideas about death, and what the purpose of the press should be.

2. Ephron offers a number of refutations to other newspapers' rationalizations for printing the controversial photographs. She points out that the photographs do not document ghetto life, since the neighborhood in question is not a ghetto; their true objective is not to educate the public about fire safety, since it's unlikely that slum landlords will truly change because of the photographs; and that a common, albeit fatal, fire in Boston is not national news. Ephron suggests that photojournalism should not be just about what is newsworthy, but about the events of people's lives—of photographs that capture "something that had happened" (para. 7). Photojournalism is powerful precisely because of its ability to capture a single moment as it unfolds, and this power brings with it the potential for intense discomfort.

3. Ephron argues that the photos are sensational in that they capture "death in action" (para. 4), but that our reaction stems partly from a "Puritan" inability to treat death as a natural part of life. The power of the photographs stems

mostly from the fact that someone was able to capture the event so vividly and depict a rare glimpse of a moment before death. The fact that the woman died, however, is not sensational itself, Ephron would argue. Yet knowing the outcome cannot help but affect the way we read a document—whether a photograph or a text. The Lusitania photograph in Morris's essay becomes poignant only after the viewer has gained knowledge of the event that took place and the meaning behind it. Morris points out that photographs have more of an impact because of their contexts. Ephron would probably agree, although she would add that effective photojournalism should grip its viewer upon the first glance.

# Jonathan Safran Foer
## LET THEM EAT DOG

### APPROACHING THE ESSAY

If your students have already read Jonathan Swift's "A Modest Proposal" (p. 831), the parallels to Foer's "Let Them Eat Dog" will be obvious. In any case, "Let Them Eat Dog" is likely to elicit a more powerful reaction, chiefly because it is contemporary: although your students are unlikely to be ruffled by anything you can say about the Irish potato famine, many (probably most) of them will be meat-eaters, so Foer's essay will present as a direct challenge to their lifestyles. The information in the essay will be new to many of your students, as well. Some of them are likely to be vocal in their disgust. Those who remain unfazed will probably be in the minority. Even students who claim to be unfazed are probably more unhinged than they are prepared to admit. Indeed, the strength of the essay lies in its ability to unhinge, and those who claim to be unfazed might very well be those who protest most loudly: eating meat is natural, they will say; eating dog is different. Many students are likely to be so unhinged that it will prove difficult to manage the discussion. As a piece of writing, "Let Them Eat Dog" is worth studying if only for that reason. Why is the essay so provocative?

There are two arguments: the ironic one (it's okay to eat dog) and the sincere one (maybe it's not okay to eat animals). The question raised by the ironic argument is certainly worth talking about: why is it okay to eat some animals but not others? Whatever your students believe, Foer's rhetorical strategy is cunning, and bears scrutiny. If your students learn anything about writing, it is likely to be as a result of an examination of Foer's logic, which seems at times irrefutable. Like Swift, Foer takes a taboo and suggests it as a reasonable option. But Swift's proposal is different, first because it is a response to an emergency situation (famine) and second because it is patently absurd: practically no one in any culture would actually consider eating children a reasonable solution to famine. Despite the comparison invoked in the subtitle of Foer's essay ("A Modest Proposal for Tossing Fido in the Oven"), the dynamics of his argument are quite different. Apparently, a lot of people find it perfectly acceptable to eat dog. In order to condemn the practice, one has to either invoke cultural superiority or concede that the taboo is arbitrary and that eating dog is no different from eating pig (and therefore perfectly acceptable). Most readers will be uncomfortable assuming cultural superiority (it smacks of racism). Forced to concede that the taboo is arbitrary and unable or unwilling to concede that it's okay to eat dog, Foer hopes the reader will go for the only remaining conclusion: that the taboo is arbitrary, and therefore it is not okay to eat pigs or cows or chickens any more than it is okay to eat dogs. Dismantling the argument in order to show your students how it works is the key to teaching the essay, but because the subject matter is so emotional that might be difficult to do. You might try illustrating the arguments with letters, instead of ideas: if A, then B or C; if A and not C, then B; and so on. Either way, it's likely to be an interesting class.

## ADDITIONAL ACTIVITIES

1. Show your students the PETA video *Meet Your Meat*, which you can easily find online. Some of them may have seen it before. Ask them how (or if) it changes their feelings about eating meat. Does the fact that the animals suffer greatly prior to slaughter change the ethical implications of eating them? How and why? Try reversing the equation: if the animals were treated well, would it be more acceptable to slaughter and eat them? You can bring the discussion back to the essay by pointing out that most dog owners treat their dogs relatively well. If treating an animal well makes eating it less offensive, you might ask, again, why we don't eat dogs.

2. You might have your students read the Peter Singer and Jim Mason article "The Ethics of Eating Meat" (found in *The Ethics of What We Eat: Why Our Food Choices Matter*), in which the authors attack the argument that it is okay to eat animals because they do not experience pain the same way that humans do: animals might *feel* the pain, but it is often argued that the emotional experience of stress and fear is much less complicated for a less intelligent animal. Singer and Mason point out that people with intellectual and mental disorders (such as intellectual disabilities) also have a lower capacity for complex emotional or intellectual experiences that accompany pain, yet we are not dismissive about their suffering. Is our only ethical obligation to members of our own species? Why or why not? Foer uses a variation on Singer and Mason's argument (without citing it) in paragraph 9.

## GENERATING WRITING

1. Have your students write an ironic essay in which they defend something they think is wrong. For example, if you have a student who feels that the death penalty is wrong, he or she could write an essay advocating a return to

public executions. Arguing in favor of public executions might serve to illuminate why capital punishment might be unethical or hypocritical, regardless of whether it takes place in public or behind closed doors. A pro-life
student might write a paper in defense of abortion, maybe advocating a free
clinic in the local high school, thereby using irony to suggest that our cultural attitudes toward abortion are too casual. A pro-choice student might
write an essay suggesting that all reproductive decisions should be made by
men and that the law should require women to have a predetermined number of children (say, 2.5?) by the time they are thirty.

2. Have the students write a sincere paper offering and defending their own
beliefs about eating meat. Do they eat meat? How much meat? How often?
Most people in America are completely removed from the reality of meat
production: by the time it gets to us, it's packaged. We don't have to think
about the animals. Confronted by Foer's argument and the video *Meet Your
Meat*, can we continue to eat meat? Is it unethical? Is it ethical in certain
circumstances? If so, in what circumstances?

## THE READER'S PRESENCE

1. Many students will be appalled by the idea of eating dog and disgusted by
the recipe. Foer clearly intends to suggest that the taboo against eating dogs
is arbitrary and that if you object to eating dogs you ought to object to eating
animals, period. His approach is certainly compelling, but your students are
likely to have such strong reactions to the idea of eating dog that it's difficult
to predict how they will react to Foer's argument. A few of them might simply say "that's different," without being able to offer a logical justification for
that point of view.

2. Again, some students are likely to react so strongly that they won't be able
to come up with a lot of rational reasons to argue against Foer. That doesn't
mean they won't disagree with him when he explains that it's illogical to put
dogs to sleep and dispose of the corpses when we could be using them to
feed the world.

3. David Foster Wallace ("Consider the Lobster," p. 839) seems to want a
thoughtful reaction. He talks about the lobster's nervous system, about leaving the room when we drop them in the pot. One might describe his tone
as professional and courteous. He establishes his credibility with that tone,
as well as by disclosing the fact that he likes to eat lobster. Foer establishes
his authority by displaying his knowledge: he's clearly researched his material, and—although he also wants to make his reader think—he uses that
research to provoke a visceral reaction, providing details of the slaughter of
a dog and the preparation of dog meat. He uses irony to make his argument,
and one might reasonably describe his tone as sarcastic. All of this serves
(or is meant to serve) to highlight the arbitrary nature of the taboo against
eating dog, thereby illuminating the criminality of eating any kind of meat.
Students will be able to find evidence of the authors' respective tones and
rhetorical strategies in almost any passage of either essay.

# John Taylor Gatto
## AGAINST SCHOOL

### APPROACHING THE ESSAY

In this essay, John Taylor Gatto, a thirty-year veteran of the New York public schools, deconstructs the purpose and value of compulsory education. He describes both students and teachers as childish and bored in a system that no longer seems relevant to its students. Gatto uses a number of rhetorical questions to propel his argument. At the end of the first section, he asks: "Could it be that our schools are designed to make sure not one of [our students] ever really grows up?" (para. 5). He then opens the next section with yet another question: "Do we really need school?" (para. 6). These questions, along with the title, attempt to push readers into completely rethinking their assumptions about the structure and purpose of compulsory education. Gatto goes on to put compulsory education into a historical context, claiming that it is based on the Prussian system that aims to produce a "manageable" population of "mediocre intellects" (para. 10). He writes that this system has six functions, first illuminated in Alexander Inglis's *Principles of Secondary Education*: adaptive, integrating, diagnostic, differentiating, selective, and propaedeutic. (You might list these six functions on the board with a short definition of each and ask students for personal examples of each type from their own schooling.) Each of these functions, as Gatto explains it, is meant to teach children obedience in order to create a controllable "underclass" within the capitalist state.

Another of Gatto's arguments is that compulsory schooling succeeds in keeping students perpetually childish by limiting their critical thinking, which makes them perfect targets for commercial marketing. Americans in general, he argues, have been trained to be childish nonthinkers in order for both business and government to use the citizenry at their will.

Gatto's essay presents a valuable lesson in the merits of thoroughly questioning even the most basic of our customs, those societal habits so ingrained as to never be questioned. His essay asks whether we can educate, rather than school, our population in a more effective way. Ask students whether Gatto suggests solutions or merely attempts to raise the question for our attention. Have them examine the second-to-last paragraph in which Gatto lays out how parents (or "you") may counteract the effects of "good" schooling. Does good parenting offer a strong enough solution to the deep-seated problems of compulsory schooling?

### ADDITIONAL ACTIVITIES

1. Have students discuss the variety and similarities of their schooling. How do factors like class size, school size, religious affiliation, public or private, boarding school, size of community, and specialization of instruction affect the basic effects of compulsory education? What remains the same despite these factors?

2. Gatto frames his argument in terms of the history of western education in a capitalist society. Have students research another country's system of education, keeping in mind the six functions of American education that Gatto lays out. What are the differences between the two educational systems? How does the country's educational system also serve to create ideal citizens?

## GENERATING WRITING

1. As a class, discuss what experiences might constitute education outside of traditional schooling. Have students write a five-page reflective essay in which they critically examine their education both inside and outside of the classroom. What do they consider the strengths of their schooling? What has been most beneficial to them? What were the negative aspects of their experiences? How would they describe their education outside the classroom? What were the biggest influences on their education? How did their learning outside the classroom compare to their schooling?

2. Every college or university has a written mission statement that should be available online. Have students read your institution's mission statement and discuss what values are highlighted. Then have each student write a short (two- or three-page) argument detailing how higher education either continues to create "servants" to be "employees and consumers" or how it breaks this pattern.

## THE READER'S PRESENCE

1. Students will likely have strong opinions on the notions of conformity and obedience taught in schools. This would be a good discussion to have in class, especially one comparing students' different educational experiences. In the essay, Gatto frames his argument in terms of the function of compulsory education to control a potential threat from the underclass, and also to shape the masses into unthinking consumers: "School trains children to be employees and consumers. . . . to obey reflexively" (para. 19). Schooling, Gatto argues, does not train students to think independently and critically, but rather to think generically to support the class system on which capitalism relies. The perpetual infantilization of students makes them more susceptible to the powers of marketing.

2. The verbs *take* and *receive* are especially important here: Gatto refers to an "education" as an active process that students engage in, while "schooling" is the passive process whereby students submit to the required curriculum. To be schooled is to submit to a prescribed way of thinking; to be educated is to learn to think critically for oneself. Gatto suggests that it is a mistake to equate schooling with success because often successful people have found education outside compulsory schooling. Gatto portrays schooling as frequently counterproductive to education; compulsory schooling traditionally

sought to control and mold students, and even today it does not encourage individualism and independent thinking.

3. In paragraph 5, Gatto asserts that "our schools are designed to make sure not one [child] ever really grows up," and Joseph Epstein ("The Perpetual Adolescent," p. 390) would no doubt agree that this objective has been realized. Both writers point to marketing and consumerism as driving forces behind America's obsession with perpetual youth. At one point, Epstein even alludes to one of Gatto's books when he remarks: "To begin with education, one wonders if the dumbing down of culture one used to hear so much about and which continues isn't connected to the rise of the perpetual adolescent" (para. 27). Some students may point out that Epstein, writing for the conservative publication *The Weekly Standard*, demonstrates nostalgia for a bygone era, in which "to violate the boundaries of any of the three divisions of life was to go against what was natural" (para. 6). Gatto's critique of compulsory schooling and its failure to raise critical thinkers who can challenge government and big business may strike some students as more politically liberal than Epstein's.

# Adam Gopnik
## SHOOTINGS

### APPROACHING THE ESSAY

In this brief essay, Adam Gopnik quietly presents an argument for gun control in America. Because gun control is such a controversial topic, you might want to canvass the class on the issue before you start discussing the essay. Some students may be able to argue rationally on the need for rifles. Others may argue for the right of collectors to collect any kind of gun. A third group may oppose gun control of any kind on principle and will possibly use the Second Amendment as part of the argument. Reading this essay in tandem with Akhil Reed Amar's "Second Thoughts: What the Right to Bear Arms Really Means" (p. 305) might be a good idea. Amar presents a considered argument for how to interpret the Second Amendment based on its historical context. Gopnik presents a similar argument but from a different point of view. Have students discuss the two points of view and how they inform each other. Which writer makes a better argument? In some respects, even though he is not a constitutional scholar and does not present a precise and developed argument, Gopnik presents a more successful essay: he makes the arguments we might make. His is, at least initially, a human-interest piece: we might know the police officers who "carried the bodies and heard the ringing" (para. 1); as parents, we might imagine the anxious hope that the ring will be answered.

Gopnik is concerned about why this is a truly American kind of tragedy. Analyze with your students those passages that suggest that Americans do not want to face this truth about themselves. Why does the Virginia governor not want to talk about gun control? What liability does a politician risk by engaging in such a conversation?

An interesting corollary to this phenomenon is presented in paragraph 2: Why are Americans reluctant in general to talk about things such as gun control, cancer and smoking, and the use of seat belts? What, if anything, do these subjects have in common? Encourage students to discuss the importance of guns (and violence) in American culture. What is the difference between American culture and other cultures when it comes to violence? What is the media's role in portraying violence? What implication does Gopnik make about the role of the National Rifle Association in places like Virginia?

## ADDITIONAL ACTIVITIES

1. Popular culture reflects—some would argue, contributes to—crime and violence. Discuss with your students movies, television shows, video games, music, and rap that glorify crime and violence. What are some of the most popular violent movies of all time? What is an "anti-hero" and when did it become a popular protagonist in American culture? Have students debate popular culture's relationship to real-life violence.

2. Language also plays a role in American violence. Instruct your class to report on the use of violent language they hear in the media, among friends, and in their families during the course of one week (they might want to keep a weekly journal). What did they notice? What words were used most frequently? What relationship, if any, do they find between the use of violent language and sexuality? Are some words used both sexually and violently? For what purpose? What states of mind were exemplified by the violent language; for instance, was violent language ever used humorously? Did the students encounter any episodes of actual violence ensuing from the use of violent language? When do women use violent language? When do men?

## GENERATING WRITING

1. Ask students to research and then write a four- to six-page paper about the history of guns in America. Why is there a fascination with guns and killing? Where did it come from? When did it begin? What sustains it?

## THE READER'S PRESENCE

1. Gopnik starts the essay with a dramatic image that speaks to the loss that is a consequence of violence, rather than the act of violence itself. Someone, somewhere, hopes the person is still alive. Furthermore, the ringing works symbolically, serving as an alarm or a wake-up call about the issue of gun

control. Gopnik is dealing with the aftermath of the tragedy. He points out that few people want to talk about gun control after the shootings, and instead focus on other topics: the mentally ill, narcissism, violence in the media, and the question of "Evil." For the reader, the ringing is harrowing, unnerving, and sad.

2. Gopnik presents opposing arguments and then rebuts them. However, his position against gun control is not absolute. In paragraph 6, he agrees that reducing the number of guns will not stop crazy people from killing or alleviate their madness. Nonetheless, making it more difficult to buy guns will mean fewer people will be killed by guns. With some reluctance, he also concedes that "rural America is hunting country, and hunters need rifles and shotguns—with proper licensing, we'll live with risk" (para. 8). Answers to the rest of this question will vary. However, acknowledging sensible counter-arguments is a strong rhetorical device.

3. Gopnik would probably agree with Akhil Reed Amar's opinions ("Second Thoughts: What the Right to Bear Arms Really Means," p. 305), using Amar's Second Amendment argument to emphasize that Americans wanted the right to collectively bear arms in a militia that drew its numbers from manda-tory participation of all adult male voters. The individual's right was not an issue for the founders of our country because everyone owned and needed a gun in the frontier environment. Amar maintains that these founding fathers never intended for madmen to have guns (let alone argue for their consti-tutional right to own a handgun or a semi-automatic). The creators of the Constitution would never have conceived of scenarios such as the ones at Virginia Tech or Columbine.

# Vicki Hearne
## WHAT'S WRONG WITH ANIMAL RIGHTS

### APPROACHING THE ESSAY

Vicki Hearne presents an unusual perspective—the idea that animals enjoy train-ing and performance. She writes of the bond between animal and trainer and the animal's joy in mastery of a task, as well as in pleasing its trainer. She relates the common idea of "animal happiness" (para. 2) to a common idea of human happi-ness—freedom from all constraint, which may extend to laziness or sloth—and challenges both. She asks whether there is a form of "suffering," in terms of work or personal challenge, that may be more pleasurable than infinite comfort.

The writer argues that opponents of animal training and performance are mis-taken in believing that the animal suffers. These same people, she argues, rally for destruction of stray animals in the mistaken belief that death is an antidote to suffering. She claims that the animal rights movement is wrongheaded and propagandist and it often acts on erroneous information. What is more, she writes, animal rights advocates often lack the firsthand experience with animals that trainers have and thus cannot comprehend the animal's perspective.

By invoking philosophy and greater questions of nature and civilization, the essay extends the argument of animal rights to the question of general values. What is happiness? Why do we privilege the natural over the human-made, when in fact it is mainly the human-made that keeps us alive? Why is possession of an animal regarded as negative, when all positive bonds involve possession as a form of mutual commitment? You may wish to begin discussion with the question of animal rights but then expand it, as Hearne does, to more general human questions. You may also wish to outline Hearne's complicated, multifaceted argument on the board and then isolate passages for students to examine and reason through slowly. How does Hearne connect the animal with the human? the particular with the general? the empirical with the philosophical?

## ADDITIONAL ACTIVITY

1. Animal rights organizations generally provide speakers to classes free of charge; contact a local organization or the American Society for the Prevention of Cruelty to Animals for a speaker willing to talk with your class. What points or cases—for instance, animal experimentation—might Hearne's essay overlook? Have students briefly restate Hearne's arguments for the speaker. What is the speaker's response?

## GENERATING WRITING

1. Have students free-write in preparation for a two- to three-page personal essay on happiness. What notions of happiness do students and their friends hold? How have these notions been challenged for them? Have students engaged in activities or habits they believed were pleasurable, only to learn that true happiness lay elsewhere? What sort of happiness does the student enjoy in the present? What sorts of happiness does the student hope to experience in the future? Recirculate essays with names removed for class discussion.

2. Have students investigate issues of animal rights for a two- to three-page position paper. Students should also prepare four-minute distillations of their arguments for class discussion.

## THE READER'S PRESENCE

1. Hearne's authority as a trainer persuades the reader to consider, if not agree with, her argument. The reader might be willing to consider, or agree with, or consider and agree with the same argument presented by a layperson but

would more likely be persuaded by the testimony of a writer with experience in the field.

2. If the reader envisions happiness in terms of comfort and freedom from work, animal trainers do indeed rob their charges of their happiness. If the reader agrees with Hearne's definition of happiness as derived from struggle and challenge, animal trainers may be seen to give animals access to opportunities they would not otherwise have. It is possible to define happiness as comfort and yet to agree with Hearne that animal training does not amount to cruelty. One overall objection, however, is that some training practices do involve cruelty (beating, starvation, captivity, and so forth) and do not involve much productive challenge for the animal. Another objection is that testing of cosmetics and other substances on animals—a major concern of the movement Hearne derides—cannot be seen to benefit the animal.

3. Hearne claims that animal rights activists focus too narrowly on the capacity of animals to experience suffering. The argument rests essentially on the assumption that animals have the capacity to experience a broader range of more complicated emotions. In this sense, animals have emotional lives similar to the emotional lives of humans: they can be happy or unhappy. Hearne invokes the Declaration of Independence, arguing that animals, like humans, have a right to the "pursuit of happiness." Presumably, this would include the right to meaningful work, like the work Hearne's dog is engaged in when he's in a dog show. Whether students will accept this is going to be difficult to predict. The allusion to slavery may alienate some of your students. The comparison between humans and animals becomes problematic when we begin to talk about principles of ownership. Hearne seems cognizant of this, and in fact invokes the comparison precisely for the purpose of reconceptualizing the way animal rights activists talk about owning animals: it's not like owning slaves, she argues, but, rather, like "having" friends.

However, the comparison is still problematic in some ways (we don't typically spay or neuter our friends) and, although the exploration of the meaning of ownership is interesting, your students will have to decide for themselves whether it's okay to compare dogs to slaves, even when the point is only that dog ownership and slavery are very different things. Does this need to be said? Given that, at least in American political history (where Hearne contextualizes her argument), African American slaves were often (and explicitly) considered subhuman by their white masters, the efficacy of the rhetoric is not its only problem.

Annie Dillard ("The Death of a Moth," p. 371) and Virginia Woolf ("The Death of the Moth," p. 625) write very different kinds of essays. Woolf turns the death of an insect into a metaphor for life and death, in general; Dillard seems to be exploring her life as a writer in more personal and particular terms. Hearne is addressing the issue of animal rights: a social, legal, or perhaps cultural idea. Hearne's purpose, then, is political; Dillard's is personal; and Woolf's is essentially philosophical. It could perhaps be argued that both Woolf and Hearne personify animals in inappropriate ways, though Woolf is deliberately metaphorical. In stark contrast, Hearne is completely sincere.

# Christopher Hitchens
## BELIEVE ME, IT'S TORTURE

### APPROACHING THE ESSAY

You may need to contextualize this piece for your students: depending on how old they are and how much they pay attention to current events, some of them may not remember when the issue of torture was all over the news. By the same token, it will be easy for them to understand what Hitchens is talking about without necessarily being familiar with or even aware of the media storm surrounding the photographs that came out of Abu Ghraib in 2004, and the subsequent court-martials. You will have to decide, on your own, whether to contextualize your discussion of the Hitchens piece with a recapitulation of the events. You might assign Hitchens first and introduce the historical context later. You might not bother with the historical context at all. But once you have made your decision about how and whether to contextualize the essay, you will probably want to focus on the question of tone.

Because the issue of tone is so important to this piece, you might begin your discussion with Reader's Presence Question 1. Hitchens's tone is at times ironic and at times matter of fact, almost clinical. At other times, his descriptions are chilling, and indeed he uses the word *chilling* at the beginning of the piece, in paragraph 1, to signal to the reader the kind of subject matter he is dealing with. The movement among the ironic, the matter of fact, and the "chilling" figurative language allows Hitchens to get his point across in a number of ways. The essay reads like a one-two-three punch: (1) of course it's torture, (2) look at the physical details of the procedure (can there really be any doubt?), and (3) it's horrifying. See Reader's Presence Question 1 for more specific commentary on the issue of tone.

When you have dealt thoroughly with the issue of tone, you'll want to move on to the larger argument of the article, summarized at the end of the essay. Direct your students to Hitchens's numbered recapitulation of Malcolm Nance's argument about waterboarding and torture (para. 12). What does Hitchens seem to be suggesting about people who argue that waterboarding is not torture? about the use of torture in general? Your students should have no trouble answering these questions, but you might encounter significant argument about their implications. Hitchens is obviously against the use of torture. Not all of your students will be. See Additional Activities for more ways to approach the discussion.

### ADDITIONAL ACTIVITIES

1. Hitchens implicitly argues not so much that waterboarding is torture but that the question—*is waterboarding torture?*—is by nature disingenuous and insincere. Disingenuous because to suggest that it might not be torture or that it is not *technically* torture is to play dumb. Insincere because those who advocate waterboarding don't actually *care* whether it is torture. They

don't advocate waterboarding because it isn't technically torture; they advocate waterboarding because *they advocate torture*. A larger and more honest question, then, is whether torture is ever justifiable. Much has been written on the subject, and merely Googling the question—can torture be justified?—will yield a bevy of results from a variety of sources. You may want to find a few articles for and against and have the students read them. At the end of his essay, Hitchens calls on Nance, author of *The Terrorists of Iraq*, to make the argument that waterboarding is deliberate torture and cannot be condoned because it opens a door that cannot be closed (para. 12). Hitchens closes his essay the way he begins it, with the reflection that waterboarding has made us too like our enemies. Do your students agree? Why or why not?

2. Recent films have also dealt with the subject of state-endorsed torture: *Unthinkable*, starring Samuel L. Jackson, has a character played by Jackson torturing a terrorist in all manner of ways. There is never any doubt that the suspect is guilty. The doubt is only as to whether it is okay to torture the terrorist to avert the deaths of millions of people. The movie seems to argue both that it *is* and *is not*. The content may be too disturbing for some viewers, but for others it will provide a useful way to approach the argument.

3. On the subject of film, a particular genre of horror film, called "torture-porn," might yield interesting fruit for discussion. Films like *Saw*, *Hostel*, and *Captivity* are just a few examples of the genre, which seems to be growing in popularity despite the fact that most of the films get horrible reviews. They consistently do well in the box office and seem to attract a young ("college age") crowd. What does this say about the popular culture at large? In what ways have Americans become desensitized to violence? Not actual violence, but film violence. Does our appetite for such fare have anything to do with the casual manner in which we accept government use of torture? Magazines like the *Atlantic Monthly*, *Harper's*, and the *New Yorker*—"intellectual magazines"—have widely publicized and condemned practices like waterboarding, but the degree of public outrage seems relatively minor when compared to the protests against the Vietnam War, in the late 1960s. It is interesting to note that many of those protests took place on college campuses, as well. Yet students today seem almost indifferent to the issue. Ask them why.

## GENERATING WRITING

1. Have the students write an argumentative research paper on the use of torture to extract information from terrorists.

2. Have the students write a piece of experiential journalism. They should *go* somewhere, *do* something, and write about it. The primary pitfall of this assignment is finding things for them to do: you don't want to actually ask them to do something dangerous, but it doesn't seem in the spirit of the Hitchens article to write restaurant reviews, either. You might just ask them to do something they wouldn't *ordinarily* do. Have the hip-hop fans spend an evening at a Country and Western bar. Have the atheists visit a church

on Sunday, or, if you have churchgoers in your class, you might ask them to attend a service at a different church. You'll want to be a bit careful, even here. You don't want to infringe on anyone's religious freedom, and bars can be dangerous places. It may be safest simply to ask the students to attend a sporting event or a flower exhibition. The important thing is only that they experience the event *as a stranger*, and write matter of factly about that experience.

## THE READER'S PRESENCE

1. This question calls the students' attention to paragraph 9, which is where the rapid vacillation between tones is best exemplified. For example, Hitchens says, "You are not being boarded. You are being watered" (para. 7). There's something almost silly about the sound of it (one thinks of watering a plant), yet it is at the same time precise: why, indeed, does the compound word "waterboard" make it sound like "board" is the verb, the action element in the equation? This sort of attention to detail is essential to the essay, because Hitchens's primary purpose is to expose the manner in which waterboarding has been misrepresented: his tone in these cases might be informally described as "well, duh." The irony is interlaced with straightforward descriptions of the experience itself: "I held my breath for a while and then had to exhale and—as you might expect—inhale in turn. The inhalation brought the damp cloths tight against my nostrils" (para. 7). This very straightforward description is followed immediately by a somewhat chilling metaphor: "as if a huge wet paw had been suddenly and annihilatingly clamped over my face." Hitchens might have confined himself to any one or two of these tones to make his argument. Some readers might feel that he should have left out the irony, avoided being snarky, and thus been more persuasive to people who might have disagreed with him prior to reading his article, but part of the point of the article is that the debate over whether waterboarding constitutes torture is dishonest and stupid: of course it's torture, he argues. He might have stuck strictly to the clinical, hence conveying that the procedure is torturous without trying to sensationalize it with metaphor, but the metaphor is meant to convey the way it *feels* to be subjected to waterboarding, so it seems essential to Hitchens's credibility. He's been through it; hence, he knows exactly what it feels like and has the authority not only to call it torture but to evoke a sense of horror in the reader with a vivid first-person account.

2. Hitchens is ashamed of not lasting long because it makes him look weak. When one of the interrogators tries to reassure Hitchens, and thus ease his embarrassment, Hitchens is grateful. Being grateful to a person who has just inflicted suffering on you is clearly a strange experience, but it is also a natural one because in the same way that the *torturer* inflicts suffering on the victim, the torturer is the only one who can *end* the suffering. This is one of the most disturbing (and, probably, effective) elements of torture: the

way it warps the mind of the one being tortured. Hitchens probably placed the observation near the end of the essay for two reasons: (1) it makes sense, chronologically; and (2) it highlights one of the most insidious aspects of torture, as a practice, and thus leaves the reader unsettled. Hitchens's article is meant to be nothing if not unsettling. It is through "unsettling" the reader that Hitchens hopes to persuade.

3. It's anybody's guess how students will react to Hitchens's and Michihiko Hachiya's ("From *Hiroshima Diary*," p. 107) essays, but they should be able to see that, in general, both authors rely on matter-of-fact language to convey their experiences. Sentence length and rhythm vary as they switch back and forth between literal—in Hachiya's case, *clinical*—and figurative language. Figurative sentences are likely to be longer, with a different sort of cadence, interrupted by the staccato rhythms of direct statements of fact. Hachiya probably uses more figurative language than does Hitchens, but this is offset by the fact that his literal language is clinical. He also steers clear of irony, which makes the pathos of the situation itself come through: Hachiya is, of course, criticizing the use of the atomic bomb, but he does so using the vehicle of memoir, while Hitchens acts as a policy critic by way of investigative and experiential journalism. Even those who would justify the use of the atomic bomb would concede that the consequences of dropping the bomb were, for the Japanese, terrible: they were meant to be. Those who advocate waterboarding are reluctant to use the word *torture* to describe the practice, so Hitchens is almost compelled to rely at least partially on irony to make his point (that waterboarding is obviously torture and to deny it is disingenuous).

# Pico Iyer
## THE INNER CLIMATE

### APPROACHING THE ESSAY

If your students have been focused on longer, more heavily researched arguments and articles, Pico Iyer's "The Inner Climate" may come as a nice surprise. It might allow them a small breath and show that writing is more than research, argument, and rigor. Writing is capable of great beauty, simply through the use of creative language, and that is exactly what Iyer's piece gives its reader: a sense of beauty.

"The Inner Climate" addresses climate change: "In California," Iyer writes, "they're all wondering where the rain has gone" (para. 2); in the Himalayas the temperatures are too high and crops are failing; and in Japan, where Iyer is, the winter is unseasonably warm. Iyer paints, though the scene is dire, beautiful pictures for his readers, allowing them to see Japan's "blue, blue, blue" skies along with roaming deer and temples. Yet it is not climate change alone that Iyer is concerned with. Rather, he is concerned with something more personal, which Iyer calls getting "the inner thermostat right" (para. 2).

For Iyer, before global change can occur that will right the planet's temperature rise, people need to begin with the self. He writes, "I'm not sure we can ever truly tend to our polluted waters, our shrinking forests, the madness we've loosed on the air until we begin to try to clean up the inner waters, and attend to the embattled wild spaces within us" (para. 3). This, for your students, will probably seem fairly radical. What does how I'm feeling have to do with the world? they might ask. Even better, they might think, how will calmly reflecting and contemplating these things make change occur? But Iyer's point is salient, timely, and crucial, and with a little help from you, your students should begin to see why. You might bring up a famous quote by Blaise Pascal, which says, "I have discovered that all human evil comes from this, man's being unable to sit still in a room." What does this mean? The Tao Te Ching asks (and it can be reasonably argued that Iyer is influenced by Eastern philosophy), "Do you have the patience to wait till your mud settles and the water is clear? Can you remain unmoving till the right action arises by itself?" (Stephen Mitchell translation). What do these quotes have to do with Iyer's piece? The answer lies in the idea, for Iyer, that if people can learn to free themselves of distraction, the right way to treat the world, our planet, should be not only obvious but a moral imperative. Highlighting the beautiful language of Iyer's piece, the small but personal examples of climate change happening, and the charge for the individual to take personal responsibility in our planet's plight are all strong, yet simple, rhetorical devices that should prompt an interesting discussion of what exactly writing has the power to do.

## ADDITIONAL ACTIVITIES

1. Give your students one of the two quotes to work with (either Pascal's or Mitchell's translation of the Tao Te Ching). Have the students compose a personal contemplation of two paragraphs, in which they try to come to terms with how the quote relates to Iyer's "The Inner Climate." Tell them to practice, if only for a moment before writing, calmly and quietly reflecting to see if that makes a difference when they approach the writing.

2. Iyer's piece focuses on the self and how to right one's inner climate. Ask your students to think of ways that the community engages in climate and environmental awareness. Is awareness enough? Try to get students to think about the environment in terms of their daily lives. In what ways are they impacted, if at all? What makes climate and environmental issues more real, both in Iyer's piece and in their lives?

## GENERATING WRITING

1. Have students research arguments about climate change and environmental issues. They should have to find two articles that support the idea that

climate change is occurring and two that argue that climate change is not a real issue. Ask them to weigh the issue and decide which they believe and why. Have them write a two-page paper, presenting the research they found (the four articles) and then have them take a stand, based on their research, arguing why they support one side over the other.

2. Have students write a personal reflection for homework. The personal reflection, however, should be tempered with the idea that it must be written directly after fifteen or so minutes of no distractions. For instance, Iyer writes that he has no cell phone, iPod, newspapers, TV, magazines, or even Internet in his small living space in order to keep himself clear. Ask the students to shut off their computer; turn off phones, televisions, and music; and just simply sit, quietly, undistracted, for fifteen minutes before writing a reflection on Iyer's piece. They might also include whether they felt different when writing this reflection compared to writing other assignments.

## THE READER'S PRESENCE

1. Iyer's essay is about how all change happens in cycles: this is why he starts the essay by describing autumn, that ending of the life cycle for plant life on a particular hemisphere. Yet, Iyer makes it clear that this is only a momentary shift, that though things change, deep down there is an enduring thing that remains the same. Iyer seems to lead off in this manner in order to show that, while climate change and environmental problems are occurring, if we learn to settle ourselves and right our "inner climate," we can tap that enduring thing that will help right our path.

2. Iyer doesn't see things in terms of "progress." All of the "small efforts" he makes are actually revulsions toward the idea of progress. All the technology that we typically see as progress, for Iyer, seem to be only things that cause distraction, and this is why he cuts himself off from Internet, an iPod, the TV; these are all distractions to the "inner climate," distractions that, for Iyer, complicate his need for clarity. Eliminating technological and worldly distractions is an amazingly helpful way to live a centered kind of life, if that is what one so desires.

3. Certainly, both Iyer and Malcolm Gladwell ("Small Change: Why the Revolution Will Not Be Tweeted," p. 411) are suspicious of technology. For Gladwell, the Web isn't a suitable medium for creating real sociopolitical change; for Iyer, the Web is just another distraction from contemplation. Gladwell, however, is much more action-oriented. Although the Web isn't the medium for certain types of change, protests, sit-ins, marches, and all physical forms of political embodiment are — Gladwell uses the Greensboro sit-ins of the civil rights movement as a perfect example. Iyer asks people to start with themselves — this isn't even a position that Gladwell considers, and here they differ greatly both in how change occurs and in what type of change they want to have occur.

# Thomas Jefferson
## THE DECLARATION OF INDEPENDENCE

### APPROACHING THE ESSAY

In this document, Thomas Jefferson discusses colonial America's quest for freedom from a world-historical perspective, lists the colonies' grievances, and declares their intention to act against England. Students may be familiar with the Declaration but are unlikely ever to have examined it as a literary, rhetorical, and possibly imperfect piece of work. Some may resist approaching it in a critical manner. You may wish to begin by outlining its points on the board, with students' help, and then isolate passages for closer investigation.

You may also wish to have students note purely rhetorical devices—high diction, declarative sentence structure, repetition, and so on—asking students what effect those devices have on their reception of the material. How would the piece read if the same points were presented in more straightforward language? What makes it a literary, as well as a governmental, document? In what ways is Jefferson's considerable literary craft evident? What other major historical documents does his style recall? How does this manifesto differ from other prose pieces students have read? Why does the manifesto refrain from considering opposing viewpoints? Does close reading afford students a new perspective on the Declaration?

Students are unlikely to disagree with the Declaration's basic tenets and statements. However, you may question what the piece fails to say or leaves out. It has been criticized for emphasizing "freedom from" rather than "freedom to" and "independence" over "interdependence"—that is, for promising removal of strictures and limitations but not mentioning rights to food, shelter, and so forth, or Americans' responsibilities to one another. You may ask students how the Declaration influences life in America today. What changes would the Founding Fathers have been unable to foresee?

One important point to be made is that the Declaration covered only the independence and rights of white Americans. African Americans would remain enslaved for another century, and Jefferson himself was a slaveholder. Have students reread the document in this light. How does this knowledge affect students' reading of the document and the struggle for "independence" in America?

### ADDITIONAL ACTIVITY

1. Break students into groups of four or so to draft their own American Declaration in the light of current events. What should we declare to other countries and each other? What are our political and economic rights and responsibilities as a nation? What are our political and economic rights and responsibilities as citizens? When disputes arise, students must negotiate, as the Founding Fathers did, for a compromise statement. Have each group read its Declaration to the class.

## GENERATING WRITING

1. Have students free-write in preparation for a two- to three-page personal essay on independence. What does independence mean to the student as a citizen? How has the student pursued independence in his or her personal life? Do Americans place too much emphasis on independence? Are there more important things in life than independence alone? Recirculate essays with names removed for class discussion.

2. Ask students to research the events leading to the writing of the Declaration. What circumstances were the Founding Fathers protesting? How old were they at the time? (The answer may surprise students.) What was Jefferson's position in the group? Why was he chosen to draft the statement? What personal danger did the Founding Fathers face? Were the Founding Fathers radicals in the modern sense of the word? How would we characterize a similar group of activists today?

## THE READER'S PRESENCE

1. Jefferson defines *independence* as freedom from outside economic and legal dominance. The declaration is made on behalf of the American people at large but may be seen to exclude at least African American slaves, who were not to be granted freedom. A counterdeclaration might stress the need for interdependence—a demand that people support each other and vow to meet all needs as a group.

2. The opening line appears to issue from a disembodied, divine, or super-human voice. The effect is of a heavenly mandate; it carries great power. The first paragraph generalizes about human events, positioning American independence as one in a chain of historic necessities. By comparing the American situation to other international situations across the ages, Jefferson allies the American struggle with other well-respected—and successful—efforts.

3. The Declaration shows the classical education of its author. Jefferson was schooled in Greek and Latin authors, as well as in the work of Enlightenment philosophers, including John Locke, Jean-Jacques Rousseau, David Hume, Adam Smith, and Francis Hutchinson. The influence of these thinkers is evident in Jefferson's rational language of natural rights, liberty, self-rule, and representative government. Akhil Reed Amar ("Second Thoughts: What the Right to Bear Arms Really Means," p. 305) insists that those seeking to understand the Constitution first need to grasp its eighteenth-century context and the Enlightenment ideals that influenced Jefferson. The call for an independent nation without a monarch—expressed in both the Declaration and the Bill of Rights—reflects the quintessential eighteenth-century emphasis on natural rights and self-rule that forms the bedrock of modern American government. Read the first paragraphs carefully, and have students infer Jefferson's definitions of these philosophical terms. How does Jefferson include God in the first and last paragraphs? Why might he have done this? Ask students to figure out what role divine providence seems to have in Jefferson's

rational vision of the ideal state. The document is also, and more basically, a list of complaints against King George III of England. Have students restate these grievances in contemporary language and discuss, point by point, what exactly the colonists were experiencing.

# Martin Luther King Jr.
## I HAVE A DREAM

### APPROACHING THE ESSAY

Reverend Martin Luther King Jr., winner of a Nobel Peace Prize, leader of the civil rights movement in the 1950s and 1960s, and advocate of nonviolent civil disobedience, began his movement in African American Baptist churches of the South. King was one of the three organizers of the March on Washington for Jobs and Freedom, where he gave his famous "I Have a Dream" speech. President John F. Kennedy was said to have feared that the march would damage the reputation of the United States internationally and would harm progress toward civil rights legislation in Congress. However, the march was influential in pushing the Civil Rights Act of 1964 and the Voting Rights Act of 1965 through Congress.

Students may be familiar with King's 1963 speech from the March on Washington but probably have never analyzed it as a piece of rhetoric. Have students make a list of the allusions in King's speech. He refers to the Emancipation Proclamation, the Gettysburg Address, the Constitution, the Declaration of Independence, and even "My Country 'Tis of Thee," in a sense challenging the nation to fulfill its promises of equality that had for so long applied only to white Americans. Discuss with students what the purpose of each of these documents is and why King focuses on them.

King piles metaphors one on top of another throughout the speech. In the fourth paragraph alone, he refers to "the tranquilizing drug of gradualism," "the desolate valley of segregation," "the sunlit path of racial justice," "the doors of opportunity," "the quicksands of racial injustice," and "the solid rock of brotherhood." You might have students rewrite a paragraph without the metaphors and then discuss their effect in King's versions. What common images and subjects does King draw on in these comparisons? What are the effects of his figurative language? his imagery?

After analyzing King's voice and rhythm, bring in a video or tape recording of his speech. How well could students hear King's voice as they read? How is the effect of hearing the speech different from that of reading it? In what ways does the speech work better orally?

Historical context will help students understand where this speech fits in the civil rights era. Make a time line of key events on the board. Then ask students what philosophy King presents in his speech. What action does he suggest (if any)? What values are most clearly expressed in his speech? This would be a good opportunity to compare King and Malcolm X as civil rights leaders.

## ADDITIONAL ACTIVITIES

1. As a class, outline the major events of the civil rights era. Where does this speech fit into the time line of events? What led to the March on Washington? What setbacks and successes did the movement experience after this speech?

2. If your classroom is equipped with computers, you might want to download and play an audio file of this speech. Ask students to follow along with the print version and note the rhythm of King's speech, including where he emphasizes certain ideas or words. How does "hearing" a writer's voice on the page compare to literally hearing the words spoken? How does hearing the speech add to or detract from the students' understanding of the speech, and how does it alter their opinion of it?

3. Bring in a copy of Malcolm X's "The Ballot or the Bullet" or "Message to the Grassroots," which are both available in print and audio from (www .americanrhetoric.com). Place students into small groups and have them analyze the two speeches and discuss the differences and similarities in how the two leaders advocate for change, position themselves against their opposition, use the language of faith, and so on.

## GENERATING WRITING

1. Assign students a paper in which they research and examine the influences present in King's speeches, from rhetorical traditions and landmark American speeches to his Christian faith. How does King draw on seminal speeches about freedom and democracy? What allusions does he make to spirituality and faith? How are these influences important to the way he envisioned the civil rights movement?

2. Ask students to consider how King's speech lays out a platform of his philosophy of nonviolent resistance and civil rights. Have students write an essay in which they discuss how his speech exemplifies his beliefs about the way African Americans should approach the civil rights movement.

## THE READER'S PRESENCE

1. King opens with an allusion to the Gettysburg Address: "Five score years ago, a great American, in whose symbolic shadow we stand, signed the Emancipation Proclamation" (para. 1). He refers to the Declaration of Independence with its "unalienable rights of life, liberty, and the pursuit of happiness" (para. 3). He also makes many allusions to biblical passages, as in "Let us not wallow in the valley of despair" (para. 9) and "the solid rock of

brotherhood" (para. 4). He holds the writers of the Declaration of Independence to a promise, saying that Americans must "live out the true meaning
of its creed: 'We hold these truths to be self-evident; that all men are created
equal'" (para. 11). King uses repetition of both theme and sentence structure throughout his speech. In paragraphs 6 and 7, many sentences begin
with "we": "We must forever conduct . . . ," "We must not allow . . . ," "We
cannot walk alone . . . ," "we must make the pledge . . . ," "We can never
be satisfied. . . ." In paragraph 9, he repeats the "go back" mantra. King's
rhythm comes from a Baptist preaching tradition and is developed through
his short repetitive phrases and metaphors.

2. In paragraphs 3 and 4, King constructs an extended metaphor of coming
to cash a check, meaning that African Americans are asking the country to
make due on past debts to them. He often uses comparisons to nature and
the environment to illustrate the struggles of his cause, as in "the dark and
desolate valley of segregation," the "sunlit path of racial justice," and "the
quicksands of racial injustice" (para. 4). Many of King's metaphors serve to
further characterize the potential pitfalls of the civil rights movement and
the goals of the movement.

3. Ho Che Anderson's graphic depiction (p. 705) helps reinforce the great
inspirational power and physical presence that King had at the march, as
well as the sheer number of people at the Mall. Anderson juxtaposes historical images like the white supremacist poster from 1890 to contextualize the
duration of African Americans' struggle for civil rights. The Lincoln Memorial appears in the background to further contextualize King's continuation
of the aims of the Emancipation Proclamation. The final scene posits King,
again in Lincoln's shadow, reflecting on the historic nature of the march and
what it meant to the people.

# Martin Luther King Jr.
## LETTER FROM BIRMINGHAM JAIL

### APPROACHING THE ESSAY

You might begin a discussion of this text by reviewing the history of African Americans' struggle to achieve equality in America. This struggle culminated in the
founding of the black civil rights movement led by the Reverend Martin Luther
King Jr. King strove both to overturn legislation that upheld segregation and to
make blacks aware of their political and legal rights even in a system in which
those rights were limited.

In 1963, King was asked by the Southern Christian Leadership Conference to assist their efforts to end segregation in Birmingham, Alabama. King and many of his followers were arrested for their participation in public demonstrations and were placed in jail. Many white moderates were critical of King; they felt he should limit his activities to his own parish in Atlanta rather than lead a crusade for civil rights throughout the South. They also questioned his judgment in breaking the law. Have students first read the clergymen's letter to King, which set the stage for King's famous letter in which he explains his actions and sets forth the difference between moral and immoral laws. Note how King responds to the criticisms point by point.

Ask your students if they can identify the major influences on King's style and method of argument. Those students with a knowledge of the New Testament will notice similarities between King's letter and those written by the apostle Paul while he was imprisoned in ancient Rome. In his Epistle to the Ephesians and again in his letters to the Corinthians, Paul encourages non-Christians to join his faith through a patient and thorough examination of religious principles. Similarly, King attempts to explain his moral position to those members of the clergy who have criticized him. Ask your students if King thought that most of his audience would recognize the biblical parallel he is making between his own situation and Paul's. Are there indications within the essay that King knows he needs to explain this connection to his audience?

In the first part of the letter, King defends his reasons for coming to Birmingham. He claims his motives were those of a Christian who must answer a brother's call for help. Consider King's rejection of criticisms that label him an "outside agitator." What phrases and rhetorical structures prepare the way for his assertion that his intervention was necessary on the grounds of universal brotherhood? Do your students find this argument morally persuasive? Is it convincing from a legal point of view?

Consider with your class King's definition of *nonviolence*. Why does King believe, as he says in paragraph 44, that his movement's means of achieving its goals must be as morally pure as the ends it pursues? Is this idea implicit to the idea of nonviolence, or is it an addition made by King himself? Compare King's ideas about nonviolence with those of the leader of the independence movement in India, Mohandas K. Gandhi. Gandhi's essays and letters on the subject can be found in various collections of his work. Examine some of Gandhi's writings with your class to find intellectual and rhetorical similarities with King's letter.

Finally, note King's tone throughout the essay. King adopts a personal tone because the criticisms were directed at him, but he does not sound defensive. He understands and remains patient with his critics because he is sure that they do not wish him or his movement ill. He also believes that if he can make his positions clear to them, they will join him in his fight. Notice also how the letter takes on the quality of oral delivery. Though the letter was meant to be read and not delivered as a speech, King nevertheless uses many of the same devices he used in his speeches. Ask students to identify moments in the letter that have a spoken rather than written quality.

## ADDITIONAL ACTIVITY

1. To further understand King's distinction between moral and immoral laws, try as a class to come up with a list of laws that most members of the class view as immoral. There will and should be debate over the immorality of certain laws. Can your students come up with a set of criteria to distinguish an immoral law from a moral law? Do those criteria differ significantly from those offered by King?

## GENERATING WRITING

1. At some time in the past, your students may, like King, have felt the need to explain their actions to people who did not understand those actions. Ask them to write a letter to these people, in which they explain why they believe they have been judged unjustly for something they did in the spirit of justice. They should follow King's technique for structuring the letter and for refuting the charges directed against them.

2. King's discussion of moral and immoral laws (paras. 15–22) lies at the center of his argument. Ask your students to examine this section of the letter closely and then to write an essay in which they reconstruct King's criterion for dismissing a law as immoral. They should be careful to distinguish "immoral" from "illegal" acts. They should also comment on whether they find King's reasoning correct or incorrect.

## THE READER'S PRESENCE

1. King's letter is an open letter addressed to anyone who agrees with the idea of civil rights for blacks but does not agree with the actions of King and his movement. The eight members of the clergy he names criticized King for his approach, not out of racism but out of fear that he might actually retard the movement toward equality for blacks by provoking too strong a reaction from whites.

2. King uses the word *hope* because, like most men and women committed to a cause, he is unsure of his capacity to remain "patient and reasonable" (para. 1) in the face of the great destructive forces that threaten him and his constituents. Though *hope* usually denotes a desired situation throughout the essay, *disappointment* indicates the failure to achieve the desired end. It is the "tension" between "hope" and "disappointment" that drives King to pursue his ends even though he cannot be sure of the outcome.

3. King's language reinforces his belief in racial harmony and equality. Balanced clauses provide equal emphasis, creating harmony within the sentence structure. Cadences create mnemonic associations, much in the same way that rhythm works in poetry and music. As with poetry, figurative language plays an important role in King's letter and speech. He depicts struggle and inaction with strong metaphors: "we still creep at horse and buggy pace" (para. 11); "Negro brothers smothering in an air-tight cage of poverty" (para.

12); "depressing clouds of inferiority begin to form in her little mental sky" (para. 12); "the tranquilizing drug of gradualism" ("I Have a Dream," para. 4). These two texts also suggest the pulpit with their sermon-like qualities and biblical references. King's memorable "I Have a Dream" speech culminates appropriately with a phrase from an old African American spiritual: "Free at last! free at last! thank God almighty, we are free at last!" ("I Have a Dream," para. 27). King writes to rouse his audience to correct behavior. He uses repetition (refrain), also used in the Bible and in music, to give his words weight.

# Laura Kipnis
## AGAINST LOVE

### APPROACHING THE ESSAY

Like John Taylor Gatto in "Against School" (p. 665), Laura Kipnis deconstructs how our culture has been taught to think about an institution commonly accepted as good and useful—in this case, love and marriage. Unlike with Gatto's critique of schooling, however, students are unlikely to readily agree with Kipnis's "treatise." Encourage them to look beyond their own experiences and concentrate on the strengths and weaknesses of her argument.

Throughout the essay, Kipnis counters the idea that the inability to "settle down" into a long-term relationship is a failure; instead, she examines the many ways in which modern marriage is a failure of love—lacking passion, requiring work to maintain it, forcing both individuals to give up a great deal in order to sustain a relationship. Kipnis approaches her subject in an impersonal and a clinical fashion. After presenting an exhaustive list of curtailed freedoms, she concludes: "Thus love is obtained" (para. 28).

Kipnis also puts love in a historical context to argue that modern romantic love is a social construction with purposes other than individual happiness; the ancient Greeks, she says, agreed that love was a temporary experience, and before the eighteenth century, marriage was considered a business partnership. Given these two perspectives, Kipnis questions our assumptions that real love will endure to sustain a relationship, and that marriage is the preferred form for our romantic instincts. Kipnis makes the slightest of nods to her opposition when she states: "Certainly, domesticity offers innumerable rewards: companionship, child-rearing convenience, reassuring predictability and many other benefits too varied to list" (para. 29). Ask students whether this nod is successful in dismissing these ideas, or whether they think Kipnis should have more adequately addressed her opposition.

Students should examine how Kipnis characterizes marriage (i.e., as "domestic coupledom"). With marriage comes "spreading waistlines" (para. 3), "grisly acts of self-mutilation" (para. 4), and "living in close proximity to someone for a historically unprecedented length of time" (para. 11). How would Kipnis define love? How does she distinguish between love and passion in this essay?

Some critics of Kipnis's book have speculated on Kipnis's own experiences in marriage and love as a means of discounting her argument. If you find any of your students making similar comments, ask them how her personal experience would affect the way they view the strength of her argument. This is a good opportunity to discuss logical fallacies, such as attacking the person.

## ADDITIONAL ACTIVITIES

1. You might have students watch two versions of the same film or story, produced in different eras or dealing with different periods or places, in which romance, marriage, or courtship is a central theme. Then have students write a comparative analysis of how ideals of love are portrayed. Some pairings might include *Clueless* (1996) and *Emma* (1996), *You've Got Mail* (1998) and *Shop Around the Corner* (1940), or *Pride and Prejudice* (1995 miniseries) and *Bride and Prejudice* (2004).
2. Place students in small groups and have them outline Kipnis's many claims. Then, ask them to list her evidence. Which claims are her strongest? Which are her weakest? How might students sum up her argument after looking at all of her claims together?

## GENERATING WRITING

1. After reading John Taylor Gatto's "Against School" (p. 665) and Lauren Slater's "The Trouble with Self-Esteem" (p. 822), have students write an argumentative essay that questions or argues against the value of a regularly accepted social institution or belief. In small groups, review drafts and discuss the various stances students took; were their arguments based on ethical, moral, political, religious, or scientific grounds? Compare tactics of argumentation to Gatto, Slater, and Kipnis.
2. Kipnis presents a short history of the rhetoric of love to contextualize her argument. In a five-page paper, have students research the history of marriage in the Western world. They might concentrate on changes in wedding traditions, popular sentiment about the purpose of and need for marriage, public debate over the place of marriage in society, or the most recent debate about gay marriage. As an alternative assignment, some students might like to do a comparison of how marriage is viewed in different cultures today.

## THE READER'S PRESENCE

1. The escape from marriage that adultery represents is evidence of how long-term monogamy is unnatural and stifling. Adulterers are implicitly saying that the contract of marriage isn't worth the sacrifice of pleasure it requires. Adultery would not be a problem if love were allowed to run its course and

the social institution of marriage did not require us to submit to a long-term arrangement, argues Kipnis.

2. Kipnis approaches the subject of love with a logical and an unemotional tone. She uses the language of medicine to deconstruct romantic love, describing it almost as a syndrome or disease. She also places romantic love in a historical context by explaining the Greeks' philosophy of love's short-lived nature and the seventeenth-century introduction of the language of romance. In general, Kipnis appeals to logic over emotion or sympathy, and she keeps her own experiences out of the discussion.

3. Society benefits from "the social stability" (para. 10) of long-term relationships by having settled families and households to raise children. Kipnis calls long-term relationships a "social institution" (para. 29) in that she believes they are socially constructed to control and regulate the population. Individuals, however, may stay in an unrewarding relationship rather than experience a series of rewarding relationships that come to a natural end. Gatto argues that schooling is a similar social institution that controls and manages the individual in order to keep alive the class system under capitalism. With compulsory schooling a potentially rebellious underclass can be properly taught and managed. The individual loses a true education in independent thinking and maturity, and instead he or she remains a child susceptible to the marketing of capitalism.

# Thomas Lynch
## INTO THE OBLIVION

### APPROACHING THE ESSAY

Adapted from a speech presented to the President's Council on Bioethics, Lynch's essay is best understood as an argument for "respecting the dead" or, rather, respecting dead bodies. He begins with the observation (an observation based on a life spent in the funeral parlor business) that, as a species, humans "deal with death, the idea of the thing, by dealing with our dead" (para. 1). In paragraph 2, he says that "the dead do not care" what happens to their bodies. They don't care about funerals. They're dead, so why should they. But the rest of the speech concerns itself with the relationship between the living and the dead, how dealing with corpses or ashes helps us deal with loss. Lynch provides a number of examples of this phenomenon: a woman putting the box of her sister's ashes in the passenger seat, instead of the trunk (para. 4); the mother of a dead teenager striking an Episcopalian deacon for saying that her daughter's body is "just a shell" (para. 6); and, of course, the first, whimsical example, the hypothetical stone age woman, disposing of her husband's remains (para. 1).

Lynch argues that the way we deal with our dead separates us from the animals, and that—whether it actually "makes sense"—there is something about the way we deal with cadavers that is essential, in both an abstract and a physical way, to human dignity. He therefore encourages the President's Council on Bioethics (and, implicitly, all of us) to consider the way we treat dead bodies carefully: to treat them, in short, "with honor" (para. 7). Ask your students what the implications of the argument might be. Is Lynch arguing against, for example, harvesting organs from the dead? Or is he suggesting only that such things should be done with a measure of reverence that we often fail to demonstrate? What would the kind of reverence he's calling for look like? What, if any, actual policy changes does he advocate?

## ADDITIONAL ACTIVITY

1. Much of Lynch's argument stems from and is concerned with the physical reality of the dead. Have your students research the actual procedures involved in harvesting organs. What, if any, effect does this research have on their view of Lynch's argument? How does an intimate knowledge of the physical reality of dead bodies—how they are harvested for organs, how they are prepared for burial or cremation, and how their bodies are ultimately disposed of—change our view of them? How does Lynch's profession uniquely qualify him to speak on the subject?

## GENERATING WRITING

1. Have students write a research paper on how we deal with the dead: sample topics might include the history of funeral rites or the legal and ethical implications of organ transplants. Their papers should reflect a philosophical concern with the issue. If they were to research, for example, ancient funeral practices—Egyptian mummification techniques or Viking funeral pyres—they should attempt to draw some conclusions about what such rites and rituals have to say about the way humans, as a species, or Egyptians or Vikings, as a culture, relate to the dead. What do their funeral practices teach us about how we deal with death? Similarly, a paper on organ transplants should grapple with the issues that Lynch raises in his essay. Do we need to show reverence for the dead when harvesting them for organs that will save lives? Why or why not? And what would such reverence *look* like, in practice?

## THE READER'S PRESENCE

1. Lynch's argument is, for the most part, abstract. He uses quite a bit of physical detail to make the argument, but what he calls for is honor and reverence, more than he calls for any specific policy change. Students are likely to have varied opinions about the effect of this strategy, but the *intended*

effect seems to be to provoke a moral reconsideration of the issues surrounding the subject of dead bodies—a reconsideration that would have deeper implications than a mere change of policy. In effect, he calls for a change of heart. Such a change of heart would reshape the way we think about the issue: it might reframe the whole subject so as to render the policy debates of the moment more or less obsolete (i.e., if we truly had reverence for the dead, or truly understood our relationship with their bodies, arguments about when and if it is appropriate to remove their organs might not even take place—not so much because we wouldn't remove organs for transplant but because we would have a better sense of the situations in which it would be appropriate, without need for a committee to debate the issue).

2. Again, Lynch is calling for something much more complicated—more *spiritual*—than a mere policy change, and as such some of his statements may seem oblique, if not opaque. The essay is full of such fodder for discussion. Draw your students' attention to paragraph 5: what does Lynch mean, for example, by "personhood"? How does the idea of personhood inform the essay? A discussion of this question will probably help lead students to answers to a variety of questions raised by the essay. The simplest explanation for the "bear us in memory" quote probably has to do with the way the dead "live on" in our memories, but it also has a great deal to do with our final interactions with the bodies of our deceased loved ones and how those interactions inform our memories. As Lynch points out at the end of paragraph 2, "The dead . . . matter to the living in ways that we're only beginning to understand." By this, he means not only our memories of their *lives*, but our interactions with their bodies *after* they are dead.

3. Both Lynch and Michael J. Sandel ("Designer Babies," p. 787) seem to have spiritual, if nonspecific, beliefs about life and death. Sandel believes that life is "a gift from the universe" (para. 8). Similarly, Lynch believes that the way we are "haunted, properly and happily in some cases, not only by [the] memories [of the dead] but also by their remnants" (para. 3). The use of the word *haunted* implies a spiritual dimension to the argument, which is made more explicit in the next paragraph, when Lynch calls for a recognition of the difference between "metabolic death, social death, spiritual death, and actual death as far as [one's] family is concerned" (para. 5). Both authors clearly feel that there is something more to life and death than biological life and death, and that, whatever it may be, "something more" is an essential part of what it is to be human: therefore, the recognition, respect, and reverence for it (life and death and the nonspecific something-more-whatever-it-may-be) is essential to human dignity. Both writers seem to value human dignity, to one extent or another, above human life, or at least above human health, as they seem to be willing to make some sacrifice of the living in favor of the dead. In Lynch's case, this means being careful about organ transplants from the dead. In Sandel's, it means being careful about using genetic engineering to control who we are at birth, even when the intention of such engineering is to avoid things like birth defects.

# Walter Benn Michaels
## THE TROUBLE WITH DIVERSITY

### APPROACHING THE ESSAY

Walter Benn Michaels has written an essay that is decidedly politically incorrect. The central issue of his essay attacks one of the sacred cows of the "tenured left" by asserting that economic inequality—not racial inequality—is the greatest problem in American society. Have students locate specific passages in which this assertion is made.

Lead students through the first few paragraphs. What is the importance of the anecdote about Ernest Hemingway and F. Scott Fitzgerald? Which of these two literary figures would probably share the author's ideas about race and class?

Ask your students to share their feelings about diversity. What role did diversity assume in their secondary education experience? How was race presented? Were the students encouraged to "celebrate" diversity? Was the concept of economic inequality (in America, not in the third world) ever engaged in their curriculum? Ask students to comment on some of the popular terms and words associated with the discussion of diversity and race in our culture. Discuss with them, for instance, the difference between prejudice and discrimination.

To what extent do Michaels's arguments suggest a conservative point of view? a liberal point of view? Ask students to find passages in the essay that support their answers. Does a social critic, such as Michaels, have to be either liberal or conservative? Would we like him to be? Why or why not?

Michaels states that "the American love affair with race—especially when you can dress race up as culture—has . . . intensified" (para. 10). Implied in this quote is a difference between race and culture. What is this difference? Is this idea radical? Do we assume that race and culture, if not identical, at least go hand in hand? Explain.

### ADDITIONAL ACTIVITIES

1. Michaels makes many simple yet almost shockingly radical statements. Present these to the class and ask students to articulate why they might be shocking, what logic drives them, and how they might fit into Michaels's overarching argument. Ask, too, if students agree or disagree with the following statements, and why: "We would much rather get rid of racism than get rid of poverty" (para. 15); "In an ideal universe we wouldn't be celebrating diversity at all—we wouldn't even be encouraging it—because . . . it would have no political significance whatsoever" (para. 20); "no issue of social justice hangs on appreciating racial or cultural diversity" (para. 20).

2. Michaels explains, "One way to look at *The Great Gatsby* is as a story about a poor boy who makes good, which is to say, a poor boy who becomes rich—the so-called American Dream" (para. 2). In groups of four or five,

have students develop a definition for the "American Dream" in the twenty-first century. Then ask the groups to share their definitions with the whole class.

3. Assign Barbara Ehrenreich's book about the working poor, *Nickel and Dimed: On (Not) Getting by in America*. Have each student prepare three discussion points, based on their reading of this book, and present the points to the class. What is the role, if anything, of race in Ehrenreich's research?

## GENERATING WRITING

1. In the penultimate paragraph, Michaels asserts, "Our identity is the least important thing about us." In a three- to five-page essay, ask students to support or refute this statement. Make sure, however, that they understand what the author means by it.

2. Michaels states that Americans don't love class. How does the public perception of a poor college student differ from its perception of a poor laborer? Ask students to write short response papers to this question.

3. Michaels states that Americans "love thinking that the differences that divide us are not the differences between those of us who have money and those who don't" (para. 8). How is the media responsible for maintaining this wrong assumption? In a September/October 2007 online article for FAIR titled "The Poor Will Always Be with Us—Just Not on the TV News," Neil deMause and Steve Rendell offer a study of network coverage of poverty. Distribute copies of this article to your class or have students download it from www.fair.org. Ask students to critique this article.

## THE READER'S PRESENCE

1. Celebrating diversity, Michaels reveals, became at some point "associated with the struggle against racism. . . . The goal of overcoming racism . . . was now reconceived as the goal of creating a diverse [and] color-conscious society" (para. 6). Focusing on celebrating diversity instead of ending poverty distracts us from the real problems at hand and from having to find solutions for them. Michaels suggests that eliminating race as a political category would allow us to focus on eliminating economic inequality.

2. Wit has always afforded writers the license to examine and criticize subjects that might otherwise be taboo. In some ways, it lessens the *immediate* impact and allows the writer to introduce difficult subjects. However, humor does sometimes anger people or allow them the opportunity to minimize the seriousness of a problem. Without the humor, Michaels's essay might still be effective, if not as readable. Examples of rewrites will vary. Rewriting a humorous passage with a more serious tone would not change the overall message. Humor is a rhetorical strategy for delivering truth and to that extent it is effective, if not overused. You might want to review with your class Jonathan Swift's classic essay, "A Modest Proposal" (p. 831), in which satire is sustained successfully throughout in order to chastise society.

3. Stephen Jay Gould ("Sex, Drugs, Disasters, and the Extinction of Dinosaurs," p. 430) states that "science works with . . . testable proposals" (para. 4). Furthermore, he would probably be critical of Michaels's statement if Michaels were presenting this statement as science. Fairness may not really be the issue here. Gould isn't saying that we shouldn't have ideas—he's just saying that we have to be careful about what we call science.

# Errol Morris
## LIAR, LIAR, PANTS ON FIRE

### APPROACHING THE ESSAY

The recognition that Errol Morris is a filmmaker may be instrumental in understanding the thesis of his essay. What is this essay about? The class will offer various answers: photography, the necessity of words, truth, ambiguity. However, once we understand the perspective from which it has been written—through the lens of a filmmaker—some of the questions that Morris asks, if not his answers, will become clearer to his readers. In what sense, for instance, is a filmmaker obsessed with captions (language)? For a filmmaker, what is the importance of pairing the right language to the right image? How does this differ from the work of other visual artists (the painter or the photographer)? Or other linguistic artists (the poet or the novelist)?

The one constant in all photographs is the photographer. Morris puts it this way: "One thing is clear. When I look at these pictures—whether it is a picture of the *Lusitania* or the *Titanic*—I imagine that someone stood on a dry dock, or some vantage point, looked through the viewfinder of the camera, and took a photograph" (para. 14). Morris does not pursue the significance of this observation except to say, "This may seem hopelessly obvious, but . . . I believe . . . that there is nothing so obvious that it's obvious" (para. 14). Ask your class to comment on the role of the photographer and compare it to the role of a writer. In what sense is "some vantage point" similar to "point of view" in writing or to perspective in drawing? Can the photographer use vantage point in any way to manipulate, or even create, a context for a picture? How has this possibility been enhanced by computer technology? How do writers create context?

Although the essay seems to be about photography, it may also be about the more important issue of language, specifically language's relationship to truth. Draw the class's attention to the following statement: "For truth, properly considered, is about the relationship between language and the world, not about photographs and the world" (para. 18). Invite students to challenge this statement. They might begin by isolating common rhetorical practices that enlist language in the pursuit of deception, propaganda, and even lies.

## ADDITIONAL ACTIVITIES

1. Have students compare Morris's essay to Nora Ephron's "The Boston Photographs" (p. 655). How do the Boston pictures support or contest Morris's assertions? What is the relationship between Morris's "captions" and
Ephron's "headlines"? How would the Boston pictures differ without captions and context? Would as many people have been as angered by them?
Why or why not?

2. Ask students to bring into class some famous photographs of the twentieth
and twenty-first centuries and present them without captions to the class.
Have students provide both context and captions for the pictures. Do the
emotional appeals of these pictures depend on captions? on familiarity? on
historical background? on graphic content? (A useful Web site for famous
photographs is www.digitaljournalist.org.)

## GENERATING WRITING

1. Assign a paper in which students compare and contrast the "ENLIST" recruit-
ment poster in Morris's essay to the first picture in Ephron's. What similar
theme or archetype do both pictures express? What emotions do viewers of
the two pictures experience? How do context and caption influence our different reactions to the two images?

2. Morris starts his essay with a variation of an old saying: "A picture is worth
a thousand words." Ask students to find a picture "shorn of all its context,
captionless, unconnected to current thought and ideas" (para. 3) and write a
thousand words (three to four pages) about it. The students should not do any
background research for this paper, nor should the photo have any personal
meaning. Rather, students should use their papers to debate whether it is
possible to understand *any* photo in this way.

## THE READER'S PRESENCE

1. Despite the fact that the pictures are old, "disconnected from the present"
(para. 6), they do not lack context. They are pictures of his family and, therefore, they have "captions" — the owner can supply them with language. The
collection reinforces Morris's ideas about images, context, and language.

2. Morris would insist that uncaptioned photography in a museum has context
as art. The artwork thus encourages the viewer to imagine a context: "Even
where there are no explicit captions . . . , there are captions in my mind.
What I think I am looking at. What I think the photograph is about" (para. 2).
The museum-goer might also know something about the photographer, the
exhibit, or the subject.

3. The two writers agree about the importance of context. For Charles Simic
("The Life of Images," p. 575), the photograph launches his imagination. He
creates elaborate stories based on the pictures. In some ways, this is similar
to what Morris says about captions: "And even where there are no explicit

captions on the page, there are captions in my mind" (para. 2). For Simic the caption *can* be as important as the picture. However, the caption is not necessary for Simic's imaginative work to begin. In fact, he takes "imaginary snapshots" all day long and believes that most people do, too. Morris seems somewhat discontented with having to accept imagination in lieu of truth. For him, the picture begins when it is given language that imbues it with context. Both writers would agree that, as Simic says, "A photograph . . . [is] full of innuendoes [and] partakes of the infinite" (para. 3). Because of infinite interpretations, the photo can have no truth *or* falsity. It has only possibility.

# Martha Nussbaum
## VEILED THREATS?

### APPROACHING THE ESSAY

Martha Nussbaum's argument might be a difficult one for some students to accept. For other students, it will be a fairly obvious matter. As Americans, we are told that the freedom of religion is inviolable. Although it can be argued that, in practice, this is not so much the case (even in the United States, which has a cultural tradition of priding itself on guaranteeing such freedoms), most students will be ready to accept the idea that Muslim women have a right to wear headscarves, and even burqas, should they wish to do so. Nussbaum considers the various arguments in favor of banning such garments one by one and flatly rejects them. This is therefore an essay that can be taught, more or less, in a straight line. It is a useful model for students, as well, precisely because it is so well structured. Nussbaum begins by establishing the philosophical traditions that inform her thinking on the subject. You can begin by discussing these traditions as articulated by John Locke (para. 5) and Roger Williams (para. 6). After that, Nussbaum enumerates the five arguments commonly made in favor of the ban, debunking them one by one. This will provide you with an excellent opportunity to teach enumeration.

### ADDITIONAL ACTIVITIES

1. If your students seem to be following (and accepting) Nussbaum's argument, you might consider challenging them with a bit of devil's advocacy. Note that Nussbaum's argument is rooted almost entirely in an Anglo American philosophical framework. The United States guarantees religious freedom; France does not. In fact, freedom of religion is *anything but* consistent with the values and traditions of Continental Europe. Given that France, for example, is culturally Catholic, might it be a mistake to judge French legislature by the standards of English or American thinkers on subjects like

religious freedom? Is it reasonable for Nussbaum to draw on American values to dictate how a nation like France should handle civil liberties?

2. The argument about the burqa certainly isn't the first one in which cultural tolerance or religious freedom might serve as carte blanche to ban institutions considered heinous by most Westerners: consider, for example, forced female circumcision in Somalia. In what ways can tolerating the burqa be likened to tolerating female circumcision? Wearing the burqa and participating in female circumcision are very different practices; circumcision is a surgical procedure. To what extent, though, are the intentions of each practice the same? It could easily be argued, for example, that both practices are meant to oppress or subjugate women. By the same token, one might argue that the intention of the burqa is to *protect* women from sexual exploitation. What do your students think about that comparison? Traditionally, feminism and liberal ideas about tolerance come from the same political and philosophical camp (i.e., one who argues for affording women a greater stake in their own destinies is also likely to argue for tolerating a multicultural society), but this is not always the case. Can your students think of other examples of conflicts between feminism and religious tolerance? Where do they stand on polygamy? abortion rights? At what point does applying the principles of Western humanism to religious tolerance become a self-contradicting (or self-defeating) enterprise?

## GENERATING WRITING

1. Have your students write an argumentative paper either supporting or refuting Nussbaum's position.
2. Have your students write an argumentative research paper about any one of the various conflicts between feminism and religious tolerance or, more broadly, Western humanism and itself.

## THE READER'S PRESENCE

1. Locke argues that the law should "not penalize religious belief, and [that laws should be] nondiscriminatory about practices, applying the same laws to all in matters [of] religious activities" (para. 5). Williams takes this a step further, arguing that the law must protect the individual's right to live in accordance with his or her conscience. Therefore, according to Williams, nondiscrimination isn't good enough because the majority will necessarily decide what is and is not acceptable, and that "even if [the resultant] laws are not persecutory in intent, they may turn out to be very unfair to minorities" (para. 6). Nussbaum essentially argues that this is the case in European nations like France, where laws have been proposed or passed forbidding the wearing of the burqa.
2. You might ask students to write a brief essay responding to this question. You might also consider using the question as a framework with which to structure your class's discussion of Nussbaum's essay. The five-point structure is

easy to follow and might be very useful in that capacity. If you have a fifty-minute class, you might even try to set a timer, giving the students ten minutes to debate each point, or you might try splitting the class into two teams, one arguing for and one against the ban, each with five minutes to support their argument on each of the five points. You could also split the class into smaller groups, requiring each group to give a short presentation on one of the five points Nussbaum enumerates. In any case, it will be important to have them cite the text of Nussbaum's argument directly.

3. The Declaration of Independence (p. 695) is very clear in its summary of the purpose of government. Governments, according to Thomas Jefferson, are created by the governed exclusively to secure the rights of the governed, and furthermore such governments are only just when they derive their powers from the consent of the governed. Therefore, according to Jefferson's theory of government, the French government has no authority whatsoever to tell people what they can or cannot wear, particularly when to do so violates their religious freedom. The situation in France is quite different from what it was in Afghanistan under Taliban rule: In Afghanistan, women were forced to wear burqas, regardless of whether they wanted to. In France, women are not required to wear burqas, so we might reasonably assume that those who do, do so by choice. Therefore, to forbid the wearing of the burqa in France has more in common with requiring the wearing of one in Afghanistan than it does with protecting women from Taliban-like tyranny. The problem with incorporating Jefferson's argument into Nussbaum's is that the Declaration of Independence is peculiarly American. As a philosophical treatise, it might be relevant, but as a government document, it has no weight under French law.

# Barack Obama
## GRANT PARK VICTORY SPEECH

### APPROACHING THE ESSAY

Many of your students will be fans of Barack Obama, which might make it difficult to take a critical approach to the essay. You might therefore be best served discussing the speech's persuasive power, without commenting too much on the way he "invokes . . . myths about America" (Reader's Presence Question 1) until you have already established that the purpose of discussing that aspect of the speech is not necessarily to criticize Obama or his presidency. Other students—conservative or Republican students, specifically—might be eager to criticize Obama and, although you want to acknowledge their points of view, you'll want to avoid allowing the classroom to fall into partisan debate. Furthermore, it is worth noting that students who dislike Obama on political grounds—Republican students—might be even more likely to buy into the "myth" of the American Dream than students who *voted* for Obama.

The object of the exercise—looking at the myths Obama invokes and ultimately denies or affirms—is to analyze Obama's rhetoric, not to praise or blame his politics or his presidency. Because he is the focal point of a great deal of emotion on either side of the political spectrum, this may be a near impossible task: a difficult one, at the very least, and (probably) important. The best way to do it might be to simply say, "Let's confine our discussion to the speech itself, rather than to Obama's actual presidency or politics." If you feel comfortable enough doing so, you might also consider asking the students who support Obama to raise their hands. Then ask for a show of hands from the students who do *not* support him. Some students won't raise their hands in response to either question. Sometimes the room will be heavily skewed one way or the other. In any case, you might consider asking those who support Obama to position themselves against him, and those who do not support him to take his side. This will prove an interesting exercise, or it will at least keep the students focused not on their preformed opinions but rather on the speech itself: its content and, more important, its rhetoric.

If you can keep your students focused on the rhetoric rather than on the political position the rhetoric is meant to serve, you might be able to have a genuinely fruitful discussion of how political speeches elicit emotional responses and persuade or fail to persuade their target audiences. Who is Obama's target audience? What is his purpose? Is his rhetoric effective? For an in-depth discussion of his rhetorical strategies—the use of myth, repetition (anaphora), and historical allusion, specifically—refer to the Reader's Presence questions in this entry.

## ADDITIONAL ACTIVITY

1. Have the students read other political speeches. You might ask them to look at Martin Luther King Jr.'s famous "I Have a Dream" speech (p. 701). You might also consider having them listen to Winston Churchill's "We Shall Fight on the Beaches" speech, or King George's VI's speech at the outset of World War II. John F. Kennedy's inaugural address might nicely serve the purpose, as well. How do these speeches work? Do the speakers use strategies similar to Obama's?

## GENERATING WRITING

1. Have the students write a political speech. They might imagine themselves being elected president, or they might write a hypothetical speech for Obama or another political figure, even a figure from history. Ask them to imitate Obama's rhetoric, to use some of the same strategies and tools. They might do this seriously or attempt to parody a politician or famous speech. Either approach will help them understand the way political rhetoric works.

## THE READER'S PRESENCE

1.  Obama says that his victory belongs to the voters (para. 10) and that his cam-
    paign was built by "working men and women who dug into what little sav-
    ings they had" (para. 12). This calls the sort of "grass roots" myth to mind:
    of course he had the support of the DNC. In paragraph 14, he says, "We as
    a people will get there," without really saying who "we" are or where we
    are going. The idea of "the American people" as a homogeneous group is
    probably a myth. The idea, in paragraph 15, that America was built "brick
    by brick" also calls a sort of mythology to mind, that America belongs to
    the working class. He calls for an end to partisan bickering, as though it is
    a myth that Republicans and Democrats cannot agree, and cites Abraham
    Lincoln to support his claim that it is possible to work together. This is par-
    ticularly interesting, in that Lincoln presided over the Civil War (hardly an
    example of "working together").
2.  Obama frequently repeats certain sentence structures. The effect (or
    intended effect) is emotional. Speeches often call on repetition; the rhythm
    of it is an effective way to rouse patriotism. You might have the students lis-
    ten to Churchill's "We Shall Fight on the Beaches" speech as an example of
    how such repetition can inspire feelings of patriotism in an audience.
3.  All of the speeches seem to invoke the idea of a perseverant American spirit,
    and furthermore a *unified* American spirit. You might have students look for
    places where Martin Luther King Jr. ("I Have a Dream," p. 701) and Abra-
    ham Lincoln ("Gettysburg Address," p. 491) repeat rhythms and sentence
    structures as they stress the importance of this unity. Have your students
    look for specific examples.

# Camille Paglia
## THE PITFALLS OF PLASTIC SURGERY

### APPROACHING THE ESSAY

Most critics of plastic surgery, particularly women, lament the fact that we are
socialized to have high regard for beauty's superficial qualities — we are all familiar
with the refrain that "beauty is only skin deep." Although Camille Paglia sympathizes with and understands the usual complaints, hers are not based on issues of
moralism, wastefulness, narcissism, or even sexism (not directly). Unlike other critics, Paglia theoretically sees nothing wrong with plastic surgery. She calls it "living
sculpture," a symbol of "the conquest of biology by human free will" (para. 1).
"Nothing," she declares, "will stop the drive of the human species toward beauty
and the shimmering illusion of perfection" (para. 4). She does, however, protest

against the type of beauty plastic surgery perpetuates—the "generic cookie-cutter sameness" (para. 12). Ask your students how they feel about these issues. What do they consider the author's real issue that is germane to the topic of plastic surgery? How does it differ from the usual moralistic and feminist arguments? Ask your students to locate Paglia's complaint and articulate her thesis in their own words.

To what extent does the success of Paglia's argument depend on her style of writing and diction? What is the effect, for instance, of her use of the words "instincts" and "mutilation" in paragraph 4? What effect does diction have on the production of tone in paragraph 6? Note the words Paglia uses to talk about "current models" of beauty: "diminished," "demeaning," "ingénue," "perky," "ingratiating," "girliness." Does the author's age have any bearing on her thesis? In paragraph 5, the author states, "I have not had surgery and have no plans to do so, on the theory that women intellectuals, at least, should perhaps try to hold out. (On the other hand, one doesn't want to scare the horses!)" In what sense is this self-parody? Why is it funny? How does the author's self-parody affect her credibility? How do we feel about her making fun of herself? How does this help or hinder the development of her thesis?

Study the final paragraph with your class. How realistic is Paglia's proposition that surgeons study art? That women refuse to perpetuate "an artificial juvenility"? What are the cultural values that are in jeopardy of obliteration?

## ADDITIONAL ACTIVITY

1. Plastic surgery is not the only form of body transformation. Have students examine the practices that Paglia describes: "from prehistory on, tribal peoples flattened their skulls, pierced their noses, elongated their necks, stretched their earlobes and scarred or tattooed their entire bodies to achieve the most admired look" (para. 4). You might want to bring in images from magazines like *National Geographic*. Discuss these practices in class with your students. What can they deduce about beauty ideals? How are these practices similar to or different from today's American expressions of beauty? What might be some historical or sociological reasons behind the evolution of these customs? Is beauty universal, in that we are all drawn to it, even if we have different cultural definitions of it?

## GENERATING WRITING

1. In a two- to four-page personal essay, have students write about some specific characteristic of their bodies, minds, or personalities that they would change and explain why they would change it. How has the characteristic handicapped the overall quality of their lives?
2. Paglia mentions the "great era of the Hollywood studio system, from the 1920s to the early '60s" (para. 7), which produced superstars like Lana Turner. Select one of these famous early Hollywood idols and analyze his or her appearance using today's standards of beauty. This assignment will necessitate researching and establishing definitions of beauty then and now. Is your screen idol beautiful? attractive? Is there a difference? Is there

anything specific (weight, height, hair color, eyes, clothing preference, even voice) that would disqualify this person from being "beautiful" today?

## THE READER'S PRESENCE

1. Paglia is ambivalent toward plastic surgery, calling it "living sculpture" (para. 1), but she is troubled by the "ruling styles of plastic surgery in the U.S. . . . , [and the] norms . . . imposed on adult or aging women" (para. 5). The author does not object, on ethical grounds, to altering one's appearance through surgery. However, she is bothered by the homogenization of beauty that the "limited repertoire of images" (para. 12) perpetuates and by the practices of "unskilled practitioners" (para. 11). Her artistic sensibility is affected by women's perpetuation of "an artificial juvenility that obliterates their own cultural value" (para. 13). The distinction between good and bad surgery, according to Paglia, is that "good surgery discovers and reveals personality; bad surgery obscures or distorts it" (para. 11).

2. Hollywood has provided our culture with its standard of beauty, which was created through "pioneering makeup techniques" (para. 7). Many of the founders of Hollywood were "European émigrés" whose "models of beauty are based on classical precedents: . . . Greek sculpture . . . or . . . Old Master oil paintings" (para. 8). These founders admired "mathematical symmetry and proportion . . . elegant aristocrats and hypnotic femmes fatales" (para. 8). However, modern film producers and directors have abandoned these standards. The model of beauty is now inspired by "snarky television sitcoms or holographic video games" (para. 9). Paglia laments today's female standard of "large breasts with a flat midriff and lean hips, a hormonally anomalous profile that few women can attain without surgical intervention" (para. 9).

3. Daniel Akst ("What Meets the Eye," p. 293), like Paglia, believes that looks do, indeed, matter, and that we all know it. Akst reinforces Paglia's assertions about body molding by pointing to sociological, psychological, and evolutionary explanations of the higher cultural status of "attractive" people.

# Michael Pollan
## WHAT'S EATING AMERICA

### APPROACHING THE ESSAY

Michael Pollan provides an unusual look at one of nature's most bountiful foods: corn. Using an ancient Mayan phrase, Pollan begins by pointing out that we are all "corn people," dependent on this "miraculous grass" for our existence. Throughout the essay, the author personifies corn and other natural agents. He calls corn "one of the plant world's greatest success stories" (para. 5); corn "came to colonize much of our land and our bodies" (para. 5); it made "the acquaintance of chemical fertilizers" (para. 8); corn is "hungry" (para. 18) for fossil fuel; the "nitrogen-guzzling monocultures of corn" (para. 21). He also personifies nitrogen, which is so important to corn's success: those "self-involved" (para. 9) nitrogen atoms; and he uses the pronoun "her" to refer to nature. Ask your students what effect this has on their reading of this essay.

Pollan's approach is unusual, too, because he seems to vilify corn: "It is no longer clear that corn's triumph is such a boon to the rest of the world" (para. 5) — an unusual move for a nature writer. Note, however, that nitrogen-hungry corn is not the real problem, nor is the nitrogen. It is the careless and greedy appropriation of the natural world by intrusive humans that has created this problem. Point out the last paragraph to your class. How does the tone of this paragraph differ from the tone of the rest of the essay? Have students compare the specific diction of this passage with that in the rest of the essay. For instance, what is the tone of "When humankind acquired the power to fix nitrogen, the basis of soil fertility shifted from . . . the energy of the sun to a new reliance on fossil fuel" (para. 15)? How does it compare to "the sun still shines" in the final paragraph? Which line seems more hopeful, and why? What is the importance of the word "still"?

The issue of corn and nitrogen runoff is part of a larger implicit issue. At what point in the essay do farms cease to be farms and become factories instead? How does the mentality of agriculture differ from the mentality of agri-business? What are some problems associated with agri-businesses that the author does not discuss in this essay?

Another issue raised in this essay is summed up in paragraph 14, the fact that "the good and evil . . . can flow not only from the same man but from the same knowledge." Ask the class to find examples of good and evil in this essay that flow from the same knowledge. How does this "double edge" complicate our solution to problems associated with the conflict between nature and humans? Why are environmental problems (and their solutions) always complicated?

## ADDITIONAL ACTIVITIES

1. A very interesting strategy used by Pollan is based on a phrase in paragraph 12: "Humans may have struck a Faustian bargain with nature when Fritz Haber gave us the power to fix nitrogen." (If students do not know the Faustian myth, briefly explain it or, better, have them research it before discussing this essay in class.) He then provides a short and sinister biography of Fritz Haber — a German Jewish chemist awarded the 1918 Nobel Prize for "improving the standards of agriculture and the well-being of mankind" (para. 13). Have students suggest ways in which Haber makes the perfect Faustian character. A respected man of science, how does he go about selling his soul? Who is the devil to whom he sells it? What does Haber get in return? What personal consequences does he seem to suffer for his "sin"? Is

the biography of Haber necessary for the development of Pollan's thesis? Why or why not?

2. Jared Diamond suggests in "The Ends of the World as We Know Them" (p. 642) that "when it comes to historical collapses, five groups of interacting factors have been especially important: the damage that people have inflicted on their environment; climate change; enemies; changes in friendly trading partners; and the society's political, economic and social responses to these shifts" (para. 3). Divide the class into five groups and assign one of Diamond's factors to each group. Have each group apply their criterion, or factor, to Pollan's essay and then report to the class their conclusions. Some factors may be more applicable than others. Some may not apply to Pollan's topic at all; if not, the group should show why. Provide the groups some research and conference time.

## GENERATING WRITING

1. In paragraph 3, the author delineates multiple uses for corn. In what ways does this explication suggest the Plains Indians' use of the buffalo? In what serious ways, however, are the two very different? What role does conservation play in both? in exploitation of natural resources? What different attitudes toward nature do the treatments of the two products (corn and buffalo) suggest? Have students address these questions in a three- to five-page paper. Some research might be required.

2. Assign an eight- to ten-page research paper on corn ethanol as a fuel. What are its advantages and disadvantages? Do scientists consider it a viable alternative to fossil fuel? How would the widespread use of corn as fuel economically affect the many other industries that rely on corn? What would be the environmental impact of using corn ethanol?

## THE READER'S PRESENCE

1. Pollan uses statistics with restraint and rhetorical consideration where they can best reinforce his thesis. The statistics reinforce our surprise, even our awe. Pollan informs us that "two of every five humans on earth today would not be alive" (para. 12) if not for the nitrogen-fixing process. A statistic that is effective, perhaps because of its simplicity. Our minds may begin to speculate about what that would mean for us personally: which of us would not be here? How would the world be different? Companies probably do not announce the abundance of corn products in our lives in order to "persuad[e] us that the 45,000 different [grocery store] items . . . represent genuine variety" (para. 4), as Pollan states. Customers might also be averse to learning about the chemistry involved in our "natural" food supply. In essence, chemical fertilizers (nitrogen) are transformed into corn by the Haber-Bosch process. Before this process was invented, crops got nitrogen through a bacterium living on the roots of legumes and through strikes of lightning. Once

synthetic nitrogen was available, farmers began to feed corn far more nitrogen than it needs in order to maximize yield. The excess nitrogen evaporates (acidifying the rain) or seeps into the water supply. The nitrogen has "alter[ed] the planet's composition of species and [shrunk] its biodiversity" (para. 20).

2. Readers of the *Smithsonian* would expect articles to be written by authors with expertise in their field, writers who also have "done their homework." They might also expect a writer who acknowledges the intellect of the reader. Pollan assumes that his readers will trust him. He also knows that tangential details will appeal to such an audience. When he opens his essay with information about the Mayan "corn people," he knows he has probably caught his readers' attention. The author can use fragments and short paragraphs as part of his writing style to captivate his readers and create a sense of urgency. Furthermore, explaining a technical subject colloquially facilitates the imparting of knowledge.

3. Both Pollan and Eric Schlosser ("Why McDonald's Fries Taste So Good," p. 558) use figurative language and break complicated processes down to manageable and comprehensible units. Schlosser's essay provides more scientific detail than Pollan's. Schlosser provides, for instance, a long paragraph of chemical names to describe the composition of "a typical artificial strawberry flavor" (para. 20). Pollan's process is probably easier to understand, but Schlosser's article analyzes more topics: the taste of McDonald's French fries, the flavor industry (particularly in New Jersey) and its history and science, the evolutionary basis for taste, how taste works and its relationship to smell, the "flavorists," "mouthfeel," and the opposition to artificial flavoring by vegetarian advocates.

# Michael J. Sandel
## DESIGNER BABIES

### APPROACHING THE ESSAY

Sandel begins by laying out some of the standard-issue arguments surrounding genetic engineering and, more specifically, the use of genetic engineering to create "designer babies." What is interesting about this essay is that he explains those arguments in order to dismiss them. He wants to deal with a less mechanical objection to designer babies: not what such technology could lead to, but what the use of it implies.

He begins with the assertion that genetic engineering is essentially the cousin of eugenics and as such belongs to a nasty tradition despite its good intentions.

He cites "a long tradition that defends eugenics in the name of 'lifting up'" (para. 2), and provides examples of respectable American progressives and reformers, including Oliver Wendell Holmes, who supported eugenics and even forced sterilization. Yet, he maintains, the legacy of Nazi Germany shows us where this sort of thinking leads, no matter how well intentioned. His next move is a marvelous example of anticipating and refuting the argument against his position. He acknowledges, in paragraph 3, that "the only thing wrong with eugenics was its coerciveness"; he then goes on, in paragraph 4, to begin his real argument: that eugenics—whether coercive or "free market"—is "morally troubling" for an altogether different reason.

In paragraph 5, Sandel again anticipates an argument, this one *in his favor* (i.e., against genetic engineering): the disparity between rich and poor would lead to a disparity in who would have access to "designer baby" technology, which would lead to a gap between economic classes that would be much more than economic in nature. But, again, he quickly dismisses the argument: there would, of course, be ways to *make* it fair. Acknowledging this further establishes his credibility as a reasonable, fair-minded thinker on the subject.

This is essential for Sandel's actual argument because his actual argument is far less tangible. What he's after is something altogether more spiritual than mechanical. We should not, he argues, attempt to master the creation of life. His objection is to exercising "our human will and our ability to remake human nature to serve our purposes and satisfy our desires" (para. 7). The rest of the essay is a reasoned evaluation of the various moral problems that arise from what Sandel calls "in part, a religious sensibility, but [a sensibility with] resonance [that] reaches beyond religion" (para. 9). You might spend some time asking your students what they think he means by this before moving on to the remainder of the essay. Ask the students how this sensibility informs the rest of the essay.

## ADDITIONAL ACTIVITY

1. Following up with the idea of the religious sensibility, ask the students how it informs the idea of the "hubris of . . . designing parents" (para. 11). What is a "Promethean assault" (para. 12)? How does a "religious sensibility [that] reaches beyond religion" (para. 9) differentiate "between providing help with health and training, and providing [it] with . . . genetic enhancement" (para. 14)? Do your students agree that there is or should be such a differentiation? Would pursuing genetic engineering technologies actually change human nature? Could "biotechnology [dissolve] our sense of giftedness," as Sandel fears in paragraph 17? How does all of this relate to Sandel's idea that "parenthood is a school for humility" (para. 19)? In what way? Sandel is particularly concerned with how we as humans view ourselves in relation to life: with humility or with hubris. Are we—or should we be—the masters of life itself? In some sense, all science aims at this sort of mastery. In another sense, its purpose is only to understand. What do your students think? What is the purpose of genetic research, if not, ultimately, genetic enhancement?

Where do we draw the line between protecting life and mastering it? These questions should provide ample fodder for classroom discussion.

## GENERATING WRITING

1. Have your students write a research paper arguing for or against genetic engineering for humans. Your students should explicitly address Sandel's concerns, framing their papers as a response to his.
2. Have your students write a paper comparing Sandel's reverence for life with Thomas Lynch's ("Into the Oblivion," p. 741) attitude toward death. In what ways do spiritual principles inform both essays?

## THE READER'S PRESENCE

1. Sandel deals with the assumption that "parents [have a right or the freedom] to give their kids the best" (para. 16), as well as the notion that we live in a "meritocratic" (para. 22) society. He cites the equalizing power of what he calls "the genetic lottery" (para. 21) to support his argument against genetic engineering, and he draws on examples ranging from the use of Ritalin in the classroom to genetic pretesting for Down syndrome. Ask your students how these examples are used, and how they relate, specifically, to genetic engineering.
2. It seems as though Sandel makes a point to identify the most common arguments for and against genetic engineering primarily to get them out of the way. For example, one of the most frequently invoked criticisms of genetic engineering is the comparison to eugenics. Sandel views this as a sound objection to designer babies, but it isn't his primary concern. Similarly, he touches briefly on the economic objections to designer babies. But all of this is preliminary to the question that he really wants to deal with: "Is there a moral objection to this genetic engineering, beyond safety, beyond fairness?" (para. 6). See the Approaching the Essay section of this entry for elaboration on these two arguments.
3. Both Sandel and Malcolm Gladwell ("Small Change: Why the Revolution Will Not Be Tweeted," p. 411) cite historical facts to make their cases. Both authors do this early in their essays: Sandel in the first few paragraphs, with the Nazis, and Gladwell immediately, with the now-famous Greensboro incident. These historical facts are meant to dramatically demonstrate the authors' points: in Gladwell's case, that real activism carries real risk; in Sandel's, that even the most well-meaning interference in the genetic lottery can lead to genocide. Ask your students if they are convinced. In what other places do they see the authors using historical facts to support contemporary arguments?

# Scott Russell Sanders
## THE MEN WE CARRY IN OUR MINDS

### APPROACHING THE ESSAY

When we think about the issue of gender and identity, we tend to focus on the problems women face in finding a place and a voice with which they can feel at ease. As Scott Russell Sanders points out, the process can be difficult for men as well. His examination of his own ideas and attitudes should spark some interesting, impassioned classroom debate.

One way to begin might be to look closely at the discussion between Sanders and his friend Anneke. Why does Sanders open the essay with their conversation? When Anneke remarks that men "have to search their souls" (para. 7), Sanders searches his, only to discover that he is "confused," his feelings a troubling "muddle." You might use this admission as a starting point, suggesting to students that they take Sanders at his word. How would they characterize Sanders's attitudes toward women? He begins the essay by stating his sympathy toward them: "This must be a hard time for women." Ask students to explain, using evidence from the text, how he acquired this sympathy. The first time he met women who "accused me and my sex of having cornered the world's pleasures," he was "baffled" (para. 19). How did he move from not understanding women's complaints to a position where he feels comfortable voicing their complaints for them?

The answer lies in the delicate question of class. This may be a hard topic to introduce among students; try to get them to respect Sanders's perspective. As a working-class man, he has experienced exclusion and oppression. He cites "dirt-poor farm country . . . mining country . . . Hispanic barrios . . . the shadows of factories, [and] Third World nations" as places "where the fate of men is as grim and bleak as the fate of women" (para. 19). Do students agree with Sanders's assessment?

Other students might point out that Sanders finds a kinship with women in their shared desires: he writes, "The daughters of such men wanted to share in this power, this glory. So did I. They yearned for a say over their future, for jobs worthy of their abilities, for the right to live at peace, unmolested, whole" (para. 21). He ends that paragraph, and the essay as a whole, with a kind of plea to women to believe in his sympathy: "If I had known, then, how to tell them so, would they have believed me? Would they now?" Ask the women in your class to respond to this question.

Some students may notice the absence of race from Sanders's discussion of exclusion. How might an African American man have portrayed the situation differently? If Sanders had been speaking with an African American friend, rather than his Dutch friend Anneke, how might their conversation have gone differently?

What if some women in the class find it hard to take Sanders's feminism at face value? What if they think he's just as "confused" at the end of the essay as he was at the beginning? What other explanations might such a reader offer, for example, for Sanders's sympathetic opening remark? What reason does *he* give for the extension of his sympathy? He says that women "have so many paths to choose from, and so many voices calling them" (para. 1) and, later, that they "feel . . . pressure to be everything, do everything. . . . Have their babies and get back to the office a week later" (para. 6). Who are these women he describes? Who were the women whom he envied for their lives of comparative "ease"? How do they differ from the women for whom he feels sorry? How would students characterize his description of women's lives in his hometown? Do they think he was seeing those lives clearly? What does the nostalgia that permeates his description of the "expansiveness" of women's days suggest about his attitudes toward women's liberation?

Some of your students may draw a distinction between the author and the narrator. After all, the author gives most of the good lines to a woman, Anneke, to whom he also awarded a mug that signifies wisdom. It is certainly worth arguing that the author was aware of some of the implications of the narrator's words — implications of which the narrator seems ignorant. But it is equally worth arguing that a first-person essay is unlikely to feature a large gap between author and narrator.

## ADDITIONAL ACTIVITIES

1. Many descriptive passages in this essay are crammed with physical detail that makes them almost palpable. Look with the class, for example, at paragraphs 11, 12, and 13. Ask students why the vivid description appears in the passages describing men engaged in brutal physical toil. It is as if the men's bodies are inscribed by the work they do. Why is there no comparable physical description of the women Sanders saw as a boy? Why don't *their* bodies "remember" their work? What connections does Sanders draw between work and identity?

2. Have students read Raymond Carver's "My Father's Life" (p. 60) and consider the following questions: How is Carver's experience similar to Sanders's? How did their childhood milieus shape them? What did their backgrounds teach them about masculinity, and how do their attitudes seem to have grown over time?

3. Students who want to do more research on the idea of masculinity and its social construction could be encouraged to read *Fire in the Belly: On Being a Man* by Sam Keen (1991) or *Refusing to Be a Man: Essays on Sex and Justice* by John Stoltenberg (1989).

## GENERATING WRITING

1. Sanders's title, "The Men We Carry in Our Minds," suggests the process by which images and their attendant ideas are formed. Given the importance of images in this essay, assign a paper in which students examine the assorted images Sanders uses in his metaphors. What do these images, taken together, suggest?

2. Early in the essay, in the context of a discussion of male guilt, Sanders wonders about the depth of the past. He asks himself, "Do I have to scour memory back through father and grandfather? Through St. Paul? Beyond Stonehenge and into the twilit caves?" (para. 10). For the purposes of his essay, Sanders apparently decides that his own personal memories go back far enough. What do students think about this? What is the statute of limitations on guilt? How far back should we feel culpable, or hold each other culpable? How much do guilt or grievances shape our identities? How much should they? This will be a difficult exploration, one that will entail both self-scrutiny and abstract thought, but for many students the mere attempt to write about such a topic will be salutary.

## THE READER'S PRESENCE

1. One of the challenges Sanders sets himself is to describe in the present tense a complex set of ideas that change over time. His questions in paragraph 10 thus must seem to emerge directly from the conversation with his friend, a dialogue that is no doubt more compressed on the page than it was in life. Sanders illustrates his conviction that "the past we must contend with is deeper even than speech" (para. 10). If there is something that rings false about the conversation—the people, the objects, the opinions seem to give off the glow of political correctness—it may stem from Sanders's desire to communicate the disconnect he felt between the men he knew and the view of male oppression he had come to believe.

2. Sanders uses the active verb *carry*, rather than *hold*, for example, as a way of introducing the image of work that is central to his portrayal of masculine identity.

3. Katha Pollitt ("Why Boys Don't Play with Dolls," p. 555) posits that children get their ideas about sex roles from their environment, which bombards children with messages about gender "from morning till night" (para 16). Sanders's childhood memories of the working men around him certainly affected his notions of gender, class, and privilege. In his essay, Sanders includes the important dimension of class when discussing gender. He points out that the underprivileged working class should not be unfairly lumped with the overprivileged class of men, as though men who act and feel entitled do so simply because of their sex and not their class. Sanders recognizes the difficulty of breaking free of conventional sex roles for both men and women.

# Barry Schwartz
## THE TYRANNY OF CHOICE

### APPROACHING THE ESSAY

This essay's topic of academic choice will resonate with the experiences of your students. Also they will certainly identify with overextension and the "choice overload" of their academic experience. You may want to begin by asking students why they have chosen to lead such hectic lives. Or first, ask them why they have chosen to go to college at all. Responses, no doubt, will focus on what they consider to be their *lack* of choice in this matter. Good jobs and salaries, early retirement, peer and parent pressure, competition, future "happiness"—all these and more will be given as reasons for traveling through life in overdrive. Challenge them by pointing out that none of these "causes" is external to their own decision-making freedom. For the first time, some of the students will recognize that it is *they* who have accepted and designed this fast-paced program for their lives.

As Barry Schwartz speaks about higher education, it becomes clear that "internal structure has largely disappeared" (para. 12). Ask students to find passages in this piece that suggest the breakdown of structure in academe. Have them suggest what has taken the place of structure. Note the penultimate line of the first paragraph: "[Students] go to a class, stay 10 minutes to see what the professor is like, then walk out, often in the middle of the professor's sentence." Do students see anything wrong with this? The breakdown of what cultural mores is suggested by this practice?

Schwartz talks about the abundance of choices primarily in education. In paragraph 20, however, the author says, "The 'liberation' of the university experience mirrors the embrace of choice in American society at large." What other institutions does he find affected by choice? What additional institutions can your class offer that Schwartz has not mentioned? How does the Internet contribute to "choice overload" (para. 6)? What about other media?

You may want to point out the conclusions that Schwartz and his colleagues derive from their study of freedom of choice: Freedom of choice does not necessarily enhance well-being; rather, "close social relations" (para. 21) play an important role. Note, however, that the author maintains that these "social ties actually *decrease* freedom of choice" (para. 22). Discuss with your students what he means by this. Are they happy with this result? Is it, for them, counterintuitive?

Finally, consider the cartoon that the author describes in the last paragraph. (Peter Steiner's cartoon can be viewed at www.thenewyorkerstore.com.) How does this cartoon epitomize Schwartz's thesis?

### ADDITIONAL ACTIVITY

1. The opposite of what Schwartz describes is illustrated in the following song lyrics, written by Kris Kristofferson and sung by Janis Joplin: "Freedom's just

another word for nothing left to lose / Nothing, I mean nothing, honey, if it ain't free." Ask your class to respond to these lyrics: Do they resonate with the new millennium generation? Why or why not? Why were the lyrics so popular with the "hippie" generation of the late 1960s (when the song was first recorded) and the 1970s? How would someone from the 1960s respond to the extraordinary and, according to Schwartz, overwhelming, freedom of choice available to today's youth? According to the lyrics, what is the sacrifice that freedom requires, and why? Why has Schwartz titled his essay "The Tyranny of Choice"?

## GENERATING WRITING

1. Assign an eight- to ten-page research paper comparing and contrasting the American higher education system to that of another country.
2. A number of essays included in *The Writer's Presence* are by college professors, such as Barry Schwartz, Michael Bérubé, and Walter Benn Michaels, among others, who write about education and the relationship between students and professors. Have students review some of these essays and then write a four- to six-page analysis on some dominant tone or thesis shared by at least three of these educators.

## THE READER'S PRESENCE

1. Metaphors of consumerism are all too commonly used in academe. Schwartz likens students to "customers," the university to an "intellectual shopping mall," available majors and courses to "goods," and selected courses to "purchases" (para. 1). However, education is not a product. The author is not against a healthy selection, but he asserts that having too many options becomes ponderous and confusing. He would not insist that students take all of the same classes as undergraduates. A suggestion could be made that better advising would eliminate the problems of choice: students could be steered by a competent mentor in the student's anticipated field. The "intellectual shopping mall" might provide enormous opportunities for intellectual development.
2. To support his thesis, Schwartz initially uses the expertise of people and writers in various fields: books by a psychologist, a political scientist, and journalists. He presents statistics to show that feelings of "happiness" have declined over the last thirty years. This kind of unbiased, empirical evidence early in his essay lays a credible foundation for the development of his thesis. Once Schwartz has established this credibility with his readers, he uses his own experience and research to further his argument. His argument becomes even more personal as he uses his own college experience as anecdotal evidence. Had the author used only statistics throughout, they would have grown meaningless and less interesting at some point.
3. Schwartz would recognize that having too many choices is probably better than having none: "There are many benefits to expanded educational

opportunities. The traditional bodies of knowledge transmitted from teachers to students in the past were constraining and often myopic" (para. 16). Although Lars Eighner ("On Dumpster Diving," p. 377) becomes more focused and aware because of his limited choices, no one—including probably Schwartz—would recommend his lifestyle. Eighner's "healthy state of mind" is not a product of living from the refuse of society; rather, it is a result of his reconciliation with and adaptation to his circumstances. He is wiser and stronger as a result of mastering his difficult situation.

# Leslie Marmon Silko
## IN THE COMBAT ZONE

### APPROACHING THE ESSAY

Leslie Marmon Silko begins and ends her essay with an explicit discussion of the need for women to believe in their right to defend themselves, and to have the skills to act on that right. Sandwiched between the beginning and end are Silko's recollections of learning to hunt and shoot: "It was great fun to take aim at a pickle jar and watch it shatter" (para. 5), and "When I was fourteen, I killed my first male deer buck with one shot through the heart" (para. 6). By the time Silko tells the story of being chased through Tucson by an angry man in a car, the reader is fully aware of Silko's status as armed and capable of using her weapon. In the reader's imagination, Silko is ready to "destroy the myth that women are born to be easy targets" (para. 25); she has her finger on the trigger of the gun that will blow away that myth, and any male predator who still subscribes to it.

Silko's essay is extremely deft in its interweaving of urgent political argument and deep cultural and personal history. The Laguna Pueblo people instilled in Silko, as in all of their children, a sense of responsibility for themselves from an early age. Silko's argument thus also includes a general critique of sexist American practices. "Women are TAUGHT to be easy targets by their mothers, aunts, and grandmothers, who themselves were taught that 'a woman doesn't kill' or 'a woman doesn't learn how to use a weapon'" (para. 24). Silko registers her mistrust of the government: "In the United States, women depend on the courts and the police" (para. 22). Even further, she states, "More than one feminist has pointed out that rapists and serial killers help keep the patriarchy securely in place," by scaring women into staying home even when they are being abused by their husbands or other male relatives (para. 9). The most radical implication of Silko's argument is that by not learning to take responsibility for their own safety, women themselves are helping to keep the patriarchy securely in place and are thus contributing to their own oppression.

Silko opens by expressing her surprise that most men aren't aware of the defensive precautions women typically take when they leave the house alone at night.

**283**

The detailed account she gives of racing through Tucson is her attempt to redress this ignorance. When she confronts the man chasing her in a parking lot, she makes explicit the connection between hunting and self-defense: "My early experience deer hunting had prepared me well. I did not panic because I felt I could stop him if he tried to harm me. I was in no hurry. I sat in the car and waited to see what choice my stalker would make. I looked directly at him without fear because I had my .38 and I was ready to use it" (para. 17). The men who threaten women and who do violence to them are predators, Silko suggests, but they are also animals. Women who take their safety into their own hands are refusing to be made prey.

## ADDITIONAL ACTIVITIES

1. Have students research the self-defense classes for women available in the local area, Take Back the Night activities, and the various programs for escorting women safely from place to place at night. Encourage them to take part in such programs; if no such programs exist (especially on a college campus), encourage them to organize one.

2. Ask students to research local handgun laws and gun-safety classes offered in the area. Have them debate the question of whether women should carry guns for self-defense.

## GENERATING WRITING

1. Following Silko's model, have students write a four- to five-page essay in which they bring together a political stand on a contemporary issue and a personal experience. Have them think about how one emerges from the other, and how that relation between experience and opinion is best rendered in their essay.

2. Have each student write a two- to three-page position paper on whether allowing people to carry concealed weapons makes a community safer. Divide students into two debate teams and organize a formal debate on the question in which students build on the points they made in their papers.

## THE READER'S PRESENCE

1. Silko identifies as a "combat zone" any place where a woman is not safe from attack by male strangers, friends, or relations. Traveling through such places—or living in them—requires showing "constant vigilance" (para. 1), "becoming strong and potentially lethal individuals" (para. 21), and "learn[ing] how to take aggressive action individually, apart from the police and the courts" (para. 24). As these (and many other) examples show, Silko develops quite deliberately metaphors of warfare. It's not simply the side with the most guns that wins but the side that knows how to use them.

2. Silko's hunting stories serve several functions in the essay. The detail of the stories is considerable and compelling; these stories above all humanize

Silko for her reader. We watch her develop from childhood through rituals of hunting and independence. We recognize her father as the prime proponent of Silko's right to bear arms. The stories also turn Silko into a larger-than-life figure, almost mythical in her fluid movement between cultures. She rides on her horse into the reader's imagination, gun slung across her chest. We appreciate the deep knowledge and skill she brings to the discussion of guns; she establishes her authority on the subject. The transition between traditional scenes of hunting and incidents of attack and self-defense confirm for her reader Silko's sense of the similarity of these wild and dangerous places.

3. Although Brent Staples describes himself as the victim of women's racial profiling ("Just Walk on By: A Black Man Ponders His Power to Alter Public Space," p. 217), Silko discusses women as victims of fear on the streets. Silko does not discuss how women judge and assess risk but instead describes situations where the threat is obvious and unquestionable. Silko says that women wrongly assume that most men are aware of their ceaseless safety precautions; however, Staples obviously is aware that women take precautions because he observes how women in particular react to him on the street at night. Like Silko, Staples admits that women have a real need to look out for their safety because they are most often the victims of street violence. He would likely disagree, however, with Silko's ending argument that women could more actively defend themselves by carrying a weapon. Some students may point out that when armed with a gun, Silko herself does not act on fear but finds calm in knowing that she is defended. An armed woman on the streets might not feel the need to run from Staples. However, his life might be in danger if armed civilians were to see him as a mugger or rapist simply because of his race.

# Peter Singer
## THE SINGER SOLUTION TO WORLD POVERTY

### APPROACHING THE ESSAY

Like other utilitarian philosophers, such as Jeremy Bentham and John Stuart Mill, Peter Singer describes himself as "one who judges whether acts are right or wrong by their consequences" (para. 5). But unlike Bentham or Mill, Singer's ethical concerns always seem rooted in his empathetic understanding of the condition of other's lives. And clearly, Singer is aware of the charges often made against his predecessors, for the title of his essay—"The Singer Solution to World Poverty"—ironically recalls the sorts of impractical and narcissistic schemes for social improvement so characteristic of nineteenth-century utilitarianism. (The most famous essay in this vein is Jonathan Swift's "A Modest Proposal," p. 831.)

Perhaps the most striking feature of Singer's essay is the way it combines lucid, reasoned argument with an acute and a merciless rhetorical address. From the opening anecdote about Dora, the central character in the Brazilian film *Central Station*, Singer's essay indicts readers for refusing to recognize their kinship to distant humans or, rather, indicts them for refusing to see that true kinship would require well-to-do readers to act to alleviate the suffering of children in Brazil or Rwanda. Singer's brand of utilitarianism never forgets the need for *utility*; that is, he never forgets that the job of the philosopher isn't merely to be right about a particular issue but is rather to be right in ways that affect how people actually live their lives.

In this instance, Singer's strategy is to alternate between sections of straightforward argumentation and increasingly direct address to readers. In three pages, Singer moves from anecdotes about Dora to the hypothetical case of the Bugatti-driving Bob, to the *actual* case of readers, whom he provides with the toll-free telephone numbers for Unicef and Oxfam America: "Now you, too, have the information you need to save a child's life. How should you judge yourself if you don't do it?" (para. 9). Time and again, he constructs arguments so that the reader is indicted by his or her own reasoning: "If you still think that it was very wrong of Bob not to throw the switch . . . then it is hard to see how you could deny that it is also very wrong not to send money to one of the organizations listed above" (para. 10).

Along the way, Singer dismantles possible opposing arguments, such as the fear that charitable giving won't reach its target or that heroic giving wouldn't be needed if everybody with means did his or her share. Ultimately, though, Singer's central goal is to construct an essay that will not allow the reader to escape the burden of his claims.

To that end, "The Singer Solution" grows increasingly direct in its address, as in the following shift from the neutral third-person to the more aggressive second-person nudge: "I trust that many readers will reach for the phone and donate that $200. Perhaps you should do it before reading further" (para. 14). "Now that you have distinguished yourself morally from people who put their vintage cars ahead of a child's life" (para. 15), the next paragraph begins, and note the understated savagery of the "now," which Singer uses to indict those readers (the vast majority) who have not, in fact, stopped reading to take action of any form. (And note Singer's audacity in writing an essay that measures success by the number of readers who stop reading midway through the piece.) "That's right," Singer insists toward the end, "I'm saying that you shouldn't buy that new car, take that cruise, redecorate the house, or get that pricey new suit. After all, a $1,000 suit could save five children's lives" (para. 21).

Have students read Singer's excerpt "Utility and the Survival Lottery" (p. 820) and compare it with paragraphs 7 through 14 in "The Singer Solution to World Poverty." Ask students to summarize the two hypothetical examples. How do they differ in authorial tone? What about the academic piece suggests that it was written specifically for an audience interested in philosophy? How do the two arguments differ in content, style, and objectives? Why does the author use a different vocabulary for each piece? Which example uses the more concrete details, and why? What is the effect of Singer's use of footnotes in one essay but not in the other? In the academic excerpt, Singer discusses John Harris's example in the light of utilitarian philosophy. In what direction do students think the essay will proceed? Do they think Singer will attempt to propose a solution to organ donation, as he does with poverty in the previous essay, or will he only focus on the philosophy behind it?

## ADDITIONAL ACTIVITY

1. Like many philosophers, Singer writes about hypothetical cases. Have your students explore the resources of this method for their own thinking, by trying to generate alternative situations that would complicate or refute those offered by Singer.

## GENERATING WRITING

1. Did students take direct action as a result of reading Singer's essay? Have students write short essays about what they did, and why, or about why they didn't do anything. Students should not be allowed to plead poverty as an excuse, unless they feel that a $200 expense for them would be equivalent to Bob's losing his leg.
2. A follow-up to question 1: Have students write an informal essay exploring why (we assume) so few direct actions took place as a result of reading Singer's essay. Or do they think that people act as they wish *despite* reasons or evidence to the contrary? What are the social or anthropological implications of their answers?

## THE READER'S PRESENCE

1. Singer chooses to describe an extreme scenario (he admits this with the phrases "most of us will immediately respond," para. 8; and "Hypothetical examples can easily become farcical," para. 16) for precise, rhetorical purposes. As he develops the implications of Bob's actions, he ropes the reader into a logically inescapable trap. "Now that you have distinguished yourself morally from people who put their vintage cars ahead of a child's life, how about treating yourself and your partner to dinner at your favorite restaurant?" (para. 15). This is one of the most painful and persuasive moments in Singer's bracing essay. The success of his argument *depends on* his reader's constant, largely unconscious rationalizations and defenses. Only after these are stimulated and drawn out can Singer begin to reason them away. Finally, with his last sentence, Singer snaps shut the trap: "We are all in [Bob's] situation."
2. The implication of this question—that world hunger is necessary as a limit on population growth—is an argument made by only the most brutal of

utilitarians. In the history of world aid, most solutions, and the best solutions, to poverty are complex, involving self-sustaining systems of food production, health, and birth control, among other things.

3. Jonathan Swift ("A Modest Proposal," p. 831) would doubtless appreciate the relentlessness of Singer's argument, its attempt to not merely suggest a solution or persuade the reader, but rather to *shame* the reader into action. Agreement is not what Singer seeks; he means to will readers into changing their lives right then and there, as they are reading. Swift's essay, as sustained satire, works by implication rather than by direct harangue, but Singer's scenarios are not without a satirical or sarcastic edge.

# Lauren Slater
## THE TROUBLE WITH SELF-ESTEEM

### APPROACHING THE ESSAY

Psychologist Lauren Slater argues that self-esteem is overrated and as a nation we put too much emphasis on the role of low self-esteem in social problems. Instead of arguing that we should all aim for high self-esteem, Slater argues that we have put undue emphasis on the value of thinking highly of ourselves. She gives evidence of experiments in which people with high self-esteem were more likely to inflict pain on others.

Our investment in self-esteem comes from a centuries-old belief that everyone is fundamentally good and valuable. Slater also believes that self-esteem is tied to our national identity and rooted in both individualism and entrepreneurialism. Most simply, we are a nation bent on finding worth in the individual, and high self-esteem is a measure of an individual's belief in that philosophy.

Slater also argues that self-esteem boosting is an industry that must promote itself. Here she reminds us of her background as a psychologist, which lends credence to her analysis: "There is a profound tension here between psychotherapy as a business that needs to retain its customers and psychotherapy as a practice that has the health of its patients at heart" (para. 17). Slater suggests self-control and self-appraisal as two alternatives to the high value put on self-esteem. Instead of valuing ourselves just because we are individuals, we emphasize appraising the work we do and the relationships we have. She refers to Freud in suggesting that our worth should come from "work and love" (para. 23).

Ask students to discuss how Slater defines self-esteem. What synonyms does she use? How does she address the issue of whether science has been defining self-esteem consistently across experiments? You might also ask students to examine how Slater establishes her credibility. How does she use personal experience? When does she bring in expert opinion? How does she use the language of psychology?

## ADDITIONAL ACTIVITIES

1. Distribute a self-esteem test to your students (The National Association for Self-Esteem offers one on its Web site at www.self-esteem-nase.org.). Analyze the questions and determine how the test appears to judge and define self-esteem. What does it take into account? What does it omit? For fun, you might have your students take the test and compare results. How effectively do they think the test measures "confidence"? "self-worth"? What other characteristics do they think the test takes into consideration?

2. Stage a class debate where one side argues for self-esteem–boosting workshops in schools and the other side argues against them. Ask the proponents to come up with concrete ideas for how children will benefit from self-esteem training. Ask the opponents to come up with an alternative philosophy.

## GENERATING WRITING

1. Assign students an analytical essay in which they evaluate Slater's argument in terms of claims, evidence, credibility, nods to the opposition, appeals, and other rhetorical strategies. Make sure that students consider the effectiveness of each technique for Slater's audience.

2. Have students read Laura Kipnis's essay "Against Love" (p. 733). Then ask them to write a comparison-and-contrast essay in which they examine how the two writers attempt to rethink and refute a social concept commonly accepted as good (marriage, in the case of Kipnis; self-esteem, in the case of Slater). What obstacles does each writer have to overcome to persuade her audience to give up a long-held belief? How does each writer use logical, ethical, or emotional appeals?

## THE READER'S PRESENCE

1. Slater's essay begins with the history of the self-esteem movement in this country and then discusses current research that debunks this obsession. She quotes numerous experts in the field, from sociologists at the London School of Economics to Sigmund Freud to practitioners of a popular Japanese form of psychotherapy called Morita. She even quotes one of her patients, a murderer who confides: "The problem with me, Lauren, is that I am the biggest piece of [expletive] the world revolves around" (para.14). Slater increases her credibility by referring to her personal experience as a psychologist and even implicating herself in her discussion of the ways in which psychologists benefit from the current fixation with self-esteem.

2. Slater traces self-esteem back to a belief in the inherent goodness in the human spirit, which bolsters the idea that believing in oneself is the same as supporting one's potential goodness. In his famous essay "On Self-Reliance," Ralph Waldo Emerson originates the idea that everyone has the capability for original and worthy creation. Slater also makes a connection between our capitalist drive and our conflation of self with worth. She claims our

entrepreneurial instincts make the "self" the most obvious target for profitable improvement. Our culture is so reliant on the idea of self-worth that psychology itself would have to rethink some of its basic tenets of therapy in order for this to change. Educational institutions would also have to give up self-esteem curriculum, and psychologists and sociologists would have to re-examine the long-held belief that social problems are caused by people with low self-esteem.

3. Slater deflates the current popularity of the self-esteem movement with a well-reasoned argument heavily supported by numerous experts in the field. As a therapist, Slater admits that psychology benefits from selling self-esteem as a cure-all. However, her line of reasoning is predominantly removed from her personal experience. In "Against School" (p. 665), John Taylor Gatto, a former teacher, argues that compulsory schooling is sold to us as the only way to succeed in life and that our educational system is a profitable business that many Americans depend on financially. Gatto also obtains credibility from his long career as a teacher: he has worked in the system as an award-winning educator and, ironically, can testify more credibly to its failures. Students may find Kipnis's argument the least convincing of the three. Although she discusses her subject matter at length, she lacks the scientific data presented by Slater and Gatto, as well as the credibility of working in a relevant field.

# Jonathan Swift
## A MODEST PROPOSAL

### APPROACHING THE ESSAY

If freshman composition can be said to have a canon, this is one of its texts. You might even begin discussion about this classic essay by inviting speculation about *why* it occupies so prominent a place in so many anthologies. Is it because its topic — cannibalism — is horrible? Or is it because of the author's masterful use of irony? Or is it the savage political satire? Do your students share the critical opinion that for decades has included this essay as a main document in composition studies?

Satirists like to kill two birds with one stone; they take a satirical attitude not only toward a topic but also toward the literary vehicle typically used to present that topic. Jonathan Swift's main subject in the essay is economic oppression, and he makes his point about it by inventing a reasonable-sounding person who offers a solution he believes is reasonable to correct a terrible problem. But he also satirizes the literary form in which such solutions are couched — in this case, the proposal. With its parliamentary style of address, its use of "official" sources, and its

statistical "evidence," "A Modest Proposal" is a remarkable parody of the governmental or "think-tank" document that purports to provide a rational solution to a
grievous social problem. You might want to point out to students that Swift lived
at a time when demographic and statistical data were just being recognized as
important sources of social information. The essay is prescient: Swift keenly seizes
on such data to show how easily they can be used for social and political control.
The speaker of Swift's "proposal" offers perhaps one of the earliest examples of
the technique we now call "blaming the victim." How can we relieve eighteenth-
century Dublin's poor and homeless? By encouraging them to sell their children to
the rich so that they can be murdered for food. It is preposterous, of course, but by
making the preposterous sound reasonable Swift achieves his ironic purpose.

One reason that this essay has played so well for so long in composition courses
is that it offers instructors a chance to teach irony. Ford Madox Ford, an English
novelist and editor instrumental in developing early twentieth-century British literature, commented that the most common error the general public makes in reading is that it doesn't distinguish between the author's opinions and those of the
characters. Ford was talking about fiction, but the same problem often occurs in
the essay, especially when the author has created a character or a "voice" that
seems identical to the writer's but isn't. Swift sustains this voice so thoroughly—that
is, he presents his plan with such a straight face—throughout the essay that many
readers in his time took his "modest proposal" seriously and were outraged.

You might get into the issue of irony here by inviting students to characterize
the unnamed person who is ostensibly writing this proposal. They should try to
identify some of his characteristics: how he presents himself as caring deeply about
Dublin's poor and wants to do something about them; how he has thought long and
hard about what to do; how in the final paragraph he identifies himself as entirely
lacking in self-interest and cares only about the public welfare (your students might
want to consider alternative explanations of the essay's final sentence). Ask them
to consider the speaker's explicit self-presentation: why do they think he wants
his readers to think of him in this way? They should also examine his language
and style, noticing his repetition and his continual efforts to appear deferential,
humble, and sincere (all words he uses). His proposal is "modest" in two senses:
it is presented as a reasonable, *moderate* plan, and it is presented by a reasonable
and *modest* person.

Obviously, there is a clash here, between the moderate tone of voice and the
violence of the plan. A large part of Swift's irony comes from this clash of moral attitudes—the speaker is appalled by the poverty and deplorable conditions of women
and children (and appalled that impoverished women would abort their pregnan-
cies), but he is not at all appalled by the idea of murdering one-year-old infants and
selling their flesh for food. Swift expects, of course, that this moral inconsistency will
tip his readers off that *his* views are not the same as his speaker's. To demonstrate
this point more clearly, invite your class to look closely at paragraph 17, where the
speaker discusses the inadvisability of a plan to cannibalize young adolescents.
The strategy (common to the rhetoric of proposals) is a good one: make your own
position appear reasonable and moderate by showing that others hold views more
extreme than your own. It even gives the speaker the opportunity to show himself

as a very feeling person: "It is not improbable that some scrupulous people might be apt to censure such a practice (although indeed very unjustly), as a little bordering upon cruelty; which, I confess, has always been with me the strongest objection against any project, how well soever intended." One of the best ways to justify one's own repugnant ideas is morally to draw the line—to say, for example: "I may propose x, but I would never propose y." Your students should notice here Swift's fine ironic touch—the speaker doesn't believe the proposal to use adolescent flesh is really cruel; he merely (and notice all the negative couching) believes that "scrupulous people" might "unjustly" think it "a little bordering on cruelty."

Other instances of inconsistency show that Swift has created a special type of "voice" here; the speaker frequently acknowledges his repetitiveness and digressions yet tells us that he is "studious of brevity." This is a joke on the speaker that Swift expects readers will notice, just as they will pick up the irony in the speaker's abhorrence for cruelty. He injects jokes on others, too: Americans come off as barbaric cannibals, though the speaker never directly says so; and we find Protestants who wouldn't mind seeing the number of Catholics reduced.

But is the prime target of Swift's irony only this individual speaker? Is he the one Swift is making fun of for his moral callousness, his officialese? You might want to discuss this issue at some length in class. You first may need to invite your students to see what this speaker represents—that behind the speaker's attitude is a dangerous rationalism willing to sacrifice human life in the name of a benevolent social program. Any plan, Swift says, regardless of how much misery it may cause or how it may harm innocent people, can be made to sound utterly reasonable, equipped with the requisite calculations and its supposed advantages. You might read aloud in class this synopsis of an article ("The Economics of Legalizing Drugs," by Richard J. Dennis) that appeared in the November 1990 *Atlantic* and ask your students how closely they think it resembles the style of argument in Swift's essay: "From a strictly economic point of view," the author argues, "legalizing illegal drugs makes a great deal of sense: It would save taxpayers billions of dollars and put drug lords out of business. And," he contends, "it would not cause an unmanageable increase in the number of addicts."

The target of Swift's irony is, students will see, the English landlords who have devastated the Irish economy. You might demonstrate this aim by examining paragraph 12: "I grant this food will be somewhat dear, and therefore very proper for landlords, who, as they have already devoured most of the parents, seem to have the best title to the children." This short paragraph opens up a problem of tone, for the speaker's attitude here seems to break out of the ironic frame and directly state the situation not as he sees it but as *Swift* apparently sees it.

You might point out the puns in this passage. The food is *dear* not only because it will be expensive and thus affordable only to landlords; but it may also be *dear* to the parents whose child it once was. Here we may assume that the speaker, whose terms are strictly monetary, may intend only one level of meaning for *dear*; the other, human level will be supplied by the reader (we thus have a lesson in irony contained in one word). But *devour* presents us with a different level of consciousness on the part of the speaker because he intends the word both literally and figuratively, to eat and eat up. It would be interesting to assess the range of student response to this passage. Do students think that it is out of character for the speaker to admit this accusation, or is it still in character? In other words, do they think Swift allows his own opinion to break directly through the ironic pose?

This is clearly a difficult discussion question—analyzing levels of irony always is—but in asking students to reflect on Swift's method you will be raising essential questions about the distance between authors and speakers that is vital to understanding literary works in their fullest complexity.

## ADDITIONAL ACTIVITY

1. Ask students to compare Swift's view of colonialism to George Orwell's experience as a British officer in Burma ("Shooting an Elephant," p. 180). Divide the class into a few groups and encourage them to find a recent proposal that promises to remedy some current social problem. They should make a copy of the proposal and bring it to class, ready to discuss its reasonableness and the self-image the proposer attempts to create. Discussion should focus on the writer's strategies to make his or her proposal acceptable to the reader.

## GENERATING WRITING

1. One good way to learn about irony is to try using it in writing. Ask students to use their opinions or attitudes about the U.S. government as a basis for an ironic essay in the manner of Swift. Students will need to invent the reasonable voice of a concerned citizen who wants society to implement his or her "benevolent" plan.

## THE READER'S PRESENCE

1. The proposal is "modest" in that it is presented as a moderate plan and the presenter claims to be humble. And with this "proposal" (with its bureaucratic language and use of statistics), Swift pokes fun at government documents that claim to propose solutions to social problems.
2. The Approaching the Essay section of this entry discusses in full the difference between Swift's attitudes and the speaker's attitudes. The speaker seems to imagine an audience that will take his ideas seriously: he is addressing powerful British landlords who he hopes will entertain his humble, modest proposal. Swift, however, imagines a reader who will appreciate the satire and who sympathizes with the Irish.
3. If readers do not anticipate Swift's vexing argument from his title, paragraph 4 should raise their hackles: the children of the poor shall "contribute to the feeding, and partly to the clothing, of many thousands." To eat children is one thing, but to wear clothes made from their skin!? In fact, by the time Swift gets to the point of describing the fine ladies' gloves that can be made from the children (para. 15), he has moved beyond the implicit and explicit comparison of the Irish poor to livestock (mothers are "dams" and "breeders," babies are "commodities") to expose the extent to which the rich are

literally sustained by the poor. Swift parodies the utilitarian views of some of his contemporaries: the best way to abolish poverty is to do away with the poor themselves. Like Swift, Laura Kipnis uses hyperbole and satire to enter into a discussion—in this case, a cultural critique—in "Against Love" (p. 733). Kipnis's overwrought language in the opening paragraphs not only draws the reader into the piece but sets the tone: "So deeply internalized is our obedience to this most capricious despot that . . . audiences seem never to tire of the most deeply unoriginal mass spectacles devoted to rehearsing the litany of its torments, fixating their very beings on the narrowest glim- mer of its fleeting satisfactions" (para. 1). By seeing love as a despotic ruler over the masses, Kipnis argues that the emphasis on lifelong love can be dangerous. Though her language is satirical, her metaphor of subjugation becomes a social critique. In the final paragraph of the piece, she says that we are always seeking fulfillment and, in a secular society, love has provided it. "But," she writes, "isn't it a little depressing to think we are somehow incapable of inventing forms of emotional life based on anything other than subjugation?"

# David Foster Wallace
## CONSIDER THE LOBSTER

### APPROACHING THE ESSAY

It's worth mentioning that "Consider the Lobster" was originally published in *Gourmet* magazine, a strange place for it, considering its approach to its subject matter. One might expect a magazine like *Gourmet* to offer advice for the prepa- ration of lobster. Instead, Wallace offers some uncomfortable speculations on the sentience of the sea creature—its level of self-awareness and its ability to experi- ence pain, as well as more complex emotions, like fear. This sort of speculation is uncomfortable because it inevitably leads to ethical questions about how lobster is prepared for consumption by humans: lobster is generally taken to be best boiled or steamed alive. For a magazine with a vested interest in keeping readers who eat lobster happy, or at least happy enough to keep their subscriptions to *Gourmet* active, publishing a piece like "Consider the Lobster" could justly be called a risky bit of business, and you might generate interest in the article by commenting to that effect when you assign the reading. In fact, when Wallace originally submitted the essay, the magazine insisted on some changes, presumably so that its readers wouldn't be (as) offended (see the Writer at Work entry for Wallace on page 855). The original version is reprinted here, but it is clear that—even in its unedited form—Wallace was making a point to be sensitive to his lobster-eating readers.

The piece begins innocently enough: Wallace writes about the Maine Lobster Festival as if he were reporting on it for any interested reader. He does not let on, at least not at first, that the essay will not include anything other than what one might expect to find in a cooking magazine: there is no suggestion, at the outset, that the reader is walking into a meditation on the ethics of eating lobster, a meditation that will almost certainly challenge the reader's beliefs. It is probably safe to assume that readers who are likely to be perusing an article on lobster in a magazine like *Gourmet* are lobster-eaters. By the end of the essay, if Wallace is successful, the reader will feel a little uncomfortable about eating lobster again. In that sense, "Consider the Lobster" is almost a trap. You might ask the students how effective they find Wallace's strategy: Is it effective? Is it honest? Should Wallace have begun with something akin to a thesis statement, expressing his reservations about the practice of boiling lobsters alive, or his doubts about whether it is true that they don't feel pain?

As it is, Wallace doesn't even mention that lobster is best put into the pot live until paragraph 12. He doesn't ask whether that's "all right" until paragraph 13. He spends much of the remainder of the essay providing evidence for why it might not be. The primary defense for boiling lobsters alive is that they don't feel pain. Wallace introduces this defense in paragraph 16, where it is articulated by his driver, Dick. In paragraph 17, Wallace tells us that this defense is "incorrect in about nine different ways." Wallace acknowledges that the experience of pain is a subjective one and that the questions surrounding our understanding of animal pain are "complex and difficult" (para. 18). He further acknowledges that the issues are uncomfortable, even for him: "As far as I can tell, my own main way of dealing with this . . . has been to avoid thinking about the whole unpleasant thing" (para. 19). This might be a good place to ask your students what they think: Do they avoid thinking about the suffering that we inflict upon animals that we eat? What effect does this admission, on Wallace's part, have on the rest of the essay? He seems to want to avoid distancing himself from his audience. Remind the students that he is writing for *Gourmet* magazine: he will likely want to avoid sermonizing his readers on the evils of eating lobster. But he does want to "consider" it. In paragraph 27, he gives the reader the impression that lobsters may actually feel pain *more* acutely than humans do. He uses a great deal of scientific terminology—mostly neurological—throughout the piece. How does the use of this language strengthen the argument that there is something morally problematic about boiling lobsters alive? What about the less scientific evidence, that when placed in pots of boiling water lobsters attempt to escape? Is the less scientific evidence also less ambiguous?

Wallace is clearly conflicted, and in his final paragraphs he refrains from asking the reader to come to any conclusions, either. Yet by the end of the essay, the evidence against traditional methods of preparing live lobster seems almost insurmountable. What does Wallace mean when he says, "There are limits to what even interested persons can ask of each other" (para. 33)? How does this relate back to his statement, in paragraph 19, that he tries not to think about the suffering inflicted on the animals?

## ADDITIONAL ACTIVITIES

1. This essay can easily be paired with Jonathan Safran Foer's piece, "Let Them Eat Dog" (p. 661). Both authors are aware of the ethical problems involved in the decision to eat animals, but Foer seems both more prepared to confront the issue and, in some ways, less equipped: there is no talk of neurology, for example, in Foer's essay. Ask your students to compare and contrast the essays, including the relative approaches of the authors. Foer includes more humor in his essay. Why? What effect does his humor have on his argument? Ask your students to consider the different audiences that the pieces were written for. Foer's essay is an outtake from his book, originally published in the *Wall Street Journal*. Wallace originally published his piece in *Gourmet*. What impact might audience have on the tone Wallace chooses? What can be said of Foer's tone, by comparison? Do we take Foer as seriously?

2. Have the students select an animal that they eat, then research the way animals of that species live and die when they are used for food by humans. Ask the students to present their findings in class.

## GENERATING WRITING

1. Related to Additional Activity 2, have the students write a research paper on the life and death of a typical animal used for food. They should feel free to select farm-raised animals or animals typically caught in the wild, as long as they can give a reasonably thorough account of what happens to the animal as it is captured, killed, and prepared for human consumption. As part of the paper, have the students evaluate the ethical implications of what they learn. Do they, like Wallace, prefer not to think about it?

## THE READER'S PRESENCE

1. Wallace wrote the article for *Gourmet* magazine. His readers were probably lobster-eating enthusiasts. He tries to establish a civil rapport with these readers by admitting that he, too, enjoys eating lobster. He questions the morality of eating lobster carefully, making a point not to attack his readers. It seems clear, however, that once he was actually at the festival, he found the practice of cooking live lobsters horrifying and the justifications for it disingenuous or absurdly flimsy, based on willful ignorance rather than authentic investigation. All of these elements—his respect for his audience, his genuine enjoyment of eating lobster, and his inability to find any decent moral justification for it—combine to make the essay a marvelous example of tactful argumentation.

2. Most magazine articles are intended either to convey information or to argue a point. Wallace truly wants to "consider" the subject matter, though, or at least ask his audience to. Essentially, the title means exactly what it says, and so does Wallace. This element of open-ended investigation is more essayistic

than the standard-issue magazine article, even if, to one extent or another, we know Wallace has already more or less made up his mind that boiling lobsters alive is probably wrong.

3. Wallace seems to have a politely condescending attitude toward tourism. He is somewhat fascinated by it, but he also seems to find it a little bit kitschy. He likes the water, loves the Bed and Breakfasts, but (at least implicitly) finds the whole affair distastefully saturated in mass-marketing. Nathaniel Hawthorne ("My Visit to Niagara," p. 438) has a similar problem with tourism and marketing but for different reasons: he's not so much bothered by the crass nature of commercialism as he is by the inability to authentically experience a thing like Niagara Falls when commercialism has established expectations in one's mind long before the actual encounter. Jonathan Swift's "A Modest Proposal" (p. 831) is ironic in nature and as such is more akin to Jonathan Safran Foer's "Let Them Eat Dog" (p. 661).

# John Edgar Wideman
## STREET CORNER DREAMERS

### APPROACHING THE ESSAY

Wideman's rather short essay reflects on the morning after the historic election of Barack Obama. The question it dares to ask is a simple one, but one that has a complex and impossible-to-determine answer: now that we have a black president, now that civil rights have come so far, now that it seems we've come so far as a nation, will such a president be able to help the victims whose lives have been destroyed by marginalization? There are no easy answers, but students should be excited about the question. Certainly, Obama has made plans for health-care reform, closing down the military base at Guantanamo Bay, and moving the United States toward more environmental uses of energy. But what about the "high percentage of youth of color" who are missing from street corners, in jail, on drugs, "alienated absolutely from school, citizenship, prospects of jobs and families?" (para. 2). Wideman implicitly asks, as a black president, what will Obama do for his own people?

The essay should generate plenty of discussion. If your students know any one thing about history, it will be this: that the 2008 presidential election was a historic one. Now, the key is to get them thinking about what this means, not only for our country, but for individual lives. Wideman considers these exact questions in his essay (your students will luckily have the advantage of hindsight). Students should notice that Wideman believes the current moment is the most fragile. Will the youth care about this historic moment? Wideman asks, "How equipped are [the youth] to imagine bridging the chasm between a White House in Washington, D.C., and a local, recently scoured public school that serves the Lower East Side's children of color and poverty?" (para 4).

Wideman's questions really have to do with appearance and reality. Students should notice that he begins by describing a poor black school's attempt to give the school a "facelift." The question for Wideman is, is this change in the school simply cosmetic, in the event of a historic election, to make things "look better" or is there real change inside the school, as well? Students should be asking themselves this question: will Obama's tenure create real change, or is his election merely cosmetic? It's a difficult question, but an important one.

As your class discusses this issue, ask them if they see any echoes from other important or famous pieces of writing. Martin Luther King Jr.'s "I Have a Dream" speech (p. 701) is referenced late in the essay, for instance, and Wideman directly brings up singer Sam Cooke's song about change. In the end, Wideman issues a call to action. Actually, it's a hope for action—a hope that the newly elected president will tell everyone to quiet down a moment, that in the face of global change and economic crisis and numerous wars, he will settle the nation and say, "Let's listen to our young people on the street corners" (para. 7). Equally in Wideman's hope for Obama to listen is the hope that youth will want to be involved, to bridge the gap between the Lower East Side and the White House, to give voice to their concerns, to speak up from the street corners.

## ADDITIONAL ACTIVITIES

1. Since Obama's election to office, many other events of note have taken place, all for the history books, including the biggest economic crisis since the Great Depression, caused by a failing housing market, and an Egyptian revolution that ousted Egypt's president. You might ask your students, has Obama effected real change? Wideman's essay is hopeful. What do students believe Wideman would say about the president's first years in office? Has he bridged that gap between the street corners and the White House?

2. Wideman refers to both Martin Luther King Jr. and Sam Cooke. Why does he do this? You might play King's "I Have a Dream" speech for your class; have them write about how the speech and Wideman's essay relate. Or, you might play them Sam Cooke's song. What does the song have to do with Obama, with what Wideman is hopeful for? Composing two-paragraph answers should help generate discussion.

## GENERATING WRITING

1. Have your students write an essay in which they support the idea that Barack Obama has created the type of change that Wideman was hopeful for in his essay. They will be arguing that Obama has, in Wideman's words, "[bridged] the gap between the Lower East Side's school and the White House in Washington, D.C." They should write a three- to five-page essay in which they research Obama's influence on education, youth culture, and poor black

areas in order to support their point. They should focus on tone and mood; because this is a hopeful notion and a rather positive and optimistic argument, their tone should match the type of argument they are making.

2. As an exercise in opposing viewpoints, give students the choice to write an essay in which they find that Obama has failed to bridge the gap between poor black areas and the White House. This will be the same assignment as in question 1 (three to five pages with research), but here they will be arguing that Wideman's concerns were valid and that Obama, like the façade of the school, was merely a president of appearances, not creating the real change that Wideman was hopeful for. After students turn in these essays and with the respective students' permission, it might be interesting for the class to read two of the best essays from each side to show that argument often isn't about what is true necessarily but about what one can research successfully and argue convincingly.

## THE READER'S PRESENCE

1. Wideman is concerned with appearances in this short article. The image of the sandblasted school is an image dealing with outward appearance: the school looks better, but is it technically any more sound, advanced, giving students a better education? In the same way, Wideman is concerned about Obama's tenure as president: will it be merely a show, a black man elected, or will real change occur? These are certainly interesting questions and ones that Wideman doesn't attempt to answer. Instead, his article is about the hope that behind the appearance, the reality of real change will occur.

2. Here Wideman is playing on the idea that rather than be incarcerated in jail, young minds should and might have the chance to be incarcerated by the "present moment" or by history unfolding. Rather than being infatuated with marginalization and drugs and poverty, they should and might be infatuated with the hope of real change. Wideman is using language here, and in other spots, ironically, to make a point about his hope for the future.

3. Wideman's essay echoes King's "I Have a Dream" speech in numerous ways. Most explicitly, however, Wideman's essay addresses King's ideas about vision of a new nation. Toward the end of Wideman's essay, he writes, "Will we become a nation converted to a new faith, a new dream, a new political consciousness and commitment, embracing Obama's complex heritage?" (para. 5). Here Wideman makes the call for the change that King saw as a possibility in his "I Have a Dream" speech. Where King dreams that one day his vision of brotherhood and equality will come to pass, Wideman wonders if that time is now, exactly now, waiting for the embrasure. However, where King's speech is concrete in its vision for the future, Wideman simply asks questions. Is this the time? Will we embrace? He says he's not "crystal-ball gazing"; neither was King, but King's vision was a bit more direct, while Wideman's vision is one of the present moment, not looking forward but asking people to embrace change now.

# Howard Zinn
## STORIES HOLLYWOOD NEVER TELLS

### APPROACHING THE ESSAY

In this speech delivered at the Taos Film Festival, historian Howard Zinn discusses how Hollywood has repeatedly failed to represent the working class, imperialism, the ugliness of war, racism, and other stories about American politics and problems. Describing Hollywood, Zinn says, "It's a structure where money and profit are absolutely the first consideration: before art, before aesthetics, before human values" (para. 2). Zinn is best known for his book *A People's History of the United States* (1980), which attempts to present American history in all the voices that have previously gone unheard, including those of minorities, women, the working class, and American Indians. In a sense, Zinn is calling for Hollywood to include these same voices in the movies it makes. Hollywood's exclusion of these perspectives is not deliberate but rather an example of the "natural selection of accidents" (para. 2), or a larger system that values money and power over art.

Most of Zinn's speech discusses versions of historical events that he believes are currently untold in Hollywood's narrative of American history. Ask students which, if any, of these stories are familiar to them. Which ones do they think are valuable stories for the American public to hear? Why might these stories have been thus far ignored by Hollywood? In some cases, films have depicted aspects of the movements that Zinn describes. From what perspective have these movies been made?

Zinn discusses Hollywood films about war, noting that most "glorify military heroism" (para. 3). Ask students if they think certain wars (such as World War II or the American Revolution) are more often depicted in this way than others (such as the Vietnam War). Have students seen any films that they feel did *not* glorify military heroism? If so, how did they feel about the film and its depiction of the war or of the people involved in it? You might discuss shifting national opinion about certain wars, particularly the Vietnam War, and note how films about war made during a period of antiwar sentiments might differ from films about war made when Americans are being encouraged to support a war effort.

Zinn's essay offers a starting point for a more general discussion on how perspective affects the way a story is told. Why is it important to understand historical events from more than one perspective? What argument does Zinn have against the stories Hollywood tells? From what perspective are movies usually made?

### ADDITIONAL ACTIVITIES

1. Your class may be interested in watching clips from some of the movies Zinn mentions: *All Quiet on the Western Front* (1930), *Saving Private Ryan* (1998), *The Long Walk Home* (1990), *Mississippi Burning* (1988), or *Roger and Me* (1989). How did the public react to these films? Which ones were critical or

financial successes (or both)? Have students bring in reviews of the films on the day you watch them in class and analyze the critics' reactions. Do the critics' reactions support or refute Zinn's suggestion that Hollywood doesn't support such films?

2. Students interested in Zinn's perspective on history may enjoy *A People's History of the United States*, a very readable alternative to history textbooks. Ask your students to present Zinn's book to the class: How does Zinn's version of American history offer an alternative take on the history that most schools teach? What different perspectives does he give? What does one gain from reading about events in American history from another viewpoint?

## GENERATING WRITING

1. Zinn mentions numerous little-known incidents of rebellion and protest throughout history. Have students choose one to research for a five-page paper. What social and political factors prompted the incident? What were the results, in both the short and the long term?

2. Assign students an essay in which they review and critique a film based on a historical event, using Zinn's critique as a guide. Students should consult some outside sources to get different perspectives on the historical event. From what perspective does the film tell the story? What perspectives does it omit? How does the film conform to traditional Hollywood ways, according to Zinn? How is the event simplified for the screen?

## THE READER'S PRESENCE

1. Zinn describes the unwritten mandate that keeps these stories from appearing in films as based not on explicit plans but at least partially on the values that drive Hollywood: "money and profit are absolutely the first consideration: before art, before aesthetics, before human values" (para. 2). Simply put, those involved in government, big business, and the military have more financial power to produce movies that promote their perspectives.

2. Zinn's audience is made up of independent filmmakers who work outside of Hollywood's big-budget studios. He is obviously speaking to a sympathetic group who will recognize that movies can be both "hateful" and loveable. Instead of focusing directly on the politics that govern movie production, Zinn uses his vast knowledge of American history to discuss the silenced and marginalized stories and perspectives that intrigue him. His teacherly, nonargumentative approach indicates his confidence that he is speaking to a largely like-minded audience.

3. Zinn is interested in history and, as indicated by the title of his essay, the stories that Hollywood doesn't tell. There are many such stories. For example, Americans generally take a positive view of the American Revolution. Hollywood gives us stories of the Revolution in which the brave colonists are the heroes. But, as Zinn points out, the war clears the way for colonists to push west of the line the British had drawn to end western expansion, so when the

British lost, it wasn't such a good thing for Native Americans of the period. Similarly, Hollywood doesn't tell us the stories of the mutinies against George Washington. Zinn seems to be a populist historian. He is interested in America as a by-the-people-for-the-people place, and he is probably reluctant, therefore, to latch on to heroes and engage in hero-worship, what is often called "the great man" theory of history. Changes are made by many people, by larger cultural trends, and by a variety of simultaneous circumstances. Furthermore, many of the events we view as positive had negative aspects to them that we ignore, like the suppression of the independence movement in the Philippines in the wake of the Spanish-American War. John Edgar Wideman ("Street Corner Dreamers," p. 856) seems to have a similar attitude toward the United States. He looks not only at the positive sides of the story (for example, that Obama is the first African American president) but also at the larger picture—the fact that many African American youths are still disaffected and living below the poverty line, regardless of whether we have an African American president. He seems reluctant to view Obama as a great man solely because he is the first African American president. It's a story Hollywood might like (America Elects African American President! Barack Obama Great Man! Everyone Lives Happily Ever After!), but as Wideman points out, many people in America have had their lives and communities destroyed by racism and other forms of marginalization, and we don't know yet what—if anything—Obama will be able to do for them. One might say that Zinn and Wideman are both a bit cynical in this regard: they tend to look at the negative. In another sense, however, they're just honest. In terms of social justice, we probably have a long way to go. It's not a story that Hollywood likes to tell, and it's not one that many moviegoers are likely to be happy to hear.

# PART 4

# THE SHORT STORY
## Seven Modern Classics

---

# Sherman Alexie
## THIS IS WHAT IT MEANS TO SAY PHOENIX, ARIZONA

### APPROACHING THE STORY

This story illustrates Sherman Alexie's usual humor and many of his common themes: alienation, loss of native culture, stereotypes of native life, community, father-son relationships, and storytelling. It is also the basis for Alexie's film *Smoke Signals*, which became the first feature film both written and directed by Native Americans.

When the story opens, Victor is at his lowest, having just lost his job and heard news of his father's death. Looking for someone to turn to in his moment of need, Victor appeals to the Tribal Council—a modern representation of this native community—but Alexie portrays it as condescending and bureaucratic. Victor ends up finding help in an unlikely place, his old friend Thomas Builds-the-Fire, whose prophetic storytelling abilities have alienated him from everyone on the reservation. When Victor first sees Thomas, he recognizes "a sudden need for tradition" (para. 24), essentially for a return to native values as well as to the sense of community and family he associates with the time in childhood when he and Thomas were friends.

Alexie structures the story to move back and forth between the present action involving Victor's trip to Phoenix and the flashbacks that reveal the childhood friendship between the two boys. The contrast between past and present reveals the distance between the two men and highlights Thomas's storytelling as the catalyst for his alienation from the community.

Alexie relies almost entirely on dialogue for characterization. Ask students to examine one conversation between the two men and analyze it for aspects of character. What is revealed about Thomas in the passage? How does the conversation add to our understanding of him? What is revealed about Victor in the passage? How does the conversation deepen or complicate our understanding of him?

Alexie twice refers to characters as "warriors": the two boys who steal a car (para. 43) and Norma Many Horses (para. 60). Ask students to describe how they think "warrior" is being defined in each instance. How is Norma a warrior? How are the two boys who steal the car warriors? What does Thomas's story about the two boys tell us about the changing nature of native identity?

Discuss the title. What does it mean to Victor to say Phoenix, Arizona?

## ADDITIONAL ACTIVITIES

1. Watch the film *Smoke Signals* (1998), which is based on this story as well as others from Alexie's book *The Lone Ranger and Tonto Fistfight in Heaven* (1993). Discuss how Alexie, who was the co-producer of the film, chose to depict Thomas and Victor on the screen. Do they look as your students imagined? Does the story's lack of physical details about the characters add to or detract from your students' enjoyment? How does seeing the short story in film change their interpretation of it? How was the story changed in its adaptation to film? What are the film's strengths? What are the short story's strengths?

2. Some students might enjoy reading Alexie's whole collection, *The Lone Ranger and Tonto Fistfight in Heaven.* Ask these students to discuss common themes throughout Alexie's stories. How would they characterize his style overall? Who might his intended audience be, and how do they know? In what way does Alexie address common stereotypes about Native Americans? Others might read his essay "The Joy of Reading and Writing: Superman and Me" (p. 27). Ask these students what issues Alexie raises in his essay. What similarities do they find between his essay and short story? How does the essay provide a background for better understanding the short story?

## GENERATING WRITING

1. Storytelling is a major theme of this short story. Ask students to write a paper that analyzes the meaning of storytelling within the context of Alexie's short story, as well as the characters' perceptions of it. Who in the story are storytellers and what does that mean for them? What are the stories they tell? How do the other characters react to these stories?

2. Assign students a paper in which they analyze the structure of the story. What is the effect of jumping back and forth between present action and memories of Thomas and Victor growing up? What do the flashback sections add to the reader's understanding of the present action? What is the purpose of each flashback section? How does Alexie use them to characterize Victor and Thomas?

## THE READER'S PRESENCE

1. Thomas's stories are sometimes prophetic, deeply revealing of character, and often touching. For instance, he predicts that Victor's father will leave his family, but he still has compassion for his limitations: "Your father's heart is weak. He is afraid of his own family. He is afraid of you. . . . Sometimes he feels like he wants to buy a motorcycle and ride away" (para. 18). For

the most part, however, Thomas's specific stories are not discussed in detail. They do not really even belong to him but are rather the "stories which came to [him] before [he] even had the words to speak" (para. 165). Alexie alludes here to a spiritual tradition of storytelling in Native American communities and the wisdom that is passed down through generations. By rejecting Thomas's stories, the community is turning away from its cultural traditions. Thomas understands his storytelling ability as a burden because no one will listen to him and no one wants to be around him while he's telling them. He's described as telling "the same damn stories over and over again" (para. 24). The ability to change the world, he suggests, lies in his community's willingness to listen, not in his ability to tell his stories: "Mine are the stories which can change or not change the world," he states (para. 165).

2. Victor starts out with nothing left to lose: he's just lost his job and he has no money when he finds out that his father has died. From the beginning, we understand that he is alienated from his father: he has not seen him in years, and initially he feels only a "genetic pain" at his passing (para. 1). This feeling will change, however, as the loss becomes "as real and immediate as a broken bone" (para. 1). Alexie hints here at the main changes Victor will go through: rethinking his role as a son. Victor also has no one to turn to for help and finally must take Thomas Builds-the-Fire's offer to lend him money, even though he identifies Thomas as an outcast. By the middle of the story, Victor has apologized to Thomas for how he treated him when they were young. At the end of the story, Victor gives Thomas half of his father's ashes, after Thomas tells him that Victor's father wanted Thomas to look out for Victor. Victor realizes that Thomas represents tradition and community, but even at the end Victor cannot promise to be his friend. He's ashamed of himself for this admission but offers Thomas the promise to listen to one of his stories. Thomas acts as the catalyst for Victor to reconsider his role as son, friend, and member of his community. The change Victor undergoes is slight, but we must assume that listening to one of Thomas's stories will be a starting point.

3. "Thomas Builds-the-Fire walked through the corridors of the tribal school by himself. Nobody wanted to be anywhere near him because of all those stories," writes Alexie of Thomas's boyhood (para. 164). Like Thomas, the young Alexie faces ridicule from his fellow Native American classmates because of his love of reading and writing stories. In "The Joy of Reading and Writing: Superman and Me" (p. 27), Alexie writes of himself: "If he'd been anything but an Indian boy living on the reservation, he might have been called a prodigy. But he is an Indian boy living on the reservation and is simply an oddity" (para. 5). In describing the Indian boys he grew up with, Alexie remarks that many of them were "monosyllabic in front of their non-Indian teachers but [able to] tell complicated stories and jokes at the dinner table" (para. 6). The boys from the reservation live in a dual world in which they must suppress their natural creativity in public, letting it free only in the privacy of the home. Thomas, who talks to himself and tells stories in public, and Alexie, who is "smart" and "arrogant," both face ridicule because they reject the failure and passivity expected of them.

# Raymond Carver
## WHAT WE TALK ABOUT WHEN WE TALK ABOUT LOVE

### APPROACHING THE STORY

If your students have already read Joan Acocella's essay, "A Few Too Many" (p. 283), they might immediately notice the use of alcohol here as both a social lubricant and a coping mechanism for some of life's tragedies. If not, no worries: Carver's piece is one of his most impressive, most thoroughly strange, and easily one of his most engaging. We all, it seems, want to know what exactly love is, and in this story Carver attempts, not an answer, but certainly a struggle with the idea of love.

Students should come away with at least one main concept after a first reading: the structure of Carver's narrative is a story-within-a-story (actually two stories-within-a-story). It might be helpful to explain to your students what this structure is even before they read the piece. In any case, students will notice that the story isn't simply about four people sitting around drinking; it's also about the tales that Mel and Terri share while drinking. This is a famous story-structuring technique, one often used by Chekhov, and here Carver uses it to great dramatic effect.

Carver sets the story on an afternoon in a cardiologist's house: the narrator and his wife, Laura, sit and drink gin with Mel, the cardiologist, and his wife, Terri. As the story progresses, it becomes clear that the narrator and Laura are in the early stages of their marriage, still in that glowy kind of love, while Mel and Terri have been at it for a while and are a bit more testy with each other. The conversation centers on the different ideas of love that Mel and Terri both have. Mel sees love as a spiritual, absolute ideal, while Terri believes that love can be more dangerous, possibly even a bit frightening, and border on the compulsive or obsessive.

The different ideas of love are presented as two anecdotes, one told by Terri and the other told by Mel, each character, respectively, defining her or his notion of love. First, Terri tells the story of an ex-lover, Ed, who stalked her, threatened Mel, was abusive toward her, and eventually killed himself, presumably because he couldn't have Terri. During this anecdote, Mel constantly says, "'If you call that love, you can have it,'" (para. 36) while Terri insists that no matter what Mel believes, her ex really did love her. This prompts some harsh words, some miscommunication, and some general awkwardness between Mel and Terri. Students should be pointed toward this tension between Mel and Terri. What is going on between the two of them? How do their different views on love create conflict? What are their attitudes toward one another?

After Terri's tale, Mel tells a story about an aging couple who he operates on after they have been in a terrible car accident. Mel can't believe they are alive, and when they are finally both stable, the old man complains to Mel that he can't see his wife. This, to Mel, is amazing: it's real love. This old man is so in love with his wife, Mel believes, that he can't go on living without being able to see her. Mel seems to not be able to fathom such a thing. Here, students are presented with Mel's idea of love, which seems vastly different from Terri's. It is worth noting how Mel eventually comes around and acknowledges that his point of view isn't necessarily the correct one. He even says that he knows Terri's ex and Terri really loved each other, which students might find surprising.

As the story progresses, it should be clear that Mel is the main character. He's the one who does the most ruminating on love and he's the one who shifts the mood of the room. Ask students how Carver accomplishes this. How does Mel's behavior and what he says change the atmosphere in the room? Also, as Mel continues to get drunk, why does he want to call his kids and why does he bring up his ex-wife? Finally, students should be thinking of where the story has gone—we start the story with two different ideas of love; by the end of the story, which one has prevailed? Are we any clearer on what love is? In what ways has Carver complicated the idea of love and made it terribly mysterious?

## ADDITIONAL ACTIVITIES

1. Ask students to create a character sketch for all the characters in the story. They should include character traits, personalities, and general worldviews. Once they have done this, students should be able to see a bit more clearly how the story is constructed. Because there is little action, Carver relies on character to create tension, movement, and general interest. How do the contrasting characters here do that?

2. Ask students to explain how the story-within-a-story (the two tales told by Mel and Terri) relate to the present action of the story (the two couples drinking around the table). In what ways are the stories told by Mel and Terri indicative of what is going on in the lives of the couples or between the couples.

## GENERATING WRITING

1. Have your students write their own perspective on what love is in response to either Mel or Terri. They should begin the paper by explaining either Mel or Terri's position on love, using quotes where necessary, and then construct their own argument of what love is. Like Mel and Terri, they should create this definition of love by using a personal anecdote that highlights their ideal.

2. Assign a paper in which students analyze the structure of "What We Talk About When We Talk About Love." Why does Carver use the multiple stories-within-a-story for this tale? What does the structure of the piece, the two stories told by Mel and Terri, allow Carver to explore with these characters?

## THE READER'S PRESENCE

1. Carver certainly doesn't want his audience to dismiss this story as drunken babbling. In fact, he uses alcohol to loosen the tongues of his characters and,

most likely, to bring them to both more honest and darker places. The use of sunlight in the story is indicative of this. The story begins with the couples beginning to drink, sun shining fully on the scene, but as things proceed and the couples get more drunk, the setting becomes less sunny, until eventually there is no light in the house at all. This darkness in the room is symbolic of where the story has taken us: rather than enlightening readers, the story has brought us to darkness, a further mystery about what love actually is. The drinking is a device that allows the characters to speak openly, probably a bit more honestly, but not necessarily with any more insight into their own situations or the idea of love.

2. Much of this is discussed in the Approaching the Essay section of this entry. However, it's important to understand that Mel's story of the old couple is exemplary of his idea of love: love as an absolute, spiritual ideal. Even though Mel believes in this kind of love, the story of the old couple and the man needing to see his wife still seems to baffle Mel. He cannot fathom it, can't even really believe it. Mel is obviously awe-stricken by the old man's need to see his wife; it begins to seem like Mel longs for this kind of love in his own life, and at this point he longs to call his children. The story greatly contrasts with Terri's story about her ex, who is abusive, threatening, and somewhat of a creep, though still in love (maybe even obsessed) with Terri.

3. In general, Carver's trademark is spare, direct prose, and the more sophisticated readers among your students will have no problem identifying Carver's voice. Even the less savvy readers will probably be able to pick up on the similarities in the prose in the two pieces with minimal nudging. In terms of subject matter, alcohol plays a major role in both the essay and the story, and indeed Carver struggled with alcoholism; he ultimately sobered up, spending the last ten years (or so) of his life in recovery, but alcoholism and recovery are common subjects in much of his work.

# Jamaica Kincaid
## GIRL

### APPROACHING THE STORY

Jamaica Kincaid makes a powerful statement about cultural conditioning in "Girl" without saying a word about it. The mother whose voice dominates this nearly uninterrupted dramatic monologue speaks in imperatives and declarative sentences that admit no backtalk. Your students will probably enjoy this story in the way one enjoys a dramatic monologue by, say, Robert Browning: they can eavesdrop on a person from another land, and, more important, they catch this person in the act of inadvertently revealing more than he or she realizes. In Kincaid's story,

the mother exposes at least one source of gender stereotyping. The Caribbean setting of this story should create enough distance for most students to feel comfortable discussing how gender stereotypes are perpetuated in the home, starting with
the example in the story, then moving closer to home. Students may get carried
away finding evidence of the mother's sexism once they realize that this is the subtext of her instructions. This is a productive first response: encourage them to find
subtler evidence for this assertion. Of course, the mother's beliefs are not idiosyncratic, and responsibility for the sexism clearly is not hers alone. The evidence that
she genuinely cares for her daughter's welfare should lead students to realize that
her warnings about sexual promiscuity spring from the same source as her instructions about etiquette: she is transmitting her culture's gender expectations to her
daughter with the probably benign intention of making it possible for her daughter
to live in that culture without friction.

If possible, have a student read this story aloud to the class; it's obviously meant
to be heard. For this reason, you might want to use this story to teach tone. Help students to identify the features, including diction and syntax, that make the mother's
voice vivid and forceful.

This story could also spark a discussion of point of view. Have students identify
the point of view and then brainstorm situations in which such a perspective might
be effective. Discuss the reader's position toward speaker and listener in such a
text. Your students probably are already familiar with persuasive methods designed
to win a reader to their point of view. Discuss indirectly persuasive methods in
"Girl" that nudge the reader into a position not directly represented in the text. Ask
about their experience with other ironic texts. Have they ever felt confused about
the position the author wished them to take? How would they construct an ironic
text so as to make the reader side with them—without, of course, directly stating
their own position?

Why does the mother give her daughter all this advice? Ask students to catego-
rize the kinds of advice she offers. Why is it sometimes difficult to sort the mother's
statements neatly into boxes labeled, perhaps, *survival*, *etiquette*, and *morality*, or
*social* and *personal*? Look at this quotation from the story: "this is how to hem a
dress when you see the hem coming down and so to prevent yourself from looking
like the slut I know you are so bent on becoming." Can your students find other
sentences in which one kind of statement slips unexpectedly into an entirely different kind of statement? What is the effect of these juxtapositions? How are seemingly discrete categories such as survival, etiquette, and morality intertwined?

Not one man speaks in this story. Nonetheless, a pervasive yet subtle male
influence stands behind the mother's words. Find the references to men and boys.
What can you tell about the men behind the scenes? What can you infer about the
mother's relationship to the father? What can you infer about the balance of power
between the genders in the community in which the daughter is being raised?

## ADDITIONAL ACTIVITY

1. Kincaid's story could be taught in conjunction with Jonathan Swift's "A
   Modest Proposal" (p. 831) in studying irony. Students will discover differing

degrees of difficulty in their attempt to pin down each author's unstated position.

## GENERATING WRITING

1. The daughter in "Girl" speaks only two lines, both of which are italicized. Still, it is possible to infer something about her character even though her mother does most of the talking. Ask students to analyze the daughter's character, both from what she says and from what she hears (if they believe that she filtered these words of wisdom from an endless stream provided by her mother).

2. In conjunction with "Girl," ask students to read Robert Browning's poem "My Last Duchess" (reprinted here). Using features of dramatic monologue drawn from both pieces, they should construct a dramatic monologue of their own. They may write in verse or prose. Remind them to use Kincaid and Browning as models for the *form*, but not the *content*, of their own work.

My Last Duchess

**FERRARA**
That's my last Duchess painted on the wall,
Looking as if she were alive. I call
That piece a wonder, now: Frà Pandolf's hands
Worked busily a day, and there she stands.
Will't please you sit and look at her? I said                          5
"Frà Pandolf" by design, for never read
Strangers like you that pictured countenance,
The depth and passion of its earnest glance,
But to myself they turned (since none puts by
The curtain I have drawn for you, but I)                              10
And seemed as they would ask me, if they durst,
How such a glance came there; so, not the first
Are you to turn and ask thus Sir, 'twas not
Her husband's presence only, called that spot
Of joy into the Duchess' cheek: perhaps                               15
Frà Pandolf chanced to say "Her mantle laps
Over my lady's wrist too much," or "Paint
Must never hope to reproduce the faint
Half-flush that dies along her throat:" such stuff
Was courtesy, she thought, and cause enough                          20
For calling up that spot of joy. She had
A heart—how shall I say?—too soon made glad,
Too easily impressed; she liked whate'er
She looked on, and her looks went everywhere.
Sir, 'twas all one! My favor at her breast,                          25
The dropping of the daylight in the West,
The bough of cherries some officious fool
Broke in the orchard for her, the white mule
She rode with round the terrace—all and each

Would draw from her alike the approving speech, 30
Or blush, at least. She thanked men,—good! But thanked
Somehow—I know not how—as if she ranked
My gift of a nine-hundred-years-old name
With anybody's gift. Who'd stoop to blame
This sort of trifling? Even had you skill 35
In speech—(which I have not)—to make your will
Quite clear to such an one, and say, "Just this
Or that in you disgusts me; here you miss,
Or there exceed the mark"—and if she let
Herself be lessoned so, nor plainly set 40
Her wits to yours, forsooth, and made excuse,
—E'en then would be some stooping; and I choose
Never to stoop. Oh sir, she smiled, no doubt,
Whene'er I passed her; but who passed without
Much the same smile? This grew; I gave commands; 45
Then all smiles stopped together. There she stands
As if alive. Will't please you rise? We'll meet
The company below, then. I repeat,
 The Count your master's known munificence
Is ample warrant that no just pretence 50
Of mine for dowry will be disallowed;
Though his fair daughter's self, as I avowed
At starting, is my object. Nay, we'll go
Together down, sir. Notice Neptune, though,
Taming a sea-horse, thought a rarity, 55
Which Claus of Innsbrück cast in bronze for me!

## THE READER'S PRESENCE

1. Most of the lines in this story represent a mother's instructions to her daughter about what a woman must know to protect herself, her family, and her image. From the mother's mode of transmission, it seems likely that she acquired these values from her own mother in a similar way; there is also some quality of folk wisdom. Three kinds of advice are offered: how to act like a lady and preserve an image of propriety, how to do the kinds of work women are responsible for, and how to relate directly to men when the occasion calls for it. Of course, much of the women's work, as domestic, is undertaken for and in response to men, so the categories intrinsically overlap. The mother's monologue calls attention to this overlap in the sentences where one kind of instruction blends explicitly into another—for instance, "this is how to hem a dress when you see the hem coming down and so to prevent yourself from looking like the slut I know you are so bent on becoming."

2. The girl's first statement is a defense against her mother's unwarranted accusation of singing benna in Sunday school. Her mother does not respond directly; this can be read as a tacit acceptance, although the mother continues to weave accusations into her instructions. The girl's second statement is a question. Here she seems more engaged, as if she has begun to accept the

general wisdom of her mother's advice and now wants tips on how to implement it. Although the mother replies critically to this question, there is some
evidence in her response that she is aware of the girl's transition toward obedience: for instance, the mother does not call the girl "slut" in her answer.

3. The main speaker assumes that a woman is responsible for managing domestic duties, keeping her image as innocent intact, and having common sense
(that is, learning the narrator's instructions). One can infer that the men are
shiftless bullies who are only interested in sex and who must be served by
their women. In "Why Women Smile" (p. 347), Amy Cunningham confesses
that "[I smile] no matter where I am or how I feel" (para. 2) and that women
"smile in lieu of showing what's really on [their] minds" (para. 3). Notice that
the narrator of "Girl" also instructs her daughter in different kinds of smiles.
Women's smiles declare them nonthreatening. According to Cunningham,
men are expected to smile less, and certainly not in situations that do not call
for it. In fact, men probably restrict their instinct to smile in order to appear
more serious and potentially aggressive than they actually are.

# Joyce Carol Oates
## WHERE ARE YOU GOING, WHERE HAVE YOU BEEN?

### APPROACHING THE STORY

"Where Are You Going, Where Have You Been?" is an early story from prolific
writer Joyce Carol Oates. Twenty years after its publication in 1966, it was made
into the film *Smooth Talk*. The story centers on a fifteen-year-old girl growing up
in 1960s America. Connie is preoccupied with typical teenage anxieties: her
looks, popular music, shopping. Oates skillfully incorporates Connie's point of view
into the third-person narrative. Readers can hear Connie's own mingled anxiety
and conceit about her good looks—and her resentment of her sister—in the narrator's description of June as "so plain and chunky and steady that Connie had to
hear her praised all the time by her mother" (para 3). Unlike June, who is homely
in both senses of the word, "Connie couldn't do a thing" (para. 3).

Like many young women, Connie feels both excited and frightened by her
newfound power to attract male attention. The story dramatizes this tension in the
strange and dangerous, yet somehow magnetic, person of Arnold Friend. Again,
Oates puts readers in Connie's shoes, preventing us from noticing how peculiar
Arnold is when he first appears. However, when Arnold appears at the house
unbidden on a Sunday when Connie's family is away, he is subtly—and then
overtly—threatening.

In the end, Connie's romantic notions and desire for attention seem destined to run head-on into adult sexuality and violence. Oates has said she sees the story as a girl's heroic struggle to "define personal identity in the face of incredible opposition, even in the face of death itself." The story's ending is left ambiguous, but the end of Connie's innocent girlhood has already come.

## ADDITIONAL ACTIVITIES

1. The story was inspired by Dan Moser's 1966 article in *Life* magazine about Charles Schmid, "The Pied Piper of Tucson," who killed several young women. Ask students to create a narrative out of an interesting newspaper or magazine article by focusing on what they think the turning point or central scene of the story would be. Encourage them to consider the emotional stance of the characters, just as Oates does in her story.

2. Watch the film *Smooth Talk*, which was based on the story. The film ends after the story does, and its ending returns Connie home to her family, not revealing what has happened to her in the intervening hours. Which version do students prefer? Why? Which version seems more true to life? Must Connie's agreeing to accompany Arnold Friend be a tragic decision?

## GENERATING WRITING

1. Oates's stories reveal an ongoing interest in the sexuality of young girls and the emotional struggles between mothers and daughters. Ask students to read Oates's short story "Shopping" and compare the mother-daughter relationship there with the analogous relationship in this story.

## THE READER'S PRESENCE

1. "Everything about her had two sides to it," writes Oates of her protagonist, "one for home and one for anywhere that was not home" (para. 5). Ironically, it is Connie's "away" persona—languid walk, bright pink smile and all—that first captures the attention of Arnold Friend. In fact, when she first notices Friend she is practically glowing with the flush of youth and freedom: "She drew her shoulders up and sucked in her breath with the pure pleasure of being alive" (para. 7). This radiant joie-de-vivre is sadly not acceptable in her critical home, and its forced public expression ultimately leads to her downfall. Friend recognizes her alienation from her family and preys on it: "They don't know one thing about you and never did," he tells her at the end (para. 158).

Like Connie, Arnold Friend (whose last name also suggests the more appropriate "fiend") has a dual-sided personality. Initially, Connie is attracted to him: she responds to the way he smiles at her at the drive-in, she likes the way he dresses, and she notices his body. It is only at the moment that she realizes how old he probably is that her heart "[begins] to pound faster" (para. 79). At this point, Friend also becomes more sinister and aggressive in his talk with Connie: "'Maybe you better step out here,' he said, and this last was in a different voice. It was a little flatter, as if the heat was finally getting to him" (para. 88). Because Connie believes only in the importance of physical beauty—"she knew she was pretty and that was everything" (para. 1)—she is unable to see beyond Friend's physical attractiveness to his darker side until it is too late.

2. Although readers may know that Oates's story was inspired by the true account of a Tuscon, Arizona, murder, we do not explicitly learn Connie's fate at the end. Even Connie, however, foretells her own death: "She thought, I'm not going to see my mother again. She thought, I'm not going to sleep in my bed again" (para. 151). As Connie sets out with Arnold and Ellie, her eyes "taken up . . . by the vast sunlit reaches of the land behind him and on all sides of him," the reader and Connie both know that she is going to her death (para. 161). The fact that Oates does not directly narrate the details of the girl's death almost forces the reader to imagine, grimly, what they might be. This adds to the haunting effect of the story.

Raymond Carver's story ("What We Talk About When We Talk About Love," p. 884) also lacks resolution, and—as in the Oates story—this lack of resolution intensifies (or seems meant to intensify) the emotional effect of the piece. The endings are otherwise quite different. At the end of "Where Are You Going, Where Have You Been?" we know what is going to happen. At the end of the Carver story, we have no idea. The stakes in the Oates piece are somewhat higher, as well: a girl is going to die. In the Carver story, the characters might get something to eat or they might have another drink. We leave them sitting at the table more or less undecided, and in silence. The narrator feels as though it is so quiet he can hear everyone's heart beat. What might be difficult for students to understand, at least at first, is that the real question hanging over the table has very little to do with whether the characters continue to drink. There is some suggestion that drinking is a problem, but nothing is dependent on this particular evening. The tension comes more from the fact that we don't know what's going to happen between Mel and his kids, Mel and Terri, and Nick and Laura. Indeed, it would be difficult to imagine any sort of resolution to the wreckage that these characters seem to have made of their lives. Everyone in the story seems a bit lost and heartbroken, and this is unlikely to change, regardless of what they have for dinner on this particular night.

In one sense, it could be argued that both stories *do* in fact resolve. The girl in the Oates story is going to die, and the characters sitting at the table in Carver's piece are going to die eventually, too, in exactly the same state of emotional suspension that they seem to live in now. Nothing is going to change very much, and if it does, it won't matter, the world is a lonely place, our relationships are tenuous and fragile and maybe not even all that meaningful. In either case, there is no *need* to write an ending.

3. Oates's description of going from draft to published story to movie adaptation helps us understand how she gets her inspiration and the work and

choices involved in crafting it into a story. Her idea did not spring from thin air but from real life. The final version of the story involves a lot of thoughtful rewriting. She casts the initial draft as a "realistic allegory" and then completely rewrites it with Connie as the story's protagonist. On the one hand, this shows that writing, even for professional writers like Oates, involves hard work and attention to detail. On the other hand, this is an encouraging message. Improving one's writing skills can be achieved through hard work; it is not a talent that one either possesses or does not. Oates recognizes that working with a different medium, like film, necessitates alterations to the original written text. She does not, however, agree with the change to the ending. For her, it seems to change the whole meaning of the tale: from a story of death and fate to one about rejuvenation.

# Tim O'Brien
## THE THINGS THEY CARRIED

### APPROACHING THE STORY

The central metaphor of Tim O'Brien's "The Things They Carried" is that, in addition to carrying various objects through the war zone, the men carry the weight of their emotions, their ideas and their imaginations, their hopes, their fears, and more. The story focuses on First Lieutenant Jimmy Cross, the platoon leader, who carries letters from a woman named Martha, a woman for whom he also "carries" an unrequited love. He has a sort of fantasy life involving her. He is fantasizing about her when one of his men, Ted Lavender, is killed. The next day, Lieutenant Jimmy Cross burns Martha's letters, to rid himself of fantasies, so that he can be a better leader for the men. The suggestion seems to be not only that he has to let go of fantasy, but that, in some sense, he has to let go of home, and let go of his attachments, in order to be effective in Vietnam.

The metaphor of "The Things They Carried" is not at all hidden, so students who ordinarily have a hard time with symbolism should find O'Brien's work fairly easy to understand. There's no real mystery to what is being said, no hidden meaning, as such, and in that sense, at least, students might find it a welcome change from the kinds of literary study they are used to. They may also find the setting of the Vietnam War interesting. You may be able to have a successful class discussion simply by asking straightforward questions: What did you think the story was about? Why did Jimmy Cross carry those letters? Why did he burn them?

You might expand the discussion in a number of directions: (1) How do we use the physical world to relate to our emotional lives? (2) How do we shut down our emotions in order to deal with difficult experiences? How do these experiences change us? In a way, it is not only his fantasy life with Martha that the lieutenant shuts down; he also severs his connection to home, to anything outside of his life and his role in Vietnam. You might explore other circumstances or other works of fiction where characters might be inclined to do similar things. For elaboration, see Additional Activity 2 of this entry.

Discuss with your students the deeper implications of the lieutenant's decision to burn Martha's letters. In one sense, it might be true that his fantasy life interfered with his ability to command. He feels like a child in a war zone and, for him, burning the letters is like "growing up." As children, for example, many of us had security blankets or favorite stuffed animals that we had to give up before we could grow up. So, in a way, Jimmy is merely growing up, accepting his adult responsibilities. He is also sacrificing his imagination and, by implication, a dream life or "life of the mind" that is an integral part of being human. In this sense, the story seems to suggest that one has to let go of a part of one's humanity in order to survive in a war. Which interpretation is more compelling? Is it possible that they are both true?

## ADDITIONAL ACTIVITIES

1. You might ask students about objects that they own and the emotional significance those objects have. Some of them might even be carrying such objects when they come to class (an item of jewelry given to them by a loved one, for example). How do these physical objects come to define or represent (or both) certain aspects of their emotional lives?

2. There is an interplay, in "The Things They Carried," between home and the war, between fantasy and reality, between one life and another that will also be apparent in other works about the Vietnam War and, indeed, in works about other wars or different kinds of traumatic experiences, both in literature and film. If you have seen a war movie, chances are you have seen this dynamic at work. In almost any war movie, characters will have pictures of their girlfriends they left back home. In many of those films, those pictures will lose their meaning or become burdens in one way or another. The thought of home becomes not a comfort but an emotional burden. Returning home, the same characters often feel like outsiders. You might show one of these movies or have your students read a book or a story by another author dealing with a similar theme. In Ernest Hemingway's "Soldier's Home," Krebs returns from World War I unable to tell his mother that he loves her. Apparently, he no longer believes in God, either. In the film *The Deer Hunter*, Nick has a picture of Linda, but after his traumatic experience, he can't bring himself to talk to her on the telephone. He doesn't go home; rather, he gets involved with an underground network of people who play (and bet on) games of Russian roulette. Michael goes home, but he can't emotionally connect to his friends anymore. In *Apocalypse Now*, a man originally sent to apprehend Colonel Kurtz ends up joining him, instead, and writing home to tell his wife to "Sell the house. Sell the car. Sell the kids. I'm never coming back." The central character of the movie, Captain Willard, played by Martin Sheen, begins the film in a similar situation, having recently returned from leave. While on leave, he divorced his wife because

he couldn't relate to her anymore; his mind has been rewired, so to speak, for survival in a war zone. You will no doubt be able to think of examples of your own, and it may be profitable to have students watch another film or read a story aside from "The Things They Carried," where they can see this dynamic at work.

## GENERATING WRITING

1. Have the students write an essay about an object that is important to them, something that has sentimental value. You might ask them to write about something they still care about (a gift from a significant other, for example, or something a deceased relative might have given them) or something they have given up (the favorite stuffed animals or security blankets, for example, that they may have carried as children; see the Approaching the Essay section of this entry). In either case, the students should examine the relationship between these physical objects and their emotional meanings or sentimental value.

2. Have the students write an essay comparing "The Things They Carried" to another piece of fiction, either a story you assign or a film, preferably about a wartime or postwar experience. What themes are common in fictional treatments of soldiers or civilian survivors of war zones? What do the similarities between these fictional accounts teach us about the way people learn to live with such experiences?

## THE READER'S PRESENCE

1. In addition to carrying physical objects, the soldiers carry their emotional lives as they move through Vietnam, both the place and the experience. Pop culture terminology might be useful to get this point across: the soldiers have, if you will, "baggage." For example, in addition to carrying Martha's letters, Lieutenant Jimmy Cross carries an unrequited love for her, the hope that she will love him in return, and the nagging question of whether she is a virgin. Similarly, Ted Lavender, the soldier who is ultimately shot and killed, prior to his death carried tranquilizers and "six or seven ounces of premium dope, which for him was a necessity" (para. 2). But he carries the objects because he is afraid. So, metaphorically, he also carries his fear, just as Kiowa carries "his grandmother's distrust of the white man" (para. 2).

2. The lieutenant burns her letters after Ted Lavender dies because he's trying to be more realistic about where he is (in Vietnam, in a war zone) and what he is doing there (commanding a platoon, which makes him responsible for his men's lives). Your students might argue any number of changes in his character: he has become more cynical or he has simply become more responsible. He tells himself, "No more fantasies" (para. 93) and plans to take responsibility for Lavender's death.

3. O'Brien's prose is generally organized in long paragraphs, full of long sentences, loaded with figurative language. When Ted Lavender dies, the

sentences are abruptly very short and factual. His body is described without metaphor, the broken teeth, the black eye. The prose becomes abruptly direct, to convey the reality of the situation, snapping us (and Lieutenant Jimmy Cross) out of the realm of imagination. There is an urgency and immediacy to the prose, which is also clearly visible in Adam Mayblum's account ("The Price We Pay," p. 164) of his experience on 9/11. When it comes to traumatic experiences, these writers convey what it is like to be in the moment. This suggests that people respond to traumatic experiences by becoming—at least temporarily—very realistic. It is not until *after the fact* that we begin to analyze the experiences and attribute meaning to them.

# Flannery O'Connor
## A GOOD MAN IS HARD TO FIND

### APPROACHING THE STORY

A southern family goes on a road trip to Florida. The grandmother would rather go to Tennessee, where she has "connections." They have been hearing about a criminal on the loose called the Misfit. The grandmother talks quite a bit and in an annoying fashion; the family does not appear overly attentive or polite to her. They stop at a restaurant and exchange platitudes with the owner about the lack of "good men" in the current day. Back on the road, the grandmother thinks she recalls a plantation she visited long ago and convinces the family to visit it, lying that the house had "a secret panel" (para. 45). As they make their way down a deserted road, she realizes she was wrong about the location. In her upset she disturbs her cat, who jumps up and causes an accident. The family members are slightly injured and wait for help. A few men come to help them. The grandmother realizes that they are the Misfit and his henchmen. He appears affable and willing to help, but eventually all the members of the family are taken into the woods and shot, except for the grandmother. She pleads for her life, invokes religion, and, at the last minute, tries to make a human connection with the Misfit, but to no avail. As she dies, one of her killers sarcastically calls her "a good woman." The Misfit protests his callousness.

Younger readers tend to resist Flannery O'Connor. They are put off by her unpleasant characters and unsentimental presentation of reality. Students may also find the story line implausible. You may wish to begin discussion from this point of resistance, showing how these difficulties stem from O'Connor's deliberate authorial choices. What words and phrases does O'Connor use to describe each character? What does the reader learn about the characters through their words and actions? What makes the characters unlikable? Why might an author choose to write a story without heroes—"good men" or "good women"? How would the story differ if it ended happily or with a sense of personal redemption, growth, or insight? Does

O'Connor appear to promote a harsh view of life in general, or just of a certain group or type of people? Why does O'Connor nickname the character "The Misfit"? Is he the only "misfit" in the story? Does it matter that the meeting with the Misfit is so coincidental? Is the Misfit meant to stand as a realistic character, or does he also function as a symbolic figure? What might he symbolize in terms of the grand-mother and the family's milieu? You may wish to isolate several passages for close reading, having students note particularly interesting or vivid turns of phrase or word choices. You might also ask students to restate a short passage in their own words. How do the two versions differ? What is lost or gained? How is the reader made aware, through the writer's "voice," of the gap between that which is and is not said?

## ADDITIONAL ACTIVITY

1. Have students read other O'Connor stories—for instance, "All That Rises Must Converge." In what ways is O'Connor's characteristic "voice" evi-dent? By what general concerns and qualities of language might this "voice" be recognized? What general picture of human nature and behavior does O'Connor's work provide?

## GENERATING WRITING

1. Have students write an imaginative two- to three-page version of the story from the Misfit's perspective, in his words. What led him to a life of crime? Why do people call him the Misfit? How does he view the events in the woods and the grandmother's attempt to connect with him? What clues in the nar-rative support this interpretation? Circulate the pieces anonymously for class discussion.
2. Assign students a passage not covered in class for a two- to three-page close reading. Students should note striking words, phrases, and techniques and then discuss what they contribute to the passage and to the story as a whole.

## THE READER'S PRESENCE

1. The grandmother appears to see herself as an authority on certain subjects and as living a meaningful life through connections to things of value. The reader is most likely to see her as annoying, small-minded, ignorant, and unloved. The writer's unrelenting presentation of her unpleasant monologue and of her family's heedlessness to her indicate the character's unlikability.
2. The grandmother thinks of herself as representative of the normal, reasonable person doing battle against the forces of the aberrant. In fact, although the Misfit is clearly deranged, the grandmother appears no less a misfit than he, and no more accepted or loved. The encounter between them is somewhere between eerie and comic. If the story were presented in a melodramatic tone, for instance, it would fail to highlight the absurdity of the characters and

their encounter. O'Connor's portrayal of the family as charmless and of the grandmother as irritating conveys a lack of respect for them; the Misfit, by contrast, who is portrayed as lively and thoughtful, is almost more compelling than the "good" citizens of the story.

3. Toward the end of "What We Talk About When We Talk About Love," Terri says she's going to put out some cheese and crackers, but she doesn't get up, and Mel turns over his glass, spilling his drink out on the table. Carver does not indicate whether Mel does this accidentally. The word *spilling* suggests an accident, but he doesn't knock over his glass or tip over his glass: he turns it over, and the word *turn* makes the action seem willful. Given the context of everything that has been said at the table prior to the action, we might take this to be a sort of "acting-out" on Mel's part. His relationship with his ex-wife is strained, and his relationship with his children is affected. His relationship with Terri doesn't seem to be that good, either. His whole life is sort of a mess. When he turns over his glass, it might be a destructive gesture, like when someone who is angry punches the wall, only not quite so dramatic or clichéd as that. It might also be meaningful that Terri didn't get up to get the cheese and crackers. Not only does she not get up for the cheese and crackers, but—after Mel spills his drink—no one makes a move to clean up the mess. It could be that these characters mess up their own lives and, rather than solving their problems, address their unhappiness only by making a bigger mess. Carver doesn't attach any explicit meaning to any of this, so it could be argued that he is interested in "mystery," the mystery of why people do the things they do. In Sherman Alexie's "This Is What It Means to Say Phoenix, Arizona" (p. 873), the key gesture is Victor's promise to listen to one of Thomas's stories someday. The promise does not go as far as Thomas would like—Victor cannot promise to be Thomas's friend—but it is a step in the right direction, one that seems likely to make each man's life better in a small way.

# John Updike
## A & P

### APPROACHING THE STORY

John Updike's classic coming-of-age story is narrated by a young, apparently working-class man who works in a grocery store. Three girls, seemingly more elite in background, self-consciously walk through the store in skimpy bathing suits. The narrator and his co-worker are mesmerized and follow the girls' every move. The narrator particularly likes the one he perceives as the leader, whom he nicknames Queenie. In "the sad part of the story, at least my family says it's sad, but I don't think it's so sad myself" (para. 12), the manager comes out and tells the girls they'll have to leave the store because their attire is not "decent." Suddenly incensed on their behalf, the narrator finds himself saying "I quit." The girls, leaving, do not hear their "hero." The manager, seemingly a friend of the family, tries to allow him a way out, but having already pronounced the words, he feels he cannot go back on them. Leaving, the narrator has a sense of "how hard the world was going to be to me hereafter" (para. 32).

Students may be tempted to read this piece as simply a straightforward tale. You may wish to use this as the basis of a lesson on subtext. What might vacationing upper-class girls, free of the constraints of town opinion and the workaday world, symbolize for the store clerk? What might the confrontation with the manager symbolize? Is the narrator's resignation simply meant to impress the girls, or is it an impulse, an error, or something more? Why does the narrator resist the manager's effort to keep him? Although he loses his job, is there something less tangible he gains through this rebellious, gratuitous act? Students are likely to enjoy this colorful piece, though some may voice reservations concerning objectification of the girls' bodies. You might wish to stress the degree to which the story is written in character, isolating a few paragraphs for close examination. What sort of person is the narrator? What do his language and preoccupations reveal about him? Does the writer appear to endorse all of his feelings and impressions? Why or why not? What clues are provided that indicate the narrator and writer are not identical? How does the writer's "voice" allow the reader to glean an understanding of the events that is unavailable to the narrator himself?

## ADDITIONAL ACTIVITY

1. Have students read other Updike works—for instance, the *Rabbit* novels. In what ways is Updike's characteristic "voice" evident? How does it differ from the narrator's? By what general concerns and qualities of language might this "voice" be recognized? What general picture of human nature and behavior does Updike's work provide?

## GENERATING WRITING

1. Have each student write a one- to two-page "pastiche," or imitation, of Updike's style, basing the story on something that has happened in their own lives. Encourage them, in particular, to pay attention to the first-person narrator. Circulate pastiches anonymously for class discussion. What did students learn about Updike's writing, and the narrative process in general, from the exercise?

2. Have students free-write in preparation for two- to three-page analytic essays on some striking aspect of the narrative—for instance, the narrator's voice, images of class, or the narrator's sudden decision and view of the future. How does the chosen feature enhance the story as a whole? What other choices might the writer have made?

## THE READER'S PRESENCE

1. The narrator's style of expression implies that he is young, enjoys slang, and is inclined toward a show of toughness or bravado. These qualities indicate that his narrative may not be wholly reliable. A less colloquial style of English might lend the narrator more credibility because he might seem—if falsely—more worldly and aware of the subtleties of his experience. Updike appears to wish the narrator to be likable, though perhaps somewhat less sure of himself than his self-presentation makes him seem. Updike presents his opinions and observations as generally sound yet clouded by youth. For instance, the objectifying language he uses to describe the girls' bodies is unlike language Updike uses elsewhere, and it says more about the boy's lack of sexual experience and his insecurity than it does about the girls themselves.

2. The deeper issue in the confrontation appears to be class. The people in the store are required to work, while the girls may amuse themselves and are buying a luxury item; in addition, the girls are dressed in a manner townspeople don't condone. The clerk is apparently inspired not only by Queenie's beauty but also by the less demeaning life she and her friends represent; the manager's stiff back indicates a deeper conflict than the one that has just occurred. The writer conveys the issue of class by having the narrator drop details—for instance, the difference in appearance between the girls and the townspeople—that the narrator fails to analyze but that indicate significant categories of experience for the reader.

3. The grocery-store check-out clerk is often on the receiving end of jokes about dead-end jobs and bleak futures. Updike skillfully conveys the dreariness of the store, with its fluorescent lighting, mothers screaming at their children, and "townies" who live five miles from the beach and "haven't seen the ocean for twenty years" (para. 10). It is therefore difficult to take entirely seriously the boss's assertion that Sammy will "feel [his decision] for the rest of [his] life" (para. 31), or Sammy's that the world is henceforth going to be hard. The intermingling of tenses throughout the story does hint at the significance of the events that day in the grocery store, but even the long alluded-to denouement is presented with tongue in cheek: "One advantage to this scene taking place in summer, I can follow this up with a clean exit, there's no fumbling around getting your coat and galoshes, I just saunter into the electric eye in my white shirt that my mother ironed the night before, and the door heaves itself open, and outside the sunshine is skating around on the asphalt" (para. 31).

   In Judith Ortiz Cofer's "Silent Dancing" (p. 68), the seemingly trivial act of watching a home movie becomes a catalyst for exploring Cofer's identity. Cofer intersects past, present, and future in her narrative to demonstrate the complexity of who she is. The dream sequence complicates the happy surface of the party and dancing with the real difficulties of her relatives' lives, making the essay's title ironic. Whereas the hyperbolic depiction of the clerk's distress ultimately undermines Updike, Cofer's narrative stands up to the somber irony of its title.

# Writing Informally About Reading

A journal is a great place for students to experience the process of writing. Because journals are not graded, they don't create the sense of pressure associated with most college writing assignments. Students also know they don't have to worry about mechanics such as grammar and spelling, and they can often direct their unfettered energy to the pursuit of ideas. Journals and other informal writing assignments can be the best cure for writer's block.

If you decide to assign journals, you have several ways of going about it. After reading these comments and suggestions, you'll be in a good position to settle on a method that will work best for you and your students.

Many instructors collect and read their students' journals once a week, although you can also set two or three deadlines during the semester when all journals are due. Journals can give you access to the pulse of the class; teachers who prefer to check that pulse often will prefer the first method. The weekly collection has an advantage for students in that it prevents extreme forms of procrastination. If students are in the habit of waiting until the night before an assignment is due before getting started, the pressure of writing five weeks' worth of journal entries in one night will destroy one reason for writing in a journal in the first place. If your schedule arranges that your slack times come twice or thrice in a semester, however, you might try the second method. Also, to keep students feeling as if they are writing the journal primarily for themselves, and secondarily for you, the infrequent due dates might help.

Because these journals are not diaries—because, that is, they are assigned rather than taken up voluntarily—the audience will almost inevitably extend beyond the writer of the journal. To create an opportunity for students to write their journals purely for themselves, and simultaneously inspiring trust, you might try *not* collecting or reading the journals, instead informing your students at the beginning of the semester that they will be responsible for handing you a written report at the close of the term on their success at keeping a journal. They should not only assess the frequency of their entries but also discuss the experience of journal writing and give an opinion on the advantages and disadvantages of being the journal's sole reader. Here is a less radical plan that still takes into account the possibility that students may not want or need a wider audience. When they hand in their journals, have them fold in half lengthwise any page they would prefer you not look at. In this way, you can make sure they've done the assignment and still ensure their right to privacy.

How might you respond to the journals you do read? Some instructors write nonjudgmental comments in the margins of journal entries, setting up a dialogue by responding to the subject—that is, to the ideas in the entry rather than to their mechanical trappings. This is one good way to simultaneously get to know your students and help them think of new directions in which to push their ideas. Other instructors don't make a mark on the journals because they take seriously the idea that the journal is the student's own place to write. The students are less likely to see their journal writing as a performance; they may even be able to forget about the audience and write for themselves. Your decision on whether to write in the margins will obviously involve a trade-off: Do you want to give each the personal touch of a dialogue and some guidance in their thinking, or do you want to give them a chance to see what they can accomplish on their own and perhaps gain a sense of their own authority? (If you're not satisfied with the thought of giving up either option, you might try assigning team journals, which are described in the next section.)

How do the journals figure into grades? Even though the journal entries themselves must be ungraded for the students to receive the benefit of writing a journal, it's a good idea to give credit for simply having done it. If you make it clear at the beginning of the semester that regularly writing in the journal—*not* the quality or even the quantity, but merely the act of participating—will affect their grade, students will be more likely to at least go through the motions. And students who start out just going through the motions often get something out of the exercise in spite of themselves. After all, exercising their minds and hands is part of the idea of writing journals in the first place. A good way to compute grades for journal writing is to give each student one point for each week in which he or she writes in the journal. Then assign a letter grade to correspond to each number—twelve entries could equal an A, eleven an A-, down to an F for zero entries. When you make up the final course grade, give the journal-writing grade the same weight you would give to a polished paper. If you make it clear that you will compute the final grade in this way, you give tangible proof that you value the writing as well as its product.

What should your students write in their journals? This question, too, has many possible answers. You might give them complete freedom to choose their subject. This option works well if you see the journal primarily as a place for finger exercises, a place for them to practice writing without external restrictions or pressures. Of course, if you'd prefer to make sure that students move past purely narrative accounts of daily life in the dorm, you might define the journal more narrowly. You could call it a *reading journal*, suggesting that they use it as a place in which to record their responses to the readings for your course. You could define it as a *writer's notebook*, in which they can write down bits and pieces of ideas for papers, a safe place to explore those ideas for themselves, free of a critical reader's gaze. You could suggest that the journal is a good place to write down personal responses to ideas brought up in class, responses that may not be appropriate for class discussion but that are nonetheless relevant to the subject. Or you might describe the journal's possibilities as combining any or all of these options.

## TEAM JOURNALS

We learned about this exciting variation on the basic journal from Elizabeth Renfro, of California State University at Chico, and we have used her idea many times with great success in our own classrooms. The primary audience for a team journal is not you and not the individual writer but the group of four to six students comprising the team. Because you do not write in the team journals—not even in the margins—your students very quickly forget that you are reading them and begin to address their entries to their teammates. The responsibility for their ideas, and their interaction, shifts to them, and they gradually gain the sense of their own authority that is so essential to their development as writers.

Here are instructions for setting up team journals. Divide the students on your class list into groups of equal size. (Five students per group works well, but four or six will also work.) Make the groups heterogeneous in gender, ability, and so on. If any students regularly attend workshops or tutorials together, or if you have put students in permanent peer-editing groups, break these groups up to form the teams for journals. The idea is to bring each student into contact with as many others as possible in your many in-class and out-of-class activities so that they will see the class as a group of friends, people with whom it is possible to carry on discussions without fear of ridicule.

Bring several new spiral-bound notebooks to class, one for each team. Divide students into the teams you have arranged, and give each team a notebook with a blank label stuck to the cover. Have them come up with a name for their journal and write it on the label. They should also write all their names inside the cover. Then they hand the journals back to you. You explain to them that they will be expected to write in the journal once a week, and that they are to address their comments to their teammates. Give any instructions or suggestions you want about their journal during the semester so that it best fits their needs. Say that you will read their journals once a week, just to make sure they're doing them, and specify exactly the hour you set aside for your weekly journal reading. You must be consistent about when you read the journals, not only because that time will precisely define the limit of each week (the deadline) but also because no students may have the journal checked out at that time.

Now tell students where they will find the journals—say, in the reserve book room of your campus library. Draw a map on the board if necessary and explain the procedure for checking out books on reserve. After class, take the journals to the library and put them on two-hour reserve. Use the titles created by the student groups when you list the journals in the card catalog. Explain to the librarian that your students have been *instructed* to write in these books. (One teacher had a difficult time persuading librarians to ignore the usual rule against writing in library books.) If possible, arrange to have librarians give you all journals at the specified time each week; otherwise you will have to fill out several charge cards each time you come in to read the journals.

And be prepared to be delighted. Instead of lugging home a stack of conventional journals each week and reading through entry after entry written by students who often don't have a clear sense of audience ("Am I writing this for me or for the instructor?") or a clear sense of what to write ("I wonder if *this* is what my instructor wants"), you will find yourself watching a fascinating journey of discovery and communication. Your students will set the tone for their journals, and they will set the intellectual pace, stimulating one another to push harder and harder on their ideas, and to explore new avenues—probably more avenues than you, with your one mind, would have thought of. And if a student writes a sexist or racist remark, you will no longer be responsible for trying to figure out a way to set it straight. Team journals are self-sufficient universes: teammates will respond as only peers can, each adding his or her voice to the discussion of the issue.

As with any other method, you may have to do some troubleshooting in the first few weeks. If some students persist, despite your instructions, in addressing journal comments directly to you ("I was absent today because my roommate twisted her ankle, but don't worry—it won't happen again"), you may have to make a second announcement in class, reinforcing the principle behind the journal's audience. If one or two groups have set low standards for themselves, writing only short, uninspired entries, you could break their cycle early by showing them an example from a productive journal. Ask the members of an active, lively team for permission to photocopy and distribute a few pages from their journal or for permission to allow members of another group to check out their journal once to get an idea of how other group journals are working. If you continue to use team journals in your classes, consider photocopying model entries, again with permission, to use as examples in following semesters. You'll want to photocopy a series of entries, at least one from each team member, to capture the spirit of communication and exchange of ideas that goes on in team journals at their best. Use these models sparingly, though, to leave enough room for each group to conceive of the journal in its own format.

At the end of the semester, let each group decide what to do with its own journal. Some will say that you can have it. Others will want to make a copy for each team member. (Copies may be too light if they've written in pencil; warn them in advance.) You may receive more creative suggestions, such as an auction or a raffle. The most satisfying conclusion—admittedly rare—comes when a group decides to continue to write in its team journal after the semester has ended, either by leaving it on reserve or by mail. This continuation is an extreme manifestation of the general effect of team journals, and the best reason to assign them. Team journals help your students take charge of their own education, to discover their own sense of authority.

## QUESTION PAPERS

The idea for this genre of exploratory writing came to us from teachers in the Bay Area Writing Project, particularly John McBratney and Jane Juska. Question papers, like journals, provide a safe environment in which your students can take intellectual risks. Also like journals, question papers do not receive a grade, but the fact that the student has written one should be registered in the final grade.

Here are instructions for a question paper. Have each student think of a question about the text you are reading, something he or she has been wondering about and really wants to know. Have each student write that question at the top of a sheet of paper and then write a possible answer to it. That answer should lead to more questions that test the limits of the first answer. Then the student should consider another possible answer to the initial question or to a question that evolves from the first one. The questions and answers should dovetail, forming a flexible dialogue in which the student talks with himself or herself in writing. Impress on your students the need to try several answers to the questions. A common problem student writers have is settling too quickly for the first answer that comes to mind, grateful to have found any answer at all. This desperate attitude is not conducive to developing ideas or complex, sophisticated essays. The spirit of inquiry they exercise while writing question papers helps enhance students' ability to develop ideas in polished essays as well.

After your students have written as many answers—and follow-up questions, and answers to those—as they can, instruct them to read over what they have written and underline the hot spot, a surprising or intriguing idea that may have appeared. This hot spot might become the starting point for a subsequent question paper, it might become the thesis statement for a formal paper, or it might come to no utilitarian end at all. Students need to understand that they are writing these question papers primarily to explore and develop their response to the text as fully as possible. If they get the impression that all question papers are ultimately mere fodder for polished essays, the old hierarchy of product over process will be reinstated.

The first time you assign a question paper, you may want to make it an in-class writing assignment because it is a new form and students may not understand the assignment. After the class has had a few minutes to think of questions, ask for volunteers to read theirs aloud. Consider reading your question aloud, too, as one model among the others. Give students, and yourself, thirty minutes or so in which to write the dovetailing questions and answers, then call again for volunteers to read theirs aloud.

Collect the papers at the end of the hour. Your written response to your students' question papers will ideally take the form of an extension of their own activity of writing them: ask any questions that occur to you when reading their papers and mark any hot spots that they might not have noticed—or merely applaud a hot spot they have chosen. Once they have the hang of this new form, you can assign question papers as homework often. We find it beneficial to alternate question papers with polished papers on our schedule of assigned writing. If you are in the habit—as we are—of assigning a rough draft before every polished essay, continue to do so. The question paper is not a substitute for the rough draft; each form has its own uses and advantages. And your students will surely discover the advantages of question papers: many who learned about them in our classes have gone on to use them to question texts assigned by teachers who had never heard of question papers. When students voluntarily adopt a strategy such as the question paper, you can be sure that they have judged it worthwhile.